CHURCH AND GOVERNMENT
IN THE MIDDLE AGES

Christopher Cheney

Frontispiece

CHURCH
AND
GOVERNMENT
IN THE
MIDDLE AGES

ESSAYS PRESENTED TO
C. R. CHENEY
ON HIS 70TH BIRTHDAY
AND EDITED BY
C. N. L. BROOKE
D. E. LUSCOMBE
G. H. MARTIN
AND
DOROTHY OWEN

CAMBRIDGE UNIVERSITY PRESS
CAMBRIDGE
LONDON   NEW YORK   MELBOURNE

Published by the Syndics of the Cambridge University Press
The Pitt Building, Trumpington Street, Cambridge CB2 1RP
Bentley House, 200 Euston Road, London NW1 2DB
32 East 57th Street, New York, NY 10022, USA
296 Beaconsfield Parade, Middle Park, Melbourne 3206, Australia

First published 1976

Printed in Great Britain
at the
University Printing House, Cambridge
(Euan Phillips, University Printer)

Library of Congress Cataloguing in Publication Data
Main entry under title:
Church and government in the Middle Ages.
Bibliography: p.
Contents: Chibnall, M. Charter and chronicle, the use of archive sources by
Norman historians. – Foreville, R. The synod of the Province of Rouen in the
eleventh and twelfth centuries. – Van Caenegem, R. C. Public prosecution
of crime in twelfth-century England. – Brooke, C. Geoffrey of Monmouth
as a historian. [etc.]
Includes index.
1. Church history – Middle Ages, 600–1500 – Addresses, essays, lectures.
2. Middle Ages – History – Addresses, essays, lectures. 4. Canon law – History –
Addresses, essays, lectures. 5. Cheney, Christopher Robert, 1906–   I. Brooke,
Christopher Nugent Lawrence. II. Cheney, Christopher Robert, 1906–   .
BR252.C54   261.7'09'02   75–41614
ISBN 0 521 21172 7

FOR CHRISTOPHER CHENEY
FROM US ALL
IN HOMAGE AND AFFECTION

CONTENTS

Frontispiece: Christopher Cheney. A drawing by Michael Noakes (1972) reproduced by permission of the Master and Fellows of Corpus Christi College, Cambridge, with the kind assistance of Dr Geoffrey Bushnell. Photograph by Edward Leigh, Cambridge.

Contents

CHRISTOPHER CHENEY

ON A SUMMER DAY in the early 1960s a visitor returned to a Lakeland cottage remote from the abodes of men to find awaiting his attention a small, tidy pile of proofs, delivered by hand. They were a part of a notable ornament to medieval scholarship, *Councils and Synods with other documents relating to the English Church*, vol. II; their arrival shows a quality which no serious user of that book, nor any reader of Christopher Cheney's other books and papers, can fail to recognise: a quiet persistence which sees every inquiry through to the end. There is about all he writes a deceptive modesty and an elegant simplicity, so that it is easy superficially to imagine that the quality of his scholarship is akin to Thomas Hearne's who, 'with learned dust besprent', was almost incapable of error in the transcription of texts. In Hearne, however, this was a natural failing, quite unaccompanied by any critical faculty; in Cheney native ability goes hand in hand with training, thought and common sense – of quite uncommon dimensions – sharpened and deepened by a mind of exceptional subtlety, perception and penetration. By these means the apparent simplicity of his productions is wrought.

His chosen field of research has been mainly in the twelfth and thirteenth centuries, and in Anglo-Norman, papal and ecclesiastical history; in these areas his mastery is widely acclaimed. But no reader of *Notaries Public in England* could fail to observe the sweep of his learning over the late Middle Ages and the whole of western Christendom, to which many of his papers bear witness. Two fields are peculiarly his. Characteristically, he represented British scholarship in the little band of experts who set up the Commission Internationale de Diplomatique; and his achievement in diplomatic was also recognised by his election in 1965 as a corresponding member of the Monumenta Germaniae Historica. He is one of the few British scholars who moves with complete assurance in the labyrinth of medieval canon law. He is the doyen of those who study conciliar and episcopal legislation. His patient, brilliant disentangling, dating and editing of the conciliar canons of the English church in the thirteenth century is enshrined in many articles and above all in *Councils and Synods*, II, one of the great works of erudition of our time. It has always been his delight to keep close to the sources of our knowledge of the past, to whose under-standing his direct contributions have been very numerous, as the Bibliography of his writings shows; and his indirect no less, for he has had a hand in many enterprises, large and small. The latest is the Centre for Episcopal Acta at York, which is adorned by his own collection of notes, and the British Academy project for their publication, which he has inspired and led.

Paul Sabatier once wrote that 'many folk see' in the scientific criticism of historical evidence 'only the hammer of destruction and demolition. That is very unjust, for when the moment comes, it can also take the mason's trowel and raise above the ruins constructions built to last.' Cheney's instruments are much subtler than hammers and trowels; but his constructions (in a different way) have as lasting a quality as Sabatier's. Many who have used his editions and papers must have felt this. It is a rare lesson in humility for any scholar to compare the papers reprinted in *Medieval Texts and Studies* (1973) with the original editions. In most cases only the slightest changes were needed – or are likely ever to be needed; yet every page and every reference has been weighed, and slight redrafting here and there, substantial rewriting in a few places where new learning has advanced the subject, reveal the intricate, meticulous skill of a great craftsman. But he is never meticulous just for the sake of it, and a measured judgement of what is useful and sensible plays over every sentence and every footnote.

This sense, and the warm humanity and human insight, which live at the root of his idea of history and link all his scholarship inextricably with the kindness and wit which are equally characteristic of him, lend depth to his work. There is more of the twelfth and thirteenth centuries in his Ford Lectures, *From Becket to Langton* (1956), than in many flashier books; and some of it is eloquently revealed. 'Did he surrender the Church's interests to the claims of the lay power?' – he asks of Hubert Walter (p. 41). 'That question touches the root problem of his career and the anomalous position of bishops in twelfth-century society. I doubt whether the question can be answered. But this much can be said. Hubert knew his Angevin masters well and was flexible and firm enough to live with them...So he was able to hold *regnum* and *sacerdotium* in England in equilibrium while he lived. That in itself was a great service to the Church. Her government, as then constituted, required the service of sinners as well as of saints.'

His judgements can be shrewd, and most of us who have worked with him have sooner or later felt as if we were Gasquet in harness with Edmund Bishop; but his criticisms are given in so plain and kindly a manner that we have never felt from him the affront sensitive minds can rarely avoid when made to face their failings. None who know him well can fail to learn from his own modesty a supreme lesson in scholarly humility. To his pupils in many places, Cairo, London, Oxford, Manchester and Cambridge, he has been a kindly and an exacting teacher, unstinting in expense of time and skill for them, never putting other men's tasks aside for his own. Many scholars could tell of advice freely given, of prompt and thorough criticism of unpublished work, of rare information supplied, of rare books and even manuscripts lent or given 'because you'll make better use of them than I shall'.

This volume is offered to Christopher Cheney for his seventieth birthday as a token of affection by a group of his friends. Our number could easily have been multiplied if the urge to produce a book of manageable compass and the exigencies of publication had not confined us. Many, we know, would wish to join us in our tribute to him. All of us have sat at his table and learned from him, and offer him our token of affection and thanks.

CHRISTOPHER BROOKE
DAVID LUSCOMBE

GEOFFREY MARTIN
DOROTHY OWEN

EDITORS' PREFACE

THE ESSAYS collected here are concerned with the history of church and government in England and on the continent of Europe between the eleventh and the early fourteenth centuries, with occasional extensions. This subject is illustrated through the eyes of different types of officials – among them English royal justices, Norman bishops and monastic archdeacons – and of scholars, such as Master Gratian, Master Vacarius and John Baconthorpe. Each essay is a discussion of a major historical text or of a vital group of documents and seeks to show how they can contribute to the common theme.

The volume is designed as a modest tribute to a deeply respected friend and colleague, Christopher Robert Cheney, Emeritus Professor of Medieval History in the University of Cambridge. Our aim has been to draw together original studies in a coherent volume related to the field of scholarship in which he has excelled. The book opens with a brief appreciation of C. R. Cheney and closes with a Bibliography of his writings.

The editors wish to thank all the contributors most warmly for their ready collaboration and help, and the Syndics and Staff of the Cambridge University Press for publishing the book. They are particularly grateful to Mrs Mary Cheney for her kindness, help and encouragement. Dr Marjorie Chibnall assisted most generously with the Index.

C. N. L. B.
D. E. L.
G. H. M.
D. M. O.

ABBREVIATIONS

AA.SS	*Acta Sanctorum*... ed. J. Bollandus and others (Antwerp, Brussels, 1643, etc.).
BEC	*Bibliothèque de l'École des Chartes*.
BIHR	*Bulletin of the Institute of Historical Research*, University of London.
BL	British Library, London.
C.	Code, in Justinian's *Corpus Iuris Civilis*.
Cant. D. & C.	Canterbury, Dean & Chapter Muniments.
CCR	*Calendar of Close Rolls* (HMSO, 1902–).
Councils II	*Councils and Synods with other documents relating to the English Church, II: A.D. 1205–1313* (2 vols., Oxford, 1964).
CPL	*Calendar of Patent Letters* (HMSO, 1893–).
CPR	*Calendar of Patent Rolls* (HMSO, 1901–).
CUL	Cambridge University Library.
CYS	Canterbury and York Society.
D.	Digest in Justinian's *Corpus Iuris Civilis*.
DNB	*Dictionary of National Biography*, ed. L. Stephen and S. Lee.
EDC	Ely Chapter Records, University Library, Cambridge.
EDR	Ely Diocesan Records, University Library, Cambridge.
EHR	*English Historical Review*.
Foedera	*Foedera, conventiones, litterae (etc.)*, ed. T. Rymer, re-edited A. Clarke, etc. (3 vols. in 6, Record Commission, 1816–30).
HMSO	His/Her Majesty's Stationery Office.
Inst.	Institutes in Justinian's *Corpus Iuris Civilis*.
JL	*Regesta pontificum Romanorum...ad annum 1198*, ed. P. Jaffé, 2nd ed. S. Löwenfeld, etc. (2 vols., Leipzig, 1885–8).
Lambeth, Reg. Reyn.	Lambeth Palace Library, Reg. Reynolds.
LRO	Lincoln Record Office.
MGH	Monumenta Germaniae Historica.
MGH. SS.	Monumenta Germaniae Historica, Scriptorum series.
Migne, *PG*.	*Patrologiae cursus completus, series graeca*, ed. J. P. Migne.
Migne, *PL*.	*Patrologiae cursus completus, series latina*, ed. J. P. Migne.
MTB	*Materials for the History of Thomas Becket*, Archbishop of Canterbury, ed. J. C. Robertson, RS (7 vols., 1875–85).
Novel	Novellae Constitutiones in Justinian's *Corpus Iuris Civilis*.
Parl. Writs	*The Parliamentary Writs and Writs of Military Summons*... ed. F. Palgrave, Record Commission (2 vols. in 4, 1827–34).

Abbreviations

PR	Pipe Roll, published by the Pipe Roll Society, London.
PRO	Public Record Office, London.
PUE	*Papsturkunden in England*, ed. W. Holtzmann. Abhandlungen der Gesellschaft der Wissenschaften zu Göttingen, phil.-hist. Klasse, neue Folge, xxv (1930–1), dritte Folge 14–15 (1935–6), dritte Folge 33 (1952). 3 vols. Berlin (1 and 2), Göttingen (3).
Regesta	*Regesta Regum Anglo-Normannorum*, vol. I, ed. H. W. C. Davis (Oxford, 1913); vol. II, ed. C. Johnson and H. A. Cronne (Oxford 1956).
RS	Rolls Series, London.
S.	Secretum (Bodleian Library, Oxford, MS. Wood empt. I).
TRHS	*Transactions of the Royal Historical Society.*
VCH	Victoria History of the Counties of England.
Wake, *Clergy*	W. Wake, *The State of the Church and Clergy of England...* (1703).
WAM	Westminster Abbey Muniments.
Wilkins	*Concilia Magnae Britanniae et Hiberniae*, ed. D. Wilkins (4 vols., London, 1737).

CHARTER AND CHRONICLE:
THE USE OF ARCHIVE SOURCES BY
NORMAN HISTORIANS

by MARJORIE CHIBNALL

To SPEAK OF 'archive' as distinct from 'narrative' sources in any part of north-west Europe during the eleventh century is something of an anachronism. This is not merely because contemporaries saw no sharp distinction between the two,[1] but because to some extent they inter-penetrated one another. Merovingian and Carolingian charters might be used to provide details for the lives of saints venerated as monastic founders and at the same time to preserve a record of former monastic lands secularised by powerful lords or devastated in war. Chronicles might be pillaged by the writers of diplomas who prefaced their gifts with a brief history of the house. As long as chanceries remained so rudimentary that many charters were drafted and written in the scrip-toria of beneficiaries, history and charter might at times be composed by the same men in much the same language. And until sealed writ-charters were generally recognised as instruments for transferring livery of seisin rather than records of previously witnessed acts of donation, a class of title-deeds clearly distinguished from the miscellaneous records of monastic houses did not exist.

Even historians dealing with more than domestic history, whether their concern was with papal pronouncements or the canons of councils, might find the frontier between document and narrative ill-defined. Rhetorical invention of dramatic speeches was so much an accepted device for conveying different opinions that a letter or even a papal bull might be invented purely to enliven the narrative. The canons of councils were not always formally promulgated in writing; attendant dignitaries carried home short summaries of canons which were not standardised when they reached the hands of historians who, while preserving many of them, diversified them still further by mixing

---

[1] See C. R. Cheney, 'The records of Medieval England' in *Medieval Texts and Studies* (Oxford, 1973), p. 3; David Knowles, C. N. L. Brooke and Vera London, *The Heads of Religious Houses in England and Wales 940–1216* (Cambridge, 1972), p. 5.

canon and commentary. The boundaries between categories of sources only gradually became clearer; even in the late twelfth century they were not always rigidly drawn.[2]

Norman historical writing proper may be said to have begun early in the eleventh century, but it drew on older traditions well-established in other provinces, and on some historical materials surviving from pre-Norman Neustria. The early records of Saint-Wandrille, which are the best preserved, illustrate the nature of these materials. From the early ninth century, a period of considerable historical activity, the *Gesta abbatum Fontanellensium* and a *Vita Condedi* survive. The author of the *Gesta* copied the *Liber Pontificalis* for the form of his work; the substance he found to some extent at least in the archives of his house.[3] He cited between forty and fifty ancient donations, including a number of royal gifts; the confusion that he shows over the date of the abbey's foundation may have arisen from a misunderstanding of two genuine diplomas of Clovis II. Besides these he made use of Carolingian privileges of immunity, records of exchanges, judicial decisions and several documents relating to the internal administration of the monastery. If one of his objects was to preserve a record of the endowment of the house, events justified his foresight. Threatened by invasions of the Northmen, the monks of Saint-Wandrille abandoned their abbey *c.* 858[4] and scattered to Chartres, Boulogne and Ghent, taking with them the relics of their saints. When the abbey was restored by Duke Richard I and the monks returned, they were obliged to leave their saints behind in Ghent and found many of their former possessions in the hands of powerful laymen. In so far as they were able to recover their lost treasures, it was with the powerful support of the Norman dukes backed, where necessary, by their own historical researches. Of their three saints, Wandrille and Ansbert were lost beyond recovery, and only after hunting for clues among the manuscripts of Saint-

---

[2] By the time of the 1148 Council of Rheims the canons of church councils were promulgated with sufficient formality for John of Salisbury to confine his account in the *Historia Pontificalis* to informal explanations of some of them (M. Chibnall, *The Historia Pontificalis of John of Salisbury* (Nelson's Medieval Texts, Edinburgh, 1956), p. 8). But secular laws in England at least were rarely so clearly formalised until later, and J. C. Holt has shown how Howden mixed text and context in recording and explaining the assizes of Henry II (J. C. Holt, 'The assizes of Henry II: the texts', in D. A. Bullough and R. L. Storey (eds.), *The Study of Medieval Records* (Oxford, 1971), pp. 85–106).

[3] For the composition of the *Gesta* see F. Lohier and J. Laporte, *Gesta sanctorum patrum Fontanellensis coenobii* (Rouen–Paris, 1936), pp. xxiv–xxvi, xxxvi–xxxvii; F. Lot, *Études critiques sur l'abbaye de Saint-Wandrille* (Paris, 1913), pp. xi–xiii.

[4] *Miracula sancti Wandregisili*, *AA.SS*, July v, 281–91.

Bertin[5] were they able to argue that St Wulfram had never left Saint-Wandrille and to make a 'discovery' of his body there in 1027 plausible enough to convince many of their contemporaries, and even such eminent later scholars as the Bollandists.[6]

The case for the recovery of former lands was supported by evidence drawn from a number of sources. For one restoration, that of the island of *Belcinnaca* in the river Seine by William, count of Arques, between 1032 and 1047, the documentation is particularly good.[7] A forged diploma of King Theoderic III, dated 673, was probably produced in the early eleventh century, slightly before the charter of William of Arques.[8] This diploma, granting the island where St Condedus had lived, was plainly based on the ninth-century *Vita Condedi*[9] and also on the *Gesta abbatum*[10] of the same period. Both these works had made use of earlier diplomas and so, by the interborrowings of charters and narratives, the tradition of possession was handed on until the property could be secured to the restored monastery with all the weight of ducal sanction. Because of the widespread loss and destruction of the earliest Norman archives,[11] few cases can be documented quite so clearly; evidence surviving from Anjou, Maine and other parts of northern France, where the early sources are richer, indicate that the story of *Belcinnaca* is typical of many others.[12]

The interdependence of charter and chronicle was closest in *Vitae sanctorum* and histories of limited scope composed in monasteries. Ducal history had other methods. It owed its beginning to the encouragement of Duke Richard I and his son Richard II in the last decade of the tenth century, when intellectual life was just beginning to revive

---

[5] H. van Werveke, 'Saint-Wandrille et Saint-Pierre de Gand', in *Miscellanea Mediaevalia J. F. Niermeyer* (Groningen, 1967), pp. 90–2.

[6] The fascinating story of the relics does not concern us here, since the monks made use only of narrative sources; the most recent treatment, with full references to earlier discussions, is by R. C. van Caenegem in 'The sources of Flemish history in the *Liber Floridus*', *Liber Floridus Colloquium* (Ghent, 1973), pp. 77–80.

[7] Printed, Lot, *Saint-Wandrille*, no. 15, pp. 56–7. This restoration was included in the genera charter of William the Conqueror (1082–7); see Marie Fauroux, *Recueil des actes des ducs de Normandie (911–1066)*, Mémoires de la Société des Antiquaires de Normandie XXXVI (Caen, 1961), no. 234.   [8] Lot, *Saint-Wandrille*, no. 1, pp. 23–4.

[9] *AA.SS*, October IX, 356–7.   [10] Lohier and Laporte, *Gesta*, pp. 39–40.

[11] See C. H. Haskins, *Norman Institutions* (Cambridge, Mass., 1925), pp. 241–9.

[12] Cf. for example the interborrowings of the early charters of St Nicholas, Angers, and the *Historia Sancti Florentii Salmuracensis* (Migne, *PL*. CLV), 481; P. Marchegay and E. Mabille, *Chroniques des églises d'Anjou* (Paris, 1869), p. 255; L. Halphen, *Le comté d'Anjou au XIe siècle* (Paris, 1906), p. x and no. 34; and the use of early diplomas by Odorannus of Sens in his life of Théodechilde (R. H. Bautier and Monique Gilles, *Odorannus de Sens, Opera Omnia* (Paris, 1972), pp. 42–4, 76–9).

after the disruption of the Norman invasions and the slow rise of the new duchy.[13] Dudo of Saint-Quentin, who undertook the task at the bidding of the two Richards, was a secular canon, later dean of Saint-Quentin, employed at the ducal court. His work, though a panegyric full of unreliable legends rather than a history, cannot be rejected out of hand and has been used with caution by historians since shortly after his own day. He owed the great bulk of his material to oral tradition and in particular to the stories of Richard I's brother, Count Ralph of Ivry, whom he addressed in one place as 'huius operis relatorem'.[14] There is no reason to suppose that even the laws of Rollo, which he described,[15] were written down in Rollo's day. Charters, at least from the time of Richard I, were a different matter; Dudo must have known, and may have used them. As a chaplain of Richard II who, on one occasion, gave himself the somewhat grandiose title of chancellor,[16] he was certainly engaged in the production of charters as well as in the writing of history. Two charters are known to have been drafted by him;[17] it has even been proved that he wrote some lines of each with his own hand.[18] Charters and history alike were composed in Dudo's bombastic, rhetorical style.[19] But, while both bear the stamp of his literary training, it must be recognised that he used earlier diplomas very rarely, and then merely as the factual basis for rhetorical speeches; he did not transmit them with the verbal faithfulness of the ninth-century monks of Saint-Wandrille. There is independent proof that the abbey of Saint-Denis had held property at Berneval in Normandy before the ninth-century invasions, and that possession was restored by the first dukes;[20] Dudo in his account of the baptism of Rollo and subsequent benefactions states that Rollo gave the property. He may have combined the stories of Ralph of Ivry with information in the 968 charter of Richard I, which restored Berneval as his father

[13] See J. Lair, *Dudonis Sancti Quintini 'De moribus et actis primorum Normanniae ducum'* (Caen, 1865), pp. 9–20.
[14] Lair, *De moribus*, p. 125.
[15] Lair, *De moribus*, pp. 171–2.
[16] It is possible that the title at this date meant no more than *scriba* or *notarius* (Fauroux, *Recueil*, p. 41).
[17] D. C. Douglas, 'The ancestors of William fitz Osbern', *EHR*, LIX (1944), 73–4.
[18] Marie Fauroux, 'Deux autographes de Dudon de Saint-Quentin', *BEC*, CXI (1953), 229–34; Fauroux, *Recueil*, nos. 13, 18.
[19] Douglas, *EHR*, LIX (1944), 73 n. 10, notes some common phrases, such as 'Dudo pretiosi martyris Christi Quintini canonicus' in the Saint-Ouen charter (Fauroux, *Recueil*, no. 18), and 'quemdam clericum pretiosi martyris Christi Quintini canonicum nomine Dudonem' in the history (Lair, *De moribus*, p. 295).
[20] Félibien, *Histoire de l'abbaye royale de Saint-Denis* (Paris, 1706), nos. XXXIII, LII, XCIII.

William and his grandfather Rollo had granted it.[21] However his brief statement, though consistent with the information in the charter, never exactly repeats its words.[22] Similarly, if he used any charters of Duke Richard I in his account of the restoration of Saint-Ouen and Mont-Saint-Michel and of the foundation of Fécamp, there is no certain echo of their language in his panegyric.[23]

A similar conclusion can be drawn from the writings of William of Poitiers, the court historiographer of William the Conqueror who, like Dudo, was a secular canon, not a monk.[24] Educated in the schools of Poitiers, he was well-read in classical authors and had at least a rudimentary training in law.[25] A man of good family, trained as a knight, he may have frequented William's court before he took orders; afterwards he was in constant attendance on William as one of his chaplains. His history shows a keen interest in laws: there are references to the *lex transfugarum*,[26] to Duke William's establishment of the Truce of God in Normandy,[27] and to the laws that he established after the conquest of England.[28] But his comments are general: they correspond only roughly to passages in the *Leis Willelme* which, though not written down until after William the Conqueror's death, were to some extent a record of practice, based on the code of Cnut which William of Poitiers may have seen.[29] His allusions do not prove research in lawbooks; very probably he owed his knowledge of the laws promulgated by William the Conqueror to his own experience of the business of the court, just as Dudo of Saint-Quentin was familiar with charters primarily because he was employed in drafting them.

Neither of these men spent his life in close contact with the resources of a monastic library. Both visited many abbeys with the duke, and had opportunities of exploring archive resources which, though probably scanty when Dudo was preparing his work, were

---

[21] Fauroux, *Recueil*, no. 3. His account has sometimes been regarded as indicating a lost charter of Rollo, but this is unlikely (*ibid.* p. 20, n. 3).

[22] Lair, *De moribus*, pp. 170–1. Dudo's words, 'Brenneval cum omnibus appenditiis' correspond only roughly with the formula of Richard I's charter, 'Britnevallem...cum omnibus suis adjacentibus'.   [23] Lair, *De moribus*, pp. 290–1.

[24] See Guillaume de Poitiers, *Gesta Guillelmi ducis Normannorum et regis Anglorum*, ed. R. Foreville (Paris, 1952), pp. vii–xiii.

[25] R. Foreville, 'Concepts juridiques et influences romanisantes chez Guillaume de Poitiers', *Le Moyen Age*, LVIII (1952), 43–83.   [26] Foreville, *Gesta Guillelmi*, p. 64.

[27] Foreville, *Gesta Guillelmi*, p. 118.

[28] Foreville, *Gesta Guillelmi*, pp. 232–4, 'Latrociniis, invasionibus, maleficiis, locum omnem intra suos terminos denegavit. Portus et quaeliber itinera negotiatoribus patere, et nullam injuriam fieri jussit.'

[29] Cf. F. Liebermann, *Gesetze der Angelsachsen* (3 vols. Halle, 1903–16), I, 497, 511; III, 277ff.

becoming much more plentiful half a century later. But neither lived long years among the traditions and records of a single great religious house. In this they differed from the third eleventh-century ducal historiographer, William 'Calculus', monk of Jumièges and contemporary of William of Poitiers. Of his early life, and whether he was an oblate monk or came to the cloister in mature years, nothing is known; however his style, so much simpler than that of either Dudo or William of Poitiers that he apologised for it,[30] suggests a monastic education, as do his written sources. His preface explains that he used a number of books in collecting his material; for the early period the stories that Dudo had preserved in a written record (*carta*) were the most important.[31] Most of his sources were chronicles, such as the *Historia Francorum Senonensis*, or *Vitae sanctorum*; he may have had a few written genealogies,[32] and he relied to some extent on oral information. Occasionally, however, the content or language of his History suggests the use of charters. His mention of the gift of the château of Dreux to Duke Richard's sister, Matilda, as her dowry, may possibly have been derived from a lost act.[33] Although his account of the restoration of his own abbey of Jumièges is not free from legend, one or two phrases have the wording of a formal deed. A lost charter may lie behind his note of William Longespée's gift to the first abbot 'cum tota villa, quam ab alodariis auro redemit';[34] the term *alodarius* is not a very common one, and occurs in this spelling in only three of the ducal charters collected by Marie Fauroux, two of which are general grants to Jumièges.[35] It was only natural that a monk, touching however briefly on the history of his own monastery, should turn for information to the charters of his house. Even in a hundred years one of the great restored monasteries of Normandy would accumulate a substantial collection of written records of various kinds.

The embodiment of traditions in charter and chronicle may be traced in other abbeys, including Saint-Ouen and Mont-Saint-Michel. At Saint-Ouen, Rouen, restoration came by slow stages, at first poorly

---

[30] Guillaume de Jumièges, *Gesta Normannorum ducum*, ed. J. Marx (Rouen–Paris, 1914), p. 1. That he was a monk of Jumièges when he wrote is known from Orderic Vitalis, *Historia Ecclesiastica*, ed. A. Le Prévost (5 vols. Paris 1838–55), II, 3, III, 85; ed. M. Chibnall (Oxford Medieval Texts, 1969ff.), II, 2–4, III, 304.   [31] Cf. Marx, *Gesta*, pp. 1, 2.

[32] Cf. Marx, *Gesta*, p. 88.   [33] Marx, *Gesta*, p. 83; cf. Fauroux, *Recueil*, p. 24 n. 19.

[34] Cf. Marx, *Gesta*, p. 40.

[35] See Fauroux, *Recueil*, no. 36, 'Do etiam…in Vado Fulmerii unum alodarium'; no. 220, 'in Amundevilla…sex homines liberos qui vocantur allodarii'. The third charter (no. 52) is for Saint-Wandrille. In three other charters the word is spelled *alodeir*, *aloter* and *aloer*.

documented. That some temporal restitution was made by Rollo is recorded in the general charter of Richard II, which says of Rollo 'partim restituit, partim et dedit, sed propriis cartulis ad notitiam futurorum minime descripsit'.[36] Legends, written down towards the late eleventh century, attributed to Rollo more extensive gifts and privileges than those recorded in Richard II's charter. These were associated with the return of the saint's relics to Rouen, when Rollo was said to have walked barefoot from the city to Longpaon to meet them. The story occurs in various records: in a collection of miracles attributed to the saint,[37] in the sermon by John the Deacon, monk of Saint-Ouen, describing the translation,[38] and in the collection of mixed legend and genuine tradition of the early dukes that circulated with the tract called the *Brevis relatio de Willelmo nobilissimo comite Normannorum*.[39] A variant version of this last collection, written after Henry I's death, can also be found in the *Additamenta* to Robert of Torigny's *Interpolations* in the *Gesta Normannorum Ducum* of William of Jumièges.[40] In spite of considerable differences of detail, there are one or two close verbal resemblances in the record of Rollo's gift. John the Deacon attributes to Rollo the following words: 'Hunc locum...amodo Longum pedanum nuncupari censeo, et ab hoc ad usque urbis moenia, omnem quae infra adjacet terram beato Audoeno liberaliter concedo.' The *Additamenta* makes him say, 'Et ego do ecclesiae vestrae et vobis totam terram, quae adjacet ab isto loco usque ad menia civitatis.' No grant in these terms occurs in the genuine charter of Richard II, but there may have been a lost document used by both. If so, it was almost certainly an interpolated version, for John the Deacon goes on to describe an immunity in terms improbable before the middle of the eleventh century: 'venerabile coenobium...juxta priscorum privilegia regum nostra auctoritate, ut immune et absolutum maneat ab

---

[36] Cf. Fauroux, *Recueil*, no. 53. The restoration of monastic life came only at the end of the tenth century (Dom Pommeraye, *Histoire de l'abbaye royale de Saint-Ouen de Rouen* (Rouen, 1662), pp. 142–6).

[37] *AA.SS*, August IV, 821ff. Cf. Fauroux, *Recueil*, p. 20.

[38] Migne, *PL*. CLXII, 1151–4. John was active in the first quarter of the twelfth century.

[39] For details of the manuscripts of this collection see T. D. Hardy, *Descriptive Catalogue of Materials relating to the History of Great Britain and Ireland*, RS (3 vols. London, 1862–71), I, no. 16. Though printed by Silas Taylor, *History of Gavelkind* (London, 1663), pp. 183–210, and J. A. Giles, *Scriptores rerum gestarum Willelmi Conquestoris* (London, 1845), pp. 1–23, it has never been critically edited. The account of William the Conqueror's life is followed by a collection of stories of his predecessors dating from the reign of Henry I; this may have come from Saint-Ouen, though gifts to Fécamp and Jumièges are described.

[40] Marx, *Gesta*, pp. 335–41.

omni judiciaria exactione, auctorizaliter constituo'. In these stories, although the legendary and apocryphal element is stronger than in the ninth-century *Gesta abbatum* of Saint-Wandrille, there is a similar attempt to use charter material.

At Mont-Saint-Michel, towards the middle of the eleventh century, the monks were engaged in interpolating two of their genuine diplomas, and the privileges so claimed were then recorded in several short chronicles and historical notes. During a protracted vacancy between 1058 and 1060, when they were resisting the imposition of an abbot from outside their own house, they produced a crude forgery of a supposed bull of John XIII granting freedom of election, and interpolated it in a genuine diploma of King Lothair.[41] They further interpolated a reference to this alleged papal confirmation and a grant of additional ducal and episcopal customs in a charter of Duke Richard II.[42] The first two documents were incorporated in a brief treatise, written *c.* 1058–60, and were later copied into a short account of the early history of the abbey. This was transcribed both into the preliminary folios of the great Cartulary of the abbey, and into a collection of historical works which included the *Chronicle* of Robert of Torigny.[43] Both these volumes were written and decorated in the early years of Robert's abbacy, shortly after 1154. Besides this, references to the supposed grant of privileges occur in several versions of the annals of the abbey. One of the earliest of these was written not later than 1070; the annals were copied into a volume, transcribed in the scriptorium of Mont-Saint-Michel, which was taken to St Augustine's, Canterbury, probably by Abbot Scolland.[44] The documents, authentic and forged, were part of the historical record of the abbey; even the illustrations

---

[41] The forgery is critically discussed in L. Halphen and F. Lot, *Recueil des actes de Lothaire et de Louis V rois de France (954–987)* (Paris, 1908), p. 53 n. 1. The diploma is printed pp. 56–7.

[42] Fauroux, *Recueil*, no. 49, pp. 158–62; cf. J. F. Lemarignier, *Étude sur les privilèges d'exemption et de juridiction des abbayes normandes.* Archives de la France monastique, XLIV (Paris, 1937), pp. 75 n. 46, 264.

[43] Bibliothèque municipale d'Avranches, MS 210 (Cartulary) and MS 211 (Chronicle); the account is printed by E. de Robillard de Beaurepaire, *Mémoires de la Société des Antiquaires de Normandie*, XXIX (1877), 871–4.

[44] BL MS Royal 13 A XXIII, fos. 96–96v. The annal for 965 reads, 'Auctoratum est sacro scripto tam a domno Papa Iohanne quam a Lothario Francorum rege ut monasterium montis sancti Michaelis perpetualiter insigniatur ordine monachili, utque nullus nomine vel officio abbatis fungatur ibi nisi quem iidem monachi de suis elegerint praeesse sibi.' This manuscript has been dated and ascribed to the scriptorium of Mont-Saint-Michel by F. Avril in *Millénaire monastique du Mont-Saint-Michel* (4 vols. Paris, 1967–71), II, 206 n. 8; J. J. G. Alexander, *Norman Illumination at Mont St. Michel, 966–1100* (Oxford, 1970), p. 28. For a fuller version of the annals written *c.* 1120 see L. Delisle, *Chronique de Robert de Torigni* (Rouen, 1872–3), II, 217.

of the great Cartulary combine legend and dramatisation of deeds of gift.[45]

No doubt the collection and preservation of these miscellaneous records was due partly to the election of the historian, Robert of Torigny, as abbot in 1154. Robert was a passionate bibliophile and a great collector; if he made very little use of archive sources in his somewhat arid *Chronicle* and his interpolations in William of Jumièges,[46] he was well aware of the place records played in the traditions of his house. One section of the great Cartulary contains *acta* of the years 1155–9, which describe donations, purchases, law-suits and all the miscellaneous business of the abbey;[47] it reads like the first draft of a projected *Liber de rebus in administratione sua gestis*. But Robert's work was also typical of an attempt, very general at that time, to arrange and preserve materials that had been steadily increasing in volume and diversity since the early eleventh century in every great monastic house.

The miscellaneous historical and semi-historical material produced in western European monasteries during the period 1049–1122 has been described as 'vast and varied';[48] and in Normandy this was true not only of more consciously written historical treatises, but also of the raw materials of administration that accumulated in increasing quantities. Too little has survived from the very early archives of Norman monasteries for any accurate assessment of their bulk to be made. But certainly in the older houses by the end of the eleventh century charters might exist in sufficient numbers to demand classification: the earliest press-marks of the charters of Saint-Ouen, Rouen, date from this period.[49] Documents regulating relationships between bishops and abbots, though rare, were beginning to appear.[50] Records were kept for various purposes, of which the preservation of titles to monastic lands and privileges was only one. The rights of patrons too needed to be

---

[45] Cf. Avril, *Mont-Saint-Michel*, II, plates XXXI, LII, LIII, LIV; Alexander, *Norman Illumination*, plate 19h; A. Boinet, 'L'illustration du cartulaire du Mont-Saint-Michel' in *BEC*, LXX (1909), 335–43. Similar collections were being made in other parts of Europe at about this date; see J. Leclercq, 'Monastic historiography from Leo IX to Callistus II', *Studia Monastica*, XII (1970), 74–5. C. Manaresi, 'Il *Liber instrumentorum seu chronicorum monasterii Casauriensis*' in *Rendiconti dell'Istituto Lombardo di Scienze e Lettere*, LXXX (1947) describes a chronicle produced in the abbey of S. Clemente di Pescara, where charters were copied beside the narrative like *pièces justificatives*.

[46] His historical work has been critically assessed by R. Foreville, 'Robert de Torigni et Clio' in *Mont-Saint-Michel*, II, 141–53.　　　[47] Printed, Delisle, *Torigni*, II, 237–60.

[48] Leclercq, 'Monastic historiography', p. 57.　　　[49] Cf. Fauroux, *Recueil*, pp. 179, 311.

[50] Cf. the document in which the monks of Saint-Evroult announced the election of Roger of Le Sap as abbot in 1099 (Orderic, *Historia* (C) v, 262–4).

safeguarded: they were entitled to liturgical commemoration and various spiritual benefits. Records of their gifts, made often in the monastic chapter, were preserved in such documents as the earliest charter-roll surviving from Saint-Evroult, which is almost as much a chapter minute book as a collection of charters.[51] The acts, mostly in narrative form, give such details as how one man granted his tithe to the abbey and received a free gift of five shillings to buy a psalter for his son whom he was sending to school;[52] or how another came into the chapter-house and promised to give himself to the abbey with all his possessions on his death, in return for the full commemoration due for any one of the monks.[53] Rolls of this kind may have been kept with the charters, or brought into the church and laid on the altar on days established for the commemoration of benefactors.[54] Among the materials intended for reading aloud to the monks in the course of the daily horarium and at special times in the commemoration of saints were passages from the lives of the abbey's saints, and accounts of the early history of the house and the gifts of its benefactors.[55] Intended primarily for the instruction of the monks themselves, they often contained passages copied from both authentic and interpolated documents.

Lastly, there is evidence that a number of official records were finding their way into Norman monastic repositories. In the later years of Duke William the *acta* of his councils appear to have been sent out in something approaching official form.[56] Papal bulls were rare until towards the close of the century, as the clumsy forgery of the monks of Mont-Saint-Michel in 1058–60 illustrates; but lists of some canons of provincial councils were being sent out. If canons of papal councils were not generally promulgated in any official form at this time, synopses of some decrees circulated: lists of canons of the 1095 Council

---

[51] Printed, Orderic, *Historia* (Le P.) v, 182–95.

[52] Orderic, *Historia* (Le P.) v, 190, no. XXXII.

[53] Orderic, *Historia* (Le P.) v, 191, no. XXXVII.

[54] Cf. the roll containing the names of benefactors and their families, preserved at Saint-Evroult (Orderic, *Historia* (C), II, 114).

[55] Cf. Pommeraye, *Saint-Ouen*, p. 248, who describes the *Livre Noir* of Saint-Ouen as 'un recueil de Vies de Saints qu'on lisoit autrefois aux collations ou conferences qui se tenoient dans le chapitre ou dans le cloistre avant complies', and Dom J. Hourlier, 'Les sources écrites de l'histoire montoise antérieure à 966', in *Mont-Saint-Michel*, II, 124–8.

[56] See M. de Boüard, 'Sur les origines de la trève de Dieu en Normandie', *Annales de Normandie*, IX (1959), 169–89, where early manuscripts containing the détails of the truce are described; also Pierre Chaplais, 'Henry II's reissue of the canons of the council of Lillebonne', *Journal of the Society of Archivists*, IV (1973), 628–32, and Orderic, *Historia* (C), III, 26, for the canons of the council of Lillebonne.

of Clermont survive from the two Norman monasteries of Séez and Saint-Evroult.[57] The monastic historian of the early twelfth century had a wide range of records on which to draw, some of them in their original semi-official form, others to some extent incorporated in annals or earlier short narratives.

Some records, notably great charters, were far from fixed and stable. The document familiar in Norman diplomatic as the pancarte grew by accretion over a period of years. The purpose of these pancartes was to preserve a record of the foundation and early endowment of a new house. The process of monastic foundation was a slow one, beginning with the first promise of endowment in a formal ceremony and often not completed until buildings had been consecrated and religious life begun several years later. The diplomatic consequences of this have been clearly explained by Professor V. H. Galbraith.[58] If when a charter of foundation was finally issued it was drafted in diploma rather than in letter form, 'the draftsman was faced by the difficulty of recording in the present tense a series of acts spread over years, and of referring to the moment of the original *donatio* much that was subsequent to it'. In a pancarte a series of gifts, each with its own witnesses, might be recorded in a single ducal charter. Subsequent ceremonies of gift might be noted in the margins of the original; when at a later stage a clean copy of the pancarte became desirable, the marginalia were inserted without much regard to chronological sequence, and new subscriptions were added to the original list. Unless any forged material happened to have been interpolated, the final copy, though chronologically confused, would be entirely genuine.[59] The document would normally contain a brief narrative of the circumstances inducing the founder to establish the house; written, possibly, in the scriptorium of the beneficiary, it was already on the way to becoming a *historia fundationis*, though without the chronological accuracy of a set of annals. If it became the basis of a more extended monastic history it might well, as a narrative, lead to misunderstanding about dates and details, whilst falling, as a charter, under suspicion of forgery in the eyes of modern

[57] Bibl. nat. MS lat. 13413; Alençon, Bibl. municipale, MS 10; see Robert Somerville, *The Councils of Urban II, Annuarium Historiae Conciliorum*, Supplementum I (Amsterdam, 1972), 83–98.

[58] V. H. Galbraith, 'Monastic foundation charters of the eleventh and twelfth centuries', *Cambridge Historical Journal*, IV (1934), 210–19.

[59] The process by which the pancartes of Holy Trinity and St Stephen's, Caen, were built up has been analysed by L. Musset, *Les actes de Guillaume le Conquérant et de la reine Mathilde pour les abbayes caennaises* (Caen, 1967), pp. 25–35.

students of diplomatic. As the charters of the two great abbeys at Caen show, copies might be made from an original pancarte at different stages of evolution, giving rise to two different 'originals', both provided with subscriptions and both equally genuine as far as the recorded concessions were concerned.[60]

When new abbeys were founded in England after the Norman conquest the Norman monks carried their diplomatic practices with them. Roger of Montgomery brought monks from St Martin's, Séez, to establish religious life in St Peter's, Shrewsbury; and Hugh, earl of Chester, sent to Bec-Hellouin for monks to restore St Werburgh's, Chester. The main foundation charters of the two houses bear all the marks of Norman pancartes and were undoubtedly written in the scriptoria of the abbeys concerned;[61] there is evidence too of copying from one house to another, for the Chester charter, *Sanctorum prisca*,[62] became the model for the great charter of Henry I to Shrewsbury Abbey, issued in 1121 and beginning with an identical formula.[63] The Shrewsbury charters in particular, with their long passages of narrative, suggest a debt to a narrative history of the abbey's foundation, and follow the Norman tradition; they provide a postscript in England to a chapter of Norman historiography. They are also a reminder that, whilst charters were as much records as title deeds, growth and variation need not imply forgery.

In Normandy itself the most effective use of charter sources came, like so much else, from the pen of Orderic Vitalis. Among the many charters that he used were more than one of the lost original pancartes of the abbey of Saint-Evroult and its dependent priories. For the abbey itself the earliest surviving copies of two lost pancartes of Duke

[60] Musset, *Actes*, no. 4; for other monasteries see also Fauroux, *Recueil*, no. 15 and *passim*.

[61] Some charters of the abbey of Bec were written in narrative form in the scriptorium of the monks as late as the reign of Henry I and then authenticated by the king's signature and seal; see M. Chibnall, *Select Documents of the English Lands of the Abbey of Bec*, Camden third ser. LXXIII (1951), p. 9, nos. xiv, xvi. The doubts there expressed about the authenticity of these charters were unfounded; see P. Chaplais, 'The seals and original charters of Henry I', *EHR*, LXXV (1960), 270.

[62] J. Tait, *The Chartulary of St. Werburgh, Chester*, Chetham Society, LXXIX (1920), pp. 13–37. The authenticity of this charter was recognised by Galbraith, 'Monastic foundation charters', pp. 218–9.

[63] Printed, *Collectanea Topographica et Genealogica*, I (1834), 191–6; also no. 35 in the new edition of the cartulary of Shrewsbury Abbey, ed. U. Rees, to be published by the National Library of Wales. I am very grateful to Mrs Rees for allowing me to see a typescript of her edition. The development of the pancartes of Gloucester Abbey, in which earlier narratives were incorporated, is discussed by C. N. L. Brooke, 'St. Peter of Gloucester and St. Cadoc of Llancarfan' in *Celt and Saxon*, ed. N. K. Chadwick (Cambridge, 1963), pp. 268–71. Abbot Serlo of Gloucester came from Mont-Saint-Michel in 1072.

William I are in the thirteenth-century cartulary.[64] Orderic's narrative of the foundation, though giving much information common to one or the other and sometimes both, corresponds exactly with neither, and adds a few details of his own. The differences could be explained if he worked from a pancarte or pancartes containing marginalia not yet worked into the text, or used an earlier narrative history incorporating such charters. Something of the kind may have been written by his master, John of Rheims; some of John's historical writings were still in the library of the abbey when Dom Julien Bellaise prepared his catalogue in 1682, and these included a treatise described by him as, 'De prioribus abbatibus Utici, et monasterii restauratione, necnon de donariis principum, nobilium, et aliorum piorum virorum'.[65] But whether Orderic worked from this treatise or directly from the charters, his account of the foundation of Saint-Evroult reveals an earlier stage in the evolution of the pancartes than that found in either of the cartulary copies.[66] Significant variations occur in the details of the process of foundation and donation and in the clause relating to freedom of elections. The election clause was certainly expanded, both in the earlier version of the pancarte and in Orderic's account of the troubles after Abbot Robert of Grandmesnil was driven into exile in 1061.[67] The clause in the later pancarte, with its insistence on the inability of the bishop of Lisieux to prevent the blessing of a properly elected abbot, was almost certainly interpolated during the period of conflict with the bishop between 1089 and 1099.[68] The author of the interpolation seems to have found his information in more than one place, possibly using an earlier narrative of Abbot Thierry's election, which Orderic also used, and adapting a grant of spiritual benefits to some bishop of Lisieux, preserved in a lost part of the abbey's chapter-rolls. The mutual borrowing of evolving pancarte and narrative, so

---

[64] See Fauroux, *Recueil*, no. 122 for critical texts and a description of the manuscript versions. The cartulary copies are also printed in Orderic, *Historia* (Le P), v, 173–80.

[65] Bibl. nat. MS lat. 13073, fos. 53v–54 (no. 129); there is an incomplete edition by B. de Montfaucon, *Bibliotheca bibliothecarum manuscriptorum nova*, II (Paris, 1739), 1268–73.

[66] Orderic, *Historia* (C), II, 16, 30–40. I hope to discuss the two pancartes and their relation to the text of Orderic more fully in volume I of my edition.

[67] Orderic, *Historia* (C), II, 90ff. An account of the early abbatial elections at Saint-Evroult is given by J. Yver, 'Autour de l'absence d'avouerie en Normandie', *Bulletin de la Société des Antiquaires de Normandie*, LVII (1963–4), 271–9.

[68] Orderic, *Historia* (C), v, 260–4. The interpolated clause relating to the bishop of Lisieux in the second pancarte runs: 'ordinante Lisiocacensi Hugone episcopo qui hoc etiam ex sua parte, ut tam ipse quam sui successores participes sint beneficii predicti loci, constituit, si ipse aliquando vel ejus successores causa alicujus non recte occasionis abbatem ordinare renuerint, illos per-recturos ad quemcumque maluerint'.

important in building up a tradition of monastic history and privilege, is reminiscent of the records of Mont-Saint-Michel at the same period.

It is plain from his handling of charter material that Orderic, writing between 1114 and 1141, thought of the documents as part of a living tradition rather than as title deeds. He drew both on the memories of other monks and on existing written annals or notices to dramatise them, and at times his memory made sense of a grant that, from the thirteenth-century cartulary copy alone, might have been condemned as a forgery. The charter of Richer of Laigle confirming the gifts of his father Ingenulf and his vassals exists only in a suspicious form: the salutation is anachronistic, and it ends with the statement that it was sealed on the day of the dedication of the church. Richer died c. 1086, and the church was dedicated in 1099. But Orderic relates that Richer's son Gilbert confirmed and augmented his father's gift on the day that the church was dedicated, when a number of lords laid tokens of their gifts on an altar still damp with the holy water sprinkled in consecration.[69] Probably Gilbert added some clauses to the record of his father's gift on that occasion, and a later scribe produced a garbled version; Orderic's narrative supports the authenticity of the gifts. Elsewhere he shows how donations briefly recorded in a single charter might be spread over a number of years and influenced by the intervening events.[70]

All this is part of a tradition of considerable antiquity, rooted in the Norman past. Established at the beginning of the ninth century, it was merely interrupted by the tenth-century wars and invasions, and was continued from the time of Duke Richard I. But in the extent of his researches among the records of the restored abbey of Saint-Evroult, in the care with which he used them, and in the wealth of archive material he incorporated in his narrative, as in so many other things, Orderic towers above every other historian writing in Normandy in his age. He may have learnt something from contemporary English historians of more comparable stature, for he knew the work of Eadmer of Canterbury and John of Worcester, though it is doubtful if he ever saw the historical writings of the greatest of them all and his only true peer, William of Malmesbury. But it is certain that, when he turned from the records of his own abbey to write a more general history of

[69] Orderic, *Historia* (C), v, 266–8; III, 130.
[70] I have discussed Orderic's handling of some of his charter material in the introduction to Orderic, *Historia* (C), II, xxv–xxix; III, xx–xxiv.

the Church, he drew inspiration and to some extent learnt his method from the giants of an earlier age: Eusebius of Caesarea and, above all, Bede. He knew Bede's *Ecclesiastical History* intimately, for he had copied almost every word of it with his own hand.[71] Probably Bede's example encouraged him to include copies of letters in his own work. Bede's *History* is particularly rich in papal letters, whereas the materials available to Orderic included few if any recent bulls; desire to imitate his model may have induced him to invent the wording of a bull to Robert of Molesme of which he had heard.[72] But the letter sent by Abbot Osbern of Saint-Evroult to Pope Alexander II, asking for absolution, is probably genuine.[73] So too is the text of the deed announcing the election of Roger of Le Sap as abbot.[74]

In his regard for the canons of the councils he was able to go beyond Bede, who was obliged to present the decisions of the Council of Whitby in the form of an imaginary debate.[75] Like his contemporaries, William of Malmesbury and John of Worcester, and perhaps responding to attempts by secular and ecclesiastical authorities to secure the promulgation and preservation of the acts of councils, he copied into his history a number of canons promulgated in his time: probably all on which he could lay his hands. These include the canons of the provincial church councils held at Rouen in 1072 and 1096, of the 1080 Council of Lillebonne, presided over by William the Conqueror, and some at least of the canons of the 1095 Council of Clermont and the 1119 Council of Rheims.[76] The machinery for promulgating ecclesiastical canons was far from perfect in the late eleventh century, and 'extant decrees are not necessarily a synod's official or final statement'.[77] They might amount to no more than incomplete lists of chapter headings; this is particularly true of the 1095 canons of Clermont. But in whatever form they reached Saint-Evroult, Orderic copied them faithfully,[78] adding information about how they were promulgated and what other business was discussed in the councils. There is a striking

---

[71] Rouen, Bibl. municipale, MS U.43 (1343); see also B. Colgrave and R. A. B. Mynors (eds.), *Bede's Ecclesiastical History of the English People* (Oxford Medieval Texts, 1969), p. lxi.

[72] Orderic, *Historia* (C), IV, 322–4. [73] Orderic, *Historia* (C), II, 108–12.

[74] Orderic, *Historia* (C), V, 262–4.

[75] Colgrave and Mynors, *Bede*, pp. 298–308. Where Bede had copies of original documents he reproduced them with meticulous care (*ibid.* pp. xxxix–xl).

[76] Orderic, *Historia* (C), II, 284–93; V, 20–2; III, 24–34; V, 10–14; (Le P) IV, 391–3.

[77] Somerville, *Councils of Urban II*, p. 21.

[78] The carefulness of his copying seems apparent from a comparison of his version with other copies of the canons of Lillebonne and of Clermont current in Normandy (Orderic, *Historia* (C), III, 25 n.3, 26 n. 1; Somerville, *Councils of Urban II*, pp. 83ff.).

contrast between his handling of these canons and of the many charters that he used; the canons were clearly separated from the supplementary narrative, whereas the charters were often written into a narrative of the grants they recorded. The canons, whatever their imperfections, were to him legal records in their own right, whereas the charters, though recording title, were still inseparable from the ceremonies of donation. Canons, unlike charters, were not drafted and written in monasteries; had he lived in the royal court, as did the English historian Roger of Howden half a century later, he might occasionally have allowed a little explanation to creep into the texts of laws.[79]

This is not the place to investigate other types of history and chronicle produced in some bulk in Normandy during the twelfth century. Apart from Orderic at Saint-Evroult, writers of general histories usually made use directly of written narrative sources, and only indirectly of archive material. Robert of Torigny collected charter material only for the history of his own house and kept his *Chronicle* to terse narrative after the manner of Sigebert of Gembloux, not even including any canons of the 1172 Council of Avranches which he had attended in person.[80] Other Norman abbeys with brilliant intellectual interests did not cherish the great traditions of ecclesiastical history that inspired Orderic and a number of his contemporaries in England to design their works on such a vast plan and include so much documentary material in them. There was a keen interest in history at St Stephen's, Caen, where part of Orderic's *Ecclesiastical History* was copied within two or three decades of his death,[81] and an anonymous annalist prefaced his brief chronicle with the confident words, 'Iocundum et utile est historias scire;'[82] but if Caen produced any more general historian it was only the secular clerk Wace, educated at Caen and later a canon of Bayeux, whose history of the Norman dukes, the *Roman de Rou*, was a vernacular epic based on narrative sources and oral tradition. Apart from anonymous chroniclers, Bec-Hellouin trained only Gilbert Crispin, who became abbot of Westminster, Robert of Torigny, who migrated to Mont-Saint-Michel, and Miles Crispin, whose *Vita Lanfranci* is a disappointing work when one considers the fine letter collections left by Lanfranc that might have been used to enrich its meagre content. The availability of archive materials did not necessarily mean that they were used. Only in the internal history of almost

[79] See above, p. 2 n. 2.
[81] MS Vatican Reg. lat. 703B.
[80] Cf. Foreville in *Mont-Saint-Michel*, II, 149.
[82] MS Vatican Reg. lat. 703A, p. 1.

every house were charter and chronicle so closely connected that narrative charter and *Historia fundationis* were both in a sense by-products of the process of endowment.[83] In Normandy until well into the twelfth century chronicles no less than charters have a place in the history of diplomatic.

[83] This is one reason why fifteenth-century chronicles often contain more reliable information about early abbots than about later abbots; see Knowles, Brooke and London, *Heads of Religious Houses*, p. 6.

THE SYNOD OF THE PROVINCE
OF ROUEN IN THE ELEVENTH AND
TWELFTH CENTURIES

by RAYMONDE FOREVILLE
Translated by Geoffrey Martin

AMONG the many institutions of medieval Europe in which the inter-action of secular and ecclesiastical government can be studied, the provincial synod of Rouen, during the eleventh and twelfth centuries, has many interesting features to commend it. The period in question is defined on the one hand by the pontificate of Leo IX (1049–54) and William the Conqueror's recovery of ducal power, and on the other by Normandy's submission to Capetian rule and the pontificate of Innocent III. Both the beginning and the end are marked by the impact of the Canon Law. Let us first bear in mind the provisions of Canon 6 of the Fourth Lateran Council (1215), which prescribed a yearly meeting for provincial synods.[1] For a study of the earlier period, the Gregorian position has a more obvious relevance. Consider, in particular, one of the most elaborate collections of canons, that of Cardinal Deusdedit. This is how it treats of the provincial synod, the tradition of which, incidentally, stretched back into the post-apostolic age and was written into the Nicean decrees.[2]

In order to proceed duly to the enquiry [into appeals against excommunication] it is the practice to assemble a council of bishops twice each year, in every province, so that they can examine such matters in a single assembly for the whole province...and those judged excommunicate by their bishop may be held excommunicate by all others until they have been judged in common...to merit some lesser sentence. (Canon 2.)[3]

The Gregorian compiler takes care, however, to emphasise the limits that apostolic authority sets to the provincial jurisdiction.

[1] *Conciliorum oecumenicorum decreta*, Centro di documentazione, Istituto per le scienze religiose (Bologna, 1962), pp. 212–13; French transl. R. Foreville, *Latran I, II et III et Latran IV* (Paris, 1965), pp. 348–9.
[2] *Conciliorum oecumenicorum decreta*, p. 7, French transl. G. Dumeige, *Nicée et Constantinople* (Paris, 1963), p. 261.
[3] *Die Kanonessammlung des Kardinals Deusdedit*, ed. Victor Wolf von Glanvell (Paderborn, 1905, repr. 1967), p. 31.

The metropolitans must air the causes of bishops and other ecclesiastical dignitaries conjointly with all the bishops of the province, in such sort that all are present and all lend their approval to the affairs of each one, provided that none shall determine his own cause, or those of his own church, nor condemn a bishop without the authority of the apostolic see. It is there that all should carry their appeals, if need be, and should seek support...You are aware that it is contrary to the Canon Law to hold a synod without that authority, and that no council can be legitimate that does not rest upon the apostolic authority. (Canon 95.)[4]

And again:

The provincial synod can be annulled by the vicars of the bishop of Rome if he so will it. (Canon 17.)[5]

Gratian goes further still when he discusses the council, noting on the one hand, one sole authority able to authorise any episcopal synod, or to validate its decrees, and on the other, the limits that are set to the competence of the provincial synod: admonition and correction, and the promulgation of the decrees of general councils. In any instance, the provincial synod has no power to define the faith, to establish constitutions, or even to pronounce a definitive sentence. Those are the prerogatives of the church of Rome:

There is no valid council that is not founded upon the authority of the church of Rome. (D.17 c.2)
Provincial councils have no substance save in the presence of the Roman pontiff. (D.17 c.6)

Finally let us consider the *dictum Gratiani*, which unites the spirit and the substance.

It follows that episcopal councils, as it appears in what has been shown, have no power to define or to constitute, but only power to correct. They are necessary to exhort and correct, for although they have no power to make constitutions, they have the authority to enjoin and enforce such things as have been enacted elsewhere, and the observance of which has been prescribed either in general or particular terms. (D.18)

Such was the Gregorian doctrine, still emphasised in the *Summa* of ancient law which recorded the growth of an authority centralised in Rome. The outcome of Gregory VII's policy was that legates were used to perform all the functions that traditionally had fallen to the metropolitan bishops. That policy was most notably maintained in the kingdom of France, where his permanent legates, Hugh of Die for France and Burgundy, Amatus of Oloron first for Aquitaine, and then

---

[4] *Ibid.* p. 78.   [5] *Ibid.* p. 36.

for the Narbonnaise, Gascony, and Spain,[6] confirmed suffragan bishops, annulled sentences of the provincial courts, and summoned and presided over synods.[7] From that vast concert, however, Normandy stood apart.

I. THE NORMAN PROVINCIAL ASSEMBLIES, C. 1040–1189

From the majority of William the Conqueror to the death of Henry II in 1189, there were twenty-seven or twenty-eight assemblies held in the ecclesiastical province of Rouen which were either explicitly documented or incidentally recorded. There can be no guarantee that the list is exhaustive. Richard Kay's research on the provincial synods of Rouen[8] relates to the thirteenth century, after the regulation of 1215, and his arguments depend upon a document unique in its kind, the Register of Archbishop Eudes Rigaud, which reveals a biennial sequence during his pontificate. By that time the synod had become a matter of ecclesiastical routine. It no longer ordinarily attracted the notice of chroniclers, and the more so because, so far as its legislative work was concerned, the statutes that it promulgated were often repeated from session to session. It was otherwise in the eleventh and twelfth centuries, when the assembly of a synod was an unusual and notable event. There are grounds for supposing, even when the incompleteness of our sources is taken into account, that only a small number of provincial assemblies would have entirely escaped the notice of the ecclesiastical chroniclers of the eleventh and twelfth centuries. There are, however, some distinctions to be drawn among the assemblies that have been recorded, which are presented here in the form of a table.

The first phase to stand out corresponds roughly with the reigns of the Conqueror and his sons Robert Curthose and Henry I. It is a period characterised by a high frequency, for it comprises no fewer than twenty-five provincial assemblies, and twenty-six if we admit the existence of a first synod in 1042, in less than a century. Of those only five met under a legate, four figure as ducal courts or councils, and two

---

[6] A. Fliche, *Le règne de Philippe Ier, roi de France* (Paris, 1912), pp. 359, 357.

[7] A. Fliche, *La réforme grégorienne* (Louvain-Paris, 1925), II. 233. The policy finds its perfect expression in the lapidary formula of the *Dictatus papae*: 'The [pope's] legate is above all bishops in a council, even if he be inferior to them in orders, and he can pronounce sentence of deposition against them' (*Registrum*, 2, 55a, ed. E. Caspar, MGH (Berlin, 1920–3), p. 202).

[8] R. Kay, 'Mansi and Rouen: a critique of the conciliar collections', *Catholic Historical Review*, II, (1966), 160ff.

Table 1. *Assemblies of the province of Rouen in the eleventh and twelfth centuries*

Date	Place	Nature	Intervention of Legates	Archbishops
1042 (?)	Caen[b]	Synod		MAUGER 1037
c. 1045 (?)[a]	Rouen	Synod		
1047[b]	Caen	Synod		
1050	Brionne	Synod		
1054[c]	Lisieux	Synod	Ermenfred, bishop of Sion	Deprived 1054
1055 (?)	Rouen	Synod		MAURILIUS 1054/5–67
1061	Caen	Council		
1063 October	Rouen	Synod		
1064	Lisieux	Synod		
1066 July	Lillebonne	Synod and Council		
[1067–9]	(?)	Synod		JOHN OF BAYEUX transl. from Avranches, 1069
1069	Rouen	Synod	Ermenfred	
1070	(?)	Synod	Ermenfred and Hubert	
1072	Rouen	Synod		
1073	Rouen	Council		
1074	Rouen	Synod		
1078 4 April	Rouen	Synod	Hubert	Resigned 1078
1079 July	Rouen	Synod		WILLIAM BONNE AME 1079–1110
1080 Whitsun[d]	Lillebonne	Synod and Council		
1082 5 September	Oissel	Council		
1091 June	Rouen	Synod		
1096 February[e]	Rouen	Synod		
1106 15 October	Lisieux	Synod		
1118 7 October	Rouen	Synod		GEOFFREY 1111–28
1119 c. Sept.–Oct.[f]	Lisieux	Synod		
November (?)[g]	(?)	Synod		
1128 November[h]	Rouen	Synod	Matthew, bishop of Albano	
				HUGH OF AMIENS 1130–64
1172 30 May	Caen	Enlarged synod	Albert and Theodwin	ROTROU OF WARWICK transl. from Evreux, 1165 Died 1183
1172 28 September[i]	Avranches	Synod	Albert and Theodwin	
1190 11 February[j]	Rouen	Synod		WALTER OF COUTANCES transl. from Lincoln 1184 Died 1208
1214 February[k]	Rouen	Synod	Robert Courson	ROBERT POULAIN 1208–22

were meetings for arbitration. The others, or rather more than half, appear to have been provincial synods properly so called.

The councils of the province meeting under a legate are distinguished not only by the smallness of their number, but also by the business performed in them. The Conqueror turned to the papal legates on particular occasions, to depose or translate bishops, for example: that is to say, in those cases which went beyond the powers of the metropolitan and invoked the authority of the apostolic see. It was thus that the legate Ermenfred, bishop of Sion, presided over the councils of Lisieux in 1054, of Rouen in 1069, and over the council of 1070, the meeting-place of which is unknown, and the legate Hubert, clerk of the Curia, presided over the council at Rouen in 1078.

At Lisieux in 1054 the council's business was to depose Archbishop Mauger, who was convicted of rapacity, of depredation of the goods of

---

Notes to Table 1

a The date 1049, which is sometimes given, cannot be reconciled with what we know of the bishops present. Robert, bishop of Coutances, is last mentioned in 1048, and his successor Geoffrey of Montbrai was consecrated 10 April 1049. Hugh, bishop of Evreux, died 20 April 1046.

b Prentout has disposed of the date 1042 for the council of Caen, in relation to the Truce of God, suggested by Dom Bessin. He admits, however, the possibility of a synod in 1042. ('La trêve de Dieu en Normandie', in *Études sur quelques points de l'histoire de Guillaume le Conquérant* (Caen, 1930), pp. 4–10.).

c The date of the Council of Lisieux (1055, c. May), is given in the chronicle of St Stephen's, Caen (J. A. Giles, ed., *Scriptores rerum gestarum Willelmi Conquestoris in unum collecti* (London, 1845), p. 165), and has been generally accepted. We did, however, question it in our edition of William of Poitiers, pp. 132–3 n. 2, on the grounds that Ermenfred is referred to as legate of Pope Leo IX, who died 9 April 1054. As Olivier Guillot has remarked in a recent work (*Le comte d'Anjou et son entourage au XIe siècle* (Paris, 1972), I, 187n.), in two acts of the Conqueror, Mauger is mentioned for the last time as archbishop on 25 December 1054, and Maurilius, his immediate successor, appears in that role in the same year (Marie Fauroux, *Recueil des Actes des Ducs de Normandie* (Caen, 1961), Mémoires de la Société des Antiquaires de Normandie, XXXVI nos. 133, 132). These acts appear to be dated by years beginning at Christmas. In consequence, the synod of Lisieux at which Mauger was deposed must have sat between Christmas 1053 and the end of April or, at the latest, the beginning of May 1054, to make allowance for the time that the news of the pope's death would take to travel.

d After the solemn celebration of the feast (31 May); presumably within the octave, at the beginning of June.

e No doubt at the beginning of Lent (Ash Wednesday fell on 27 February).

f Before the general Council of Rheims, but probably after the battle of Brémule (20 August 1119).

g After the Council of Rheims (20–30 October).

h During Archbishop Geoffrey's last illness: he died 28 November.

i This was essentially a Norman council. Nevertheless, the archbishops of Tours and Dol came to submit to the legates the dispute that had arisen between them over metropolitan jurisdiction (cf. *Gesta regis Henrici II*, ed. W. Stubbs, (RS, 1867), I, 34 and Roger de Hoveden, *Chronicle*, ed. W. Stubbs, RS (1868–71), II, 40).

j 11 February, the first Sunday in Lent.

k In 1214, the first Sunday in Lent fell on 16 February.

his church, of sexual incontinence, and of defiance of the apostolic see.[9] To those delicts we may add a personal grievance on the part of the duke against his uncle for having meddled in the rebellion of William of Arques, for denouncing his union with Matilda as one within the prohibited degrees.[10]

At Rouen in 1069 there were certainly two sessions of the synod, in the course of one of which Lanfranc, prior of Bec, was elected to the metropolitan see in succession to Maurilius, who died in 1067 having himself succeeded Mauger. The other was occasioned by Lanfranc's refusal to accept the see, and followed his embassy to the Curia to seek the translation of John of Bayeux from the see of Avranches to the metropolitan church.[11] After the deposition of Stigand as an intruder upon the see of Canterbury, by the legates Ermenfred and Hubert, Lanfranc's nomination was announced by the same legates in the council of the bishops and abbots of Normandy, on a date between 15 and 29 August 1070.[12] Finally, at Rouen in 1078, the legate Hubert, having inquired into the illness of Archbishop John, who had become incapable of discharging his duties, either obtained his resignation or deposed him in a synod of bishops, abbots, and the canons of the metropolitan church.[13]

A similar situation must have arisen in 1128, when the provincial council was assembled on the orders of King Henry by the legate Matthew, bishop of Albano, during Archbishop Geoffrey's last illness.[14] On all those occasions, whilst they involved reserved cases, the legate's intervention, requested by the prince, ended in his deference to the prince's wishes by the final choice, election, or nomination of some *persona grata*.

Two assemblies, those of 1073 and 1082, stand apart. They cannot have been other than tribunals convened for a closely-defined purpose.

9 Guillaume de Poitiers, ed. R. Foreville (Paris, 1952), pp. 130–2. Mauger was deposed by the duke 'in public session of the holy synod, the apostolic vicar and all the bishops of Normandy having...given their unanimous assent to the sentence'. Orderic Vitalis also notes that Mauger was deposed by the prince's will, but upon the pope's decree (*Historia ecclesiastica*, ed. Le Prévost (5 vols., Paris, 1838–55), III, 233; ed. M. Chibnall (Oxford, 1968–   ), IV, 73, 74, 84–5). For the date of the council (1054) see table 1, n. c.

10 Orderic Vitalis, ed. Le Prévost, I, 184; William of Malmesbury, *Gesta regum*, ed. W. Stubbs, II, RS (London, 1889), 327.

11 Orderic Vitalis, ed. Le Prévost, II, 170; ed. Chibnall, II, 200.

12 Orderic Vitalis, ed. Le Prévost, II, 212; ed. Chibnall, II, 252 and note.

13 Gregory VII, JL 5074 (4 April 1078); Dom Bessin, *Concilia Rotomagensis provinciae* (Rouen, 1717), Pars I, p. 66.   14 Orderic Vitalis, ed. Le Prévost, IV, 496–7.

Summoned and presided over by the Conqueror, the sessions at Rouen in 1073 examined the dispute that had arisen between Archbishop John and the abbot of Saint-Ouen over the solemn celebration of the patronal feast (24 August) of the great abbey, a close neighbour of the cathedral. The celebration occasioned a disturbance that the archbishop punished with interdicts. The sanctions directed against certain monks rebounded, however, upon the prelate himself, who was subjected to a heavy fine of 300 *livres* for his proceedings against a ducal abbey.[15] A similarly limited council met in 1082, consisting chiefly of lay magnates and several abbots of Upper Normandy, besides the bishop of Durham: the only Norman bishops present were those of Evreux and Lisieux, the sees adjoining the archdiocese. It was concerned solely with the arbitration of a dispute between Archbishop William Bonne Ame and the abbot of Fontenelle (Saint-Wandrille) over the primate's juridical rights in four parish churches, dependent on the abbey, concerning the blessing of the iron used in the ordeal.[16]

In their references to the assemblies of 1047, 1061, 1066 and 1080, the chroniclers show them in the character of a court or a ducal council. In fact such courts, however formal, were entirely compatible with the assembly of a lesser council of the Norman bishops and abbots. The matters discussed could be expected to engage the support of the clerical members, although they concerned both clergy and laity, and affected the general public interest.

In 1047, not in 1042 or 1061 as has sometimes been argued, the famous synod upon the Truce of God was held at Caen. It is not impossible that a preliminary synod was convoked in 1042. Be that as it may, the truce was established by the duke and his bishops after the troubles of William's minority and the victory at Val-ès-Dunes, on the model of the measures taken a little earlier in Burgundy. There can be no doubt that a synodal decision was involved, because the sanctions envisaged required an episcopal authority: thirty years' penance performed beyond the diocese involved, for anyone who broke the truce, seven years' within the diocese for anyone who took another's goods during the time of truce, and finally, an oath and the ordeal of hot iron for anyone who professed to have infringed the truce unwittingly. We also know that a sanctuary was raised and dedicated to

---

[15] Dom Bessin, pp. 63–4, after the *Chronique de Caen*, A.D. 1073.
[16] Dom Bessin, pp. 75–6.

the Holy Peace to mark the event and commemorate the solemn assembly.[17]

In 1061, also at Caen, there were decrees on the curfew and upon the discovery of criminals, and against abbots and prelates from rural areas frequenting the towns near their churches.[18] At Lillebonne, in July 1066,[19] there was a veritable ducal council. The bishops, at least those of princely family, were designated by their affiliations: Odo, Duke William's half-brother, bishop of Bayeux, John, the son of Ralph, count of Bayeux, bishop of Avranches, Yves, son of William of Bellême, bishop of Sées. The business was to make the final dispositions for the expedition against England, which concerned the *proceres*, but also to send a delegation to Pope Alexander II to seek his blessing upon the enterprise.[20]

We do not know where or at what date the council met which decided, after the Conquest, the penances to be imposed on those who, during that campaign, had killed, pillaged, committed rapes and adultery, or had as clergy borne arms.[21] It cannot have been earlier than the new king's first return to Normandy (29 September 1066– March 1067), and might belong to one of the sessions of the synod of 1069, unless it came before the death of Archbishop Maurilius on 9 August 1067.

The assembly at Lillebonne at Whitsun 1080[22] is justly remembered for the importance of its decisions, which include the renewal of the Truce of God and measures to check the violation of churches. Above all it regularised the work of the spiritual courts and defined their authority, confirming that of the duke's justice over the clergy as well as the laity in causes touching seisin, in conflicts of jurisdiction and in offences against the forest laws. It should be noticed, however, that many of the decrees published on that occasion related to ecclesiastical

[17] Dom Bessin, pp. 39–40. On the circumstances of the Peace Council and its date, 1047, not 1042 (Bessin) or 1061 (de Bras, followed by the early historians of Normandy), see H. Prentout, *Études sur quelques points de l'histoire de Guillaume le Conquérant* (see Table I above, p. 23, n. b), pp. 4–10, and the passage cited from Wace, *Roman de Rou* (ibid. pp. 6–7). Prentout here invalidates the arguments of Charles de Bourgueville, sieur de Bras, *Recherches et Antiquités de la duché de Normandie* (Caen, 1588, in 4°), p. 15, accepted by Du Moulin, *Histoire générale de Normandie* (Rouen, 1631, in folio), p. 160.

[18] Dom Bessin, p. 48. The text of Canon I is undoubtedly corrupt.

[19] Orderic Vitalis, ed. Le Prévost, II, 121–2; ed. Chibnall, II, 140–2.

[20] The authenticity of Alexander's blessing has been questioned in C. Morton, 'Pope Alexander and the Norman Conquest', *Latomus*, XXXIV (1975), 362–82.

[21] Dom Bessin, pp. 50–1.

[22] Orderic Vitalis, ed. Le Prévost, II, 315–23; ed. Chibnall, III, 24–34; Dom Bessin, pp. 67–71.

discipline, taking up the decrees of earlier councils, both general and purely Norman. They cover marriages within the degrees of consanguinity, clerical concubinage, the prohibition of laymen sharing the revenues of churches, the regulation of archidiaconal visitations and the rights of sanctuary. They strengthen the bishop's authority over priests who neglect their ministry, the obligation to celibacy, and attendance at diocesan synods.

That concern is less evident in the meeting that King Henry I held at Lisieux on 15 October 1106, shortly after the victory of Tinchebrai, which assured his possession of the duchy. According to Orderic Vitalis, 'the king came to Lisieux; he called together all the *optimates* of Normandy and held a council most useful to the Church, that assured a firm peace throughout all Normandy'.[23] The decrees that have come down to us provide for the repression of the supporters of Robert Curthose and the recovery of lands by those dispossessed during the civil wars, the deportation to England of the unfortunate Duke Robert, who had fallen into his brother's hands, the punishment of false moneyers and so forth. There is nothing that specifically concerns ecclesiastical discipline.

Those councils made decisions on matters of high policy, or took measures concerning peace and public order in the duchy. In such assemblies the Church helped determine its own terrestrial fortunes, through the disposition of its property and no less by the discipline that it exercised over clergy and laity. Beside them there were other provincial councils, no less numerous, by which there were introduced into the duchy the reforms that the papacy was then endeavouring to impose upon the Christian West.

During Mauger's pontificate, at a date which is uncertain, but was earlier than the year 1049 which some have suggested and which, from the presence beside the archbishop of Robert, bishop of Coutances (d. 1048) and Hugh, bishop of Evreux (d. 20 April 1046), must have been close to 1045, there was an ecclesiastical synod at Rouen: 'placuit sacerdotalem inter nos fieri conventum' in the words of the synodal letter.[24] The nineteen canons that have survived cover, after the profession of the catholic faith, simoniacal practices in taking orders and in the distribution of the sacraments and conditions for the promotion of clerks, education and canonical age. They inveigh insistently

---

[23] Orderic Vitalis, ed. Le Prévost, IV, 233–4.   [24] Dom Bessin, pp. 40–2.

against the ambition of bishops, abbots, archdeacons and ordinary clerks who seek promotion through the favour of the prince or his entourage, be it by supplanting a colleague or usurping a benefice.

Duke William made time, during the siege of Brionne in 1050, to convene there an 'assembly of many wise men from all over Normandy' ('conventus multorum ex tota Normannia sapientum'). Its purpose was to confound Berengar of Tours in person, about the same time as his theories on the Eucharist, recently examined by a synod at Rome, were carried before a Roman council at Vercelli (1 September).[25]

A reforming synod must have been summoned at Rouen by Maurilius shortly after his accession. This synod would have fulminated against simony and – a novelty in Normandy – against the marriage of priests, their offspring and hereditary succession to the fathers' churches. Such canons, of which we know only the general tenor, were evidently found relevant at Rouen in 1055. They show the same spirit as the deposition of Mauger and attest the reforming zeal of the new primate, a product of the monastic life, chosen deliberately by the duke. So does the accord of the bishops of the province, gathered around their metropolitan at his first council.[26]

The synod held in 1063,[27] also by Mauger and the six suffragans, in Duke William's presence, on the occasion of the consecration of the celebrated metropolitan basilica, was no less remarkable than its predecessors. It must have borne an even more solemn aspect, and before it proceeded to the business of the hour, notably the question of clerical continence, an anti-Berengarian profession of faith was pronounced by the assembled clergy. The formula was transcribed in the *Liber pontificalis rotomagensis ecclesiae* at the instigation of the bishops. It therefore took its place in the *ordo* for the synodal assemblies of the province at the end of the creeds of the great councils, and it became an obligation upon the bishop on the day of his consecration. The Church in Normandy had declared itself upon a question of faith, and the more

[25] The date 1050 was attributed to the synod of Brionne by Dom Bessin. Various authors have questioned both the date and the sequence of Lanfranc's and Berengar's journeys, the Norman synod and the councils at Rome. The best discussion of the evidence, with a definitive argument in favour of 1050, is to be found in J. Heurtevent, *Durand de Troarn et les origines de l'hérésie bérengarienne* (Paris, 1912), pp. 139–41, especially 139 n. 2. On Berengar's doctrine and the controversy over it, see Heurtevent, *op. cit.* and more recently, Jean de Montclos, *Lanfranc et Bérenger: La controverse eucharistique du XIe siècle*, Spicilegium Sacrum Lovaniense: études et documents. fasc. 37 (Louvain, 1971).

[26] Dom Bessin, p. 47. For this synod, see n. 8 above.

[27] Orderic Vitalis, ed. Le Prévost, II, 373; ed. Chibnall, III, 92; Dom Bessin, p. 49.

emphatically because in Lanfranc's own person it might have been suspected of some sympathy with the views of Berengar.[28]

The metropolitan church, the reconstruction of which had been begun by Archbishop Robert (d. 1037) and had now reached an advanced stage of completion, had established itself as the setting for the synods of the province. It was at Lisieux, however, that there assembled in 1064 one of the most important of all the provincial councils of Rouen, unknown among the ancient compilers of synodal collections and happily discovered by Léopold Delisle in a Cambridge manuscript.[29] Ten canons have come to us in an abbreviated form, in a summary of the council's decrees. After reference to the profession of Trinitarian and Eucharistic beliefs, certainly anti-Berengarian in the terms proposed by Lanfranc (Canon 1), the synod dealt with clerks who had taken wives since the Council of Rouen: that of 1063 in Delisle's view, but possibly that of 1055. Those in major orders were commanded to put their wives aside; those in minor orders were to be persuaded to do so (Canons 2 and 3). Various measures were directed to maintaining the peace. The Truce of God was renewed (Canon 10); all violence offered to clerks and their goods was condemned (Canon 4); clerks were forbidden to carry arms, to practise usury, to serve laymen as agents (Canons 5, 8). The most novel and important of the decrees of 1064 are surely Canons 2 and 3. If they are not, as Delisle supposed, an advance upon the so-called Gregorian legislation they certainly reflect, less than five years after their promulgation and precisely in the terms they use (*introducta mulier*), the measures decreed by Pope Nicholas II at the Roman council of 1059. We must see in them the hand of the reforming prelates, themselves monks: Archbishop Maurilius, and Lanfranc, at that time abbot of St Stephen's, Caen. The full force of William of Poitiers' testimony can be felt here when he asserts both the duke's concern for the Church and the responsibilities that he placed upon Lanfranc: 'It was to him that [the duke] committed the duty of an unsleeping watch over the entire order of clergy in the whole of Normandy.'[30] Thus did the province of Rouen enter, perhaps

---

[28] Not in Normandy, but at the Council of Rome (29 April 1050) where he was present and had to make his excuses for the terms in which Berengar's letter referred to him. (Heurtevent, *Durand de Troarn*, pp. 131–4 and 131 n. 6).

[29] Trinity College Cambridge MS R 16 34. Published by L. Delisle, 'Canons du Concile tenu à Lisieux en 1064', in *Journal des Savants* (1901), pp. 516–21. The articles are reproduced in C. J. Hefele, *Histoire des Conciles*, trans. and ed. H. Leclercq (8 vols. in 16, Paris, 1907–21) IV, App. 9, pp. 1420–3. *See also* Heurtevent, *Durand de Troarn*, pp. 113–14.

[30] ed. Foreville, p. 127.

as early as 1055, and certainly not later than 1063, upon the age of the reforming synods initiated by Archbishop Maurilius and maintained by his successor, John of Bayeux, who was translated from the see of Avranches.

Archbishop John's pontificate is marked by two great councils, both assembled in the cathedral at Rouen. The first, in 1072, decreed twenty-four canons upon liturgical order and discipline.[31] The preparation and distribution of the holy chrism, the celebration of the mass, baptism, and confirmation, the observation of Ember Days, the fast of Lent, the Paschal office, the use of the sanctoral and temporal, adult and infant baptism, were all objects of regulation. No less important were the decrees concerned with discipline and morals. Clandestine marriages were condemned, and an enquiry prescribed into the degree of kinship of all intended spouses. Second marriages were forbidden with a concubine or during the lifetime of a wife entered into religion. In the same way, a wife was forbidden to remarry if her husband had not returned from a distant voyage, but there was no certainty of his death. The second canon of Lisieux, against priests, deacons and subdeacons who were married or who kept mistresses, was renewed.

The council of 1074 shows some intellectual refinement both in what it derived from the great councils for the Trinitarian creed, Nicea, Constantinople I, Ephesus and Chalcedon and in reference to the papal decrees upon ecclesiastical promotions. The expression 'simoniacal heresy' also reveals the influence of those known as the Gregorians. The rule of St Benedict was made obligatory for all houses of monks and nuns. The ordinary was warned to be watchful for false testimony, whether from the laity seeking to replace an unwanted husband or wife, or from clerks who alleged some irregularity in ordination to escape from their orders.[32]

After the great assembly at Lillebonne in 1080, where as we have shown many decrees of former councils were restated, the provincial synod met much less frequently in Normandy. Robert Curthose succeeded William the Conqueror, and Normandy was torn by war between the rival brothers. Two synods of the province are recorded, in 1091 and 1096, under Archbishop William Bonne Ame (1079–1110),

---

[31] Orderic Vitalis, ed. Le Prévost, II, 237–43; ed. Chibnall, II, 284–92; Dom Bessin, pp. 54–7. It would have been celebrated in the Conqueror's presence (*Annales Uticenses* in Orderic Vitalis, ed. Le Prévost, v, 128).

[32] Dom Bessin, pp. 64–6.

and two more in the time of Henry I and Archbishop Geoffrey, in 1118 and 1119.

Within the octave of Pentecost, that is to say, in June 1091, the archbishop held a synod of bishops and abbots in the presence of Duke Robert.[33] We know only that it discussed the church of Sées, which had been vacant for several months. The bishop-elect, Serlo of Orgères, abbot of Saint-Evroult, must have been consecrated on 22 June. William Bonne Ame held another synod at Rouen in February 1096.[34] The Norman church had appointed two bishops, Gilbert of Evreux and Serlo of Sées, as delegates to the great council under Pope Urban II at Clermont in November 1095. The synod at Rouen promulgated some of the decisions taken at Clermont: those relating to the Truce and the Peace of God, to simoniacal practices and the intrusion of laymen into benefices. Like the earlier Norman councils it makes no reference to lay investiture, though it does forbid any act of homage by the ordained clergy to a layman (Canon 8).

In 1119, as in 1096, the provincial synod based its acts upon the decisions of a general council, this time the one that Calixtus II assembled at Rheims from 20 to 30 October. There seem to have been two sessions, the first at Lisieux in September or October, and the second at some place unknown after the meetings at Rheims where the presence of a Norman bishop, Audoen le Barbu, of Evreux, is attested.[35] This synod had political overtones, from the mediation that Calixtus had taken upon himself between Henry I and Louis VI, who were then at war. It opposed the promulgation within the province of at least one of the reforming decrees at Rheims, the second canon, which forbade 'absolutely any investiture of bishops and abbots by the hand of a layman'. Even at Rheims that proposal had met with strong opposition: its discussion had necessitated an extra session, and it had undergone important modifications during its drafting.[36]

A year earlier, on 7 October 1118, Archbishop Geoffrey had summoned a synod in the metropolitan church which illustrates well the complex nature of these Norman assemblies: a great gathering about the king, with debates of high import both for the Anglo-Norman kingdom and for the Christian church. Orderic Vitalis, who may have been an eye-witness, describes the proceedings in detail.

[33] Orderic Vitalis, ed. Le Prévost, III, 379; ed. Chibnall, IV, 232; Dom Bessin, pp. 76–7.
[34] Orderic Vitalis, ed. Le Prévost, III, 470–3; ed. Chibnall, V, 18–25; Dom Bessin, pp. 77–9.
[35] Orderic Vitalis, ed. Le Prévost, IV, 378.
[36] Orderic Vitalis, *ibid.* p. 391.

There, King Henry discussed the peace of the realm with the archbishop of Canterbury, Ralph, and the other barons whom he had summoned together. There the archbishop of Rouen, Geoffrey, talked of the condition of the Church with four of his suffragans, Richard of Bayeux, John of Lisieux, Turgis of Avranches, and Roger of Coutances, and with many abbots, those of Fécamp, Jumièges, Bec, Caen, Préaux, Troarn, and others whom it is unnecessary to name....There Conrad, a clerk of Rome sent by pope Gelasius, complained in an eloquent discourse...of the emperor...and deplored the activities of the anti-pope Bourdin; he also announced the arrival on this side of the Alps of pope Gelasius, exiled by the rebels' enmity...[37]

The interest of the text is that it illustrates the autonomy of the provincial synod, on the one hand by its relation to the council of the Anglo-Norman kingdom, and on the other, by the precise and limited mission performed by the pope's envoy.

The councils of 1118 and 1119 end the active period of the Norman synod and another, of a rather different character, begins. From that time onward there was no council of the province of Rouen without a legate present, and as opposition to the entry of legates grew after Henry II's accession, in both the duchy of Normandy and the kingdom of England, the provincial synod practically disappeared. We have referred already to the council that Matthew, bishop of Albano, the legate of Honorius II, held at Rouen in November 1128. It forbade the faithful to attend masses celebrated by married priests and ordered them to restore to the bishop's hands any churches or tithes that they had detained (Canons 1 and 3).

More than forty years passed before another council assembled in Normandy. It required, what is more, an exceptional occasion: the reconciliation of Henry II in 1172, after the murder of Thomas Becket, archbishop of Canterbury, by the legates of Alexander III, the cardinals Albert and Theodwin. There were, in the event, two sessions, of which the first, on the Wednesday in the octave of the Ascension (30 May), must have been for the solemn display in the abbey church of St Stephen, Caen, of the results of the decisions taken at Avranches on 19 and 21 May.[38] The second was held at Avranches on 28 September, where twelve canons were promulgated, under the legates' presidency,

---

[37] Orderic Vitalis, *ibid.* pp. 329–30; Dom Bessin, p. 80. Serlo, bishop of Sées, pleaded illness and advanced age; Audoen, bishop of Evreux, the defence of the cathedral city (he would have denounced, at the Council of Rheims in 1119, the burning of his cathedral by Amaury de Montfort). Both sent representatives.

[38] R. Foreville, *L'église et la royauté en Angleterre sous Henri II Plantagenet* (Paris, 1943), pp. 339ff.

against abuses, notably in promotions to ecclesiastical charges. Many of these points were taken up again by the Third Lateran Council (1179) in its third, fifth, and thirteenth decrees. All the same, the Norman bishops showed some opposition to certain measures seeking to prevent payment for the sacraments, absolutions and benedictions.[39]

Such was the history of the Norman councils during one and a half centuries, for the assemblies of 1172 stood alone in Henry II's reign. It took the death of the first Plantagenet, the impulse of the general council of 1179, the organisation of the third crusade and its despatch by Richard I, to convene once more, in 1190, the Norman synod.

2. THE CHARACTERISTICS OF THE PROVINCIAL SYNOD IN NORMANDY

A review of the historical facts relating to the provincial assemblies in Normandy in the eleventh and twelfth centuries reveals a number of distinctive characteristics. They derive from the general nature of the synod, its composition, frequency, its reforming tradition, and from the impact of the work of the Gregorian reformers and of the papacy. Those matters can only be fully appreciated in the light of comparative history and of the evolution of the institution.

The Norman councils do not all display the same features, and it is by no means easy to discern their exact nature through the medium of the brief and sometimes incidental notices that we have of them. In the eleventh century the council was usually summoned by the prince and discussed in his presence matters which in various ways concerned the duchy as a whole.[40] It displayed upon occasions the character of a ducal council, and of a feudal, rather than an ecclesiastical, kind, attended by faithful men called to give their counsel and, above all, their consent to propositions set forth by the duke's officers. Such decisions might well relate as much to ecclesiastical discipline as to the public weal, and even to both domains at once, as with the Truce of God, or when the

[39] *Ibid.* pp. 336–7. See Table 1 on p. 23, n. i. For the council's decrees, see Dom Bessin, p. 86.

[40] William of Poitiers shows clearly the interest that William the Conqueror took in ecclesiastical synods and the rôle that he assumed. 'Every time that, at the duke's order and according to his advice, the bishops assembled, the metropolitan and his suffragans, to discuss the state of religion, of the clergy, of monks and of the laity, he took every care to be present as the arbiter of these synods, both to stimulate by his presence the application of the most zealous, the wisdom of the best-advised, and because he did not wish to depend upon the report of others to learn how they had dealt with matters which he wished to see determined in full accordance with right, the law, and religion.' (ed. Foreville, p. 124).

competence of the Church courts had to be delimited against the duke's own jurisdiction. What is more we find upon occasions both assemblies of bishops sitting apart to pursue some special commission, and then participating in the general meeting and mixed sessions, in which barons and lay-vassals take part in the debate of ecclesiastical issues.[41] Those again take various forms: the examination of matters under litigation, the enforcement of disciplinary rules upon clerks and laymen alike, and elections in which there took part, either separately or with the cathedral chapter, the episcopal college and the abbots of the province on the one hand, and on the other the representatives of the king.[42] An occasion of that kind was an important episode in the administration and even in the government of the duchy. The composition of the assemblies was quite widely drawn. Around the duke, first William the Conqueror, then Robert Curthose, and the metropolitan, there assembled the bishops of the six suffragan dioceses, and the heads of the great abbeys, chiefly those of the diocese of Rouen. The others were not excluded, but their assiduity seems to vary in inverse proportion to their distance from the court, at least when we turn to Lower Normandy.

Whereas in the other provinces of the kingdom of France the provincial council was readily open to the bishops of neighbouring

---

[41] The practice is described exactly in the words of an order addressed by the Conqueror to his subjects: 'Sciatis vos...qui in Anglia manent quod *episcopales leges*, quae non bene nec secundum sanctorum canonum praecepta usque ad mea tempora in regno Anglorum fuerunt, *communi consilio, et consilio archi-episcoporum et episcoporum et abbatum et omnium principum regni mei* emendendas judicavi.' (*c.* 1075–1080) [My italics]. Mansi, xx, col. 605. The most recent editions are in *The Registrum Antiquissimum of the cathedral church of Lincoln*, ed. C. W. Foster and K. Major, I (Lincoln Record Society xxvII (1931)), p. 2 and *Early charters of St Paul's, London*, ed. M. Gibbs, Camden 3rd Series LVIII (1939), no. 4. The date *c.* 1076 is proposed by C. N. L. Brooke and G. Keir, *London 800–1216* (London, 1975), p. 372, because of its link with the Council of Winchester. I am obliged to Professor Brooke for the reference.

[42] Canon 28 of Lateran II (1139) ordered that the election of bishops should be made with the advice of regulars, that is of abbots or their representatives: 'We forbid upon pain of anathema the canons of episcopal chapters to exclude the religious from the election of bishops: it is with their advice that an honourable and capable candidate is to be chosen. If the religious be excluded from an election, any result that does not enjoy their consent and approval shall be held null and void.' (*Conciliorum*, p. 179; French transl. Foreville, *Latran*, p. 193.) The prescription is repeated in Gratian D. 63 c. 35. Nevertheless, many chapters must have obtained the exclusive right to elect their bishop: Arras, 1131; Bourges, 1145; Coutances, 1146, Agde, 1173. For the practice of elections in the presence of 'religious' and the other suffragans, see M. Pacaut, *Les élections épiscopales sous Louis VII* (Paris, 1957), pp. 47–9; Foreville, *L'Église et la royauté, passim*, especially pp. 9, 102–4, 374–7, 479–80 and 486–7. It was Innocent III, upon the occasion of the dispute at Canterbury in 1205–6, who reserved the election to the chapter of the see alone (A. Potthast, *Reg. pontificum Romanorum 1198–1304* (2 vols. Berlin, 1874–5), 2939, 2940; *The letters of Pope Innocent III...concerning England and Wales*, ed. C. R. and M. G. Cheney (Oxford, 1967), nos. 726–7).

provinces and even to travelling bishops, the Norman council was closed. Upon two occasions only, during a century and a half, is the presence of a bishop from outside the province noted. At Rouen in 1128, when the cardinal legate Matthew, bishop of Albano, presided, Geoffrey of Lèves, bishop of Chartres, and Joscelin of Vierzy, bishop of Soissons, were present, though no explanation of their presence was offered. On the other hand, at Caen on 30 May 1172, the exceptional nature of the occasion dictated, as we have seen, an exceptional ceremony. The legates Albert and Theodwin had summoned, besides the Norman episcopate, the archbishop of Tours and his suffragans. The king made his entry in the middle of the assembly. It was, in fact, proper that his readmission to the Church, already effected at St Andrew of Avranches, should be celebrated also in the ducal city, before the clergy of the ancestral provinces of his continental domain of Normandy, but also of Maine and Anjou, of Touraine and even of Brittany which was dependent upon the metropolitan of Tours.

The frequency of the councils in the province of Rouen seems to set them apart from those of similar assemblies held in the other provinces of the kingdom of France. It is true that Dr E. W. Kemp[43] has counted thirty-six over two centuries in the province of Narbonne (996–1195). We have found twenty-nine in Normandy, from *c.* 1040 to 1190, or the space of a century and a half, which gives for the one an average frequency of five and a half years, and for the other, five years. In a recent study, M. J-Cl. Tillier has written 'the history of the provincial councils of Aquitaine is rich: forty-eight of these assemblies appear between the fourth and the nineteenth centuries'.[44] That shows an average frequency of 31 years three months. What then should we say of Normandy? The province of Rouen stands apart even from that of Narbonne if we consider the Gregorian age alone. From 1042 to 1128, with twenty-six meetings, the average frequency is narrowed to three years four months; from 1042 to 1119 the meetings were triennial, from 1042 to 1096, they occurred every two and a half years or less.

Paradoxically, the frequency of provincial assemblies in Normandy in the eleventh century, and at the beginning of the twelfth, is a mark of the refusal of its episcopate to take part in the synods that papal

---

[43] E. W. Kemp, *Counsel and consent* (London, 1961), p. 36.

[44] 'Les conciles provinciaux de la province ecclésiastique de Bordeaux au temps de la réforme grégorienne, 1073–1100', *Bulletin philologique et historique* (jusqu'à 1610), Comité des Travaux Historiques, 1968 (Paris, 1971), p. 563.

legates held in the neighbouring provinces, as is also the weakness of the delegation which represented it at the papal councils of Clermont in 1095 and Rheims in 1119. Whilst the legates Amatus of Oloron and Hugh of Die summoned many councils, the former at Poitiers, Gerona, Bordeaux, Issoudun, Charroux, Saintes, and elsewhere; the latter at Anse, Clermont, Dijon, Autun, Poitiers, Lyons, Avignon, Bordeaux, Béziers, and Toulouse, and during the first third of the twelfth century, Gerard of Angoulême, himself the permanent legate of successive popes, presided over eight councils in the provinces of Tours, Bordeaux, and Auch, the duchy remained aloof from the movement. We know of Hugh of Die's unsuccessful efforts to impose himself, and the reproaches that Gregory VII addressed to Archbishop William Bonne Ame, for having neglected to seek the pallium, to visit the Holy See, or even to approach the legates, are notorious.[45] His predecessors had received similar reprimands. Now, in no other province of the French kingdom did the constituents of the provincial system, metropolitan and synod, work together as smoothly as in that second Lyonnaise, which was precisely the territory from which the legates were kept at arm's length. As soon as it can be distinguished from the ducal council, the provincial council appears there in its 'pure form', that is to say, 'held by the archbishop in his province, with none but the clergy of his suffragan dioceses'.[46]

Although in England the primacy of the see of Canterbury allowed its occupant to hold councils in his province, but for the whole kingdom, until the death of St Anselm (1109), the Norman synods did not extend beyond the borders of the province of Rouen. Examining Gregory VII's interventions, Dr Kemp[47] subscribes to an opinion of Augustin Fliche's[48] which asserts that the provincial synods could only have made decisions of importance under the presidency of papal legates, because the bishops' causes had been withdrawn from the metropolitan's jurisdiction. That belief must be qualified. It cannot be applied to the Anglo-Norman kingdom: in the eleventh century, and still in the early twelfth, reforms were introduced into England under the king's aegis, beyond or beside the actions of the legates, by the primate, 'metropolitan of all Britain', in councils binding upon the whole kingdom. And if, in the kingdom of France, the legates' inter-

---

[45] *Registrum*, VIII, 24; JL 4204; Dom Bessin, p. 74.
[46] J. Gaudemet, in F. Lot and R. Fawtier, *Histoire des institutions françaises au Moyen Age*, III, *Institutions ecclésiastiques* (Paris, 1962), p. 315.
[47] Kemp, *Counsel and consent*, p. 33.   [48] Fliche, *Réforme grégorienne*, II, 114-16.

vention changed the nature of the synod and extended it over several provinces, there is one that stands apart. Preserved from the legates' authority by an exceptionally strong power, and one intent upon defending its rights, secure in a territory corresponding with a political entity, the second Lyonnaise, the province of Rouen, which barely extended beyond the boundaries of the duchy in the French Vexin, presents in the eleventh century an almost perfect image of the provincial synod. It is true that the Norman synods did not all contribute equally to the cause of moral and disciplinary reform. There is no question, however, of the effectiveness of the councils of 1063, 1064, 1072, 1080, and 1096; that is to say, of the synodal assemblies convened by Archbishops Maurilius, John of Bayeux, and William Bonne Ame. Those were reforming synods, even though despite the Roman decrees they never discussed lay investiture by the staff and the ring.[49]

In the twelfth century Normandy ceased to be the nursery of the provincial synod and resisted, in all but the most exceptional circumstances, the intervention of legates. To our knowledge there is no trace, during the seventy years between 1118 and 1190, of a synod within the province of Rouen save those summoned by the legates in 1128 and 1172. That development is not peculiar to Normandy; a similar situation obtained in the other regions of the Christian West.[50] An anonymous compiler of decretals, the author of the *Summa Bambergensis* written in Gaul between 1206 and 1210,[51] bore witness to that state of affairs when, defining and distinguishing councils as general, particular or provincial and local, that is to say, diocesan, he added his own comment. 'In our day, we see that metropolitans do not convene provincial councils, although they have the power to do so (D.18, *Dict. Grat.* ante c.1).'[52]

At the very end of the twelfth century there are signs of a revival: the provincial synod reappears and begins to take its place once more

---

[49] The Norman synods from 1063 to 1096 could not remain uninfluenced by the Roman decrees against simony and nicholaism. By contrast, the Norman practice of lay investiture was entirely consistent. Orderic Vitalis describes the delivery of the abbacy of Saint-Evroult to Osbern, prior of Cormeilles, in these terms: 'Normannicus dux...(ei)...*per cambucam* (*cambutam* eds) *Maurilii archiepiscopi* in sinodo Rotomagensi curam Uticensis abbatiae commendavit.' [My italics] (ed. Le Prévost, II, 82; ed. Chibnall, II, 90–2.)

[50] Cf. R. Foreville, 'Royaumes, métropolitains, et conciles provinciaux' in *Le istituzioni ecclesiastiche della 'Societas Christiana' dei secoli XI–XII: Papato, cardinalato ed episcopato. Atti della quinta settimana internazionale di studio: Mendola, 26–31 agosto 1971*. Miscellanea del centro di studi medioevali, VII (Milan, 1974), pp. 293ff.

[51] E. M. de Groot, *Doctrina de jure naturali et positivo humano in Summa Bambergensi* (DD. 1–20) (Druten, 1970), p. 27.　　　[52] *Summa Bambergensis*, p. 83.

as an essential feature of the life of the Church, just as the diocesan synod elaborates statutes as a preliminary to what has been called 'the pastoral revolution' of the thirteenth century.[53] Normandy entered upon the new movement. On the eve of his departure on crusade,[54] in February 1190, the archbishop of Rouen, Walter of Coutances, revived the metropolitan tradition and held a provincial council in his cathedral with his suffragans, many abbots and others.[55] Twenty-three canons were promulgated, some of them based upon decrees of the Third Lateran Council. They covered liturgical practice, making the use of the metropolitan church of Rouen obligatory in the province, church ornaments, the dress and behaviour of priests and tithes. They regulated interdicts and excommunications, archidiaconal visitations and the right of sanctuary; they condemned arsonists, forgers, the contumacious and so on. The whole life of the Church and its role in society were reviewed. It was a comprehensive exercise necessitated by a long quiescence and stimulated by the new crusade, for which the decrees of Popes Urban II, Gregory VIII, and Clement III were renewed and had to be observed (Canon 17).

By the time that Robert Courson and his colleague Peter of Benevento, Innocent III's legates, came in to the kingdom of France to hold the preparatory councils for the Fourth Lateran Council, Normandy had been separated from the English crown for some ten years. The council held at Rouen in February 1214[56] showed none of that Norman particularism that had manifested itself so often in the past, even to the extent of rejecting some papal decrees. The assembly was a single link in a chain extending from Paris (summer 1213) to Bordeaux (June 1214) and Montpellier (January 1215). Well-disposed and well-instructed, it reproduced the canons of the Parisian council, regulating in detail the discipline of secular clerks, prelates, monks and nuns, and prescribing the duties of pastoral care. Its models were decrees of the Third Lateran Council, the diocesan statutes of Eudes de Sully, bishop of Paris, and the constitutions published for the diocese of Paris by the legate Guala in 1208.[57]

---

[53] Cf. R. Foreville, 'Les statuts synodaux et le renouveau pastoral du treizième siècle', *Cahiers de Fanjeaux*, VI (1971), 119–50.

[54] Canon 31 condemns clerks and laymen who fraudulently withhold revenues from the archbishop, unless they make amends before his departure ('antequam iter peregrinationis arripiat').

[55] Dom Bessin, pp. 94–8.

[56] R. Foreville, *Latran I, II, III et Latran IV* (Paris, 1965), pp. 242–3.

[57] Dom Bessin, pp. 107–8.

Made obligatory by the Fourth Lateran Council, freed from the tutelage of the prince and from the attentions of legates, the provincial synod now recovered, after the long inactivity of the twelfth century, its proper place, in Normandy as elsewhere, in the system of ecclesiastical government. As defined in the sixth canon of the great council of 1215, its business was to mend morals and punish offenders; it was the natural channel of communication between the general council and the diocesan synod. In the same period, the nation itself began to take shape. The kingdoms of France and England had acquired a certain political and administrative competence by the development of specialised institutions and no longer needed to lean upon the Church's system. Henceforth the history of the provincial council belongs not to the world of high policy in Church and State in which we find it in the Gregorian age, but in the system of pastoral care perfected and dignified by the Fourth Lateran Council.

PUBLIC PROSECUTION OF CRIME IN TWELFTH-CENTURY ENGLAND

by Raoul C. van Caenegem

THE public prosecution of a suspected criminal before the law courts is an indispensable feature of modern society: as soon as sufficient evidence is available the grand jury or the director of public prosecutions formally incriminates the suspect and the trial ensues, to establish his guilt or innocence, to condemn or to acquit. Private complaint by the victim or his relatives plays a minor role in present day criminal procedure. This used not to be the case and public prosecution, as we know it, is the product of a long development. Originally most criminal offences were considered as violations of private rights and led to extra-judicial vengeance or compensation. With the emergence of law courts and the judicial settling of claims, the need arose for a formal complaint to set the criminal plea in motion (except when the criminal was taken in the act and summarily dealt with). For centuries the right to bring this complaint belonged to a private person and the criminal plea was a contest, where accuser and accused fought on an equal footing under the formal guidance of the court; they fought with oaths, sworn by themselves and their oath-helpers (fore-oaths and purgatory oaths), with sticks or swords in judicial combat, or with other primitive modes of proof. Both parties ran heavy risks: at worst, the accuser who failed to prove his case might undergo the punishment he had hoped to obtain for his opponent (unless he had already fallen in judicial combat); at best he would suffer some minor penalty. Leaving the impleading of criminals to the uncertain and very risky initiative of private avengers was quite inadequate for the defence of public order and led, with the emergence of modern ideas about the state, to the replacement of the accusatorial by the inquisitorial procedure. Then the prosecution of crime was entrusted to an official organ, proceeding *ex officio*, and purgatory oaths and ordeals were replaced by modern means of inquiry. This transition is a common European phenomenon and, without belittling the attempts of the Carolingian monarchy, it may safely be

41

considered a product of the emergence, from the twelfth century onwards, of the centralised state.

The English development is no exception to this general picture: we find a transition, beginning roughly in the twelfth century, from the archaic procedure of appeal, undertaken by a private plaintiff at his own risk and entailing archaic modes of proof, to a modernised procedure based on indictment under the aegis of the state and using rational modes of inquiry. Nevertheless, the traditional English procedure contains some striking features of its own and none more so than the essential role played by the jury of presentment (later the grand jury) and the almost total absence, until very recent times, of the prosecution of crime by an individual official of the state, such as the continental *procureur* or advocate-fiscal. For eight centuries at least, from the Assize of Clarendon till the creation of the office of Director of Public Prosecutions in 1879 and the abolition of the grand jury in 1933, suspected criminals had to stand trial, not on the basis of a *réquisitoire* pronounced by an official of the state, but of an indictment pronounced by a jury of their fellow citizens.[1]

The story of this 'grand jury' of accusation, still an important feature of the American legal landscape and so called in opposition to the 'petty' or 'trial jury' which had to pronounce a verdict of guilty or not guilty, begins with the Assize of Clarendon. Issued by Henry II in 1166 with

---

[1] In the absence of a comprehensive study on a European scale, the reader will find some basic information in the following works: H. Brunner, *Die Entstehung der Schwurgerichte* (Berlin, 1871); A. Esmein, *Histoire de la procédure criminelle en France et spécialement de la procédure inquisitoire depuis le XIIIe siècle jusqu'à nos jours* (Paris, 1882); J. F. Stephen, *A History of the Criminal Law of England* (London, 1883), I; P. Guilhiermoz, *Enquêtes et Procès. Étude sur la procédure et le fonctionnement du Parlement au XIVe siècle* (Paris, 1892); F. Pollock, 'The King's Peace in the Middle Ages', in *Select Essays in Anglo-American Legal History* (Boston, 1908), II, 403–17; *The Continental Legal History Series*, V: *A History of Continental Criminal Procedure with special reference to France* (Boston, 1913) (= mainly a transl. of Esmein, with some additions and short pieces on other countries); G. Salvioli, *Storia della procedura civile e criminale* (Milan, 1927), II, 356–69: *Il procedimento inquisitorio o di ufficio*; M. Palasse, 'Le paradoxe de l'inquisitio franque', in *Études d'histoire du droit privé offertes à P. Petot* (Paris, 1959), pp. 423–30; P. Devlin, *The Criminal Prosecution in England* (London, 1960); J. Cerdá Ruiz-Funes, 'En torno a la pesquisa y procedimiento inquisitivo en el derecho castellano-leones de la edad media', in *Anuario Hist. Derecho Esp.*, XXXII (1962), 483–517; E. Schmidt, *Einführung in die Geschichte der deutschen Strafrechtspflege*, 3rd edn. (Göttingen, 1965); G. Landwehr, 'Gogericht und Rügegericht' in *Zeitschrift der Savigny-Stiftung für Rechtsgeschichte*, G.A., LXXXIII (1966), 127–43; E. S. Procter, *The Judicial Use of Pesquisa (Inquisition) in León and Castille 1157–1369* (London, 1966), *EHR*. Supplement, 2; *Handwörterbuch zur deutschen Rechtsgeschichte*, fasc. 10 (Berlin, 1973), s.vv. *Gemeindezeugnis, Inquisitionsbeweis, Inquisitionsprozess* and *Inzicht*; J. Bellamy, *Crime and Public Order in England in the later Middle Ages* (London-Toronto, 1973), pp. 121–61. For classical Roman law: J. Dahyot-Dolivet, 'La procédure pénale d'office en droit romain', *Apollinaris*, XLI (1968), 89–105 and W. Kunkel, *Untersuchungen zur Entwicklung des römischen Kriminalverfahrens in vorsullanischer Zeit*, Bayer. Akad. Wiss., Philos.-hist. Kl., Abh. N.F. 56 (Munich, 1962).

the consent of the magnates of the kingdom, it was expanded in 1176 in the Assize of Northampton.[2] The main features of these two assizes, or royal enactments, were the following. The king undertook to repress specified forms of serious crime in a nation-wide, centrally conducted operation. The duty of indicting the suspected offenders was imposed on local juries composed of the more lawful men of hundreds and vills, who presented criminals without the intervention of a private appellor and by-passing the traditional local courts. The indicted persons, if they had not already fled, stood trial before the royal justices who were sent on eyres (*itinera*) round the country, and the mode of proof was the ordeal of water. The punishment for those who failed was mutilation, those who succeeded but stood in very bad repute in their communities were sent into exile (as if success in the ordeal justified a pardon but was not a proof of innocence).[3] When the ordeals disappeared in the early thirteenth century they were gradually replaced by the trial jury, which remains the central feature of the English criminal process till this day. The chattels of the condemned criminals and of the fugitives were the king's. Nothing was changed in the traditional appeal procedure, which continued to be important and frequent for centuries.[4] Some changes took place between Clarendon and Northampton: in 1166 the presentment was made to sheriffs or justices, in 1176 the justices in eyre alone are mentioned; also the list of crimes under the assizes had become longer and punishment harsher. The first assize was, in our view, conceived as a unique emergency measure to deal with years of violence in the aftermath of the 'Anarchy', but from 1176 onwards temporary steps developed into a permanent system, not least because the justices in eyre became the dominating element in English judicial organisation.

Of all King Henry's interesting innovations it is the jury of present-

[2] W. Stubbs, *Select Charters*, 9th edn by H. W. C. Davis (Oxford, 1913), pp. 167–73 and 178–81. On the authenticity of the Assize of Clarendon, see J. C. Holt, 'The Assizes of Henry II: the Texts' in *The Study of Medieval Records. Essays in honour of Kathleen Major*, ed. D. A. Bullough and R. L. Storey (Oxford, 1971), pp. 85–106.

[3] The *Leges Edwardi Confessoris* (18, 2) insist that a pardoned murderer must abjure the realm: quoted by N. D. Hurnard, *The King's Pardon for Homicide before A.D. 1307* (Oxford, 1969), p. 15.

[4] A. L. Poole, *Obligations of Society in the XII and XIII Centuries*, Ford Lectures, 1944 (Oxford, 1946), p. 87, quotes a Lincolnshire assize of 1202 where approximately 353 prosecutions were brought by personal appeal and 77 by jury presentment; see also *Placita Corone or La Corone Pledee devant Justices*, ed. J. M. Kaye, Selden Soc. Suppl. Series, IV (London, 1966), pp. xxiv–xxxviii.

ment that occupies us here. Few historians will deny that it appears in the full light of day, and with its definite, classical features, in the Assizes of Clarendon and Northampton and that from 1166 onwards its development can be followed continuously.[5] But no such consensus exists concerning the period before 1166, indeed the origin of the jury of presentment is a much debated problem and in the pages that follow we hope to make a few tentative suggestions towards its solution.

One of the questions invariably posed about the institutions of Norman and Angevin England is that of their continental or Anglo-Saxon origin. The jury of presentment has not escaped this fate and it is to the claim of its Anglo-Saxon origin that we shall first turn our attention. In the Code of Wantage of Aethelred II of A.D. 978–1008, c. 3, a famous passage occurs concerning the twelve leading thegns of the wapentake and with them the royal reeve, who are to go out and swear on relics taken into their hands that they 'will neither accuse any innocent person nor protect any guilty one'.[6] This is so similar to the twelve presenting jurors of the Assize of Clarendon that the idea of a continuous practice from Anglo-Saxon till Angevin times seems natural: the accusing jury of Aethelred's day, so the theory would run, was part and parcel of English society and continued to lead a not very well-documented existence until it came into the full light of the Assizes of 1166 and 1176 and was systematised and incorporated into the grand new scheme of Henrician justice. Miss Hurnard explored

---

[5] Pollock, 'The King's Peace', p. 415: 'As early as 1166 the old accusation by the common report of the country-side became a "presentment" by definite persons representing the local knowledge of all classes, who were bound to inform the king's judges or the sheriff'; F. W. Maitland, *Select Pleas in Manorial and other Seignorial Courts*, I, Selden Soc., II (London, 1888), xxxviff; F. Pollock and F. W. Maitland, *The History of English Law before the Time of Edward I*, 2nd edn (Cambridge, 1898), pp. 130–2; T. F. T. Plucknett, *A Concise History of the Common Law*, 5th edn (London, 1956), pp. 428–9; S. F. C. Milsom, *Historical Foundations of the Common Law* (London, 1969), pp. 356–8.

[6] III Aethelred, 3, 1. Text in F. Liebermann, *Die Gesetze der Angelsachsen*, 1 (Halle, 1903), 228 and in D. Whitelock, *English Historical Documents*, ed. D. C. Douglas, I (London, 1955), 402. This Code is concerned with the Danelaw and the regional law it records naturally betrays many Scandinavian features, just as its terminology is essentially Scandinavian. See F. M. Stenton, *Anglo-Saxon England*, 3rd edn, The Oxford History of England, ed. G. N. Clark (Oxford, 1971), pp. 500–4; D. Whitelock, *The Beginnings of English Society*, Pelican History of England (Harmondsworth, 1965), II, 146–7. There is no argument in favour of the thesis of H. G. Richardson and G. O. Sayles, *Law and Legislation from Aethelberht to Magna Carta* (Edinburgh, 1966), p. 25 that the legislation for the Danelaw seems as a whole plainly to be the extension to it of English institutions (on p. 118 the authors bluntly state that 'in tenth-century England the English jury, or at least its ancestor, was introduced into the Danelaw from Wessex', without offering any evidence); cf. S. B. Chrimes's review in *Law Quarterly Review*, LXXXIII, 607.

the possibilities of this theory most thoroughly, and indeed defended it, in a remarkable article thirty years ago.[7] Although its rich documentation and close reasoning were much admired, the 'Hurnard thesis' was not generally accepted. As S. B. Chrimes put it, 'Miss Hurnard's argument undoubtedly contains a certain amount of probability, but in the absence of sufficient evidence to support it, can hardly be regarded as convincing...and if, as Miss Hurnard believes, a form of the jury of presentment was in common and continuous use from late Anglo-Saxon times, it is certainly remarkable that so little, if any, direct evidence of it survives', and the author concludes that, although due weight must be attached to it, Miss Hurnard's argument is not strong enough in itself to undermine the view held by Maitland and most other scholars on the subject.[8] There are indeed some formidable obstacles in the way of the Hurnard thesis and the absence of 'direct evidence' during a period of a century and a half is the most striking, but not the only one. The argument *a silentio* should, of course, be used with circumspection: in the case of Normandy before 1066, for example, it would have very little value, but England between Aethelred II and Henry II is a very different proposition, for the surviving documents are so numerous and varied that the absence of any clear mention of an important institution such as the jury of presentment is a grave argument. Not only do we have thousands of charters and a considerable number of letters, chronicles and other narrative writings, but also legal treatises such as the *Leges Henrici Primi*, where the numerous and detailed chapters and paragraphs dedicated to the question of criminal accusations fail to mention the jury of accusation of twelve thegns and a reeve. Miss Hurnard tried to overcome this difficulty by making the most – and in our view too much – of certain passages in the only surviving Pipe Roll of Henry I and by quoting documents from a period after 1166 as throwing light on older practices. The Pipe Roll of 31 Henry I mentions judges and jurors who are amerced for unspecified shortcomings or who pay to

---

[7] N. D. Hurnard, 'The Jury of Presentment and the Assize of Clarendon', in *EHR*, LVI (1941), 374–410. D. M. Stenton, *English Justice between the Norman Conquest and the Great Charter 1066–1215*, Jayne Lectures for 1963 (Philadelphia, 1964), p. 71, speaks of 'the line of descent from the chief thegns of Æthelræd's Wantage code through the jurors of the Pipe Roll of 31 Henry I to the presenting jurors of the Assize of Clarendon'.

[8] S. B. Chrimes, *Introductory Essay*, in W. S. Holdsworth, *A History of English Law*, I, 7th edn (London, 1956), 49*–50*. Maitland, *Select Pleas*, p. xxxvi speaks of the lack of a 'stepping stone' between the Laws of Aethelred and the Assize of Clarendon, definitely disclaiming the idea of continuity.

be set free from their perilous duties.[9] However, the Pipe Roll does not specify that the jurors are members of a presenting jury, nor do we know exactly what fault cost them so dear. From all we can tell from those laconic entries, the *juratores* might be presenting jurors and they might not: they might be sworn party witnesses or oath-helpers (possibly summoned by royal writ), or jurors called up to serve in one of the numerous and well-known sworn inquests into the king's rights and amerced for not turning up, failing in their oaths, or not telling (all) the truth and hiding certain information of (financial) interest to the crown. There were so many occasions on which jurors were called upon and so many things they could do wrong and be amerced for, that no certainty can be obtained from the entries in this Pipe Roll; we are likewise ignorant of what the judges and 'little (judging) men' who were fined by the travelling royal justices had done wrong.[10] Nor is it certain, as Miss Hurnard believes, that 'communal presentments' were necessarily involved in the amercement 'for hiding a plea' in the Pipe Roll of 1158[11] or for 'hiding a murder' in the Pipe Roll of 1163.[12] Hiding a case of murder or another royal plea, and thus cheating the royal treasury of the *murdrum* fine or some other form of income, could happen in any community of wily villagers

[9] *Magnum Rotulum Scaccarii*..., ed. J. Hunter, Record Commission (London, 1833), p. 27, 'Et idem vicecomes reddit compotum de 31 m. arg. de 9 judicatoribus comitatus de eisdem placitis;' p. 28, 'Idem vicecomes reddit compotum de 336 m. arg. et 5 s. et 6 d. de minutis judicibus et juratoribus comitatus de eisdem placitis'; p. 34, 'Judices et juratores Eboraciscir' debent 100 li. ut non amplius sint judices nec juratores'; p. 69, '...3 d. de placitis G. de Clint' de juratoribus comitatus;' p. 103, 'Idem vicecomes reddit compotum de 40 s. de placitis G. de Clint' de juratoribus et minutis hominibus comitatus.' Pp. 27, 28 and 34 refer to Yorkshire, p. 69 to Sussex and p. 103 to Bedfordshire. There had been visitations of Yorkshire by Geoffrey de Clinton and by Walter Espec and Eustace FitzJohn. H. G. Richardson and G. O. Sayles, *The Governance of Mediaeval England* (Edinburgh, 1963), pp. 181–4 think they recognise juries of presentment in the *judices*, and trial juries in the *juratores*, thus finding the thirteenth-century scheme of grand and trial jury in the time of Henry I.

[10] To be amerced for one of the innumerable possible faults in connection with courts and pleas was one of the commonest risks of life. One might easily apply to England what has been said of Normandy, i.e. that 'almost every court action ended with an amercement of plaintiff, or defendant, or both' (J. R. Strayer, *The Administration of Normandy under Saint Louis* (Cambridge, 1932), p. 51) – and oath-helpers as well as the parties were liable. On amercement in England, 'one of the chief burdens which fell upon all men during this period', see A. L. Poole, *Obligations of Society*, pp. 77–91. The *minuti judices* and *minuti homines* belong presumably to the judicial personnel of minor local courts, communal and feudal, i.e. the Old English lawmen pronouncing judgements in county and hundred courts and the vassals doing the same in their lords' courts; see on this point Richardson and Sayles, *The Governance of Mediaeval England*, pp. 181–4.

[11] Pipe Roll 2–4 Henry II, p. 127, an amercement of ten marks 'de Blafeldhundredo pro placito celato'; cf. Pipe Roll 5 Henry II, p. 9 and 6 Henry II, p. 2.

[12] Pipe Roll 9 Henry II, p. 65: the sheriff of Cambridgeshire and Huntingdonshire accounts for two marks due 'pro murdro celato in Lehtunestan hundredo'.

without pre-supposing the existence of communal presentment. The *placitum celatum* of 1158 may have been a case of treasure trove, which was a plea of the crown. *Murdrum* had to be notified to the reeve, and the hundred was supposed to name the culprit and catch him or pay the fine of forty marks (how this was done the *Leges Henrici* do not tell, nor do they mention a presenting jury, although they state (92, 11) that the murdered person's English nationality will be 'established by the oaths of twelve substantial men of the hundred').[13] The temptation to hide the murder, bury the body and not to tell the officials must have been strong for villagers who were suddenly threatened by yet another demand for payment into the bottomless pit of the royal treasury. Even less helpful is Miss Hurnard's 'assumption' that the reeve, the priest and the four men from each vill who had to attend the hundred and county courts were there to make presentments, because she finds it 'difficult to understand this requirement except on the assumption that these village representatives were to make presentments'.[14] As to the post-1166 evidence quoted by Miss Hurnard, it might reflect older practices, but, again, it might not: the standardised form of presentment of the Assizes was applied throughout the kingdom and could quickly be imitated in local courts.

It seems to us that the silence of the texts presents a real and grave difficulty for the theory of the unbroken existence of the accusing jury from the tenth to the twelfth century. Nor should it be forgotten that there are substantial differences between the jury of Aethelred and that of Henry: the thegns swear with the reeve, whereas in the Assizes the

[13] *Leges Henrici Primi*, ed. L. J. Downer (Oxford, 1972), c. 75, 6ff.; 91, 1–4; 92, 1–19a. The accusation by the hundred is described in the following terms: 'si hundretum compellet aliquem quod murdrum fecerit...' (92, 16). The *murdrum* procedure was very special, created to meet the exceptional circumstances in an occupied country, and is too untypical to allow generalisation, but Miss Hurnard has to admit (p. 385) that her evidence for the communal duty of accusation 'comes mainly from the regulations concerning the murder fine' and even in that context we find no express mention of an accusing jury.

[14] Hurnard, 'The Jury of Presentment', p. 383. There are other instances of 'probable' examples of presentment, where the texts are too vague and other interpretations equally plausible; thus the interpretation (p. 384ff.) of a writ of Henry I for Nottinghamshire about the sending of representatives to the shire court and the king's pleas, and the statement (p. 393) that since the establishment of a murdered person's Englishry is done by the oath of twelve men 'it is highly probable that the accusation was made in the same way'. Other examples occur in her *King's Pardon*, p. 18, where the impleading at the king's suit does not necessarily imply the use of communal presentment and where there is no reason to state that Serlo de Turlauestona had 'apparently' been presented, since this is nowhere mentioned or even alluded to ('Serlo de Turlauestona deb. 10 m. ut habeat disrationationem suam si appellatus fuerit ab aliquo de morte cujusdam unde retatus est' (Pipe Roll 12 Henry II, p. 57) – on the notion of *retatus*, see below, p. 48 n. 18).

meliores homines present to the sheriffs or justices. There are also indications that the leading thegns are the principal local doomsmen, i.e. an upper bench of judges, who accuse suspected criminals and then leave the judgement to God in the ordeal,[15] whereas the jurors of Henry II are ordinary people, not invested with any judicial authority, and their accusation leads to a trial before judges. Finally, it is not easy to explain how a Scandinavian technique, belonging, as the Code of Wantage makes clear, to the peculiar customs of the Danelaw, should have become a general practice among the English – not the normal trend in the Anglo-Saxon kingdom.[16] Yet, if we feel obliged to cast grave doubts on the 'Hurnard thesis', it does not mean that English society was totally unprepared for the jury of presentment introduced by Henry II. Ever since Anglo-Saxon times the communities of vills and hundreds had been taught to bear collective responsibility for the fight against crime, in the system of *friborh* and tithing and frankpledge, the collective responsibility in case of *murdrum*, and the duty of hue and cry, of pursuing cattle thieves and of helping to arrest criminals caught in the act.[17] The important notion of the '*tihtbysig* man', the untrustworthy man of bad repute 'who had often been accused' and for whom the usual proof of innocence was made very difficult, was certainly an important weapon of law enforcement in a peasant community, where few things remained secret (how one's reputation of *tihtbysig* was established we do not know, the words of some older people and the murmur of approval of the crowd attending the local court may have been sufficient).[18] However, these old-English attitudes

---

[15] Stenton, *Anglo-Saxon England*, pp. 503ff. speaks of the 12 leading thegns as an 'upper bench of doomsmen within their wapentake', the 'fate of the suspects being settled by the ordeal, and not by the judgement of the thegns who had presented them'. The twelve leading thegns are compared with the 'lawmen' of Lincoln, York, Stamford, Chester and Cambridge by Whitelock, *Beginnings of English Society*, pp. 146ff.

[16] See p. 44 n. 6. Sensing this difficulty Miss Hurnard writes ('The Jury of Presentment', p. 376) that although these Wantage decrees 'were drawn up for the Danelaw', it is not proved 'that they were peculiar to it', i.e. the institution of the accusing thegns and reeve may also have existed in non-Danish parts of the country. This possibility can, of course, not be excluded, but no text mentions it, not even the corresponding code, concerning 'the law of the English', issued at Woodstock, probably about the same time.

[17] Pollock and Maitland, *History of English Law*, I, 554–7; Holdsworth, *History of English Law*, I, 13–15, 76–8; Stenton, *Anglo-Saxon England*, pp. 295, 404; Poole, *Obligations of Society*, p. 87; Plucknett, *Concise History of the Common Law*, pp. 86, 97ff; G. O. Sayles, *The Medieval Foundations of England*, 2nd edn (London, 1950: Univ. Paperbacks, 1966), p. 335; F. Joüon des Longrais, 'La Preuve en Angleterre', in *Recueils de la Société Jean Bodin*, XVII: *La Preuve*, II: *Moyen Age et Temps Modernes* (Brussels, 1965), 200–3.

[18] The notion of *tihtbysig* was as real and important as it is vague. The *tihtbysig* man is the man of ill-repute, the *ungetrywe*, the *infamatus*, *incredibilis*, *rectatus*, *redté e testimoniet de deleauté*, as opposed to the *homo legalis*, the law-abiding man. We can follow the notion from the tenth

48

and practices did not amount to the formal juries of presentment of Henry II's day, although they may well have prepared the ground, as they were expected to voice the conviction of the neighbourhood.

If Henry's presenting juries are not an old Anglo-Saxon institution, are they perhaps of Norman origin, introduced by the same conquerors as judicial combat and the sworn inquest? Here again there is neither proof, nor likelihood, that the Norman knights brought the accusing jury with them when they crossed the Channel in October 1066, but the sworn inquests on royal command may well have prepared the ground for the sworn presentment of criminals to royal justices of Angevin times[19] (in the duchy traces of accusing juries in lay

century to the enactments of Henry II and other twelfth-century texts. The *infamatus* suffered grave disadvantages; he might be sent to the triple ordeal, or undergo harsher penalties, or be arrested, or need more oath-helpers, or he might be sent into exile, even though he succeeded in the water ordeal, as in the Assizes of Henry II. Who decided that somebody was *tihtbysig*, and how, is obscure, but having been accused repeatedly was one of the main indications, hence such expressions as *accusationibus infamatus* and *ante culpatus*, to render *tihtbysig*; we also find a justice asking the *lagemanni* and *meliores* of borough, hundred or vill about somebody's reputation: 'de quali vita ipse est et si antea audierunt eum calumpniari de exlegalitate' (*Leges Edwardi*, 38, 2). The main texts are VI Aethelstan I, 4 (Liebermann, *Gesetze der Angelsachsen*, I, 174, A.D. *c.* 930–40); III Aethelred 3, 2–4 (*ibid.* p. 228, A.D. 978–1008); III Eadgar 7 (*ibid.* p. 205, A.D. 959–*c.* 962), repeated in II Cnut 25, 25a (*ibid.* p. 329, A.D. 1027–34) and in *Leis Willelme*, 47 and 47, 1 (*ibid.* p. 518, A.D. 1090–1135); II Cnut 30 and 30, 1 (*ibid.* p. 330, A.D. 1027–34); *Leis Willelme*, 14, 15 (*ibid.* p. 503); *Leges Henrici Primi*, 8, 5; 61, 18c; 64, 9; 65, 3; 67. See Liebermann, s.vv. *Bescholtene* (II, p. 305), *tihtbysig* (II, p. 210) and *Rechtsgang* (II, pp. 625ff.). The notion is comparable to the ecclesiastical *infamia* of that period, see P. Landau, *Die Entstehung des kanonischen Infamiebegriffs von Gratian bis zur Glossa Ordinaria* (Cologne–Graz, 1966); R. H. Helmholz, 'Canonical Defamation in Medieval England', in *The American Journal of Legal History*, xv (1971), 256–68. Eadmer, in his *Historia Novorum in Anglia*, ed. M. Rule, RS (London, 1884), p. 194, mentions the *publica parochianorum fama*, in connection with the prosecution of clerics who did not obey the new legislation on celibacy, and we find *fama publica* in *The Letters and Charters of Gilbert Foliot*, ed. A. Morey and C. N. L. Brooke (Cambridge, 1967), no. 9, p. 46, A.D. 1139–48.

[19] Neither Brunner nor Haskins mentions any. It is possible that we have traces of a Norman practice in the inquest through sworn accusers conducted in Bruges in September 1127 by the Norman William Clito, Robert Curthose's son, who had become count of Flanders after the murder of Charles the Good in March of that year and who wanted to round up and punish all those implicated in the conspiracy against the late count. However, this jury of accusation, reminiscent of, and in all probability descended from, the Frankish royal *inquisitio per testes*, may have been Flemish and not imported from Normandy. There are no other instances in Flanders around that time, although the *dorghenga* and *franca veritas* were frequent techniques of criminal inquest in later times (R. C. van Caenegem, *Geschiedenis van het Strafprocesrecht in Vlaanderen* (Brussels, 1956), pp. 35–50), nor is there any in Normandy. It is probable, however, that the punishment meted out by William of Normandy to some of the conspirators, who were thrown to their deaths from a tower in Bruges, was a Norman practice, unknown in Flemish criminal law (R. C. van Caenegem, *Geschiedenis van het Strafrecht in Vlaanderen* (Brussels, 1954), p. 168, n. 3; cf. Galbert, c. 81, and J. Le Foyer, *Exposé du Droit Pénal Normand au XIIIe siècle* (Paris, 1931), p. 231). The story of the inquest is in Galbert of Bruges, c. 87, ed. H. Pirenne, *Histoire du meurtre de Charles le Bon* (Paris, 1891), pp. 131ff. (= *The Murder of Charles the Good, Count of Flanders by Galbert of Bruges*, transl. by J. B. Ross,

courts are very faint before Henry II's time and even thereafter they are not prominent).[20]

Our conclusion must be that Henry II's accusing jury was neither of Anglo-Saxon nor of Norman origin (the question of a possible ecclesiastical origin will be discussed later). To this some readers may object that no society could defend itself against criminals by relying solely on private initiative: surely, they would argue, 'it is hard to imagine that the prosecution of criminals should have been left entirely and completely for several hundred years to the initiative of merely private persons',[21] and if so, what else but a presenting jury was available? Although one should not underestimate the role of appeal, even in 'state crimes' such as treason,[22] there is no doubt that pressure for public prosecution of serious crime, independent of the hazardous procedure of appeal, was strong in England as in other countries, where the state and central authority were growing fast and the financial proceeds of the struggle against crime and the power entailed in expanding jurisdiction were powerful considerations. The English kings of the twelfth century, who were amongst the most powerful of the age and greatly concerned both with public order and the state of their treasure, were loth to leave such an important business as the prosecution of criminals to the hazards of private initiative. However, it is our contention that in the reign of Henry I and Stephen and the

Records of Civilization, LXI (New York, 1960), pp. 258ff.): '...meliores et magis fideles simulque castellanum Gervasium jurare precepit comes pro honore terrae ut vera assertione profiterentur quis Karolum comitem occiderit...igitur post conjurationem consederunt simul in domo comitis et accusaverunt...'. The full list of names produced by this jury of accusation is given in Baldwin of Avesnes's Chronicle of Hainaut, c. 130 (MGH. SS, XXV, 441-3).

[20] Brunner, *Die Entstehung der Schwurgerichte*, pp. 464ff., only mentions passages in the thirteenth-century *Summa de Legibus* dealing with *infamia* or *fama publica*. Strayer, *The Administration of Normandy under Saint Louis*, p. 23, mentions an inquest by a bailiff or viscount and twenty witnesses, which is something like an English grand jury.

[21] Sayles, *Medieval Foundations*, p. 335, discusses the accusing thegns of the Code of Wantage.

[22] Examples of appeal of treason by private persons: Henry of Essex was accused of treason by Robert de Montfort and beaten in the ensuing judicial combat, the normal mode of proof in the appeal procedure (Plucknett, *Concise History of the Common Law*, p. 428 – the story is in the Annals of Jumièges and in Robert of Torigny); an appeal for *laesio regiae majestatis* was brought against Gerard de Camville in 1194 (J. C. Holt, *Magna Carta* (Cambridge, 1965), p. 74, the story is in Roger of Hoveden); in the rolls of the *curia regis* for 1199 we hear of the appeal by Richard fitz Troite of Robert of Hodelme 'quod ipse nequiter dereliquit dominum suum regem Henricum et mentitus est ei fidem suam' and allied himself with the king of Scotland, King Henry II's mortal enemy (F. Palgrave, *Rolls and Records of the Court held before the king's Justiciars or Justices*, Record Commission (London, 1835), II, 30-1). It is not clear from either Henry of Huntingdon or Orderic Vitalis who falsely accused Geoffrey de Clinton of treason in 1130, but it looks like a case of private accusation, see R. W. Southern, 'The Place of Henry I in English history', in *Proceedings of the British Academy*, XLVIII (1962), 139.

early years of Henry II the crown resorted to other means than presenting juries to achieve this end: the English rulers, among the very first to do so in Europe, introduced an innovation of the utmost importance, i.e. the systematic prosecution of suspected criminals by individual royal officials acting on their own authority. In their fight against crime and for the rights arising from crown pleas, English kings had for several generations resorted to the prosecution *ex officio* by royal officials, until Henry II in a series of dramatic moves stopped the practice and replaced it by the juries of presentment.

To prove our point we shall quote from legal treatises, charters and narrative sources, but first a few words must be said about the officials who, with their underlings, played the key role in this new development. These were the local justices, who took their place as the principal judicial agents of the crown at the side of the sheriffs and played a considerable role until their sudden and surprising suppression by Henry II in the 1160s. Earlier historians have underestimated their role, and it was Lady Stenton who pointed out how important it had been.[23] In recent years they have received a good deal of attention and the outline of their office is now reasonably clear.[24] Under the Conqueror and his sons sheriffs of baronial rank were top men in their own right (as well as being royal servants with a great variety of tasks). In order to reduce his independence and power Henry I appointed royal justices in the local courts to deal specifically with judicial work and to keep and hold pleas of the crown. The very first traces of the new office appear towards the end of William II's reign, but under Henry I it was firmly and systematically established and continually extended in counties, hundreds and boroughs 'to safeguard the jurisdictional rights of the crown and to provide for the hearing of the pleas which belonged to it':[25] London obtained its own justiciar *c.* 1130.[26] The creation of this new type of royal servant fits in very well with the general tendency

[23] *Cambridge Medieval History*, v (Cambridge, 1926), 584ff.

[24] See Sayles, *Medieval Foundations*, pp. 310, 330ff.; Richardson and Sayles, *The Governance of Mediaeval England*, pp. 173ff., 195ff.; Richardson and Sayles, *Law and Legislation*, pp. 88ff.; W. T. Reedy, 'The origins of the general eyre in the reign of Henry I', in *Speculum*, XLI (1966), 688–724; R. F. Hunnisett, 'The origins of the office of coroner', in TRHS, 5th series, VIII (1958), 85–104; R. F. Hunnisett, *The Medieval Coroner*, Cambridge Studies in English Legal History (Cambridge, 1961), pp. 1ff.; H. A. Cronne, 'The office of local justiciar in England under the Norman Kings' in *University of Birmingham Historical Journal*, VI (1957), 18–38; H. A. Cronne, *The Reign of Stephen 1135–54. Anarchy in England* (London, 1970), pp. 255–8.

[25] Cronne, *Stephen*, p. 257.

[26] For a recent discussion of London's administration during the period under review, see S. Reynolds, 'The rulers of London in the twelfth century' in *History*, LVII (1972), 337–57.

under Henry I, the creator of a complete new class of people 'who depended on royal government for their rise, and on its continuance for their survival'.[27] Under Stephen the office acquired even greater importance and was occupied by some very powerful men. Justices threatened to become, like the sheriffs before them, local potentates rather than mere 'trusted and experienced servants of the crown' responsible 'de placitis et forisfactis que pertinent ad coronam'. Henry II at first conserved the office. He had agreed in 1153 with Stephen that only men who would not take advantage of it to gratify private revenge or extend indulgence to crime would be appointed, and, according to William of Newburgh, Henry appointed in all districts 'ministers of right and law to coerce the boldness of the wicked'[28] – was it because they disappointed the king that the great criminalistic drive of 1166 became necessary? However this may be, it is clear that until the system of general eyres was well established, reliance continued to be placed on the local justices: the breakthrough of the former coincides with the disappearance in the years 1166–8 of the latter. Royal distrust of too powerful justices with local roots and a general tendency towards centralisation must have been important considerations in their suppression (a few years later the Inquest of Sheriffs and their massive dismissal taught those officials a sharp lesson too). However, the itinerant justices could not deal with everything and part of the job of the local justices was eventually taken over by the coroner, created in 1194.

The local justices 'upon whose shoulders the burden of royal judicial activity from early Henry I till c. 1166 must have fallen',[29] had subordinate officials (and we find one such serjeant in the Pipe Roll of Henry I).[30] It is clear that these justices, specially entrusted with looking after the judicial interests of the crown, were not likely to leave known criminals in peace, solely because no appellor wanted, or dared, to stand up and accuse them: they must have been under pressure to take the initiative and to proceed *ex officio*, when private parties were passive. Public order and royal interest demanded it and elsewhere similar steps

27 Southern, 'Henry I', p. 132.
28 Cronne, 'Office of local justiciar', p. 38.
29 Reedy, 'Origins of the general eyre', p. 719.
30 Benjamin, a Norfolk man, in 1130 paid 56s. 8d. as part of a debt of £4. 5s. 'ut custodiat placita que corone regis pertinent' (Pipe Roll 31 Henry I, p. 91). He appears in a charter of that time as Benjamin the king's sergeant and should be considered a subordinate official of the county justiciar whose duties were numerous and whose 'jurisdiction extended over at least one whole county' (Hunnisett, 'Origins', p. 101).

were being taken.[31] Not only was this likely to take place, but we dispose also of such positive and abundant texts that one wonders why so many historians have overlooked them.[32]

An obvious work to turn to for information on royal justices and legal procedure in the period under review is the *Leges Henrici Primi*, written probably in 1116–18 in Wessex by an anonymous cleric who was professionally occupied with legal business, possibly in the service of some great lord or even the king.[33] The author deals extensively with the problem of prosecution of crime and leaves no doubt that, besides the private appeal and various archaic communal techniques of keeping the peace, the new procedure of prosecution *ex officio* by the local royal justices, 'a new method of impleading' as he calls it, had arisen (6, 4). Thus, when he states the rule 'Nemo a rege inplacitatus cogitur per legem alicui respondere donec ei qui dominus omnium est satisfecerit' (43, 1), or writes of the case 'si quis a justitia regis inplacitatus ad consilium exierit' (48, 1a), or of somebody who 'de proprio placito regis inplacitetur a justicia ejus' (52, 1 – *inplacitare* is quite different from *submonere*!); or when we read that one is excused for staying away from one's lord's court because of *regis inplacitatio* (61, 6) and that somebody who 'a vicecomite vel justitia regis legittime inplacitetur de furto...ad triplicem ladam jure sit applicandus' (in the case of a private accusation the required proof of innocence is more difficult) (66, 9; 66, 8), there is little doubt that the local *justicia* could prosecute a suspected criminal in the king's name on his own authority and initiative, without jury or private plaintiff. Yet, if any doubts are left, the following lines will certainly allay them: 'De inplacitatione

---

31 For example in the county of Flanders (Van Caenegem, *Strafprocesrecht*, pp. 35ff., 55ff. French summary pp. 325–7) and in the Church, see below p. 61.

32 Only W. Ullmann, *Principles of government and politics in the Middle Ages*, 2nd edn (London, 1966), p. 156, n. 2, says clearly that in the Norman period the king's justices also intervened in criminal matters *ex officio* and without complaint by a party (following Liebermann, *Gesetze*, II, 630, s.v. *Richter*, who refers to *Leges Henrici*, 92, 14, a rather obscure article, but there is better evidence). Miss Hurnard, 'Jury of Presentment', p. 392, n. 1, confronted with the evidence pointing towards prosecution *ex officio*, rejects it on the grounds that 'had ex officio prosecution in such cases been lawful before 1166 it is hardly to be believed that Henry II would have given up this prerogative, even in favour of presentment by the jury' – no reasons for this disbelief are given nor does the author consider the fact that presentment might be more efficient than prosecution by a simple official, and that Henry II may have had good reason for rejecting it – see below, p. 68. Lady Stenton thought that the *sacrabar* (the word is Scandinavian) was an official from pre-feudal days whose duty it was to act as public prosecutor in a shire or hundred (*English Justice*, pp. 55ff., 124–37, followed by Holt, *Magna Carta*, p. 58, n. 3), but her interpretation was rejected by J. M. Kaye, 'The Sacrabar', in *EHR*, LXXXIII (1968), 744–58, who sees in the *sacrabar* a private plaintiff in an ordinary procedure, not a court official who prosecuted *ex officio*. 33 *Leges Henrici Primi*, ed. Downer, pp. 34–45.

judicis fiscalis. In causis ubi judex fiscalis aliquem inplacitet de socna sua sine alio accusatore, sine sagemanno, sine investitura, si quis se tertio vicinorum suorum purget, satis est propter justitie reverentiam' (63, 1), i.e., 'Concerning impleading by a royal judge. In causes where a royal judge, acting with the authority of his own jurisdiction, without another accuser, without an informer, without the culprit being caught in the act, impleads a person, if the accused man clears himself by his own oath and that of two neighbours, this satisfies the respect due to justice.'

Our anonymous author's evidence is corroborated by some very interesting London material, relating to the end of Henry I's or to Stephen's reign. We find it in the London Municipal Collection of the Reign of King John (BL Add. MS 14252), which Miss Bateson so carefully analysed.[34] The manuscript is the work of an anonymous author, probably attached to the Gildhall, and was compiled in the early thirteenth century, or slightly later. The author probably had before him an account of London's legal customs written as the result of the city's self-administration granted by Henry I's charter of 1129–33.[35] The first passage, de plaiz de corune, that interests us contains a reference to the London justiciar, who disappeared early in Henry II's reign, and therefore belongs to the period of late Henry I or Stephen (it also contains a reference to ordeals). Here we read: 'Si le rois siut vers aucun hume plai de corone senz clamif et die ke celui est blamé et le roi le mescroit, l'em lui doit esgarder k'il s'en defende soi setime main, et s'il en chiet, si est autant cum il fust s'il eust eu clamif encuntre lui', or, in Miss Bateson's translation, 'If the king prosecutes any man for a plea of the crown without an appellor and says that this man is blamed and the king suspects him, it shall be awarded to him that he defend himself with six compurgators, and if he fail, he is adjudged the same penalty as if there had been an appellor against him.'[36] Clearly the absence of a private accuser is no obstacle to the royal official prosecuting in the king's name and bringing the suspect to trial and

---

[34] M. Bateson, 'A London Municipal Collection of the Reign of John', in EHR, XVII (1902), 480–511, 707–30.

[35] See C. N. L. Brooke, G. Keir and S. Reynolds, 'Henry I's charter for the City of London' in Journal of the Society of Archivists, IV (1973), 558–78. The authors are not certain of the authenticity of the charter, but argue that if it really was granted by Henry I, it should be dated 1129–30 or soon after, not later than 1133; they believe that it might very well be a forgery of Stephen's time or an authentic charter from Stephen which was later erroneously attributed to Henry.

[36] See Bateson, 'A London Municipal Collection', pp. 707ff. Text and transl. in M. Bateson, Borough Customs, I. Selden Soc., XVIII (London, 1904), 47.

everything proceeding as if the traditional accusation had taken place. (This 'proceeding *as if* something had happened' is a nice example of the use of legal fiction, but we cannot go into this here.)[37] The second passage, dating from the same period, is equally clear: 'Nullus scelere comprehensus vel confitens potest appellare hominem de civitate si tamen boni testimonii sit, nec ei in aliquo respondeat, sed justicia, si voluerit, eum se septima manu sacramento constringere potest', i.e., 'No one who has been found, or has confessed himself to be guilty can appeal a man of the city who is of good character, nor need (the accused) answer such (an accuser) in aught, but the usticiar, if he chooses, can put him to the oath, himself the seventh hand.'[38]

The first traces of this independent impleading by royal officials may go back to the late eleventh century and, without insisting too much on a brief passage in Domesday Book and the corresponding entry in the Inquisition of St Augustine's Canterbury,[39] we are on more solid ground with a charter of William II who ordered the restitution to Ramsey Abbey of a sum of 100 shillings 'quos Radulfus Passelewe inplacitavit'. Ralph Passelewe was justiciar in Norfolk in the period 1091-5 – the time of that other great *placitator et exactor*, Ranulf Flambard.[40] Religious houses soon began, of course, to obtain exemptions from impleading by such royal *placitatores*. A charter by Henry I for Tewkesbury ('non inplacitentur ab aliquibus meis placitatoribus')

---

[37] It is striking that when Count Philip of Alsace introduced prosecution *ex officio* in the Flemish towns, he used exactly the same formula: 'si alii assultui interfuerint de quibus clamor factus non sit, si comes super hoc veritatem scabinorum requisierit, scabini veritatem inquirere debent et quotquot veritate scabinorum de assultu tenebuntur unusquisque 60 librarum reus erit *ac si* de eo clamor factus esset' (charter of Ghent, A.D. 1177 or shortly before, c. 2, ed. A. C. F. Koch, *Vroeg middelnederlands ambtelijk proza. Gentse keuren van voor 1240* (Groningen, 1960), p. 4f). See a similar phrase in a statute of Ravenna of 1241: 'si forcia vel forfacta facta fuerit, et notorium et manifestum seu publicum aut mihi denunciatum fuerit, quamvis non sit querimonia facta mihi, tamen inquiram *ac si* querimonia mihi facta esset' (Salvioli, *Storia della procedura*, II, 356, n. 2).

[38] See Bateson, 'A London Municipal Collection', pp. 711-13. Text and transl. in Bateson, *Borough Customs*, I, 25.

[39] A. Ballard, *An eleventh-century inquisition of St. Augustine's Canterbury.* Records of the Social and Economic History of England and Wales, IV (London, 1920), 31: 'Et si abierit domum non apprehensus vel divadiatus tamen minister regis eum sequetur et c. solidis emendabit' (Domesday Book), 'Et licet abierit inde domum non calumpniatus nec divadiatus tamen sequeretur illum prepositus regis ubicunque fuerit et regi c. solidos emendabit' (excerpts).

[40] W. MacRay, *Chronicon Abbatiae Rameseiensis*, RS (London, 1886), no. 188, p. 211. *Regesta*, I, no. 448, with the date 1087-1100, but Ralph Passelewe was local justiciar in Norfolk in 1091-5 and the first known member of a family much employed in the king's service (see Stenton, *English Justice*, p. 65). Florence of Worcester called Flambard *placitator ac totius regni exactor* (*Chronicon*, ed. B. Thorpe (London, 1849), II, 46).

(A.D. 1107 or 1114)[41] and a privilege for Ely granted by the same king in 1123–9 after bitter complaints by Bishop Hervey that everybody 'calumpniabatur, impellebatur, injuriis afficiebatur, dives et pauper angustiabatur' by the king's officials, are relevant here.[42] Ramsey, Tewkesbury and Ely may only involve fiscal impleading, but the distinction between royal proceeds from fiscal or feudal dues and from criminal pleas was not so sharp that we ought to overlook them altogether.

Law books and charters are not our only evidence, however. The chronicles fortunately tell us a few anecdotes that make the faceless officials of the treatises come to life and appear human, if not very attractive beings. Again our first story comes from the late eleventh century and concerns the 'perverse exactions' to which the monks of Ely were subjected by the serjeants of Sheriff Picot, and particularly by one Gervase who was constantly impleading people and getting them condemned: 'hunc dampnabat, hunc frequenter in causam vocabat, hunc crudeliter attrectabat...', until St Etheldreda could stand it no more and appeared to the overzealous man in a horrible vision that gave a salutary fright to this and other *judices et ministri*.[43] From about this time we have a letter of Herbert de Losinga (d. 1119) complaining that he had constantly to defend himself 'adversus accusatores et bedellos, quorum tanta est copia quo vicini nostri: adversus hos vigilamus nocte, laboramus die, et nulla conceduntur tempora, quin eorum dolis aut fraudibus, aut rapinis reluctari cogamur': sheriffs and reeves, accusers and beadles, are all fraudulent and full of wiles and 'venerate nothing but money', so one should beware of the *astutia accusatorum*![44] Eadmer's *Historia Novorum in Anglia*, which fails unfortunately to explain how the fifty men were prosecuted in the famous forest case,[45] tells us a good deal about how Henry I prosecuted through his officials the unfortunate clerics who had failed to obey the canons of the Council of London on celibacy. Eadmer sees it as an oppressive means

[41] J. Conway Davis, *Cartae Antiquae Rolls* (London, 1960), no. 604, p. 187 (older ed. H. Hall, *Formula book of English official historical documents* (Cambridge, 1908), I, no. 17, p. 23) – *Regesta*, II, no. 853.

[42] *Liber Eliensis*, III, c. 39, 40, ed. E. O. Blake. Royal Historical Society, Camden Soc., 3rd series (London, 1962), p. 277f. – *Regesta*, II, no. 1420. The bishop had to go overseas to obtain satisfaction.

[43] Blake (ed.), *Liber Eliensis*, II, c. 132, p. 212ff.

[44] R. Anstruther, *Epistolae Herberti de Losinga* (London, 1846), no. XXX, p. 60ff.

[45] Ed. Rule, p. 102: 'capti sunt et calumniati quod cervos regis ceperint...negant illi, unde statim ad judicium rapti judicantur injectam calumniam examine igniti ferri a se propulsare debere'. Eadmer then talks of the 'malitia hominum eos impie destruere cupientium'.

of raising money and calls it a *crudelis et immanis exactio*, but the fact is that the clergy in question were trespassing against prohibitions issued by the ecclesiastical and lay authority of the land and were therefore liable to prosecution. How this was done is quite clear from Eadmer: 'hoc ergo peccatum rex inpunitum esse non sustinens suos ministros eos implacitare et pecunias eorum...praecepit accipere'! We know from other sources that Henry had the reputation that 'he could not bear to leave anything unrevenged'[46] (and it is a pity we are not told exactly how the miserable false moneyers were brought to justice in 1125), but Eadmer surely exaggerates when he says that the king and his officials invented new misdeeds in order to prosecute people who seemed to have some wealth and did not dare stand their ground in a trial against the king.[47]

The case of Bricstan and Malarteis of 1116, one of the most famous of the reign of Henry I, is also most instructive for our problem. The story of Bricstan was told by Bishop Hervey of Ely (whose complaint about the zeal of the king's ministers we have already met) and recorded in Orderic Vitalis's *Historia Ecclesiastica*.[48] His tale of woe concerns one of those ministers, a certain Robert 'Malarteis' (he had deserved this nickname, we are assured), who 'seemed to have no function except to catch men out' and set about it by 'accusing all equally whenever he could, striving with all his might to harm everyone'. So keen was his desire to get people condemned that 'if he could find no valid reason for condemning them, he became an inventor of falsehood'. One of his victims was Bricstan, an inhabitant of the village of Chatteris, a man of perfect reputation and moderate means, who sometimes lent money to needy neighbours, though not at usury, so we are told. In unexplained circumstances (presumably because he was guilty and had taken fright, though Bishop Hervey would not countenance this at all: the Ely version speaks of illness) he expressed the wish to put on the habit of religion among the monks of Ely. However, the royal official Robert

---

[46] William of Malmesbury, *Gesta Regum Anglorum*, ed. W. Stubbs, RS (London, 1889), II, 487: 'nihil patitur inultum quod a delinquentibus commissum dignitati suae non esset consentaneum'.

[47] *Historia Novorum*, p. 172. As to the false moneyers, William of Jumièges only says: 'Iratus ergo rex, et propter militum suorum injuriam, magis autem ob justitiam temeratam, sententiam dictavit, mandans et praecipiens illis quos in suo loco in Anglia dimiserat [the royal justices?] ut omnes nummularios qui hujus impietatis juste argui valerent...multarentur' (*Gesta Normannorum ducum*, book VIII, c. xxiii, ed. J. Marx (Rouen–Paris, 1914) (Soc. Hist. Normandie), p. 297).

[48] Book VI, c. 10, ed. M. Chibnall, *The Ecclesiastical History of Orderic Vitalis*, III, Oxford Med. Texts (Oxford, 1972), 346–59. A slightly different and shorter version occurs in Blake (ed.), *Liber Eliensis*, pp. 266–9.

Malarteis accused him of having found hidden treasure and retaining it (and trying to escape punishment in Ely). Treasure trove was a very serious business, for keeping the treasure that belonged to the king was not only a fiscal case, but a positive crime, akin to treason and called a quasi-theft by some authors[49] and 'larceny and usury' by Malarteis, who forbade the bishop to give shelter to the culprit and managed to send him to trial under surety ('sub fidejussoribus missus ducitur ad judicium'). The royal judge who, presiding over the county court of Huntingdon, tried the case was the severe Ralph Basset.[50] To him Bricstan was presented and Malarteis's false accusation repeated; Bricstan denied the charge, but was adjudged in the king's mercy ('ipsum cum omni omnino possessione ditioni regis tradendum') and imprisoned in London, where he never 'ceased to call on St Benedict and St Etheldreda', and one night was miraculously freed. Here we see how people were charged by minor though very zealous royal *ministri*, who, in all probability, were specially appointed for keeping pleas of the crown as helpers of the local justices – we may call them 'serjeants' or 'reeves', in the thirteenth century the term 'bailiff' will become more general.[51] Though we may have doubts about St Etheldreda's and St Benedict's miracles, Robert Malarteis was real enough: he owned land in Huntingdonshire and Bedfordshire and was still holding office in 1130, as we know from the Pipe Roll of that year.[52]

This same Pipe Roll contains several instances of people owing sums of money to the king 'to have peace' in respect of some homicide; in one case, that of William fitz Roger, the Pipe Roll expressly adds that obtaining this does not mean that an appeal by the victim's relations is excluded (a normal proviso in grants of pardon in later centuries).[53] This implies that, beside the traditional appeal, an independent prosecution on the initiative of the king or his justices was also

---

[49] Pollock and Maitland, *History of English Law*, II, 498.

[50] The man of whom Roger of Wendover said that he was appointed 'ut evelleret, destrueret, raperet et disperderet et omnia hominum bona ad fisci commodum comportaret', calling him 'hominem perversum et ad omne scelus paratum...et regni Anglorum subversorem' (*Flores Historiarum*, ed. H. O. Coxe, II (London, 1841), 165). See on him D. M. Stenton, *Pleas before the King or his Justices 1198–1212*. Selden Society, LXXXIII (London, 1967), III, xlviiiff; A. L. Poole, *From Domesday Book to Magna Carta 1087–1216*, 2nd edn (Oxford, 1955), pp. 388, 404; Richardson and Sayles, *Governance*, pp. 174–7, 180–6, 249.

[51] See Hunnisett, 'Origins', p. 92.

[52] Cf. Richardson and Sayles, *Governance*, p. 186; Stenton, *English Justice*, p. 61.

[53] Pipe Roll 31 Henry I, p. 102: 'Willelmus filius Rogeri de Ponte Alerici debet 2 m. auri ut habeat pacem de morte Willelmi del Rotur. Et si quis eum appellaverit defendet se legali lege', see Hurnard, *King's Pardon*, p. 16.

possible. The conclusion seems to impose itself that, in Miss Hurnard's words, 'William fitz Roger's pardon fits into – indeed it presupposes – the situation in which prosecution at the king's suit was fast encroaching on the private appeal'[54] (Miss Hurnard has communal presentment in mind, whereas we are thinking of royal justices as agents of this public prosecution).

It is always interesting to keep an eye on Normandy when studying the law of twelfth-century England. Although their institutions were not identical, the two countries lived in a sort of osmosis, under the same ruler (most of the time) and under the same class of knights and prelates. Information on criminal prosecution *ex officio* by ducal justices is very scarce, yet not completely absent. Thus, in a generally addressed notification of 1129 from Rouen, Henry I states that his court has recognised the right of Abbot Roger of Fécamp to £21 (or £20) from each plea of arson and £20 from each plea of homicide arising in the lands of the abbey and concerning which the king's justice had impleaded the culprit ('unde justicia mea placitaverat') and a judicial combat on the charge of arson had been held in his court.[55]

There can thus be little doubt that the prosecution *ex officio*, or 'impleading by a royal justice' as contemporaries called it, was part and parcel of the legal landscape from Henry I onwards. The reaction of the public must have been twofold. People cannot have failed to notice the defects of the old appeal procedure: vexatious appeals and intimidation of the victim, bribery,[56] the fear that the appeal might go wrong on

---

[54] *Ibid.* p. 17. There can, however, be no absolute certainty about this laconic entry. It is conceivable that the culprit had been arrested in, or very shortly after, the act – without formal procedure of prosecution – and was paying for his release (see the case of the London robber, Richard Bucuinte, who was caught and delivered to Richard de Lucy, the royal justice, who locked him up, A.D. 1177: *Gesta Regis Henrici Secundi Benedicti Abbatis*, ed. W. Stubbs, RS (London, 1867), I, 156). It is also possible that William FitzRoger was buying off certain financial rights of the crown in this plea of homicide. Transactions throwing light on the financial gain that could be expected from crime are not hard to find, see, for example, the recognition by Henry I of the right of Roger, abbot of Fécamp, to £21 (or £20) from each plea of arson and £20 from each plea of homicide arising in the lands of the abbey and tried in his, the king's court (Conway Davies, *Cartae Antiquae Rolls*, no. 543, p. 149 – *Regesta*, II, no. 1579, A.D. 1129). Agreement among parties was one thing, the judicial revenues of king and lords were another and the two spheres had to be distinguished. See, for example, the city charter of Wells of 1136–66, granted by Bishop Reginald of Wells, allowing the citizens to come to an agreement in case of crime 'justicia nostra nullam inde exigente consuetudinem vel emendationem', except in case of 'mortale vulnus vel dampnum perpetuum corpori inflictum' and 'salva in omnibus justicia regis et dignitate' (D. O. Shilton and R. Holworthy, *Wells City Charters*, Somerset Record Soc., XLVI (1932), xii). [55] See n. 54.

[56] The Jews of Norwich, who were suspected of St William's murder, so Thomas of Monmouth tells us, 'resorted with prayers and money to Robert the brother of the murdered boy...to whom the business of the accusation was chiefly entrusted' ('cui accusationis negotium maxime

some technical fault,[57] or that the appellor might not find the necessary suit to support him,[58] not to mention the mortal risk of judicial combat or the not always pleasant duty for the victorious appellor of carrying out the execution of mutilation of his adversary,[59] all this made appeal very inadequate.[60] The old communal organizations with their duty of arrest, hue and cry, frankpledge and so on, may well have been seriously disturbed by the turmoil in English society that followed the Conquest. There certainly was something to be said for strong kings, bent on law and order, prosecuting at least the worst forms of crime, independently of other considerations and on their own authority, and to this advantage society cannot have been blind. On the other hand the prosecution by officials implied grave dangers and various authors we have already quoted were very vocal about them. The power to prosecute could lead to arbitrary oppression and to sheer extortion: 'quis custodiet custodes?' Who was to decide that there were serious grounds for suspicion and who was to stop the overzealous or downright dishonest from pressing people for money under threat of pro-

incumbebat'), but he refused and later told the author 'that he could have had ten marks from the Jews if he had hushed up the charge' ('si calumpniam de nece fratris unde impetebantur quietam acclamaret') (A. Jessop and M. R. James, *The Life and Miracles of St. William of Norwich by Thomas of Monmouth* (Cambridge, 1896), pp. 91ff.). The same author has a story (pp. 28ff.) about how the Jews promised a hundred marks to the sheriff, who forced the plaintiff to pledge under oath 'quod judeos super visis non infamaret neque visa...detegeret'.

57 The *Leges Henrici* threaten loss of the tongue or payment of wergeld for a false accusation that might have led to capital punishment (34, 7; 59, 13); the fine of 60s. for failure to prove a charge by winning the judicial combat, known as *recreantisa*, is less fierce (Hurnard, *King's Pardon*, p. 10). The *Leges Henrici*, 24, 2 order compensation to be paid for an unproved accusation.

58 On the suit of 'witnesses' see Bateson, *Borough Customs*, II, xxx, and *Leges Henrici*, 5, 9a.

59 Execution of the condemned criminal by the appellor was a very old form of justice, and we find it until the late Middle Ages, see Bateson, *Borough Customs*, II, xxvi. The *Miracula Wulfstani* of c. 1240 contain a very nasty story of the appeal of Thomas filius Estmeri who was beaten in judicial combat (and lost an eye) in Gloucestershire in 1221 and should have been executed, but was spared his life and condemned to blinding and emasculation instead. This was done by the family of the victorious appellor and led to some disgusting scenes ('testiculos...ita ut juventus lasciva illos inter mulierculas huc illucque pedibus suis recriproce jactaret') (ed. R. R. Darlington, *The Vita Wulfstani of William of Malmesbury*, Camden Soc., XL (London, 1928), II, 16, pp. 168ff.).

60 Kaye (ed.), *Placita Corone*, pp. xxiv–xxviii, discusses how the royal justices attempted to improve the procedure 'in such a way as to preserve their essential and valuable features whilst discarding the objectionable ones'. See also the discussion in Hurnard, *King's Pardon*, pp. 10–11, of the forms of pressure being put in the twelfth century on recalcitrant appellors to bring the appeal, or to discourage the withdrawal and unauthorised compromising of appeals, cf. *Leges Henrici*, 59, 27, 28. The appellor is obliged to give gage or pledge to maintain his appeal (*suire sa clameur*: Bateson, *Borough Customs*, I, 26, London, twelfth century) and even if the appellor drops his appeal, the accused man remains in prison (*ibid.* p. 27, Romney, A.D. 1352), or the case proceeds at the king's suit (*ibid.* p. 28, Fordwich, fifteenth century) – these last two texts may reflect late developments.

secution and its uncertain outcome? We have seen what Bishop Hervey thought of the king's ministers, and we may well conclude this paragraph with a quotation from the *Leges Henrici*, where we read, no doubt about this particular innovation, that 'to the greater confusion of all a new method of impleading is sought out, a new trick for inflicting injury is devised, as if too little damage follows from what has been done before, and he who does most harm to most people is valued the most highly'![61]

However, the state was not the only place where this wicked new method of impleading was being tried. The Church was doing exactly the same, and her prosecuting ministers reaped an even more abundant harvest of protest and abuse. It is to this aspect of our inquiry that we shall now turn and nobody who is aware of the close links between Church and State in Anglo-Norman lands, where the same clerics often served in royal and ecclesiastical courts, will be surprised that we find it necessary to do so.

Speaking generally, until the twelfth century the prosecution of crime – or rather sin – in the courts of the Latin Church proceeded either by the old private accusation, clearly the most important in the *Decretum* of Gratian (*c.* A.D. 1140), or by the communal accusation before the bishop by (seven) 'synodal witnesses' (or, as we might call it, the presentment to the bishop of culprits (*diffamati*) by sworn members of the parish), which went back to Carolingian times and is expounded notably in Regino of Prüm's *De synodalibus causis* of A.D. 906 as a normal machinery of prosecution; trial followed by ordeal or compurgation. To these traditional methods, which constitute the criminal process of Gratian, was added the prosecution by an ecclesiastical

---

[61] *Leges Henrici*, 6, 4; the author states repeatedly the traditional rule that there should be a lawful accuser in a criminal suit: criminal causes start either by the seizure in the act or by a formal *accusatio* (5, 7a; 5, 9a; 9, 1a; 9, 6; 62, 3, 3a). The boroughs clung tenaciously to the old rule 'Wo kein Kläger ist, ist auch kein Richter' (Bateson, *Borough Customs*, II, xxvi). Quoting the above passage from the *Leges Henrici* in translation (6, 4 and also 6, 3), F. M. Stenton, *The First Century of English Feudalism 1066–1166*. Ford Lectures (Oxford, 1932), pp. 218–19, writes that the new system which the anonymous author deplores because of the 'temptations which it offered…and the hardship with which it bore on the common people', was 'evidently connected with the process by which in the reign of Henry I criminal offences in increasing number were being brought under the cognisance of the king's justices, and with the new significance of the king's writ as a means of beginning civil pleas', and he goes on to say that 'an element of extortion entered into the judicial reforms of Henry I'. Let us not forget that 'since England was mainly valuable as a source of treasure for foreign war, the agents of government who provided this treasure had an importance and freedom which they could scarcely otherwise have obtained; Henry I left a large liberty to the men in England who provided him with the sinews of war' (Southern, 'Henry I', p. 135) – impleading his subjects on criminal charges was one of the liberties those agents resorted to.

dignitary (a bishop or a member of his judicial personnel) *ex officio* and on his own initiative – the basis for his action could be a denunciation of ill repute (*infamia*). A parallel change in the law of evidence replaced the old purgatory modes of proof by the *inquisitio*, a rational inquiry by the judge. Though it is older in certain churches, notably in Normandy and England, we find the new method proclaimed generally as early as the Council of Tours (1163) and it gained strength by enactments of Lucius III, Innocent III, Gregory IX and the Fourth Lateran Council and by its use in the *inquisitio hereticae pravitatis*.[62] In England and Normandy, as in the rest of the Latin Church, we find the old accusatorial procedure (the most notorious example is the accusation of poisoning Archbishop William of York, brought against Osbert, archdeacon of York, by Symphorian, a clerk of the household of the late archbishop)[63] and the presentment by synodal witnesses. England and Normandy were an integral part of the Latin Church and there is no reason why episcopal visitations, synodal witnesses and primitive proofs of innocence should not have been practised there as elsewhere; the Norman Church was, after all, just a provincial offshoot of the Frankish Church where the 'synodal system' had originated and was widely used. Nevertheless, facts and documents are better than the most logical deduction and fortunately they are not lacking.

The financial aspects of institutions have often made the clearest

---

[62] See, as well as the literature mentioned, p. 42 n. 1: Brunner, *Die Entstehung der Schwurgerichte*, pp. 458–63; *Realencyclopädie für protestantische Theologie und Kirche*, 9th edn, s.v. *Send, Sendgericht* XVIII (Leipzig, 1906), 209–15 (by A. Hauck); A. Koeniger, *Die Sendgerichte in Deutschland*, I (Munich, 1907); A. Koeniger, *Quellen zur Geschichte der Sendgerichte in Deutschland* (Munich, 1910); E. Jacobi, 'Der Prozess im Decretum Gratiani und bei den ältesten Dekretisten', in *Zeitschr. Savigny-Stift. Rechtsg.*, K.A. III (1913), 223–343; H. Barion, *Das fränkisch-deutsche Synodalrecht des Frühmittelalters*, Kanonistische Studien, v, VI (Bonn–Cologne, 1931), 284–94; J. F. Lemarignier, J. Gaudemet and G. Mollat, *Institutions ecclésiastiques* (F. Lot and R. Fawtier, Histoire des institutions françaises au moyen âge, III (Paris, 1962)), pp. 14–18; W. Hellinger, 'Die Pfarrvisitation nach Regino von Prüm', in *Zeitschr. Savigny-St. f. Rechtsg.*, K.A. XLVIII (1962), 1–116; XLIX (1963), 76–137; *Handbuch der Kirchengeschichte*, ed. H. Jedin (Freiburg, 1968), III, ii, 130ff., 267ff.; J. Dahyot-Dolivet, 'La procédure judiciaire d'office dans l'église jusqu'à l'avènement du pape Innocent III', in *Apollinaris*, XLI (1968), 443–55. We are greatly obliged to Dr D. Lambrecht, who is preparing a study of synodal witnesses and placed his valuable material at our disposal.

[63] *The Letters of John of Salisbury, I: The early Letters (1153–1161)*, ed. W. J. Millor and H. E. Butler, revised by C. N. L. Brooke, Nelson's Medieval Texts (London, 1955), no. 16, pp. 26–7., and appendix III, pp. 261f. (the case belongs to late Stephen and early Henry II). Also, *The Letters and Charters of Gilbert Foliot*, ed. A. Morey and C. N. L. Brooke (Cambridge, 1967), no. 127, pp. 164–5. In a case concerning the king of England, Ivo of Chartres made a sharp distinction between *legitima accusatio* and mere *pravorum delatio conjecturarum divinationibus palliata*; this sort of irresponsible denunciation does not deserve any formal defence or *purgatio* (Letters, Migne, *PL.* CLXII, no. 74, col. 95ff.).

mark on the records and this is so with the synodal system. The link between the visitation and the synod on which it is based is expressed in the constant coupling of *circadae et synodalia*, payments made by the parish priests to the bishop on the occasion of visitations and synods. The numerous Norman charters and other texts from the tenth century onwards concerning episcopal (or what should have been episcopal) rights (*consuetudines*) in synods and visitations are evidence of the continued existence of the synodal system there.[64] In his *Norman Institutions* Haskins specially discussed an arrangement made in 1061 between the bishop of Avranches and the abbot of Mont-Saint-Michel. He rightly concluded that it concerns synodal *testes*, 'a Norman link midway between Regino and the decrees of Henry II'. The men of the Mount 'cogebantur enim venire Abrincas ad respondendum de quacunque accusatione contra christianitatem'. (They were summoned to the bishop's synod at Avranches to answer under oath questions put to them, thus presenting offenders against Christian discipline, one sin explicitly mentioned is 'illicit marriage'.) The text then explains that this led to expense and troublesome oaths, 'sepe in forifacta et emendationes episcopales incidebant et sepe iuramentis fatigabantur': if lawful witnesses came forward to make accusations, the cases should be heard before the bishop and by purgatory oaths the sins which had been committed against the law should be dissolved according to the law.[65]

For England also explicit texts are available. At a council held in London in 1102 legislation had been passed to enforce celibacy. In 1108 further decrees were issued in the presence of King Henry containing important precisions as to the procedure to be followed in bringing transgressors to justice, i.e. the accusation by two or three synodal

---

64 J.-F. Lemarignier, *Étude sur les privilèges d'exemption et de juridiction ecclésiastique des abbayes normandes depuis les origines jusqu'en 1140* (Paris, 1937), pp. 64–83 (esp. p. 74, n. 43), 108–10 (several texts specifically mention the misdeeds concerned; sometimes 'synods and visitations' are mentioned expressly, more often they fall under the general term of (episcopal) 'customs'); Lemarignier, Gaudemet and Mollat, *Institutions ecclésiastiques*, pp. 14–18.

65 C. H. Haskins, *Norman Institutions*, Harvard Historical Studies, XXIV (Cambridge, Mass., 1918), pp. 227ff. See also some instructive charters in L. Musset, 'Les actes de Guillaume le Conquérant et de la Reine Mathilde pour les abbayes caennaises', Mém. Soc. Antiquaires Normandie, XXXVII (Caen, 1967), no. 13, pp. 98–102 (A.D. 1079–1083), no. 19, pp. 122–25 (late eleventh century, containing elements of A.D. 1066–83); they concern the jurisdiction *de criminalibus peccatis* shared between the abbey of St Stephen and the archdeacon of Bayeux. There is an example of seven monks-accusers charging the abbot of Jumièges with incontinence in a letter of Arnulf of Lisieux (ed. F. Barlow, *The Letters of Arnulf of Lisieux*, Camden Soc., 3rd series, LXI (London, 1939), no. 17, p. 22, A.D. 1159): 'super quo septem accusatores, monachos sacerdotes, et novem postmodum testes, monachos itidem, sed diversorum ordinum, produxerunt'.

witnesses or public fame (of which the witnesses are supposed to be the expression), leading to compurgation with six compurgators in the case of a priest, four in the case of a deacon and two of a sub-deacon.[66] A letter of Innocent II of 1136, very much in the Norman tradition of exemption of monasteries from synodal dues, is another proof of the synodal system in England. It concerns the synodal obligation of St Mary's Abbey at Cirencester and declares that the canons are only obliged to send one of their members 'quando episcopus sinodum celebravit ut consuetudines episcopales audiat et suscipiat et fratribus referat'.[67] Nor should we forget that c. 6 of the Constitutions of Clarendon of 1164, recording under the authority of barons and prelates the customs of the time of Henry I (and in fact 'representing not unfairly the practice of the past'),[68] contains the old principle of accusation in Church courts by *certi et legales accusatores et testes in presentia episcopi*, i.e., by synodal witnesses before the bishop.[69] The practice continued in the following century, from which a fair number of regulations concerning synodal inquests has been conserved.[70]

It is into this traditional picture of private accusation and parochial presentment through the voices of synodal witnesses, that a new system was introduced, i.e. the prosecution of offenders by individual ecclesiastical officials, who acted on their own authority and knowledge,

[66] 'Si vero in duobus aut in tribus legitimis testibus vel publica parochianorum fama aliquis eorum accusatus fuerit quod hoc statutum violaverit, purgabit se...' (Florence of Worcester, ed. Thorpe, II, 58; Eadmer, ed. M. Rule, p. 194), cf. the comments of Hurnard, 'Jury of Presentment', p. 395, who also sees a presenting jury in this passage. The term *testes* was unfortunately used for sworn accusers as well as for presenting jurors and could be misleading. See, for example, W. Holtzmann, *Papsturkunden in England*, II (Berlin, 1935), no. 61, pp. 222–6 (A.D. 1149), where *accusatus est testibus* gives the impression that we are dealing with synodal witnesses, but no. 64, p. 229, A.D. 1150, being more explicit, makes clear that it is a private accusation with supporting 'witnesses'. On the other hand a letter of Alexander III, describing the trial by Richard, archbishop of Canterbury, of a husband and wife accused of marrying within the prohibited degrees ('in plena sinodo...seniores et prudentiores producti sunt testes in quorum audientia contrahendi matrimonii fuerat denuntiatio celebrata'), although 'unfortunately we are not told how these proceedings were initiated' seems indeed 'to presuppose the machinery for collecting *fama publica*' (C. R. Cheney, *English Synodalia of the Thirteenth Century* (repr. with new introd., Oxford, 1968), p. 29).

[67] Holtzmann, *Papsturkunden in England*, III, no. 30, pp. 150–3.

[68] Z. N. Brooke, *The English Church and the Papacy from the Conquest to the reign of John* (Cambridge, 1931), p. 202.

[69] Stubbs, *Select Charters*, p. 165 (c. 6, § 1): 'Laici non debent accusari nisi per certos et legales accusatores et testes in praesentia episcopi, ita quod archidiaconus non perdat jus suum nec quicquam quod inde habere debeat'.

[70] Cheney, *English Synodalia*, pp. 5–9, 26–33, 122. For texts, see F. M. Powicke and C. R. Cheney, *Councils and Synods with other documents relating to the English Church*, II: *A.D. 1205–1313* (2 vols., Oxford, 1964), General Index, s.v. Inquest, and comment: I, 262.

suspicion or denunciation. The procedure was rooted in the bishop's duty to discipline his flock swiftly and authoritatively, independently of the uncertainties of accusing juries or private plaintiffs.[71] However, what was gained in efficiency was lost in safeguards for individual parishioners: the archdeacons and deans, to whom the bishop delegated this inquisitorial duty, were at best apt to be rash and overzealous and at worst to turn into oppressors and blackmailers, imperilling their own souls and making people's lives hell. In Anglo-Norman lands the first traces of the prosecution by 'ministers of the Church' appear as early as the Council of Lillebonne of 1080. Here we find a repetition of the condemnation of clerical marriage made in the earlier Councils of Lisieux and Rouen, but with an important precision on the procedure to be followed against an offender. We find that there are two ways in which he could be brought to trial, either on the basis of an accusation made by ministers of the bishop ('si per ministros episcopi inde prius fuerit accusatus'), or of an accusation made by parishioners or lords ('si vero parrochianorum vel dominorum suorum aliquis eum prius accusaverit'). In the former case the accused cleric will purge himself in the bishop's court, in the latter in the parish he serves, in the presence of the bishop's officers: accusation by episcopal officials is clearly mentioned as a possibility of prosecution beside that by one's own community.[72] Significantly, the canons of the same council also contain a stipulation about possible abuse, for we read that 'bishops and their officers are not to compel priests either by force or by threats to give them more than the lawful episcopal dues, pecuniary fines are not to be exacted if they keep women'[73] – but this is exactly what did happen, as later texts make abundantly clear. The question of clerics keeping women has already been mentioned in connection with the English decrees of 1102 and 1108. The problem was taken up again at a council in Westminster in 1127, but then prosecution was not left to synodal witnesses voicing the *publica parochianorum fama*, but was firmly made the duty of archdeacons and other ecclesiastical dignitaries: 'archidiaconis vero et ministris, quibus hoc incumbit, auctoritate Dei et nostra praecipimus ut omni studio et sollicitudine procurent ab

[71] Dahyot-Dolivet, 'Procédure judiciaire d'office dans l'église', p. 443ff.; Acta Apost. 5: 1–11; I Cor. 5: 1–5; F. X. Funk, *Didascalia et Constitutiones Apostolorum* (Paderborn, 1905), pp. 40, 60–76.
[72] *The Ecclesiastical History of Orderic Vitalis*, v, 5, ed. M. Chibnall, III, Oxford Medieval Texts (Oxford, 1972), p. 26.
[73] *Ibid.* p. 28.

aecclesia Dei hanc perniciem omnino eradicare'.[74] The king confirmed the acts of the council, and the archdeacons and ministers of the Church went to work with all the required zeal. We find them again, this time in Normandy, in the time of Stephen. His predecessor, King Henry I, had proclaimed in Rouen in 1135 a decree concerning the Peace of God in Normandy in a solemn charter which includes details on the mode of proof to be used (judicial combat) and the mode of prosecution (the traditional appeal) ('si occisorem illum aliquis duello appellare voluerit, duellum illud in curia mea tenebitur'); the charter goes on to say that if no appellor turns up, 'ipse occisor in ecclesia Dei per manus ecclesie et judicium se purget'.[75] The passage is not so clear as one would wish: it could mean that the suspected man will be prosecuted in some other way and that he will purge himself by his and oath-helpers' oaths in church and judgement then given. More probably it means that the suspected murderer should be accused in church by the oaths of synodal witnesses and prove his innocence by undergoing the ordeal. However this may be, a charter of Stephen of 1136–9, confirming much of the previous document, is clear enough: if there is no private accuser, the suspect will be prosecuted by the ministers of the Church and sent to the ordeal of water or hot iron ('si vero defuerit qui occisorem in trevia Dei duello probare voluerit, tunc ille occisor per ministros ecclesie vocatus aperta lege judicii aut aque aut ignis sese purgabit').[76] One gains the impression that the mode of proof has not changed, but that the oaths of synodal witnesses have been replaced by impleading by ecclesiastical officials.

Thus the archdeacons and deans, the immediate judicial collaborators of the bishop, went to work and prosecuted sinners, laymen as well as clerics, to enforce Christian discipline. Unfortunately, as could be expected, many of them abused their newly-found powers to enrich themselves and oppress the faithful. The question 'whether an archdeacon could be saved' was one of the sick jokes of the age and several writers forcibly voiced the unrest of the public. Thus John of Salisbury, a learned, wise and well-informed man, who believed that suspects should lawfully be forced to stand trial,[77] repeatedly expressed his

---

[74] J. R. H. Weaver, *Anecdota Oxoniensia. The Chronicle of John of Worcester* (Oxford, 1908), p. 24 (also in H. Spelman, *Concilia* (London, 1639–64), I, 410 and in Florence of Worcester, *Chronicon*, ed. Thorpe, II, 87), c. 5. In c. 6 the *ministri ecclesiae* are made responsible for the arrest of the concubines of priests and canons so that they can be punished *episcopali judicio*.

[75] E. J. Tardif, *Coutumiers de Normandie* (Rouen, 1881), I, I, no. 65 – *Regesta*, II, no. 1908.

[76] *Regesta*, III, no. 609, A.D. 1136–9.

[77] *Letters*, I, ed. Millor, Butler, Brooke, no. 100, p. 158: 'Verum si personae suspectae sunt, ad legitimam purgationem urgeri possunt'.

worries about those to whom this task was given. Sometimes he did so in a paternal warning to some archdeacon not to give the impression 'that you are thirsty for the money of the delinquents, keep your hands from the sordid gains of false accusations, lest the office of judge...may seem to be a sort of business';[78] sometimes he grew sarcastic and wrote that 'deans and archdeacons seemed to think the spoliation of a poor man to be good sport' and called them 'ambisinistrous' (a wonderful word, with several connotations).[79] On other occasions he became vitriolic and talked of a 'genus of men who in God's Church are given the name of archdeacons', positively rejoice in 'calumnies', 'eat and drink the sins of the people'[80] and to whom applies the biblical word 'in quorum manibus iniquitates sunt, dextera eorum repleta est muneribus'.[81] 'Ask the King of the English and Duke of the Normans and of Aquitaine what he thinks of those people', thus John of Salisbury, 'and he will answer that there is no evil in the clergy of which they are not guilty.'[82] We shall come back to Henry II in a moment, but he was not the only one in high authority to know of the 'archidiaconorum decanorumque tirannie, quibus parere intolerabile est et non parere dampnosum',[83] and of the misdeeds of those who 'should conserve God's law and do not'.[84] Popes also came to hear of this social menace, which scandalised the Church. Alexander III, in a letter of 1174–81 to the archbishop of Canterbury, mentions specifically the archdeacons of Coventry as guilty of various forms of oppression sprouting 'de radice cupiditatis et avaritiae',[85] and Pope Lucius III heard such dark things about English archdeacons and deans and their 'officials', who dragged Templars before the courts 'to get hold of their money rather than to inflict due penance for their sins', that he issued a special bull addressed to the English hierarchy ordering them to put an end to this abuse, since it would be particularly undignified 'if the aforesaid brethren, who ask for alms in order to defend the eastern Church,

---

[78] *Ibid.* no. 100, p. 159: Archbishop Theobald orders Robert, archdeacon of (almost certainly) Lincoln, to proceed against a certain priest who squanders church property on a concubine (A.D. 1153–61).

[79] *Ibid.* no. 118, pp. 193–5, A.D. 1160–1, letter to Bartholomew, archdeacon of Exeter, about the complaint of a Londoner who had been despoiled by one of his deans.

[80] Letter to Nicholas de Sigillo, archdeacon of Huntingdon, Migne, *PL.* CXCIX, no. CLXVI, col. 156f.

[81] *Policraticus*, V, c. XVI, ed. C. C. I. Webb (Oxford, 1909), I, 353ff. [82] *Ibid.* p. 354.

[83] J. Laporte, *Epistolae Fiscannenses*, in *Revue Mabillon*, XI (1953), 30; the letter belongs to the early years of Henry II (before 1161) and complains about the misfortunes of Fécamp with its English possessions; see D. J. A. Matthew, *The Norman monasteries and their English possessions* (Oxford, 1962), p. 51. [84] John of Salisbury, letter quoted n. 80.

[85] JL 14,315; text in E. Friedberg, *Corpus Juris Canonici* (Leipzig, 1881), II, 88off. (c. 3, X, 5, 27).

should suffer any loss in their possessions': if any Templar should deserve correction, let it not be a pecuniary one.[86] That there was something seriously wrong with this sort of prosecution *ex officio* was evident to many. But not all went to the root of the problem in the way the learned and austere Gilbert Foliot did: more serious than the misconduct of individuals, he found, was a defect inherent in the institution itself, i.e. that one person, bishop, archdeacon or dean, was at the same time a prosecutor inculpating a suspect and a judge holding a trial.[87]

All these complaints, misgivings, sarcasms and admonitions did not stop the firmly rooted prosecution *ex officio* by deans and archdeacons. They carried on in their bad ways, possibly encouraged by the crisis of authority under Stephen, until in the early years of Henry II's reign they went too far and came up against a powerful, headstrong ruler with an instinct for justice. A number of scandalous cases came to the king's notice – it was the period when the question of the criminous clerks was coming to a head – and caused a crisis, which led to a dramatic decision of far-reaching consequence. The king ordered that this form of ecclesiastical prosecution, which he considered iniquitous and probably suspected of being one of the products of the *tempus guerre* under Stephen, should be stopped and the courts should revert to the traditional accusation by synodal witnesses, one of the respectable customs of the good days of his grandfather. That King Henry – and many with him – believed the accusation by the Christian community to be the rightful old custom we know from the Constitutions of Clarendon (c. 6); that he issued an edict forbidding the new form of prosecution in his very first years we know from an event of 1158, when he protested against the violation of the said edict (it is called a *lex prohibitionis* and a *constitutio*, the text is lost, the date obviously is

---

86 J. Delaville le Roulx, *Cartulaire général des hospitaliers de Saint Jean de Jérusalem* (Paris, 1894), I, 2, no. 752, p. 479, A.D. 1185. The nuns of Godstow were freed by Alexander, bishop of Lincoln 'ab omni archidiaconali exactione sive aggravacione ut in hospitiis exigendis aut capellanis inplacitandis ceterisve ejusdem ecclesie ministris in causam ducendis' – a precious privilege for their chaplains and other personnel (cartulary, London, PRO E 164/20, fo. v, A.D. 1139). There is a good discussion of the exactions of the archdeacons and rural deans, 'one of the serious abuses of the twelfth century', in Haskins, *Norman Institutions*, pp. 330–2.

87 The learned abbot of Gloucester voiced his unease in somewhat involved terms in an interesting letter to Simon, bishop of Worcester (*Letters and Charters of Gilbert Foliot*, ed. Morey and Brooke, no. 9, p. 46f., A.D. 1139–48). Though he could see that a dignitary of the Church might be forced to act against a sinner as *fame publice prolocutor*, he had misgivings about the same person being *accusator* and *judex*. See the discussion of the letter by the editors and the texts of the *Decretum* to which they refer for the rule that the judge should not also be the accuser unless the offence is notorious.

1154–8). Our information comes from a good contemporary source, William FitzStephen's Life of St Thomas, who tells us that King Henry was angry with the English clergy, took badly the insolence of some of their members and was particularly incensed when, in York in 1158, a citizen of Scarborough complained that a dean had extorted 22s. from him by vexing his wife and accusing her of adultery *sine alio accusatore*, a practice which the king had forbidden by law. As if this violation of a royal edict was not enough, the king met with clerical opposition when he wanted to try the guilty dean: John, treasurer of York and archdeacon of the East Riding of Yorkshire, felt that the money should be given back to the plaintiff but that the dean should be handed over to his archbishop, which Richard de Lucy countered with the words: 'and what will you adjudge to the lord king against whose constitution this man has trespassed?' The dispute dragged on for a while, but soon afterwards the king went overseas and stayed there for several years.[88] When he came back in 1163, he was told of the misdeeds of the archdeacons 'who exercised tyranny, plagued laymen with their calumnies and clerics with their unjustified exactions',[89] and he complained bitterly about the 'violence of the archdeacons who turned the delicts of others into profit for themselves and demanded a price for sins', stating that he did not want 'anybody to be accused by them without the agreement of a royal official'.[90] In 1164, in the Constitutions of Clarendon, he repeated his prohibition, but soon the great quarrel with Becket broke out and attracted even more attention. At Falaise at Christmas 1159, as we know from the *Continuatio Beccensis* of Robert of Torigny, he had repeated the English prohibition for Normandy, forbidding deans to accuse anybody merely on their own authority and requiring the support of the testimony of

---

[88] J. C. Robertson, *Materials for the History of Thomas Becket*, III, RS (London, 1877), pp. 43–5. The dean maintained that the woman had been accused by a deacon and a layman and that her husband had given the money (20s. to the archdeacon and 2s. to the dean) in order to obtain a more 'lenient' treatment at the trial, but the witnesses called before the king did not prove this and Henry demanded that the dean should be punished, exclaiming that 'the archdeacons and deans of his kingdom every year pressed more money from its inhabitants than he received himself'.

[89] Anonymous Life of St Thomas, ed. Robertson, *Materials*, IV, 95ff.

[90] Robertson, *Materials*, IV, 201ff: 'Conquestus est de archidiaconorum violentia, quod aliorum delicta in sua verterent lucra, quod peccatorum exigant pretia…dixitque se velle ne archidiaconi quemquam, quantumcumque infamem, super aliquo crimine conveniant praeter officialis sui conscientiam.' From a letter of John of Salisbury, quoted above, n. 9, we hear that the offended Londoner had complained to Henry II, who had ordered an investigation; the letter leaves no doubt that the king meant business and that the guilty dean was in serious trouble.

neighbours enjoying good repute for any inculpation in ecclesiastical courts.[91]

The re-imposition of the accusing witnesses, a real ecclesiastical jury of presentment, certainly dealt with the iniquities of public officials putting a man in jeopardy simply by their bare words alone, but the *testes synodales* also had their disadvantages: what happened, the king may have been asked, if the parishioners who should accuse somebody refused to do so, because they were frightened, corrupted or on the culprit's side? Could the Church just look on and be idle? Henry II had a remarkable answer, which, however, was foiled by Becket's opposition. We learn from c. 6 of the Constitutions of Clarendon that he placed royal power, represented by the sheriff, at the disposal of the bishop to force twelve lawful men from the neighbourhood or vill to make truthful accusations and we may well feel that, whatever their personal fears and dislikes, the terror inspired by a royal master like Henry II would make them speak up.[92] Such then, in the years preceding 1166, was Henry's attitude to the impleading by one man *simplici loquela sua* (to use a phrase from Magna Carta, c. 38) in Church courts: he forbade it and replaced it by the older communal sworn accusation, preferably under the supervision or with the collaboration of a royal agent. The king's motives were outrage at the injustices the incriminated system entailed, the exploitation of 'his' citizens by the Church, the general feeling that clerics had – because of Stephen's 'Anarchy'? – grown too powerful in the state and should be put in their place and, possibly, the conviction that indicting juries were more efficient for bringing crimes to light and culprits to justice than individual endeavours.

91 R. Howlett, *Chronicles of the Reigns of Stephen, Henry II and Richard I*, IV, RS (London, 1890), 327: 'Rex Anglorum Henricus ad Natale Domini fuit apud Falesiam et leges instituit ut nullus decanus aliquam personam accusaret sine testimonio vicinorum circummanentium, qui bonae vitae fama laudabiles haberentur'; cf. Haskins, *Norman Institutions*, pp. 329ff.

92 Stubbs, *Select Charters*, p. 165: 'Et si tales fuerint qui culpantur, quod non velit vel non audeat aliquis eos accusare, vicecomes requisitus ab episcopo faciet jurare duodecim legales homines de visneto seu de villa coram episcopo quod inde veritatem secundum conscientiam suam manifestabunt'. It is very hard to decide which 'customs' of the Constitutions are old and which are recent. Considering the antiquity of the synodal system, the first part of c. 6 certainly reflects an old practice in the English Church, but the paragraph here quoted is so different from tradition and so startlingly novel that it is probably an innovation introduced by Henry II, that 'subtle inventor of new legal forms'. Similarly c. 9 on the plea *utrum* reflects old law, but the stipulation that it should be held before the chief justiciar looks new (W. L. Warren, 'Royal Justice in England in the twelfth century', in *History*, LII (1967), 173). C. 6 makes the point that it is not because the accusation is made by synodal witnesses that the archdeacons should lose the judicial revenues to which they may be entitled.

It is time to turn our attention again to procedure in the lay courts. Here too the uncertainties of the past demanded a solution. Henry II, as his Assizes and the immense efforts of his itinerant justices prove, certainly wanted to repress crime in a big way and on a national scale and was ready to mobilise considerable forces for it. To rely on private appeals only was out of the question, but relying on the prosecution by the single royal justice was equally difficult. We have already seen some of the misgivings of public opinion, and John of Salisbury in his *Policraticus* (A.D. 1159) is equally vocal about the *accusantes Herodiani*, the *officialium clamor* and the awfulness of the ministers of the king who believe that everything is allowed them.[93] That nobody should be put in jeopardy by a single, even official accuser was a traditional notion.[94] Magna Carta, c. 38[95] and various other charters prohibiting accusation by an official *simplici loquela sua* leave no doubt as to the continuing strength of this feeling, even after the juries of presentment had become standard practice.[96] Also, it must have been difficult for the king to

---

[93] Book VI, c. 1, ed. Webb, II, 6: there are, however, some people who deny 'ministris [Cesaris] universa de jure licere'; the judicial officers are a terrible lot: 'they all from the greatest to the smallest are given to extortion rather than to justice and they plague ("debaccantur") the people so much that what one of them leaves in peace, the other soon takes away' (*ibid.* p. 5). From around this time, A.D. 1165, we have the story of St Gilbert of Sempringham, who was 'falsely' accused *a fidelibus regis et ministris* and forced, with various heads of houses of his order, to stand trial before royal judges, who imposed compurgation; the saint refused and a royal mandate came from overseas that the case should be postponed until the king could deal with it personally (Life of St Gilbert, Dugdale, *Monasticon Anglicanum*, VI, 2, pp. *xviiff.).

[94] On the necessity of a suit for the accuser see Pollock and Maitland, *History of English Law*, II, pp. 604ff. Bateson, *Borough Customs*, I, 167; II, xxx; T. F. T. Plucknett, *The Medieval Bailiff*, Creighton Lecture in History, 1953 (London, 1954), p. 11: the defendant answers with a flat denial or maintains that he need not answer at all the *simplex dictum* or *simplex vox* of the plaintiff; this applied in appeal as in other cases and it seemed fair to demand that official accusers should also produce suitors. We sometimes find, however, that a citizen must answer another citizen, but not a stranger, without suit (Pontefract, 1194, Bateson, *Borough Customs*, I, 167).

[95] 'Nullus ballivus ponat de cetero aliquem ad legem simplici loquela sua, sine testibus fidelibus ad hoc inductis'. See Pollock and Maitland, *History of English Law*, II, 604; W. S. McKechnie, *Magna Carta. A Commentary on the Great Charter of King John*, 2nd edn (Glasgow, 1914), pp. 369–75; Plucknett, *Mediaeval Bailiff*, pp. 9–13; Holt, *Magna Carta*, p. 226.

[96] Wallingford, *c.* 1154: 'Et si ipse prepositus eos aliqua occasione sine calumpniatore implacitaverit, non respondeant' (Bateson, *Borough Customs*, II, 30); Pontefract, 1194: 'Si serviens pretoris locutus fuerit versus burgensem, non respondebit sine teste' (*ibid.*); Leeds, 9 John, taken over from Pontefract (T. D. Whitaker, *Loidis and Elmete* (Leeds, 1816), p. 7); in 1207–9 Peter de Brus, Lord of Darby and Skelton, issued a charter granting to the knights and free tenants of Cleveland that none should be summoned or impleaded in the wapentake of Langburgh except by consideration of the wapentake, or through a reasonable *sacrabar*, nor should they be troubled by pretence of a plea (Holt, *Magna Carta*, p. 58); 'Magna Carta' of Cheshire of Earl Ranulf II, 1215–16 (J. Tait, *The Chartulary or Register of the Abbey of St. Werburgh, Chester*, Chetham Soc., New Series, LXXIX (Manchester, 1920), I, 102–3): 'si vicecomes meus aut aliquis serviens in curia mea aliquem hominum suorum inculpaverit, per thwertnic se defendere poterit...nisi secta eum sequatur'; *Leges quatuor Burgorum*, *c.* 1270 (Bateson, *Borough Customs*, II, 30); Fordwich, Swansea, Dover, fourteenth century (*ibid.* I, 25, 26).

impose in his own courts a procedure which he so ostentatiously criticised and even forbade in the Church courts.[97]

Thus, here also, royal policy veered towards the use of a jury of accusers from the neighbourhood. We can first glimpse the shape of things to come in the forementioned Edict of Falaise, for immediately following the article on the Church courts the text goes on to say that Henry II, speaking of the lay courts in Normandy 'de causis similiter quorumlibet ventilandis instituit ut, cum judices singularum provinciarum singulis mensibus ad minus simul devenirent, sine testimonio vicinorum nihil judicarent', i.e., at the monthly meetings of the courts, nobody was to be condemned unless the accusation had been supported or brought by witnesses from the neighbourhood (a perfect corollary to the preceding ecclesiastical paragraph).[98] This was still rather vague,[99] but the procedure became more precise in the Constitutions of Clarendon, c. 6, when we hear for the first time of a jury of presentment of twelve lawful men summoned by a royal sheriff. This jury of 1164, although it is mentioned only in connection with ecclesiastical jurisdiction, is an important breakthrough. The stage here reached was crucial. Here we have the sheriff empanelling a local jury of twelve lawful men to present suspected trespassers to the bishop for trial. It was only one step to the empanelling of a local jury of twelve lawful men to present criminals for trial to the travelling justices under the Assizes of 1166 and 1176. The essentials of the presenting jury on royal command are there. Can we at last say where it came from, whether it was of Anglo-Saxon, Norman, or ecclesiastical origin?[100] The answer seems to be that none of the elements taken separately was new (the sworn inquest, with the sheriff empanelling local juries to answer questions of interest to the crown, the panel of local men accusing co-parishioners

---

[97] We know, however, that some of his subjects had been illegally imprisoned, those namely 'qui capti essent et retenti per voluntatem regis vel justitiae ejus, qui non essent retenti per commune rectum comitatus vel hundredi vel per appellationem' – they were ordered to be released upon Henry II's death (Hurnard, 'Jury of Presentment', p. 409f.).

[98] *Continuatio Beccensis*, ed. Howlett, *Chronicles of Stephen*, IV, 327.

[99] Haskins, *Norman Institutions*, p. 329 presses the evidence when he speaks without reservation of the 'requirement of the accusing jury, which here makes its first appearance under the Anglo-Norman kings'.

[100] Pollock and Maitland, *History of English Law*, I, 130ff. prudently hint in this latter sense; Cheney, *English Synodalia*, p. 29 is equally prudent; Ullmann, *Principles*, p. 195 is definite that 'both the inquisition and the replacement of the ancient accusatorial principle by the inquisitorial judicial proceedings...stemmed eventually from canon law'; Sayles, *Medieval Foundations*, p. 336, is equally definite that we ought to 'abandon the Norman and ecclesiastical origin of the jury which presented criminals'. A most instructive discussion of the interplay of forces round Henry's presenting jury can be found in Plucknett, *Mediaeval Bailiff*, pp. 9–12.

of various misdeeds to the ecclesiastical authorities, had all been seen before), but the combination of these elements into one form of process, with the sheriff empanelling twelve local jurors to present criminals for standing trial, was an innovation, as was the systematic character and the 'stern uniformity'[101] with which it was used by the crown. As so often, Henry II had developed something new and efficient out of a choice of existing materials. His decision betrays his legal insight, for it avoided the disadvantages of prosecution *ex officio simplici loquela*, without giving up the advantage of prosecution by the state independently of private initiative; also, it laid a good deal of the burden and responsibility of this public task on the population, a familiar technique of English kingship.[102] It is hard to distinguish the various strands in his jury of presentment. It owed obviously a good deal to the synodal witnesses of ecclesiastical and Frankish origin. To the Normans it owed the technique of the sworn inquest on the king's command, whereas the old-English state certainly prepared the ground with its communal responsibility in the pursuit of crime and its strong network of local institutions. Thus, what became a distinctively English procedure was of an international, truly European origin.

Let us see how the sworn presentment developed in the years after the Constitutions of Clarendon. To understand what happened we must keep in mind the development of the royal judiciary, for in those years a momentous centralisation took place. The great experiment with the local justices, that had been going on for three generations, was discontinued and a court of central justices – touring the country or sitting at Westminster – was given full priority and developed into a permanent and powerful instrument of enforcement and creation of English law. The sheriffs were given a subaltern role in this new scheme of things, particularly after the devastating Inquest of 1170, which must have confirmed the government's distrust of local independence in judicial matters.[103] When Henry II decided in 1166 to take the repression of crime into his own hands and issued the stern Assize of Clarendon, he took up again the indicting jury of 1164, but this time in the frame not of episcopal but of royal justice. Judicial organisation in those years

---

[101] Stenton, *English Justice*, p. 71.
[102] Joüon des Longrais, 'La Preuve en Angleterre', pp. 201–3.
[103] Richardson and Sayles, *Law and Legislation*, p. 98; Hunnisett, 'Origins', p. 104. The history of the office of sheriff seems to be one of continuous erosion, first with Henry I's local justices, then with Henry II's central courts, followed by the creation of such royal officers as the coroners in 1194, the escheators and the *custodes pacis* in the thirteenth, and the justices of the peace in the fourteenth century.

was in a state of flux: the sheriffs were still powerful agents of the law the local justices still played their role in the local courts, but the king was just about to relaunch the eyres of his grandfather in a big way: Geoffrey de Mandeville and Richard de Lucy toured seventeen counties from the south-east to the north between spring and autumn 1166. The Assize of Clarendon reflects this state of affairs: it mentions sheriffs and justices, leaving open the question whether local or central (travelling) justices are meant. From the Pipe Roll it appears that in some counties 'the Assize was enforced locally by sheriffs or local justiciars without the intervention of justices in eyre',[104] whereas elsewhere the latter were clearly enforcing it, with much better results.[105] Precious lessons were learnt. The Inquest of Sheriffs made abundantly clear that they had misbehaved in the enforcement of the Assize of 1166: the country was asked such pointed questions as whether 'anyone had been unjustly accused in the Assize of Clarendon, for money, promise, hatred or some other unjust reason, and whether one of the accused was released or declared guilty for money, promise or love and who received money therefore'.[106] The Assize of Northampton understandably left out the sheriffs. Was it fair to entrust local dignitaries, tied by so many links to their communities, with the execution of so stern and new an edict? They certainly proved unequal to the task. The returns in the Pipe Rolls make abundantly clear that the justices in eyre were much more efficient than the local chiefs in carrying out the king's policy: one reason why the local justices were replaced with advantage by judges travelling from the centre. The consequences can be seen in the Assize of Northampton of 1176: the local justices are gone and even if the local sheriff, though hardly mentioned in the Assize,[107] continued to play a certain role in empanelling juries, all trials under the Assize and later under the Articles of the Eyre had to take place before the itinerant justices. In 1176 they toured the country in six groups, each consisting of three judges, they continued the work in 1177, and from 1179 onwards they were a permanent and ever-expanding feature of English life: it has been said with good reason

---

[104] Holt, 'The Assizes of Henry II', pp. 103ff.

[105] *Ibid.* p. 105: 'The Assize was enforced much more effectively in those counties which the justices visited; it seems inescapable that the justices were the men responsible'. In view of Holt's detailed investigation the opinion of Stenton, *Pleas before the King*, III, liii, that judgement under the Assize of 1166 exclusively belonged to the travelling justices is untenable.

[106] Stubbs, *Select Charters*, p. 176, c. 6.

[107] He appears in c. 12 which says that the sheriff shall guard a thief taken in the act.

that in 1176–7 'a true general eyre system was in existence',[108] which gave the jury of presentment its classical shape as a technique of public prosecution.[109] By welding the local juries to the central body of royal justices, the Assizes of 1166 and 1176, as enforced by the ensuing general and special eyres, solved for centuries a problem that had been urgently posed early in Henry II's reign. That the Anglo-Norman monarchy was the first to introduce prosecution *ex officio* by state officials is not surprising, since England happened to be the strongest and best organised nation-state in Western Europe at the time, but it is a paradox that it was precisely at the moment when England was rejecting this experiment[110] that the continent began to introduce it.[111] However, this continental development is a different story into which we cannot enter here.

[108] Reedy, 'Origins of the general eyre', p. 716.

[109] See on the eyres of that period: D. M. Stenton, *The Earliest Lincolnshire Assize Rolls A.D. 1202–09*, Lincoln Record Society XXII (Lincoln, 1926), xvii–lxxxii; D. M. Stenton, *English Justice*, pp. 71ff.; F. J. West, *The Justiciarship in England 1066–1232*, Cambridge Studies in Medieval Life and Thought, n.s., XII (Cambridge, 1966), 46–8; Reedy, 'Origins of the general eyre', pp. 716ff.; D. M. Stenton, *Pleas before the King*, III, liiiff.; W. L. Warren, *Henry II* (London, 1973), pp. 286ff.; A. Harding, *The Law Courts of Medieval England*, Historical Problems: Studies and Documents, XVIII (London–New York, 1973), pp. 32–85. On the interplay of county courts and justices in eyre and the changes in the local character of the presenting (and grand) jury, see Milsom, *Historical Foundations of the Common Law*, pp. 357ff. It should be noted that Henry's legislation which compelled borough juries to appear before the justices in eyre, put an end to any criminal jurisdiction which the cities and boroughs might have had; see on the case of Oxford, M. D. Lobel, 'Some Oxford Borough Customs', in *Miscellanea Mediaevalia J. F. Niermeyer* (Groningen, 1967), p. 189.

[110] Prosecution by state officials was not altogether absent from English law in later centuries, since there was the rather shadowy procedure of 'criminal informations', see Stephen, *History of the Criminal Law*, I, 294–7; Pollock and Maitland, *History of English Law*, II, 658ff.; Plucknett, *Concise History*, p. 430; Bellamy, *Crime and Public Order*, p. 135. This procedure of obscure origin may go back as far as Edward I; it was certainly known in the Star Chamber and was regulated by Acts of Parliament. The Attorney or Solicitor General used it only in cases of public importance; there were numerous complaints about its disadvantages for defendants. Even within the formal framework of the jury of accusation the justices of the peace in fact became prosecutors in course of time, but we cannot go into this here.

[111] For the Latin Church and the county of Flanders, see p. 53 n. 31. In Spain 'there is not much evidence of the use of *pesquisa* in penal cases before the mid-twelfth century, although this may be partly the result of the loss of royal archives' (Procter, *Judicial Use of Pesquisa*, p. 20) – the *pesquisidores* carried out the inquiry without any private accusation (*ibid.* p. 28), and 'royal *pesquisidores* had been functioning since the last quarter of the twelfth century' (p. 34). Cerdá Ruiz-Funes, 'En torno a la pesquisa', p. 490, says that 'since the twelfth century the importance of *pesquisa* on judicial initiative became accentuated'. There are traces in France in the second half of the twelfth century, see M. Boulet-Sautel, 'La preuve dans la France coutumière', in *Recueils de la Société Jean Bodin*, XVII (Brussels, 1965), 282. Generally speaking the breakthrough of the inquisitorial process did not come until the thirteenth century and met with resistance in several quarters. In Normandy the Anglo-Norman law was gradually replaced by French royal procedure of romano-canonical inspiration and in Scotland, where the monarchy was much weaker, in spite of some legislation on English lines around the middle of the thirteenth century, the jury of presentment never took firm root, nor did the justices in eyre after the

English model exist there: thus England with its grand jury stood isolated (I. D. Willock, *The origins and development of the jury in Scotland*, Stair Soc., xxiii (Edinburgh, 1966), 144; *An Introduction to Scottish Legal History*, Stair Soc., xx (Edinburgh, 1958), 426; *The Acts of William I King of Scots 1165–1214*, ed. G. W. S. Barrow with the collaboration of W. W. Scott (Edinburgh, 1971), p. 43; G. W. S. Barrow, 'The Scottish Justiciar in the twelfth and thirteenth centuries', in *The Juridical Review* (1971), 123).

GEOFFREY OF MONMOUTH AS A
HISTORIAN

by CHRISTOPHER BROOKE

GEOFFREY OF MONMOUTH's *History of the Kings of Britain*[1] purports to be a history of the rulers of Britain from the foundation of the British race by Brutus, great-grandson of Aeneas, in the second half of the second millennium B.C. to Cadwallader in the seventh century A.D. It is a shapely, well-conceived book, written in Latin in the style of contemporary histories; its climax and centrepiece is the account of King Arthur, the greatest of the British Kings; its comparatively matter-of-fact approach is only once set aside for more than a moment, in the 'Prophecies of Merlin'. It purported to be history, and history it

[1] There is no fully satisfactory modern edition; my citations are by book and chapter, and by page, to *Historia Regum Britanniae*, ed. A. Griscom (New York, 1929); I have also used the edition of E. Faral, in *La légende arthurienne*, I, iii (Paris, 1929). The English version is usually my own, though I have made some use of Thompson–Giles (in the form in J. A. Giles, *Six Old English Chronicles* (London, 1882)); and I have derived much pleasure and profit from the translation and notes by L. Thorpe (Harmondsworth, 1966). Thorpe gives a useful short bibliography and list of editions and translations (pp. 46–7, 31–4). The fullest commentary is J. S. P. Tatlock, *The Legendary History of Britain* (Berkeley and Los Angeles, 1950); a useful general study by J. J. Parry and R. A. Caldwell is chap. 8 of *Arthurian Literature in the Middle Ages*, ed. R. S. Loomis (Oxford, 1959). Interesting recent studies are H. Pähler, *Anglistik: Strukturuntersuchungen zur 'Historia Regum Britanniae' des Geoffrey of Monmouth* (Bonn, 1958), W. F. Schirmer, *Die frühen Darstellungen des Arthurstoffes* (Cologne–Opladen, 1958), chap. I, and R. W. Hanning, *The Vision of History in early Britain* (New York and London, 1966), pp. 121–72, 221–47. There is a handlist of MSS in Griscom's edition, supplemented by J. Hammer, 'Some additional manuscripts of Geoffrey of Monmouth's *Historia Regum Britanniae*', *Modern Language Quarterly*, III (1942), 235–42; but it is sad that Hammer's full studies and projected edition have not yet been published. The status of the variant version, shorter than the vulgate text (ed. J. Hammer (Cambridge, Mass., 1951)), is still under discussion. On the whole it is probably an abbreviation, not a first draft; but if it were to become clear that it was a draft, only minor modifications of my argument would be needed. Also important is the second variant, on which H. D. Emanuel wrote in *Medium Aevum*, XXXV (1966), 103–10 (it is sad that Mr Emanuel did not live to complete his penetrating work on Geoffrey's text).
On Geoffrey in his context as a historian, see now A. Gransden, *Historical Writing in England c. 550 to c. 1307* (London, 1974), esp. pp. 200–9. On his historical influence, see W. Ullmann, 'On the influence of Geoffrey of Monmouth in English History', in *Speculum Historiale*, ed. C. Bauer, L. Boehm, M. Müller (Freiburg–Munich, 1966), pp. 257–76.
In the notes that follow bibliographical references have had to be kept to a minimum, since the full literature on this, as on every aspect of the Arthurian tradition, is immense; it is listed annually in the Bibliographical Bulletin of the International Arthurian Society (Société Internationale Arthurienne).

was taken to be: with only a few dissentient voices the Latin world immediately accepted it as genuine, and gave it a tremendous reception. And this is remarkable, since we now know that hardly a word of it is true, that there has scarcely, if ever, been a historian more mendacious than Geoffrey of Monmouth.

His achievement was essentially literary; he produced one of the most popular of medieval Latin chronicles, and he floated Arthur as matter for serious historical enquiry, thus playing a crucial role in making him respectable throughout western Europe, and the centre of the Matter of Britain. Geoffrey's interest as a historian is that he reveals the aims and methods of one of the most flourishing schools of medieval historical writing – that of southern and western Britain in the early twelfth century – untrammelled by the limitations and exigencies of evidence and source. No modern scholar would look for reliable historical evidence in Geoffrey, even though all acknowledge that he had access to sources now lost.[2] In a sense it may matter little for our enquiry whether he was a serious student troubled, like a number of other chroniclers of the tenth, eleventh and twelfth centuries, by an incurable incapacity to distinguish truth from fiction; or a deliberate 'liar', to use a contemporary phrase intended to distinguish 'history' in the sense used by Bede or William of Malmesbury, from the fiction of the courtly romance.[3] Indeed, it is not clear to some modern scholars that Geoffrey would entirely have understood the distinction. Yet for his interpretation it seems to me fundamental to establish at the outset whether he designed his book to read like history out of serious purpose or a desire to parody. Nor

[2] See Tatlock, *The Legendary History, passim*; and for his use of Welsh sources, some now lost (which Tatlock tended to minimise), see especially the penetrating paper by S. Piggott, 'The Sources of Geoffrey of Monmouth', *Antiquity*, xv (1941), 269–86, 305–19 and R. Bromwich in H. M. and N. K. Chadwick *et al.*, *Studies in Early British History* (Cambridge, 1954), pp. 125–8. Piggott doubted if bks. ii–iii could be entirely of Geoffrey's invention, since the use of materials is sometimes clumsy; but the effect of this is always to enhance his likeness to other historical writers, and he is never so clumsy as his most substantial earlier source, the *Historia Britonum*; nor does any serious scholar doubt that his work is a mosaic, not pure invention. For a recent contribution to his sources, see E. M. R. Ditmas, 'Geoffrey of Monmouth and the Breton families in Cornwall', *Welsh Hist. Rev.*, vi (1972–3), 451–61.

[3] For a rather different view from mine, briefly expounded but with great penetration, see Sir Richard Southern, 'Aspects of the European tradition of historical writing, 1...', *TRHS*, 5th Series, xx (1970), 173–96, esp. pp. 193–6 (also pp. 191–2 on the Norman Dudo). Walter Map described himself as 'a foolish and dull poet – yet not a writer of lies; for he does not lie who repeats a tale, but he who makes it' (*De nugis curialium*, i. 25, trans. M. R. James), perhaps answering Hugh of Rotelande's accusation that he was an expert in the art of lying, and, more remotely, taking up Bede's famous definition of 'uera lex historiae' (*Eccl. Hist., praef.*): cf. K. G. T. Webster in *Speculum*, xv (1940), 272–9. The point will be discussed in the forthcoming reissue of M. R. James's text and translation of Map's *De nugis*, to be published in Oxford Medieval Texts.

shall we expect to find a simple answer to a question from which all ambiguity cannot be removed; for parody may be as serious as imitation.

There are certain passages in Geoffrey's *History* which can hardly be based on anything but bravado. The Laws of Molmutius, he alleges, were established by Dunuuallo Molmutius in some remote period B.C. (a generation or so after the death of King Lear) and 'are famous among the English to this day'; and he proceeds to specify some of them.[4] Later he observes that Belinus, one of Molmutius's sons, confirmed the laws, 'and if anyone is curious to know what he decreed concerning them [the highways] let him read the Molmutine laws, which Gildas the historian translated from British into Latin, and King Alfred into English'.[5] This passage is very characteristic of Geoffrey. He takes famous names and genuine authors, thus lending to an implausible tale a certain verisimilitude, and uses them out of context.[6] There has been much argument as to how much he invented, and this will never be concluded, for no one doubts that some of his sources are lost.[7] What the patient researches of Tatlock and others have made abundantly clear is that he liked to create, as it were, a mosaic pattern in which most of the pieces had some existence in his material, some of the pieces were recognisably historical, but most of the pattern was invention.

Another characteristic of this passage is the use of the *topos* of translation. This was to have a great future: in numerous courtly romances and similar works the author claims that his work is simply based on a translation – from a Latin original discovered by Walter Map, from an Arabic version by Kyot the Provençal, to name only two of the most famous.[8] In the majority of cases the point of these *topoi* is that the statement, though significant, is obviously false. It seems rarely to have been intended to deceive contemporaries as it has often deceived modern critics. The most important use of this *topos* for our purpose is Geoffrey's claim that his whole work is a translation from a book in the 'British' tongue discovered by Walter, archdeacon of Oxford;[9]

---

[4] *Historia*, ii. 17, ed. Griscom, p. 275. [5] *Historia*, iii. 5, ed. Griscom, p. 282.

[6] Good examples of his misuse of authors are his references to Homer and Gildas in *Historia*, i. 14, 17, ed. Griscom, pp. 245, 252; for his use of classical names, see esp. Tatlock, *The Legendary History*, chap. IV. [7] See esp. Bromwich, in *Studies in Early British History*.

[8] Map is named in the *Queste del Saint Graal* and the *Mort Artu* of the prose Lancelot cycle; Kyot in Wolfram's *Parzival*.

[9] Walter was archdeacon from *c*. 1111–12, or earlier, to his death in 1151, and a friend of Geoffrey (*Letters and Charters of Gilbert Foliot...*, ed. A. Morey and C. N. L. Brooke (Cambridge, 1967), p. 537 and references, esp. to H. E. Salter, 'Geoffrey of Monmouth and Oxford', *EHR*, xxxiv (1919), 382–5). 'British' has been variously interpreted as Breton and Welsh, though perhaps Welsh is more probable; but the ambiguity may well be deliberate.

and to this we shall return. For the moment, let us observe that it sits on the face of the passages we have just inspected that Geoffrey can hardly have expected serious belief in the Laws of Dunuuallo Molmutius.

This passage, then, is evidently a literary adventure; but whether the intent was wholly frivolous cannot be established from one part of the book alone. The most revealing passage elsewhere is the famous account of Arthur's court and crown-wearing at Caerleon-on-Usk, which is in a sense the climax of the whole book. It contains a long list of lesser worthies, which are now known simply to be an extract from a Welsh genealogy.[10] It is doubtful if a Welsh audience would have been deceived, likely enough that an English or Anglo-Norman audience would have believed that this was a genuine list of names. The greater magnates included 'the three archbishops of the three metropolitan sees, London, York, and Dubricius of the City of Legions. This prelate, who was primate of Britain ("Britannie primus"), and legate of the apostolic see, was so eminent for his piety that he could cure any sick persons by his prayers...'[11] There follows the crown-wearing over which Dubricius, as bishop of the see of Caerleon, presided, and all the panoply of a royal court; finally the business of the day and ecclesiastical appointments. 'St Dubricius, from a pious desire of leading a hermit's life, made a voluntary resignation of his archiepiscopal dignity; and in his room was consecrated David, the king's uncle, whose life was a perfect example of that goodness to those whom he had taught.' This and other passages imply some knowledge of the ecclesiastical organisation of Roman Britain in the fourth century: how much, we cannot say, for this had been the subject of much speculation in the early twelfth century by supporters of the claims of London and St Davids against Canterbury in the primacy disputes of the age. What is clearer is Geoffrey's interest in these contemporary controversies. We know of four which flickered or flared between the Norman Conquest of England and the composition of the *History* in the 1130s. First, the controversy of Canterbury and York, opened in 1070 by Lanfranc's claim to be primate of all Britain, a title used by his successors when receiving the professions of their suffragans, and naturally attributed by Geoffrey to Dubricius. When Geoffrey wrote it was dormant, for in spite of the Canterbury forgeries of *c.* 1121 the popes had recently supported York in its claim

---

[10] S. Piggott, *Antiquity*, xv (1941), 281–2.
[11] *Historia*, ix.12, ed. Griscom, p. 463 (and for what follows, p. 458).

not to be subject to Canterbury.[12] Next there was the claim based partly on ancient history, partly on the declared intentions of Gregory the Great and partly on obscure passages in eighth-century history, that London should be the seat of the archbishopric – or at least that the bishop should have a pallium. This claim is echoed not only in the reference to London in this passage, but also in the 'Prophecies of Merlin', Geoffrey's seventh book, where it is forecast that the pallium of Canterbury shall adorn London. Both passages gave heart to Gilbert Foliot in his fight against Thomas Becket in the 1160s;[13] but long before Foliot's accession, Bishop Richard de Belmeis I had tried to revive such a claim in 1108.[14] Next there was the struggle of the Welsh and Scottish churches for independence of the English metropolitans. In this the Scots were successful; the Welsh failed. But the claim that St David himself had been an archbishop and that his see should be archiepiscopal was still very active in the early twelfth century, and its major protagonist, Bishop Bernard (1115–48), still very much alive when Geoffrey wrote.[15] It had not, however, commended itself to the founders of the diocese of Llandaff, who raised what appears to be a counter claim, 'that their own founders, Teilo, Oudoceus – and Dubricius himself – had been archbishops.[16] Finally, soon after Geoffrey's book had been issued, Henry of Blois, bishop of Winchester, was to demand a pallium and an independent province.[17]

It cannot be supposed that Geoffrey wrote this passage in support of any contemporary cause. Of Canterbury he naturally makes no mention, since he is writing of an epoch earlier than Augustine; but if

---

[12] See esp. R. W. Southern, 'The Canterbury Forgeries', *EHR*, LXXIII (1958), 193–226.

[13] A. Morey and C. N. L. Brooke, *Gilbert Foliot and his Letters* (Cambridge, 1965), pp. 151–62, esp. pp. 156ff.

[14] *Ibid.* p. 151 and n. For the earlier history of this claim, see D. Whitelock, *Some Anglo-Saxon bishops of London* (London, 1975), esp. p. 14.

[15] C. N. L. Brooke in N. K. Chadwick *et al.*, *Studies in the Early British Church* (Cambridge, 1958), pp. 214ff.; corrected by the text of the new edition of *Rhigyfarch's Life of St David*, ed. J. W. James (Cardiff, 1967); M. Richter, 'The *Life of St David* by Giraldus Cambrensis', *Welsh Hist. Rev.*, IV (1968–9), 381–6; M. Richter, 'Professions of obedience and the metropolitan claim of St David's', *National Library of Wales Journal*, XV (1967–8), 197–214.

[16] Brooke in Chadwick, *Studies in the Early British Church*, pp. 218ff.; among more recent studies of the Book of Llandaff and its context see esp. Wendy Davies, 'The Early Charter Memoranda of the *Book of Llandaff*' (London Ph.D. Thesis, 1970); W. Davies, 'St Mary's Worcester and the *Liber Landavensis*', *Journ. of the Soc. of Archivists*, IV, no. 6 (1972), 459–85; W. Davies, 'The Consecration of Bishops of Llandaff in the Tenth and Eleventh Centuries', *Bulletin of the Board of Celtic Studies*, XXVI, pt. i (1974), 53–73.

[17] John of Salisbury, *Historia Pontificalis*, ed. and trans. M. Chibnall (Nelson's Medieval Texts, 1956), p. 78; cf. Morey and Brooke, *Gilbert Foliot and his Letters*, pp. 158–9.

his story was taken as literal truth, it could deal a deadly blow at Canterbury, as Foliot saw. Against St Davids and Llandaff he strikes impartially, since he makes Caerleon the metropolitan see of Wales and enthrones there in succession Dubricius and David himself. Nor could York or London gain much comfort from being made subject to a Welsh primate (as they would have understood it); and in any case when Geoffrey wrote London and Llandaff were vacant, as was Canterbury. Thus he declared a pox on all their houses, and can have intended nothing but mockery and mischief.

There is curious confirmation of his mischievous intent in the manner in which the book was issued. Early copies were dedicated to King Stephen, the earl of Worcester, the earl of Gloucester, and to the bishop of Lincoln:[18] it is evident that Geoffrey wished it to circulate widely among possible patrons (as was shortly to be shown) of varying political complexion in the disputes of Stephen's reign soon to flare into civil war. But the first recorded reader was Henry, archdeacon of Huntingdon, who was a colleague of Geoffrey in the diocese of Lincoln, fellow archdeacon of Geoffrey's accomplice Walter of Oxford, and one of the best known chroniclers of the day.[19] It would have been natural for Geoffrey to take Henry into his confidence and to consult him in the process of compiling his history. Yet Henry was left to discover it in peculiar, and, one might have supposed, suspicious circumstances. For early in 1139 Henry visited the Norman abbey of Le Bec in company with Archbishop Theobald, en route for the papal curia.[20] At Bec Henry's attention was drawn to Geoffrey's book by his fellow-chronicler, Robert of Torigny, as he himself tells us in a letter he wrote to Warin Brito, full of the excitement of his discovery, which both Henry and Robert entered in their chronicles.

Henry is directly referred to in the epilogue to Geoffrey's *History*,

---

[18] The 'Prophecies of Merlin' (bk. vii) have a separate dedication to Alexander, bishop of Lincoln; one known MS is dedicated to King Stephen and Robert, earl of Gloucester; several to Earl Robert and Waleran, count of Meulan and earl of Worcester; the large majority to Earl Robert alone. See the useful summary of the evidence in Thorpe, pp. 39–40, n. 7; see also esp. Parry and Caldwell in *Arthurian Literature* (cited n. 1), p. 80, n. 2.

[19] A new edition of Henry of Huntingdon's *Historia Anglorum* by A. Gransden is in preparation; see her *Historical Writing* (cited in note 1), pp. 193–200. The Rolls Series edn by T. Arnold (1879) is incomplete, since it only includes one of the letters which are an integral part of the book, and gives a very inadequate account of the complex and interesting MS tradition.

[20] Henry's letter is given most fully in Robert of Torigny, *Chronique*, ed. L. Delisle (2 vols. Rouen, 1872–3), I, 97–111. For the context of this journey, see A. Saltman, *Theobald, Archbishop of Canterbury* (London, 1956), pp. 14–15.

which is missing from some manuscripts and may be an afterthought, but bears all the marks of authenticity.[21]

> The kings who have ruled in Wales from that time I leave as a theme for Caradoc of Llancarvan, my contemporary, and those of the Saxons for William of Malmesbury and Henry of Huntingdon: but I forbid them to say anything of the kings of the Britons, since they have not that book written in Breton (or Welsh) which Walter archdeacon of Oxford brought out of Brittany (or Wales); which is a true account of their history; and which I have thus in these princes' honour taken pains to translate into Latin.

Caradoc was author of saints' lives of little substance – the word 'contemporaneus' may or may not hint that Caradoc was a historian of Geoffrey's ilk;[22] William and Henry were the best known English historians of the day. In the light of the passages we have inspected, we may surely take the last two clauses quite literally and presume that Geoffrey's confidence that William and Henry could not have access to the Welsh book was based on his knowledge that it did not exist.[23] But it is so couched, as with the translation of the Molmutine laws, to disguise the implication from a gullible reader – and modern interpreters very far from credulous have failed to draw the conclusion. Since we know that no Welsh book could have contained more than a tiny portion of Geoffrey's narrative, and that his only other use of the *topos* of translation is a palpable fiction, it would in any case seem reasonable to conclude that Geoffrey already used the *topos*, like later writers, to hide a fiction. For myself, I think his success as a historian was beyond his expectation and that the epilogue expresses the daring of a man who cannot believe that he will continue to be taken seriously.

In any case he took elaborate pains to make his book seem like history. Although the materials are rich and varied, his idea of how history should read seems to owe most to William. For at its best it consists of a string of narrative reconstructed with great ingenuity from tenuous evidence, embellished and turned into readable narrative by

---

[21] *Historia*, Epilogue, ed. Griscom, p. 536; cf. Brooke in Chadwick, *Studies in the Early British Church*, pp. 231–2.

[22] *Ibid.* p. 232 attempts to see special meaning in the use of a rare word; but the material for the new *Dictionary of Medieval Latin from British Sources*, kindly shown me by Mr R. E. Latham, shows that the word was in fairly common use in this period.

[23] The contrary view is expressed by Southern, *TRHS*, 5th Series, xx (1970), 194: 'Personally I am convinced that the source which he claimed to have received from Walter, archdeacon of Oxford, really existed. But when we observe the freedom with which other historians in the same tradition treated their sources, we shall not expect any exact correspondence between Geoffrey's source and the "translation" which he made of it.'

frequent recourse to stories beautifully told. The difference is that William's ingenuity was exercised in genuine historical research, in fitting annals and charters and stories into a single whole; but the effect on a credulous reader is much the same. The long stretches of fairly jejune succession stories are also reminiscent of Henry of Huntingdon, and Geoffrey shared the interest both William and Henry showed in antiquities. He follows Henry in describing the making of Roman roads, and he seems to have created a whole romantic chapter on the basis of a Roman inscription in Carlisle, already noted and mildly misinterpreted by William.[24] His method and his fancy enabled him to carry this interest further, and out of Caerleon and its Roman remains he created the chief city of Arthur's empire. Yet through most of the *History* the tone is tolerably matter of fact; there is a little magic, a few references in the Christian epoch to miracles; but much less of the marvellous than in other contrived narratives of the early or mid-Middle Ages. Even the making of Stonehenge is attributed to technology of a kind rather than to magic.[25]

To the comparatively rational tone of the history there is one notable exception. Outside the seventh book there is comparatively little mystification; in the seventh book there is little else. King Vortigern built a tower, and the more he added to the top, the more the foundations sank into the ground. His magicians declared that the only solution was to sprinkle the foundations with the blood of a child born without a father. After elaborate search, such a child was found. But Merlin (for such was the child's name)[26] turned the tables on his persecutors: he not only knew what was in the minds of the magicians, but he was able to explain the mystery of the tower, in a highly rational way. Under the foundations was a pond: the tower was sinking into the mud. His predictions continued. At the bottom of the pond were two stones and under the stones two dragons. The pond was cleared at Vortigern's command, and the dragons were duly found; they came out of their lair and proceeded to fight with one another. The king enquired of Merlin what these dragons signified and so compelled the sage to tell Vortigern of the fate of his people. The dragons were symbols of the British and the Saxons – and thus we are launched on a lengthy pro-

---

[24] William of Malmesbury, *Gesta Pontificum*, ed. N. E. S. A. Hamilton, RS (1870), pp. 208–9; cf. Tatlock, *The Legendary History*, p. 20.   [25] *Historia*, viii.10ff., ed. Griscom, pp. 410ff.

[26] *Historia*, vi.17–19, and vii, *passim*, ed. Griscom, pp. 380ff. On Merlin, see esp. references in Bromwich (Chadwick *et al.*, *Early British History*), pp. 125–6 and n. 3; J. J. Parry's introduction to the *Vita Merlini* (University of Illinois, 1925).

phecy in symbolic language stretching far into the future. The first
section carries the story to the reign of Henry I – that is, to Geoffrey's
own day – and most of the details can be interpreted after a fashion.[27]
But this only accounts for less than a quarter of the whole. The next
section is also comparatively clear: it represents the messianic hope of a
pan-Celtic revival, although there is no suggestion that Arthur is to
be the messiah. 'Cadwallader shall call upon Conan and take Albania
into alliance' seems to mean that Wales (or South Britain as a whole)
shall join with Scotland and make common cause, to expel the foreigner
and set up a native Celtic or British kingdom again.[28] A little over half
the prophecy remains, and it has been from that day to this utterly
unintelligible. The idiom is much the same as before, but no sort of
interpretation can be made of it and no picture emerges of the prophet's
intention. The final passage is apocalyptic and astrological.

There was plenty of precedent for planting political prophecy into
a historical narrative; and also for the kind of prophecy which gives
itself plausibility by opening with an account of recent events put into
the mouth of a great figure of the past. Both, for instance, occur in the
Book of Daniel, although Geoffrey, needless to say, could not have
known that Daniel 7, like his own seventh book, was written in the
middle of its prophetic vision.[29] From Daniel and the Psalms come the
animal symbolism, the composite animals and the rhythm and style of
the prophecies. The opening story and start of the prophecy come from
Nennius's history, into which Geoffrey has inserted the name Merlin;
the astrological catastrophe at the end comes, in garbled form, from
Lucan's *Pharsalia*.[30] There seems little doubt that the inspiration of the

[27] There is no full modern attempt to follow the medieval commentaries into 'that Serbonian
bog, interpretation of the Prophecies' (Tatlock, *The Legendary History*, p. 403), but Tatlock's
own account (chap. XVII) is extremely useful, with references to earlier, respectable literature.
For 'findetur forma commercii: dimidium rotundum erit' (vii.3, ed. Griscom, p. 387), cf.
P. Grierson and C. N. L. Brooke, 'Round Halfpennies of Henry I', *British Numismatic Journ.*,
XXVI (1951), 286–9. The Prophecies have a separate dedication (to Alexander, bishop of Lincoln)
and sometimes appear by themselves in MSS. I am grateful to Dr Chibnall for reminding me
of the conclusive evidence of Orderic, xii, c. 47, that the Prophecies were known *c.* 1134–5.
Cf. R. H. Fletcher in *Proc. Med. Lang. Assoc. of America*, XVI (1901), 468.

[28] For discussion of Geoffrey's political interests, see Tatlock, chaps. XVI, XVIII; and the interesting
paper (suggesting glorification of the Norman dynasty) by G. H. Gerould in *Speculum*, II
(1927), 33–51, esp. 48–9. Doubtless there are obscure hints here and elsewhere of sympathy
with Celtic aspirations; but Geoffrey's chief patron was a great marcher lord, and this section
of the Prophecies can equally be read as a glorification of the Norman dynasty – was early
read, not unnaturally, as prophecy of the Angevin empire.

[29] Cf. E. W. Heaton, *The Book of Daniel* (London, 1956), esp. pp. 57–8.

[30] *Historia*, vii.4, esp. ed. Griscom, p. 397; on the influence of Lucan see Tatlock, pp. 405ff. and
references.

piece is Celtic; that it owes a great deal to a type of prophecy popular among contemporary Celts. But in detail it is Geoffrey's composition, and it is as difficult to find precise Celtic elements here as elsewhere in the *History*.[31] It has been suggested that the unintelligible sections of the prophecies were taken over from a Celtic source more or less whole-sale; and it is reasonably certain that they were as unintelligible to Geoffrey as to us. But this kind of jigsaw puzzle of nonsense is danger-ously easy to compose, and the only satisfactory explanation is that when the original purpose of the prophecy was fulfilled the parodist's pen carried on. In the summary of this prophecy which Geoffrey gave in his other book, the *Life of Merlin*, the later part is wholly omitted.[32]

Geoffrey followed his *History* after about ten years, or a little more, with the *Life of Merlin*, a strange and horrifying fairy-story, in which the portrait of Merlin is in some ways quite different from that in the *History*.[33] It serves to show that Geoffrey had an abiding interest in prophecy, for he repeats in summary form the intelligible part of the earlier prophecies, adds a supplement to bring it up to date and yet another account of the messianic hope. But in the main it underlines by an extraordinary contrast the comparatively matter-of-fact tone of the *History*.

Some students of medieval historical writing are inclined always to search for political motives and political bias and to see these as a force more powerful in the historian's mind than an interest in the past or the love of historical truth; to others, disciples of the school of *Geistes-geschichte*, chronicles are primarily expressions of a world of ideas. Both approaches explain too little and too much. When the Venerable Bede, after a lifetime spent in other work, came in his grey hairs to write the *Historia Ecclesiastica*, he revealed a profound curiosity in the story of the conversion of the English people as well as an extraordinary gift for fitting scattered and disparate materials into a flowing narra-tive.[34] When Bede wrote there was no fashion and little precedent, save in ancient narratives, for writing history. Geoffrey of Monmouth wrote in a milieu in which history flourished: in the wake of Eadmer,

---

[31] But see above, p. 78 n. 2.

[32] The *Vita Merlini*, ed. J. J. Parry (University of Illinois, 1925), pp. 65–73, ll. 580–688.

[33] *Ibid.* esp. p. 13: in the *Historia*, Merlin is essentially the Ambrosius of Nennius; in the *Vita* 'he has many of the traits of the Celtic Myrddin'; cf. above, p. 84 n. 26.

[34] This is well brought out in D. P. Kirby, 'Bede's native sources for the *Historia Ecclesiastica*', *Bulletin of the John Rylands Lib.*, XLVIII (1965–6), 341–71. A new edition of *Bede's Ecclesiastical History*, ed. B. Colgrave and R. A. B. Mynors (Oxford Med. Texts, 1969), with full commen-tary ed. J. M. Wallace-Hadrill, is in preparation.

William of Malmesbury, John of Worcester and Henry of Hunting-don.[35] We may discount the love of historical truth as a motive for his work; but it is well to explore for a moment the possibility of political bias and a fascination with historical reconstruction and historical story-telling as possible motives; and his place in a *Geistesgeschichtliches* scheme.

The prophecies and the *Life* were dedicated to successive bishops of Lincoln;[36] the *History* to various secular potentates, including both Robert, earl of Gloucester, and King Stephen. This does not suggest any particular predilection for one side or the other in the civil wars of Stephen's reign; rather, perhaps, an inclination to hedge his bets. But if we are right in thinking that the book was completed in 1138, a year before the Empress entered England, it may not have been clear even to an intelligent observer that civil war was on the way.[37] The dedications suggest that the narrative of the *History* was expected to appeal to men who liked good secular narratives, the prophecies to men of a more learned and sophisticated turn of mind. None of them is known to have had Celtic ancestors in the recent past, although the chief recipient, Robert of Gloucester, was a great marcher lord with much Welsh territory under his rule.[38]

The history gives the British element in the island's past a massive boost, and the prophecies obscurely hint at a pan-Celtic revival.[39] But neither is calculated to bring this home to any audience likely to pay attention: we have no reason to suppose that any of the dedicatees would have viewed such a movement with sympathy – quite the reverse – and any wish to stir such a movement might have been better expressed, less obscurely, in Welsh. It is much more likely that Geoffrey was deliberately obscure in presenting expressions of sympathy for his fellow-Celts.

More substantially, he portrays a golden age in British monarchy in

---

[35] See Southern in *TRHS*, 5th Series, xxiii (1973), 246ff.; C. N. L. Brooke, *Twelfth Century Renaissance* (London, 1969), pp. 166ff.; Gransden, *Historical Writing in England, c. 550–c. 1307*.

[36] See above, p. 82 n. 18; Parry, pp. 30–1, 119.

[37] On the date, see Brooke in Chadwick, *Studies in the Early British Church*, p. 231, n. 2. The evidence of the dedications has sometimes been used to suggest a date as early as 1136; and the combination in one MS of Stephen and the Empress's half-brother Robert of Gloucester makes a date as late as 1139–40 difficult to accept. But the fact that Henry of Huntingdon could 'discover' the work in Normandy early in 1139 makes it almost incredible that the work was circulating more than a few months earlier than this.

[38] On Robert of Gloucester as a patron, see *Complete Peerage*, revised edn, v, ed. V. Gibbs and H. A. Doubleday (London, 1926), pp. 683–6 and 686n.

[39] See p. 85 and n. 28.

the past, in the reign of Arthur; he makes Arthur appear in all his lineaments like a very grandiose version of Henry I; and the prophecies of the future might be read as referring to the Angevin empire rather than to a Celtic revival. The glorification of British, or Anglo-Norman, monarchy seems strangely ill-timed: by 1138 it can hardly have seemed that Stephen would be a worthy successor to Arthur; yet it would have required considerable prescience to foresee the triumph of Henry II, then a small boy of five. But it is in the nature of medieval monarchy that it most needed propaganda when it was weak, and there is nothing impossible in Geoffrey conceiving in the 1130s that it was an acceptable time to boost the monarchy by setting beside Edward the Confessor as the source of monarchical legend – and in rivalry to Charlemagne[40] – the heroic figure of Arthur.

Such an idea may or may not have entered Geoffrey's head; it can hardly in any case have accounted for most of the book that we know. This is a literary work of remarkable skill: a skill in story-telling above all and in reconstructing the past out of fragmentary materials. It is in this sense that he takes his place both among the major literary figures and among the most ingenious historians of the age. He was perhaps the most popular of all medieval historical writers: close on two hundred manuscripts testify to his success; even Bede, with a four-hundred-year start, cannot quite muster 150.[41] More than that, he played a substantial part in creating one of the great literary fashions of the Middle Ages. Even those scholars who have been most concerned to belittle his role in the creation of the Matter of Britain could hardly deny him that.

Equally striking to a modern reader is the way in which he has created out of genealogies, king lists and such documents as lay to hand, as well as out of a copious imagination, the kind of reconstruction of history which impresses the modern scholar in William of Malmesbury and the authors of the Book of Llandaff. It has long been known that William of Malmesbury attempted to reconstruct lists of kings, bishops and abbots by fitting together succession lists, annals and charters; above all, that he understood in principle – even if he floundered in practice – how charters could reveal the relative epochs

---

[40] See F. Barlow, *Edward the Confessor* (London, 1970), chap. 12; R. Folz, *Le souvenir et la légende de Charlemagne dans l'empire germanique médiéval* (Paris, 1950).

[41] Griscom, pp. 550–84 (cf. pp. 31–41), lists 185; this has been supplemented by the studies of Hammer and others (above, p. 77, n. 1). For Bede, see R. A. B. Mynors's introduction to *Ecclesiastical History*, ed. Colgrave and Mynors, pp. xxxix–lxx, lxxv–lxxvi.

of kings and ecclesiastics.[42] It has been argued that a similar technique, even more brilliantly though less truthfully applied, explains the lists of bishops in the Book of Llandaff.[43] In recent years Dr Wendy Davies has accumulated formidable evidence to suggest that this was much over-stated: that in fact the authors had authentic charters or *notitiae* of some kind to work on and failed effectively to unite them with the genealogies.[44] Even so, it seems clear that they knew and attempted to use, however inadequately, William of Malmesbury's techniques. Essentially, it was a kind of jigsaw they were constructing; and in piecing together a convincing history out of often tiny fragments commonly belonging to quite a different context Geoffrey was imitating their technique. In this way he reflects contemporary fascination with history as a reconstruction of obscure past events.

Geoffrey also owed a debt to one greater than William of Malmesbury; and his technique appears at its most refined and effective when he is closest to the Venerable Bede.[45] The early to mid-seventh century was the last British heroic age in his eyes, and he understandably closes his *History* with Cadwallon and Cadwallader, for the former was a major figure in history as well as in legend. But it was also a notable age in English history, and the closing section had to encompass two of Bede's heroes, Edwin and Oswald, as well as the rise of Mercia under Penda. There is plenty of other evidence that there was a Welsh tradition of this epoch with different emphasis from Bede's; and details such as the story that Edwin was nurtured in Wales, and Cadwallon's flight to Ireland,[46] seem almost certainly to prove that Geoffrey knew and used these traditions. Doubtless he realised that there were divergences between his sources; and this provided the need, and the challenge, for a measure of novelty. The result is calculated to appeal to a Welsh audience and to seem not too out of line to one acquainted with Bede; and yet there are stings for both. Readers of Bede were and are surprised to find the whole scene dominated by Cadwallon, to

[42] See esp. J. Armitage Robinson, *Somerset Historical Essays* (London, 1921), chaps. I, II; Southern, *TRHS*, 5th Series, XXIII (1973), 253ff. (and the context, pp. 249ff., emphasising the wider interest in charters and documents of many kinds in 11th–12th-century England).

[43] Brooke in Chadwick, *Studies in the Early British Church*, pp. 218–33.

[44] See above, p. 81, n. 16.

[45] On Geoffrey's use of Bede, see Faral, I, ii, esp pp. 317ff.; and on this section esp. Tatlock, pp. 251–3. The essential passages are Geoffrey's *Historia*, bk. xii, ed. Griscom, pp. 511ff.; Bede, *Eccl. Hist.*, ii.20, iii, esp. cc. 1–3, 6, 9 (ed. Colgrave and Mynors, pp. 202–45).

[46] For these details and the other sources, see J. E. Lloyd, *History of Wales* (3rd edn, London, 1939), I, 182ff., esp. 183, 185.

whom Penda is a mere satellite – a cunning improvement on his role of ally, as portrayed by Bede; Cadwallon survives his defeat by Oswald to preside over Oswald's later destruction and to participate in the battle of Oswestry (though Geoffrey follows Bede in making Penda destroy Oswald) and to die a natural death in the time of Oswiu. To bemuse his Welsh audience, after Cadwallader, Cadwallon's son, had made an edifying end borrowed from the English Caedwalla,[47] Geoffrey unkindly associates the decline in British power with the change of name to Welsh, tries out one or two etymologies of the word, but concludes that it may just refer to their barbarity. Thus the whole section reveals Geoffrey at his most characteristic: piecing together genuine sources and ancient legends, twisting them a little to his purpose, improving a notable saga; save in skill and inventiveness little different at first sight to the *Historia Britonum*, or Dudo on Norman origins, or much twelfth-century hagiography, in honourable fudging. Yet there is an edge to Geoffrey's work rarely evident among his rivals; and when he introduces Cadwallader he covers over the fact that Bede never refers to the last great British king by boldly asserting that Bede called him Chedwalda,[48] a characteristic touch of bravado, in some sense preparing us for the confusion with Caedwalla which follows. There is little in this to suggest a substantial political or 'patriotic' motive, although it is a fitting tail-piece to a wonderful vision of the British past. But the motive most in evidence is the desire to display the literary gifts of a historian.

Thus at the end of the day it is the more purely literary achievement, the construction of a history enshrining heroic legend, which most impresses us. If the Celtic hope was uppermost in his mind, or the Norman empire, he could easily have made his interest much clearer. The adventure of Henry of Huntingdon may suggest personal spite on Geoffrey's part or just anxiety about his book's reception. None of this can be taken very seriously. The conversion of Arthur from a minor hero in one small part of Europe into the central figure in the most popular legendary cycle of the French- and German-speaking world is quite another matter. We must not attribute everything to Geoffrey.

[47] Bede, *Eccl. Hist.*, v.7 (ed. Colgrave and Mynors, pp. 468–73); cf. next note.
[48] Faral's reading; and something of the kind must be intended, though in the present state of knowledge of the MSS Geoffrey's spelling cannot be confidently affirmed. Clearly, as Tatlock pointed out (p. 253n.), it is 'a reminiscence of Bede's "Caedualla, iuuenis strenuissimus de regio genere Geuissorum"' (*Eccl. Hist.*, iv.15, p. 380). This serves to underline Geoffrey's bravado.

But the basic achievement is his. The Latin chronicles connected with the Charlemagne cycle had helped to foster the legends of Saint-Denis and Roland, but hardly to make Charlemagne respectable, for that he was pre-eminently before. In Arthur's case this was not so. William of Malmesbury had seen the possibility. 'Arthur is he of whom the Breton ditties today still burble; but he was worthy – not to be dreamt of in bogus legends – but to be described in a genuine history, since he long sustained his failing country, and urged the unbroken spirit of his fellow-countrymen to war.'[49] It was just such a 'genuine' history which Geoffrey purported to provide, and this remarkable sentence may well in a measure have inspired him.

---

[49] William of Malmesbury, *Gesta Regum*, ed. W. Stubbs (RS, 1887–9), I, 11; cf. Brooke, in Chadwick, *Studies in the Early British Church*, pp. 231–2 and *Twelfth Century Renaissance*, p. 166.

Plato in Gratian's *Decretum*
(MS Vat. lat. 1370, fo. 3v)
(Foto Biblioteca Vaticana)

[Facing p. 93

GRATIAN AND PLATO

by STEPHAN KUTTNER

IN the course of his often analysed discussion of natural law, Gratian tackles the problem of private ownership in the section the school designated as Distinction Eight. It has often been observed that one could describe the whole introductory part of the *Concordia discordantium canonum* as an expanded commentary on the chapter *de legibus* of Isidore of Seville's Etymologies;[1] thus Dist. 8 partly serves to illustrate the words 'communis omnium possessio' in Isidore's description of the *ius naturale*.[2]

Here, by way of introducing St Augustine's famous challenge of the right of the Donatists to own property,[3] Gratian presents the thesis that by the law of nature all things are common to all men ('omnia communia omnibus') and finds this vestigial communism not only practised by the early company of believers of whom we read in the Acts of the Apostles, but also prefigured in the pre-Christian philosophers:[4]

Unde apud Platonem illa ciuitas iustissime ordinata traditur in qua quisque proprios nescit affectus.

The terse dictum on 'not knowing one's own attachments' remained a puzzle for most of the medieval glossators. Modern writers, for all their interest in Gratian's general doctrine of law, have all but bypassed it and certainly made no efforts at finding its source.[5] Only a few, by now

---

[1] See J. Gaudemet, 'La doctrine des sources dans le Décret de Gratien', *Revue de droit canonique*, I (1951), 5–31.   [2] D.1 c.7: Isidore, *Etymologies*, v. 4.1.

[3] D.8 c.1: Augustine, *In evangelium Joannis* VI. 25. For the medieval discussion of common (public) and private ownership in relation to natural law, see R. Weigand, *Die Naturrechtslehre der Legisten und Dekretisten von Irnerius bis Accursius und von Gratian bis Johannes Teutonicus*, Münchener theologische Studien, Kanonistische Abteilung XXVI (Munich, 1967), 307–61.

[4] D.8 pr.: '...quod non solum inter eos seruatum creditur de quibus legitur,..."Multitudinis autem credentium erat cor unum et anima una" [Act. 4:32], uerum etiam ex precedenti tempore a philosophis traditum inuenitur. Unde...'

[5] Among the very few who even mention it, derivation of Gratian's dictum from the pseudo-Clementine passage on 'Grecorum quidam sapientissimus' in C.12 q.1 c.2 (see at nn. 44ff. below)

93

forgotten, twelfth-century decretists recognised *proprios nescire affectus* as a quotation. But it was a quotation out of context, and we may safely assume that Gratian himself was unaware of the contextual meaning of the phrase he quoted: or else he would have chosen a less embarrassing parallel to the communal property of the first Christians than the communal marriage bond and common offspring of the Guardians in Plato's ideal State.

For Gratian's phrase can be traced back to the book that occupied the central place in medieval Platonism: the *Timaeus* in its Latin version (*c.* A.D. 400) by Calcidius.[6] Some of the influence the dialogue exerted on legal thought of the twelfth century has been discussed elsewhere: it came chiefly from the opening pages, where Plato had Socrates recapitulate major points of 'yesterday's discourse', i.e., the *Republic*; it also came from Calcidius's commentary and the contemporary glosses of William of Conches and others.[7]

The Guardians of Plato's City, the *Timaeus* reminds us, have no property of their own. Their women must be moulded according to the same values and conventions as the men.[8] Regarding marriages and children, Socrates recalls, 'we ordained that all should have all in common, so that no one should ever recognise his own offspring (ὅπως μηδείς ποτε τὸ γεγενημένον αὐτῷ ἰδίᾳ γνώσοιτο) and all should regard all as their kinsmen'.[9] But Calcidius chose the Latin *affectus* (plural) in the extremely rare[10] meaning of 'the loved ones' for rendering Plato's τὸ γεγενημένον, 'the offspring':[11]

de existimandis communibus nuptiis communique prole, *si suos quisque minime internoscat affectus* proptereaque omnes omnibus religionem consanguinitatis exhibeant...

has been baldly asserted by D. Composta, 'Il diritto naturale in Graziano', *Studia Gratiana*, II (1954), 151–210 at p. 179; Ch. Leitmeier, 'Das Privateigentum im gratianischen Dekret', *ibid.* 361–73 at p. 365. Weigand, *Naturrechtslehre*, p. 311 and n. 15, rightly expresses doubt but considers the source unknown.

6 *Timaeus a Calcidio translatus commentarioque instructus,*...adiuncto P. J. Jensen ed. J. H. Waszink; Corpus Platonicum medii aevi, ed. R. Klibanski: Plato Latinus, IV (London–Leiden, 1962). This now replaces J. Wrobel's edition, *Platonis Timaeus Chalcidio interprete* (Leipzig, 1876).

7 S. Kuttner, 'Sur les origines du terme "droit positif"', *Revue historique de droit français et étranger*, 4e série, XV (1936), 728–40; and 'A forgotten definition of Justice', in the forthcoming *Mélanges G. Fransen*; S. Gagnér, *Studien zur Ideengeschichte der Gesetzgebung*, Studia iuridica Uppsalensia, I (Stockholm–Uppsala, 1960), pp. 211–40.

8 *Timaeus* 18 B-C.

9 *Timaeus* 18 C-D (see R. G. Bury's translation in Loeb Classical Library, p. 21).

10 Lucan, *Pharsalia*, VIII.132 and Julius Capitolinus, *Vita Maximini*, c.23, are the chief instances quoted in Lewis and Short's *Dictionary, s.v.*

11 ed. Waszink, p. 9; ed. Wrobel, p. 7.

Thus *affectus* became the key word for Gratian (*proprios nescit affectus*) and his interpreters. But very few, if any, could guess the original and rather recherché connotation of the term as indicating not emotions but persons.

Stephen of Tournai was the first of the Bolognese to comment upon the passage in Gratian, and he set the pattern for its traditional explication. In that great fictional republic of Plato's, he says, all things are common and no one must prefer affection (*affectus*) for one's own to that for others; that is, all must love all in equal measure.[12] This formula comes close to the ultimate goal in the Platonic scheme, and it was repeated in one way or another by many of the glossators.[13] Some also pointed to the parallel with St Paul's description of Charity 'which does not seek its own'.[14] But all these explanations remain unaware of the specific foundation, the *communes nuptiae*, on which the equal love for everyone's offspring was to be based in Plato's City.

The only twelfth-century comment on Gratian's Dist. 8 that shows a direct acquaintance with the context of the passage in the *Timaeus* is that of the *Summa Antiquitate et tempore*.[15] Its anonymous author belonged to the French school of the 1170s and probably taught for some time at Cologne.[16] He begins his discussion with a critique of the Master's *omnia omnibus communia* which, he says, cannot be called a characteristic of the natural law if we maintain (with Gratian) the

---

[12] Stephanus Tornacensis, *Summa*, D.8 pr.v. *nescit proprios affectus*: 'Sic enim dixerat Plato esse in illa maxima ciuitate cuius rem publicam fingebat omnia communia et neminem suorum affectus aliis preponere debere, idest omnes ab inuicem equaliter diligendos esse' (Vatican MS Borgh. 287, fo. 13va). The text in Schulte's selective edition (Giessen, 1891), p. 17, is marred by serious misreadings.

Hereafter, glosses and other material from manuscript sources will be printed with their full text only in appendix I below; in the footnotes, references to MS and folio will be given only for short texts not included in the appendix.

[13] Johannes Faventinus, *Summa*, Dist. 8 pr. (with only minor verbal variants); *Summa De iure canonico tractaturus* (Laon MS 371 bis); Alanus, *Glossa Ius naturale*; Johannes Teutonicus, *Glossa ordinaria*. For Laurentius and Huguccio see n. 36 and text at n. 84 below.

[14] *Glossa Ecce uicit leo* Dist. 8 pr. v. *nescit*: 'idest nescire debet, uel *nescit*, tantum. Similiter caritas nescit que sua sunt' etc. (see appendix I below for full text); cf. 1 Cor. 13:5. The gloss 'tantum' is derived from Huguccio's exegesis; cf. the text at n. 84 below.

[15] Göttingen MS 159, fo. 11ra/b; published only in part and without adequate explanation by H. Singer, 'Beiträge zur Würdigung der Decretistenlitteratur, II', *Archiv für katholisches Kirchenrecht*, LXXIII (1895), 70-1; full text in appendix I below. The inferior MSS of the *Summa* omit this important piece together with several other passages in Dist. 4-10; see J. F. von Schulte, *Die Summa magistri Rufini* (Giessen, 1892), pp. l-lvii and Singer, 'Decretistenlitteratur', pp. 35-40; hence not discussed by Weigand, *Naturrechtslehre*, who only consulted one MS, Mainz 477 (52), cf. p. xv.

[16] S. Kuttner, *Repertorium der Kanonistik (1140-1234)*, Studi e testi, LXXI (Vatican City, 1937), 178f.; S. Kuttner and E. Rathbone, 'Anglo-Norman canonists of the twelfth century', *Traditio*, VII (1949-51), 279-358 at p. 299.

equation of natural and divine law.[17] Then, after citing scriptural proof from the Decalogue, the Old and the New Testament, for the right to own property, he goes on to say: 'We could pass over this text (*locus*) if he (Gratian) had not confused matters by appending examples to show that nothing is one's own', and refers to the quotations from Acts and from Plato.[18] In a somewhat sophistic argumentation, which echoes another work of the early French school, the *Summa Magister Gratianus in hoc opere* (*Summa Parisiensis*), our author charges Gratian with the blunder (*peccauit*) of having drawn a universal conclusion (*omnium omnia*) from limited examples: first, the common possessions of those early Christians 'with one heart and one soul' were not possessions of 'all', since they did not include unbelievers;[19] and the second blunder is 'obvious to all who understand Plato':

For only the Guardians (*milites*, φύλακες) of that City were to have their expenses in common, lest, being concerned with their own [affairs], they give less service to the common good of their guardianship.[20]

This is pure *Timaeus*, followed by the platitude that this does not mean common to 'all': at least the enemies are excluded.[21] After some more sententious remarks – on worthy Homer nodding, on property beginning with Adam's sons[22] – the author concludes that Gratian's examples were only meant to show what *ought* to follow from the natural law. They may be insufficient but remain useful: 'non sufficiunt

---

[17] *Antiquitate et tempore*, Dist. 8 pr.: 'Set quod iste non sit effectus iuris naturalis ex his innotescat: ius nature inferius appellat ius diuinum et illud dicit contineri in scripturis diuinis. Quod si scripturam diuinam appellat decalogum preceptorum, patet quoniam secundum illud aliqua sunt propria', etc.

[18] *Ibid.* 'Sic transiri posset locus iste, nisi rem turbaret exemplis suppositis. Duo enim subiungit exempla quibus conatur ostendere nulla esse propria, quorum unum sumptum est de actibus apostolorum...alterum a Platone, scilicet de ciuibus platonice ciuitatis', etc.

[19] *Ibid.* 'Set in utroque exemplo peccauit: in priori quia, etsi singulorum quorum erat cor unum et anima una non essent aliqua propria, tamen que eorum erant communia non erant "omnium" communia, quia infidelium non'; cf. *Summa Parisiensis*, Dist. 8 pr.: 'set laborat in positione exemplorum, et salua pace sua melius potuisset de his tacere, quia que erant apostolorum inter se erant communia, set non omnibus aliis' (ed. McLaughlin, p. 7, emended: see appendix I below).

[20] *Antiquit. et temp.*: 'Quod in secundo exemplo peccauerit palam est intelligentibus Platonem, quia tantum milites illius ciuitatis debebant expensam habere de communi, ne propriis intenti minus ad communem utilitatem milicie deseruirent.'

[21] *Ibid.* 'Nullatenus tamen "omnium" erant communia que possidebant ibi ciues, quia saltem non inimicorum.'

[22] *Ibid.* 'Ad hoc dicendum non esse mirum si quandoque bonus dormitat Homerus...quia modo non est iste effectus iuris naturalis, nec fuit forte ex quo Adam filios habere cepit, quia probabile est quod statim ceperint esse propria.'

set proficiunt'.[23] Here again he follows in the steps of the *Summa Parisiensis*, which had called them 'non...exempla set quoquo modo uestigia exemplorum'.

When *Antiquitate et tempore* turns to the exegesis of Gratian's 'in qua quisque proprios nescit affectus', the author's familiarity with the Calcidian text – and, presumably, its twelfth-century commentaries – becomes once more apparent. The single manuscript, however, stands here in need of some emendation:[24]

quia 'quisque' minores se dilexit[a] ut filios, maiores ut parentes,[b] et sic non habuit 'proprios' uel speciales[c] circa unum 'affectus'...

[a–b]dilexit inter filios maiores. ut parentes. MS   [c]spirituales (sp̄uales) MS

This renders the thought of a kinship pattern which Plato expressed at this point in the *Timaeus*:[25] to treat all one's elders as parents, all one's juniors as sons (the third Platonic relation, equals as brothers or sisters, is omitted). In his vocabulary, however, our author seems closer to the medieval glosses than to the Latin dialogue itself.[26] A brief speculative remark follows about the equal distribution of goods 'if there really were people who had no greater *affectus* for one than for another',[27] and only then, for the first time, the author of *Antiquitate et tempore* alludes to the specific context of all this, the communal marriages in Plato's City. He does so in a rather oblique fashion:

Nota quod quidam [quia MS] dicunt Platonem loqui ibi de nuptiis catarorum et eum sensisse illas esse celebrandas.

The marriages of the Cathari – this indeed leads us far afield into a Manichean world where the absolute rejection of the flesh made all monogamous unions as 'evil' as any fornication or sexual perversity. Not only in popular Catholic belief but also in learned opinion, the

---

[23] *Ibid.* 'Verumtamen ostendit hic M. G. qualis deberet esse effectus iuris naturalis....Si ergo M. G. non ponit exemplum usquequaque sufficiens, est tamen quod dicit in parte proficiens: ista enim exempla non sufficiunt set proficiunt.' Cf. *Summa Paris.* ad loc: 'dici potest quod hec non sunt exempla set quoquo modo uestigia exemplorum' etc.

[24] The following is one of the passages omitted by Singer, 'Beiträge', p. 71.

[25] *Timaeus*, 18 D.

[26] Compare William of Conches, *ad loc.*: '...maioritas ut pater, mater, minoritas ut filius, equalitas ut frater, soror,...docuit Plato ut maiores etate diligeremus ut maiores sanguine', etc. in the edition by E. Jeauneau, *Guillaume de Conches: Glosae super Platonem*, Textes philosophiques du moyen âge, XIII (Paris, 1965), 78. The *Timaeus*, on the other hand, goes into greater detail, specifying *religio* not only *parentum* but also *auorum atque atauorum*; and it calls the juniors *infraque filii* and *nepotes*, but not *minores*: ed. Waszink, p. 9.

[27] *Antiquit. et temp.*: 'Et forte si aliqui essent qui non maiorem ad unum quam ad alium affectum haberent et illi omnibus equaliter cuperent ⟨dare?⟩, et talium bona omnibus essent communia.'

Catharist rejection of marriage was tantamount to a licence for promiscuous intercourse;[28] and there is reason to believe that within the Catharist establishment not a few *credentes* shared this view, leaving the suppression of the body to the *perfecti*.

To arrive at this equation between the 'unlimited' marriages of the Cathari and the community of wives and children among the Guardians of Plato's State was an intellectual feat which testifies to the sophistication of the unknown French or Rhenish canonist who wrote *Antiquitate et tempore*. It belongs in the same intellectual climate as Alan of Lille's observation concerning the Cathari's promiscuity (which he took for granted in his *Contra hereticos*): 'They say that marriage is contrary to the Law of Nature, because Natural Law prescribes that all should be common to all.'[29]

With a final remark, 'But we are accustomed to excuse Plato when we read his book', our author follows the lead of William of Conches and other glossators of the *Timaeus*, all of whom defended the philosopher against the imputation of lewdness (*turpitudo*) and tried to get around a literal understanding of the *communes nuptiae et communis proles*.[30] We shall have to return to this exegesis in discussing the second Platonic text of the Decretum.

The thoughtful commentary of *Antiquitate et tempore* left disappointingly little trace among the glossators of Gratian's Dist. 8. There is a brief passage in the *Summa Tractaturus magister* repeating the criticism of the Master's 'insufficient but useful' example;[31] and we have a remarkable gloss by an academic (i.e., non-scribal) hand in the Biberach manuscript of Gratian, to Dist. 8 pr. v. *nescit*:[32]

idest non internoscit. maiores enim minores ut filios diligebant et hii illis ut patribus obsequebantur.

[28] See e.g., Alan of Lille, *Contra haereticos*, I. 63: 'Dicunt enim quidam eorum quod omnibus modis se homo debet purgare ab eo quod habet a principe tenebrarum, idest a corpore, et ideo passim et qualitercumque fornicandum esse, ut citius liberentur a mala natura', in Migne, *PL*, ccx, 365–6. Further references and discussion in A. Borst, *Die Katharer*, MGH Schriften, xii (Stuttgart, 1953), 2, 179, 182; J. T. Noonan, *Contraception: A history of its treatment by the Catholic theologians and canonists* (Cambridge, Mass., 1966), pp. 183–8. See also G. Couvreur, *Les pauvres ont-ils des droits?*, Analecta Gregoriana, cxi (Rome, 1961), p. 128 and n. 398.

[29] *Contra haeret.* I. 63: 'Dicunt etiam coniugium obuiari legi naturae, quia lex naturalis dictat omnia esse communia', col. 366B.

[30] *Antiquit. et temp.*: 'Set nos eum excusare solemus in legendo librum ipsius'; cf. William of Conches: 'Hic quidam...Platonem turpitudinis arguunt,...Nos uero dicimus Platonem non imperasse turpitudinem sed affectum', ed. Jeauneau, p. 78.   [31] Text in appendix I below.

[32] Biberach MS B 3515 fo. 12ra. On the MS and its several layers of glosses see R. Weigand, 'Die Dekrethandschrift des Spitalarchivs Biberach an der Riss', *Bulletin of medieval canon law*, N.S., ii (1972), 76–81; on its decretals also S. Kuttner, *ibid.* iii (1973), 61–71.

The use of *internoscere* even suggests a direct knowledge of Calcidius's text; all the same, a relation also exists between this layer of glosses and *Antiquitate*: a little earlier on the same page, the glossator of the Biberach manuscript mentions the existence of a copy of the *Codex Theodosianus* in Chartres – an assertion that has its only known parallel in our *Summa*;[33] and this in turn is related to a similar remark of the *Summa Parisiensis* on copies of the Theodosian Code in Orléans and in St Denis.[34]

No other texts have come to light to indicate an influence of the *Summa Antiquitate et tempore*. Among the later Bolognese glossators, Alanus Anglicus had read the *Timaeus*, though at Dist. 8 he limited himself to a mere mention of the dialogue.[35] But in the early thirteenth century, some must still have had a notion of the original meaning of Calcidius's vocabulary: they were rebuked by Laurentius Hispanus when he glossed (*c.* 1210–14) the words *quisque nescit proprios affectus* in Dist. 8 pr.: 'Do not understand this as if everyone ought not to know his own sons, or were permitted to sleep with his own daughter' – and then followed instead the conventional exegesis: those words mean, to accept strangers like one's children.[36] The rejected interpretation may, in its second part (*coire cum filia*), easily have been made up for polemical purposes, perhaps by Laurentius himself, as a *reductio ad absurdum*. But its first part (*ut nesciat filios suos*) renders of course Plato's true sense. It may, together with its negation, somehow be derived from the gloss of William of Conches on the passage *de communi prole* in the *Timaeus*[37] – though by what channels, we could at present not say.

---

[33] The Biberach gloss to Dist. 7 c.2 v. *Theodosianum* is partly hidden in the fold of the volume and hence not fully legible on the microfilm: '///dicem carnotensis ///cut dicitur ut (?) quedam scripta ///decretis habentur'; cf. *Summa Antiquit. et temp. ad loc*: 'Hunc codicem adhuc habent Carnotenses, unde in decretis Iuonis multa ab hoc codice excepta inueniuntur' etc.; Göttingen MS 159, fo. 10vb.

[34] *Sum. Par.* C.2 q.6 c.24: 'Sed cum Theodosianus codex non sit in Lombardia, est enim [*leg.* tamen?] Aurelianis et apud sanctum Dionysium' etc.; ed. McLaughlin, p. 109. The testimonies of the two *Summae* have been frequently discussed and variously evaluated, ever since Maassen first published the text from *Sum. Par.* in 1858; see *inter al.* Th. Mommsen in the *Prolegomena* of his edition of the Theodosianus I.1 (Berlin, 1905), lxxviii, cv; and A. von Wretschko, 'De usu Breviarii Alariciani...', *ibid.* p. cccxlix, with bibliography in nn. 3–5. (Note that the word 'excepta' in *Antiquit. et temp.* [n. 33] is always misquoted 'excerpta'.)

[35] *Glossa Ius naturale*, Dist. 8 v. *Platonem*: 'in Thimeo. *proprios*: idest tanta affectione' etc. (More at n. 47 below).

[36] *Glossa Palatina*, Dist. 8 pr. v. *nescit*: 'Non ita intelligas ut nesciat filios suos et ut ei liceat cum filia sua coire, set ita: idest eodem affectu suscipit extraneos quo et filios proprios' etc.

[37] According to William of Conches some believe that Socrates and Plato ordained 'quod... cum aliquis coire uellet, prefectus quam uellet tenebris supponeret, ignorante utroque cui commisceretur et ita nec proprium filium cognosceret'; but we take Plato's meaning 'ac si diceret: unusquisque uxorem et filios alterius in bono diligat ac si sui essent', ed. Jeauneau, p. 78; and see at n. 81 below.

Even further remote is the chance that the opinion Laurentius rejected was a late echo of Abaelard's teaching. Peter Abaelard in his *Theologia christiana* appears to have been the only major writer of the twelfth century who held that Plato here meant what he said. The interpretation of the passage from the *Timaeus* is part of Abaelard's exposition of the 'harmony of evangelical and philosophical doctrine' in respect of the active life.[38] But in placing – as Gratian would do after him – the Acts of Apostles and Plato next to each other, Abaelard for one left no doubt that 'illud decretum Socratis in Timaeo Platonis inductum' really meant community of wives, so that 'nullus proprios recognoscat liberos'.[39] This led him to a rhetorical question on *turpitudo* and *abominabilis obscoenitas* in so great a moral philosopher and hence to a digression quoting Jerome's harsh censure of passion and ardour in the act of marriage ('nihil est fedius quam uxorem amare quasi adulteram').[40] He concluded that the marital communism decreed by Socrates was not intended for the delight of sexual unions but for their fruits – thus ending in a sombre, utilitarian kind of *caritas* in which the individual possesses anything he has, children and all, for the sake of the common weal alone.[41] And as if to clinch his point, Abaelard related the story from Valerius Maximus how Aulus Fulvius, when his son went over to Catilina, had the lad seized and put to death, proclaiming, 'I did not sire my son for Catilina against my country (*patria*) but for the country against Catilina'.[42]

[38] Abaelard, *Theologia christiana*, II. 45–8, ed. E. M. Buytaert, Corpus Christianorum, Continuatio mediaeualis, XII (Turnhout, 1969), 150–1; Migne, *PL*. CLXXVIII, 1180A–81A. (The term 'euangelicae ac philosophicae doctrinae concordia' is from c. 44, ed. Buytaert, p. 150, lines 619–20.) See also his *Dialogus inter Philosophum, Iudaeum et Christianum*, Migne, *PL*. CLXXVIII, 1653B–C. Both texts briefly mentioned by Couvreur, *Les pauvres* (n. 28 above), p. 171.

[39] *Theol. christ.*, II. 46 (lines 648–51).

[40] *Ibid.* c. 47, from Jerome, *Adversus Iovinianum*, I. 49: Migne, *PL*. XXIII, 281. On this text and its use in Gratian, C.32 q.4 c.5, see Noonan, *Contraception* (n. 28 above), pp. 79–80, 196–7; and authors cited in P. Weimar's 'Addenda and corrigenda' to the reprint of H. Kantorowicz, *Studies in the glossators of the Roman law* (Cambridge, 1938; repr. Aalen, 1969), no. 20, pp. 328–9.

[41] *Theol. christ.*, II. 48: 'Vxores itaque uult communes esse secundum fructum, non secundum usum, hoc est ad utilitatem ex eis percipiendam, non ad uoluptatem in eis explendam, ut uidelicet tanta sit in omnibus caritas propagata, ut unusquisque omnia quae habet, tam filios quam quaecumque alia, nonnisi ad communem utilitatem possidere appetat'; ed. Buytaert, p. 151, lines 673–9.

[42] *Ibid.* lines 679–85. After the present pages were written Professor John Benton kindly called my attention to the recent paper by T. Gregory, 'Abélard et Platon', in *Peter Abelard: Proceedings of the International Conference, Louvain May 10–12, 1971*, Mediaevalia Lovaniensia, ser. I, Studia II (Louvain–The Hague, 1974), 38–64. Professor Gregory discusses *Theol. christ.*, II. 45–8 on p. 59 and apparently finds no great difference between Abaelard's exegesis and that of William of Conches ('un commentaire analogue'). Yet it was one of William's chief concerns to shield Plato from a literal understanding of the *communes nuptiae*; see nn. 30, 37 above and 81 below.

This austere reading of the *Timaeus* seems to have found no followers in the Middle Ages.

With the exception of the few authors thus far mentioned, all canonists took their information on the sharing of wives in Plato's State from another text in the Decretum. This was the Pseudo-Isidorian Letter Five of Pope Clement I, to St James and the brethren in Jerusalem, on having all things in common. Gratian presented this text as one of his authorities (c.2) in discussing the first question of *Causa* 12: whether clerics may have any possessions of their own.[43] 'Clement' backed his counsel on *communis vita* and *communis usus omnium* with various maxims, scriptural proofs, and the affirmation that 'one of the wisest of the Greeks said that friends must have all in common: but "all" includes without doubt the wives' ('in omnibus autem sunt sine dubio coniuges').[44]

It was, on the whole, a troublesome text. The glossators found it difficult, for instance, to explain a passage which preceded this one and declared that iniquity was at the root of all private ownership.[45] It was even harder to admit that St Clement should have followed a pagan philosopher and recommended the sharing of wives. They knew that the *sapientissimus* was Plato, reporting in the *Timaeus* on his imaginary republic;[46] a gloss by Alanus even cited the exact paragraph of the Latin text.[47] (The glossators could not know, of course, that the source behind the pseudo-Clementine reference was the *Republic* itself: for only there all things are said to be 'common to friends', κοινὰ τὰ φίλων, while in the *Timaeus* it reads 'common to all', κοινὰ τὰ...πᾶσιν.[48]) What is more important, however, is that several canonists refused to

---

43 Clemens, *ep.* 5 in *Decretales Pseudo-Isidorianae et capitula Angilrammi*, ed. P. Hinschius (Leipzig, 1863), pp. 65–6; Gratian, C.12 q.1 c.2.

44 *Ibid.* 'Denique Grecorum quidam sapientissimus, hec ita esse sciens, communia debere ait esse amicorum omnia: in omnibus autem' etc.

45 Cf. Weigand, *Naturrechtslehre* (n. 3 above), pp. 310–60; Couvreur, *Les pauvres*, pp. 121–54.

46 Rufinus, *Summa* C.12 q.1 c.2 v. *Grecorum quidam*: 'scilicet Plato in Timeo'; ed. H. Singer (Paderborn, 1902), p. 321. Stephanus Tornacensis, *Summa*, *ad loc.* v. *coniuges*: '...ex uerbis Platonis...qui in re publica illa quam fingebat uxores et liberos communes esse dixit' etc. Cf. Johannes Faventinus and Huguccio *ad loc.*; also the *Summae Magister Gratianus in hoc opere*, *Omnis qui iuste*, *De iure canonico tractaturus*, and *Tractaturus magister*.

47 Alanus, *Glossa Ius naturale* C.12 q.1 c.2 v. *coniuges*: 'supra di. viii. § Differt. In Platone c. de feminis; set intelligas' etc. See *Timaeus* 18C, tr. Calcidius: 'De feminis quoque opinor habitam mentionem...de existimandis communibus nuptiis' etc.; ed. Waszink, p. 9.

48 *Republ.* 423E–424 on marriages and the procreation of children, κατὰ τὴν παροιμίαν πάντα ὅ τι μάλιστα κοινὰ τὰ φίλων ποιεῖσθαι, 'the proverbial goods of friends that are common' (P. Shorey's translation, Loeb Classical Library; and see his discussion of the proverb and Plato's use of it, I, p. 330 note *b*); 449C on wives and children, ὅτι κοινὰ τὰ φίλων ἔσται. The wording of *Tim.* 18C is given in the text at n. 9 above.

accept it. 'I do not believe', Stephen of Tournai said, 'that Clement placed this sentence of Plato's into the letter' ('non credo hoc apposuisse Clementem'), and others adopted or at least reported these doubts.[49] One gloss ascribes the passage to forgers, 'a falsatoribus dictum est',[50] while a French anonymous *Summa* observes that the words are Clement's but the meaning is Plato's.[51]

None of these writers was aware that a number of manuscripts of the (Pseudo-Isidorian) Decretals, especially of Hinschius's class A–2, indeed omitted the offensive words 'in omnibus autem' etc.[52] They were also omitted by one of the earliest major users of the Decretals in the A–2 form, the *Collectio Anselmo dedicata* of the late ninth century.[53] Two hundred years later, the canonical collection of Anselm of Lucca, in its recension B, presented this expurgated version of the letter as the first chapter of a cluster of texts on the *vita communis* at the beginning of Book VII (it is absent from the other recensions).[54] Hence Anselm cannot be the model of Gratian's text: the chapter is derived from another tradition, which has its fountainhead in the so-called *Collectio Tripartita* of Ivo of Chartres and has not been noted before.[55] This version cuts out some parts and reverses the order of others in the pseudo-Clemen-

---

[49] Stephanus, *Summa* C.12 q.1 c.2 v. *coniuges* (preceding the reference to the *uerba Platonis*, n. 46 above); 'non credo...' also in Johannes Faventinus, *Summa ad loc.*; the *Summae Omnis qui iuste* and *De iure can. tract.* merely have 'hoc non dicunt Clementem apposuisse' etc.

[50] Cues MS 223, gloss *ad loc.* v. *coniuges*.

[51] *Summa Tractaturus ad loc.* v. *in omnibus autem*: 'hec sunt uerba Clementis, tamen ex sensu uerborum Pla. sumpta' etc.

[52] See Hinschius, *Decretales Pseudo-Isid.* p. 65 n. 6; H. Fuhrmann, *Einfluss und Verbreitung der pseudoisidorischen Fälschungen*, MGH Schriften, XXIV (3 vols. Stuttgart, 1972–4), I, 55 n. 134 (at p. 56).

[53] *Coll. Ans. dedic.*, VI.1: Vercelli, Cathedral Chapter MS XV, fo. 141rb. For the collector's general dependence on the A–2 class of Pseudo-Isidore see P. Fournier–G. Le Bras, *Histoire des collections canoniques en Occident* (2 vols. Paris, 1931–2), I, 237; Fuhrmann, *Einfluss und Verbreitung*, II (1973), 429–30; for the distribution of parts of Clem. *ep.* 5 in the collection, see the tabulation in Fuhrmann, III (1974), 828.

[54] Ans. Lucensis, *Collectio* (rec. B) VII.1: MSS Vat. lat. 6381, fo. 161r; Vat. lat. 1364, fo. 161r. Already Antonio Agustín [Augustinus], *De emendatione Gratiani dialogorum libri duo* 1.15 (in the posthumous edition, Tarragona, 1587, p. 151; *Opera omnia*, III (Lucca, 1767), 80) and the *Correctores Romani* commented upon the difference from Gratian's text; moreover Agustín recorded in the margin of his MS of Anselm (today Vat. lat. 6381) the absence of the chapter in another MS he had collated (today Venice, Marc. lat. IV.55; recension A). The chapter is also in recension C, VII. i: MS Vat. lat. 4983, fo. 331r. I have discussed some of Agustín's work on these three codices in 'Some Roman manuscripts of canonical collections', *Bulletin of medieval canon law*, N.S. 1 (1971), 16–20. For Anselm see further Fuhrmann, *Einfluss und Verbreitung*, II, 511–20; on Ans. B VII.1 also *ibid.* I, 56n.

[55] *Coll. Tripart.* I.1.23–4; also the chronological collection of decretal letters in MS Vat. lat. 3829 (on which see Fournier–Le Bras, *Histoire*, II, 210–18), fos. 14v–15r (11v–12r, old foliation). This should not have been overlooked since another fragment from the same pseudo-Clementine letter in Gratian Dist. 37 c.14 is correctly traced to *Tripart.* I.1.25 in Friedberg's edition, n. 137 *ad loc.* and Fuhrmann, III, 829 n. 303.

tine letter and labels it as *epistola quarta*.[56] But Gratian, as Ivo before him, had no qualms about leaving the reference to Plato intact.

It is almost touching to see how similar the worries of sixteenth-century scholars about this passage were to those of the early glossators on Gratian. Until it was recognised and admitted that the decretals of Clement were all spurious, the only way to save the text of *ep.* 5 was to declare the passage on sharing the women to be interpolated. In 1551, Petrus Crabbe's collection of the *Concilia omnia* still left the letter unchanged[57] as it had been printed by Merlin, but from Surius on (Cologne 1567) all the great conciliar collections excised the words 'in omnibus autem...coniuges'.[58] The *Correctores Romani* of Gratian first addressed themselves to the problem in the meeting of 17 October 1570, as we learn from their (much too little-known) manuscript volumes of minutes and drafts in the Vatican Library.[59] The line the *doctores* took then was essentially the same as twelve years later when the edition went to press: the minutes record no discussion of the authenticity of the letter itself, but the incriminated passage, they say, should be branded as absent from the original and as added by some Nicolaite heretic. By right the words ought to be cancelled, if it were not for the editorial principle that all parts of the text commented upon in the *Glossa ordinaria* must be maintained.[60] Instead, there would have to be a note warning the reader that the words are *pessime addita*, as well as a theological refutation; also, the collection of Anselm of

---

[56] Details in appendix II below.

[57] *Conciliorum omnium tam generalium quam particularium* Tomus I (Cologne, 1551), p. 52b; see also his first edition, *Concilia omnia...*, I (Cologne, 1538), fo. xxvi r. In both printings, Crabbe's marginal note to *Grecorum...sapientissimus* reads: 'Pythagoras philosophus'. Cf. Diogenes Laertius, X.11, καθάπερ τὸν Πυθαγόραν κοινὰ τὰ φίλων λέγοντα.

[58] Cf. Ph. Labbe and G. Cossart, *Sacrosancta concilia* I (Paris, 1672), 115 [= J. D. Mansi, *Sacrorum conciliorum nova et amplissima collectio*, I (Florence, 1759), 143], marginal note v. *sapientissimus*: 'Platonem intelligit'; *omnia*: 'In MS. atque editis Merlini et Crabbi pauca interseruntur, de quibus in notis. Ea Surius et post eum alii resecuerunt' etc. (The promised *notae* were not printed.) Cf. also J. Hardouin, *Acta conciliorum* I (Paris, 1715), 62 not. marg.

[59] MSS Vat. lat 4889–94, 4913; cf. S. Kuttner, 'Brief notes', *Traditio*, XXIV (1968), 505; 'Some Roman manuscripts', pp. 13 n. 25, 14, 17 n.46, 21; A. Theiner, *Disquisitiones criticae* (Rome, 1836), pp. xi, xiii n. 1 (wrong reference); and for Vat. lat. 4913, Ae. L. Richter, *De emendatoribus Gratiani dissertatio historico-critica* (Leipzig, 1835), pp. 1, 39–45; K. Schellhass, 'Wissenschaftliche Forschungen unter Gregor XIII. für die Neuausgabe des Gratianischen Dekrets', in *Papsttum und Kaisertum: Forschungen...Paul Kehr zum 65. Geburtstag dargebracht*, ed. A. Brackmann (Munich, 1926), 674–90.

[60] See the *Leges constitutae...in correctione Decreti*, no. v, published by Theiner, *Disquis.* Appendix I, pp. 4–5; cf. Friedberg's *prolegomena* to his edition, p. lxxvii; also the preface of the *Correctores*, *ibid.* p. lxxxv. H. von Schubert, *Der Kommunismus der Wiedertäufer in Münster und seine Quellen*, Sitzungsberichte der Heidelberger Akademie, philos.-hist. Klasse 1919, No. 11, p. 56, seems to believe that the *Correctores* eliminated the offensive passage.

Lucca was to be collated.[61] In the end this resulted in a long *notatio* of the printed text in which the *Correctores*, before quoting some patristic material to refute the offensive passage, reported that it was absent from Surius's edition of the Councils, from two old manuscripts (of the papal letters) and from Anselm's collection.[62]

Even a scholar of the stature of Antonio Agustín would not commit himself further than this, although briefly and cautiously ('ni fallor') he referred to the true source of the words which are read in Gratian but not in Anselm's collection (of which Agustín owned an important manuscript) nor 'in melioribus Clementis libris'.[63] This is quite in keeping with his well-known reluctance to arrive at a final conclusion on the Pseudo-Isidorian problem.[64]

Then came St Robert Bellarmine. The Jesuit controversialist has never been properly credited with his share in unmasking Isidorus Mercator, because his treatise entitled *Epistolas Summorum Pontificum quae in primo tomo Conciliorum habentur a sancto Clemente usque ad Siricium supposititias esse* remained unpublished until 1913.[65] Bellarmine probably wrote it about 1589 as an expert opinion for Cardinal Carafa's committee in charge of editing the decretal letters of the popes.[66] As a piece of historical erudition and critical sensitivity it leaves Dumoulin's invectives[67] and the embittered diatribes of the Magdeburg

---

[61] Text in appendix III below.

[62] *Notatio correctorum*, see ed. Friedb. col. 675 *ad loc.* and appendix III below for Michael Thomasius's draft. The *duo codices manuscripti* cited in the *notatio* – one *Vaticanus* and one *bibliothecae S. Marci Florentiae* – are probably Vat. lat. 3788 and Florence, Bibl. Naz. MS Conv. soppr. J.III.18 (Nos. 71 and 18 in S. Williams, *Codices Pseudo-Isidoriani*, Monumenta iuris canonici, Subsidia, III (New York, 1971)). Couvreur, *Les pauvres* (n. 28 above), p. 129 n. 400 misunderstands this note in assuming that there are variations in the Gratian MSS at this point.

[63] *De emendatione Gratiani*, I.15: 'In Anselmi veteri libro (*marg.* Ans. lib. 7 c.1) haec de coniugibus non sunt. Omittuntur etiam in melioribus Clementis libris, sed sumuntur, ni fallor, ex Recognitionibus Clementis'. (See also n. 54 above.)

[64] See his *Hadriani papae capitula cum notis*, to which the Dialogue here refers but which was published only posthumously at Cologne in 1618 by S. Binius, *Concilia generalia et provincialia*, III.I.I pp. 436–50 (whence Ant. Aug. *Opera omnia*, III, 349–69), *passim* on Angilramnus, cc. 7, 8, 22, 23, etc.; and especially at c.63 on the Pseudo-Clementines, ed. Binius, p. 449a; *Opp.* III, 367. Cf. F. Maassen, *Geschichte der Quellen und der Literatur des canonischen Rechts im Abendlande* (Graz, 1870), pp. xxxi–xxxiii.

[65] *Auctarium Bellarminianum: Supplément aux oeuvres du Cardinal Bellarmin*, ed. X.-M. Le Bachelet (Paris, 1913), no. 50, pp. 490–3. Not mentioned in Fuhrmann, *Einfluss und Verbreitung*, I, 10 (on Bellarmine), but see I. A. Zeiger, *Historia iuris canonici* (2 vols. Rome, 1939), I, 49 and n. 48, quoting C. Silva Tarouca's comments in the *Liber Annualis* of the Gregorian University for 1931 [not seen]. [66] Le Bachelet, *Auctarium Bellarminianum*, p. 490 n. 2.

[67] *Decretum Divi Gratiani…resectis verò nothis, absurdis, difficilibus ijsdemque inutilibus…pseudographijs…* (Lyons, 1554). The anonymous editor – 'impius Carolus Molinaeus' to the Roman canonists, see Th. Manrique's *censura* of 1572 in Theiner, *Disquis.* p. xv, n. 3 – alludes to his name in the *praefatio* and signs the marginal notes, 'C.M.' These were republished by F. Pinsson in

Centuriatores[68] far behind, and perhaps even surpasses the lawyer–humanist Antoine Le Conte's critique, or at least what is preserved of it.[69] But in the congregations of the Curia, it was Bellarmine's confrère Francisco Torres who won the day: 'propter aliquos canonistas' the false decretals were included in Carafa's 1591 edition, though set off from those of Siricius and later popes; '...neque Turrianus magnam laudem assecutus est ex defensione harum epistolarum', as Bellarmine laconically noted years later.[70] Had his views been accepted at the time – if we may indulge in some day-dreaming – there might have been no need for David Blondel's scathing classic, *Pseudo-Isidorus et Turrianus vapulantes* in 1628.

The fifth letter of St Clement was one of Bellarmine's main pieces of evidence. He showed that it was a forgery based to a considerable extent on the pseudo-Clementine *Recognitiones*,[71] the early Christian romance which survived in Rufinus of Aquileia's translation, and where *inter al.* the pagan philosopher Faustinus espouses the doctrine of 'Grecorum quidam sapientissimus' on the common possession among friends of all goods and women and is properly refuted by St Clement.[72] It goes beyond the limits of this paper to speculate why Bellarmine's

Caroli Molinaei *Opera omnia* (Paris, 1681), IV, 1–67. Cf. Richter, *De emendatoribus*, pp. 24–8. The historical value of Dumoulin's notes has been overrated. His remark on the letter of Anacletus at Dist. 22 c.2, 'ut sit manifestum hoc capitulum et alia pleraque multis postea seculis a monachis vel Papis conficta esse' (p. 66a; *Opp.* IV, 5b with Pinsson's note), has often been quoted; it is about his only contribution to the Pseudo-Isidorian question.

68 *Ecclesiastica historia...congesta per aliquos studiosos...in urbe Magdeburgica* (Basle, 1560ff.), centuria II, 142–53; III, 177–85; IV, 575–82. Cf. Fuhrmann, *Einfluss und Verbreitung* I, 5–7, with bibliography in n. 2.

69 *Decretorum canonicorum collectanea...* (Antwerp, Plantin 1570 and, with new title page, Paris, Du Puys 1570). The original edition, for which Du Puys had a *Priuilege du Roy* dated 23 October 1556, never appeared; as Le Conte himself tells in his *Lectiones subsecivae iuris civilis*, I.10 (Antonii Contii *Opera omnia* (Naples 1725), p. 15a), it was carried off to Antwerp, heavily censored, and printed 'tandem post longum exilium amputatis dedicatoriis epistolis et proprio titulo,...mancum et lacerum'. But a few comments on false decretals escaped the Spanish censor, thus to Dist. 16 c.13, C.30 q.5 c.18 (ed. 1570, pp. 47, 988); and a fragment of the original dedicatory epistle to the Chancellor Michel L'Hôpital, with its general critique of the papal letters prior to Siricius, was published by Pinsson in Dumoulin's *Opera omnia*, IV, pp. viij–x. See J. Doujat, *Praenotationum canonicarum libri quinque*, IV.13 (5th edn Venice, 1748) p. 397; Richter, *De emendatoribus*, pp. 28–36. Hence H. E. Troje, *Graeca leguntur*, Forschungen zur neueren Privatrechtsgeschichte, XVIII (Cologne–Vienna, 1971), p. 79 n.16, is mistaken in believing that the 1566 edition exists.

70 *Auctarium Bellarminianum*, no. 111, 'Observatio ad secundam partem Antimornaei...', pp. 679–80.

71 *Auctarium*, no. 50, sec. 4.2 (p. 491b). Cf. Antonio Agustín, *De emendatione Grat.*, 1.15 (quoted n. 63 above), whose hesitant statement Bellarmine may or may not have seen.

72 Bellarmine, *Auctarium*, '...ad uerbum desumptus est ex libro 10 Recognitionum, ubi ista dicuntur a Faustiniano haeretico [al. ethnico] et a Clemente refelluntur'. See *Recogn.* x.5 and 7: Migne, *PG.* I, 1422C-D and 1423B-C; ed. B. Rehm and F. Paschke, *Die Pseudoklementinen*, II, in Die griechischen christlichen Schriftsteller, LI (Berlin, 1965), 327.12–19 and 328.8–23.

censura had to remain hidden; and also why in the fourth volume of his *Controversiae*, several years later, he resumed it only in a slightly softened manner which left the alternative of a genuine but interpolated epistle,[73] thus returning to the rather cautious approach he had taken before he came to write the treatise of 1589.[74] It remains to be investigated whether all this is connected with the troubles Bellarmine had during the pontificate of Sixtus V on account of his denial of a direct power of the pope *in temporalibus* – a doctrine for which he narrowly escaped being put on the Index, and which was to delay the process of his canonisation for centuries.[75] But it should also be recorded that his observations on this pseudo-Clementine *ep.* 5, even in the less outspoken formulation of the *Controversiae*, provided one of the very rare instances in which Blondel, the relentless critic of popish (*pontificii*) scholars, would exclaim, 'Quandoquidem Bellarmini iudicio per omnia subscribimus', before he proceeded to refute Torres.[76]

From this long digression let us retrace our steps to the medieval exegesis of the pseudo-Clementine letter (in C.12 q.1 c.2) by the glossators of Gratian. Since they could not throw out its *auctoritas*, they endeavoured to render it less embarrassing by giving the crucial passage a harmless interpretation. Thus we find 'in omnibus autem sunt sine dubio et coniuges' explained as if the words were an exercise in grammar: *in omnibus*, that is, in the word 'all', *sunt coniuges*, that is, there must be understood or included [the word] 'wives'.[77] The passage thus serves as an occasion for legal maxims such as 'general words must

---

73 Bellarmine, *Disputationum de controversiis christianae fidei*, Tomus IV (Venice, 1596), controv. 3, *De bonis operibus in particulari*, III.11: '...constat enim eam epistolam aut non esse Clementis aut ab aliquo valde corruptam ac depravatam' (p. 597a in ed. Venice, 1721, here used), as against the treatise of 1589, sec. 3: 'Epistolae istae videntur omnino compositae ab uno atque eodem auctore' (*Auctarium*, p. 491a).

74 *Disputationum*...Tomus I (Ingolstadt, 1586), controv. 3 *De summo pontifice*, II.14: 'at quamvis aliquos errores in eas [*sc.* epistolas] irrepsisse non negaverim, nec indubitatas esse affirmare audeam; certe tamen antiquissimas esse nihil dubito' etc. (p. 316a in the Venice, 1721 edition). Authors discussing Bellarmine on Pseudo-Isidore usually refer only to this passage.

75 The Index affair is summarised in P. Dudon's article 'Bellarmin', *Dictionnaire d'histoire et de géographie ecclésiastiques* VII (Paris, 1934), 798–824, at col. 806–7. E. A. Ryan, *The historical scholarship of St. Bellarmine*, Recueil de travaux...d'Histoire et de Philologie, 3e sér., XXXV (Univ. de Louvain, 1936), 151, sees the main reason for Bellarmine's caution in the *Controversiae* as stemming from the purpose of the work: he did not want to furnish weapons to the Protestants, since any concession made in this matter would be exaggerated.

76 David Blondellus (Blondel), *Pseudo-Isidorus et Turrianus vapulantes* (Geneva, 1628), p. 99.

77 Thus in the gloss composition *Ordinaturus magister* (e.g., MSS Cues 223, Vat. Ross. 595), incorporated in Huguccio's *Summa* C.12 q.1 c.2 v. *in omnibus*: 'idest in eo uocabulo, scil. "omnia", *sunt coniuges*: idest intelliguntur et comprehenduntur coniuges,' etc. See also *Glossa Animal est substantia, Glossa Palatina*.

be taken with a general meaning', or 'words generally uttered include all particulars'.[78]

More significant than these commonplaces were the efforts to purify Plato's saying. From Rufinus onwards, all asserted that wives were to be held in common not as regards the flesh ('quo ad carnis usum', 'coniunctionem', 'amplexandi dilectionem'), but by common respect, affection, deference, courtesy ('honesta servicia', 'obsequium', etc.), and dutiful love.[79] This text, we are told, gives no licence to do anything sordid; and one temperamental glossator calls those stupid (*stulti*) who take the passage about the wives literally (it was the same glossator who proposed the alternative that it had been put in by forgers).[80]

All this is quite in line with the twelfth-century glosses on the *Timaeus*. William of Conches, as mentioned before, defended Socrates and Plato against the *quidam indocti* who accused them of *turpitudo*, unaware perhaps that thereby he placed Tertullian and Lactantius and other early Fathers among the unlearned. By the words 'de existimandis communibus nuptiis et communi prole', William affirms, Plato had not commanded promiscuity but common affection: for he had not said that marriages and children 'are' common (*essent communes*) but 'should be considered' (*reputarentur*) common. This clears the way for an interpretation where all is reduced to the principle of showing the same love for strangers as for one's own[81] – and the canonists who

---

[78] Huguccio continues *loc. cit.*: 'et est arg. quod uerbum generale est generaliter intelligendum' etc. *Gl. Ordinaturus* in Vat. Ross. 595: 'et est arg. quod in uerbo generaliter prolato comprehenduntur particularia' etc. Thus also *Gl. Palat.*; the gloss of Alanus follows Huguccio's phrasing.

[79] Rufinus, *Summa* C.12 q.1 c.2 v. *coniuges*: 'non quo ad carnis usum sed quo ad dilectionis officium', ed. Singer, p. 321. Cf. Stephanus Tornacensis, Johannes Faventinus, the *Summae Omnis qui iuste* and *De iure can. tractaturus*: '…set quantum ad dilectionem et obsequium'; *Summa Tractaturus*: 'quantum ad honesta seruicia'. Similar formulations in the *Summa Parisiensis*, the glosses of the Biberach MS and Leipzig, Univ. MS Haenel 18; in Huguccio, Alanus, Bernard of Compostella, the *Glossa Animal est substantia*, and the *Gl. ordinaria*. Cf. also Couvreur, *Les pauvres* (n. 28 above), p. 129 n. 400.

[80] *Glossa Ecce uicit leo*, v. *coniuges*: '…quo ad effectum [*sic*] caritatis et seruitium licitum, non autem quo ad turpe aliquid committendum'. Cues MS 223, gl. v. *coniuges*: 'A falsatoribus dictum est, uel dictum est non quantum ad carnis usum ut stulti putant, set quantum ad dilectionem' (cf. at n. 50 above).

[81] William of Conches, *Glossae super Timaeum* 18C: 'Hic quidam indocti Socratem et Platonem turpitudinis arguunt, credentes eos precepisse omnes mulieres esse communes sic quod omnes …ignorante utroque cui commisceretur;…Nos uero dicimus Platonem non imperasse turpitudinem sed affectum. Non enim dicit quod "essent" communes sed "reputarentur". Ac si diceret: Unusquisque uxorem et filios alterius in bono diligat ac si sui essent' (ed. Jeauneau, p. 78). Cf. nn. 30, 37 above. Similarly the glosses of Uppsala MS C.620, ed. T. Schmid, 'Ein Timaioskommentar in Sigtuna', *Classica et Mediaevalia*, x (1949), 220–66, at p. 230: '*De extimandis*: Hic quidam imponit Platoni quod uoluisset communes esse mulieres

adopted this formula for the text of 'Clement' in Gratian thus came around full circle to what had been their understanding of Gratian's dictum on Plato and the *nescire proprios affectus*.[82]

Now this might seem hardly worth saying if it were not for the fact that the first generations of Bolognese glossators remained as unaware as Gratian himself of the true context from which his observation on the Platonic City was derived. To be sure, the letter of Clement was placed by some early gloss compositions as a cross-reference in the margin of the opening dictum of Dist. 8: 'infra xii.q.i. Dilectissimis', so they write,[83] but this indicated no more than a parallel, a verbal concordance:

Gratian	C.12 q.1 c.2
iure nature sunt omnia	communis enim usus omnium
communia omnibus...	...omnibus hominibus esse debet;...
	communia debere ait esse amicorum
	omnium...
unde apud Platonem...	Grecorum quidam sapientissimus...

Slow as the development may seem to us from hindsight, it took an Huguccio to make the connection between the two texts and to discover that the wives (from Plato in C.12 q.1) must be included in the *omnia* (from Plato in Dist. 8 pr.), of course with the proper understanding that this means equal affection for strangers as for one's own, etc.:[84]

Huguccio Dist. 8 pr.	Stephanus Dist. 8 pr.
nescit proprios affectus: idest	*nescit proprios affectus:*
tantum se ipsum diligere.	
Confinxit enim Plato quandam suam	Sic enim dixerat Plato esse in illa
rem publicam, quam fingendo sic	maxima ciuitate cuius rem publicam
disposuit ut omnia omnibus essent	fingebat omnia communia
communia, *etiam coniuges quo ad*	
dilectionem et obsequium,	

omnium, sed falso;...uoluit intelligi quod unusquisque pari dilectione suam et alterius mulierem et prolem diligeret: unde dixit "extimande", non "esse" communes.' On the problem of authorship for the Uppsala glosses see Jeauneau, p. 14.

[82] Stephanus Tornac. *Summa* C.12 q.1 c.2: 'ex uerbis Platonis...uxores et liberos communes esse dixit, idest affectum dilectionis communiter exhibendum ait suis et extraneis; non communes dixit uxores quantum ad carnis usum' etc. See also Johannes Faventinus and the *Summae Omnis qui iuste* and *De iure can. tractaturus* at C.12 q.1 c.2. Compare Stephanus (n. 12 above), Johannes and *De iure can. tractaturus* at Dist. 8 pr. Ph. Delhaye, 'Morale et droit canon dans la Summe d'Étienne de Tournai', *Studia Gratiana*, I (1953), 447–8, considers this interpretation 'assez proche de celle d'Abélard', but see nn. 41 and 42 above.

[83] Thus MSS Leipzig Haen. 18, fo. 3va; Vat. Ross. 595, fo. 16ra; Cues 223, fo. 3ra; also in the *Summa Tractaturus.*

[84] In the text of Huguccio that follows (Admont MS 7, fo. 9vb), from 'Confinxit enim' on, I have set off his expansion of the traditional gloss, which goes back to Stephen of Tournai (MS Vat. Borgh. 287, fo. 13va).

et omnibus equaliter dilectionis affectus exiberetur, scilicet tam suis quam extraneis, *ut xii. q.i. Dilectissimis.*

et neminem suorum affectus aliis preponere debere, idest omnes ab inuicem equaliter diligendos esse.

From here on we can follow the few brief flashes of true insight. There was Alanus who combined, at C.12 q.1 c.2, his precise indication of the passage in the *Timaeus* with a telling cross-reference to Gratian's dictum at Dist. 8. There were those unnamed writers whose correct understanding of the Calcidian term *nescire affectus* was rejected by Laurentius.[85] But in the *Glossa ordinaria*, Johannes Teutonicus left all this by the wayside.[86] The few bits salvaged in Guido de Baysio's *Rosarium* from the pre-*ordinaria* glosses[87] were not enough to keep the interest in Gratian's use of Plato alive during the later Middle Ages. Guido Terreni, who read the Decretum very much with the eyes of a fourteenth-century schoolman, would comment upon the two passages[88] only to point out that Aristotle in the *Politics* had criticised the communism of Plato's State.

APPENDIX I

Texts from manuscripts: Summae and glosses on Gratian

Stephanus Tornacensis, *Summa decretorum* (Bolognese school; Orléans, after 1160)

(D.8 pr.) *nescit proprios affectus:* Sic enim dixerat...diligendos esse.
  Vatican Library, MS Borgh. 287, fo. 13va, printed above, note 12, to replace Schulte's faulty edition (Giessen, 1891), p. 17.

(C.12 q.1 c.2) *quidam Grecorum:* Plato in Thimeo.[1] *sunt et coniuges:* Non credo hoc apposuisse Clementem, cum tamen ex uerbis Platonis hoc haberi possit, qui in re publica illa quam fingebat uxores et liberos communes esse dixit, idest[2] affectum dilectionis communiter exhibendum ait[3] suis et extraneis. Non communes dixit

---

[85] See nn. 47 (Alanus) and 36 (Laurentius) above.

[86] *Glossa ord.* Dist. 8 pr. After the conventional remark on 'tantum diligit alium ut se', Johannes merely writes: 'Finxit enim Plato quandam rem publicam: in qua omnia enim sunt communia' (the Latin is rather rough).

[87] Guido de Baysio, *Rosarium* at Dist. 8 pr. first quotes Laurentius's gloss 'non ita intelligas' etc. ('dicit lau. sic...') and then Huguccio's 'idest tantum seipsum diligere' ('secundum hu.').

[88] I am grateful to Dr Kenneth Pennington for having called my attention to the pertinent passages in Guido Terreni's *Commentarium super Decretum* and for the copies he took from MS Vat. lat. 1453; see appendix I below. For this commentary see P. Fournier, 'Gui Terré (Guido Terreni), théologien', *Histoire littéraire de la France*, XXXVI (1927), 432–73, at pp. 464–8, 'Expositorium Decreti' (which appears as title in the Paris MS, B.N. lat. 3914). I have not consulted B. Xiberta, *Guiu Terrena, carmelita de Perpinyà* (Barcelona, 1932) nor I. Melsen, *Guido Terreni (1260?–1342) iurista* (Rome, 1939).

uxores quantum ad carnis usum set quantum ad dilectionem et obsequium.

MS Borgh. fo. 62vb, ed. Schulte, pp. 213–14.

[1] *gl. om. Sch.*   [2] ubi *Sch.*   [3] a *Borgh.*

Johannes Faventinus, *Summa decretorum* (Bologna, after 1171)

(D.8 pr.) *nescit proprios affectus:* Sic enim dixit[1] Plato…diligendos esse.
Reims MS 684, fo. 4vb (repeats Stephen's text).

[1] dixerat *Steph.*

(C.12 q.1 c.2) *quidam Grecorum:* Plato[1] scil. in Timeo.   *sunt et coniuges:* Non credo hoc…et obsequium.
MS Rem. fo. 79ra (repeats Stephen's text).

[1] prelato *Rem.*

Summa Magister Gratianus in hoc opere (Parisiensis) (French School, c. 1170)
(D.8 pr.) *Differt:* Differentiam ostendit inter effectus iuris naturalis et constitutionis siue consuetudinarii, set laborat in positione[1] exemplorum, et salua pace sua melius potuisset de[2] his tacere, quia que erant apostolorum inter se erant communia, set non omnibus aliis, et in illa ciuitate quam fingit Plato multi propria habebant, set se debebant equaliter diligere. Ideo dici potest quod non sunt hec exempla set quoquo modo uestigia exemplorum, scilicet ex quibus ⟨uidetur quod⟩ quoquo modo[3] omnia sint communia iure nature. Verum quicquid dicat Gratianus enititur probare auctoritate Augustini dicentis: *Quo iure.*[4]
Bamberg MS Can. 36, fo. 2vb; ed. T. McLaughlin (Toronto, 1952), p. 7.

[1] i poñe *Bb,* imponere *McL*   [2] ab *Bb McL*   [3] uidetur quod *scripsi:* ex quibus quoquo modo *Bb,* ex quibus, quo, quomodo *McL*   [4] D.8 c.1

(C.12 q.1 c.2) *sapientissimus:* forte Plato.   *et coniuges:* quia communes debent esse non usu carnis set quantum ad exhibitionem caritatis.
Ed. McLaughlin, p. 156 (with MS readings).

Summa Antiquitate et tempore (French school, after 1170)
(D.8 pr.) *Differt autem ius nature:* Assignauit supra differentiam iuris naturalis ad cetera iura, scil. ius consuetudinarium, quod est ius non scriptum, et ius constitutionis, quod est ius scriptum, dicens ipsum inter omnia iura precellere et tempore et dignitate. Consequenter eiusdem ad alia iura assignat differentiam secundum effectum, dicens hunc esse effectum iuris naturalis quod omnia sint omnibus communia. Set secundum ius consuetudinis uel constitutionis aliqua sunt propria, hoc meum, illud alterius. Set quod iste non sit effectus iuris naturalis ex his innotescat: ius nature inferius appellat ius diuinum et illud dicit contineri in scriptis diuinis. Quod si scripta diuina appellat decalogum preceptorum, patet quoniam secundum illud aliqua sunt propria: ibi enim continetur, 'non concupisces rem proximi tui';[1] ergo aliqua est res proximi. Item ibi fit mentio furti, furtum autem non fit nisi ubi fit contrectatio[2] rei aliene inuito domino;[3] quod si omnia essent omnibus communia, nulla essent aliquibus aliena. Quod si diuinum ius appellat quod continetur in ueteri testamento, scil. in libris Moisi, secundum illud etiam aliqua sunt propria, quia ibi promissa est Iudeis terra

promissionis ut hereditario iure eam possiderent, et postea data est eis et possederunt eam.[4] Et item ibidem dicitur quod si attenuatus fuerit frater tuus et emeris eum, seruiet tibi vi. annis et vii°. liber erit etc.[5] Sin autem ius diuinum uocatur quod continetur in euangelio, secundum hoc etiam aliqua sunt propria, unde in euangelio: 'Reddite Cesari que sunt Cesaris et que Dei Deo'.[6] Item non negauit Cesari dandum tributum, set filium regis debere dare negauit.[7] Ex his palam est quod quicquid hic appelletur ius diuinum, secundum illud aliqua sunt propria. Nam quod dicit, 'iure diuino Domini[8] est terra et plenitudo eius',[9] uerum quidem est set minus pertinet ad rem dictam, quia omnia sunt Domini per creationem et hoc non prohibet aliqua esse propria. Ad hoc tandem post omnem disquisitionem dicendum est diuinum ius hic appellari primam illam equitatem que a prima creatione naturaliter mentibus hominum indita fuit, secundum quam unusquisque ita rem ad usum suum habere deberet ut et alius[10] ad suum usum eandem haberet dum ei esset necessaria.

Sic transiri posset locus iste nisi rem turbaret exemplis suppositis. Duo enim subiungit exempla quibus conatur ostendere nulla esse propria, quorum unum sumptum est de actibus apostolorum, hoc scil. 'multitudinis credentium erat cor unum et anima una',[11] alterum a Platone, scil. de ciuibus platonice ciuitatis, idest illius ciuitatis quam Plato iustissime ordinatam fuisse testatur. Set in utroque exemplo peccauit: in priori quia etsi singulorum quorum erat cor unum et anima una non essent aliqua propria, tamen que eorum erant communia non erant 'omnium' communia, quia infidelium non. Quod in secundo exemplo peccauerit palam est intelligentibus Platonem, quia tantum milites illius ciuitatis debebant expensam habere de communi, ne propriis intenti minus ad communem utilitatem milicie deseruirent. Nullatenus tamen 'omnium' erant communia que possidebant ibi ciues, quia saltem non inimicorum. Ad hoc dicendum non esse mirum si quandoque bonus dormitat Homerus.[12] Preterea M. Gra. competentia exempla habere non potuit, et ideo indulgendum est ei si ista posuit, quia modo non est iste effectus iuris naturalis nec fuit forte ex quo Adam filios habere cepit, quia probabile est quod statim ceperint esse propria. Verumtamen ostendit hic M. G. qualis deberet esse effectus iuris naturalis. Sicut enim illis omnia erant communia quorum erat cor unum et anima una, et sicut[13] milites platonici de communi uiuebant, ita iure naturali omnibus omnia deberent esse communia. Si ergo M. G. non ponit exemplum usquequaque sufficiens, est tamen quod dicit in parte proficiens: ista enim exempla non sufficiunt set proficiunt.

in qua quisque proprios nescit affectus: quia 'quisque' minores se dilexit ut filios, maiores ut parentes,[14] et sic non habuit 'proprios' uel speciales[15] circa unum 'affectus'. Et forte si aliqui essent qui non maiorem ad unum quam ad alium affectum haberent et illi omnibus equaliter cuperent ⟨dare⟩,[16] et talium bona omnibus essent communia. Nota quod quidam[17] dicunt Platonem loqui ibi de nuptiis catarorum et eum sensisse illas esse celebrandas. Set nos eum excusare solemus in legendo librum ipsius.

Göttingen MS 159, fo. 11ra/b.

---

[1] *Gen.* 20:17　　[2] contrectio *Gt*　　[3] cf. *Inst.* iv.1.6　　[4] cf. *Exod.* 6:8; *Lev.* 20:24, 25:46; *Deut.* 1:21 etc.　　[5] cf. *Lev.* 25:35, 39–40　　[6] *Mt.* 22:21　　[7] cf. *Mt.* 17:24–5　　[8] dictum (dc̄m) *Gt*　　[9] *Ps.* 23:1 *ap. Augustinum* (D.8 c.1)　　[10] aliis *Gt*　　[11] *Act.* 4:32　　[12] *Horat.*

Ars poet. 359 [13] Sicut...sicut] Sic...sic *Gt* [14] ut filios—parentes *scripsi*: inter filios maiores. ut parentes. *Gt* [15] spirituales (sp̄uales) *Gt* [16] *om. Gt* [17] quia *Gt*

Summa Tractaturus magister (French school, *c.* 1181–5)

(D.8 pr.) *multitudinis credentium:* Non est exemplum sufficiens set proficiens, quia etsi inter eos omnia communia, quod non uidetur, non tamen extraneis.[1] *apud Platonem:* et c. xii. q.i. c.ij. *iustissimus ordo:* si talis possit inueniri.

    Paris, B.N. lat. 15994, fo. 3vb.

    [1] Non—extraneis *etiam apud* Weigand, *Naturrechtslehre (laud. supra n.* 3), *p.* 316.

(C.12 q.1 c.2) *Grecorum quidam*: Plato in Timeo. *in omnibus autem:* Hec sunt uerba Clementis, tamen ex sensu uerborum Platonis sumpta. *coniuges:* quantum ad honesta seruicia.

    MS Par. fo. 53vb.

Summa Omnis qui iuste (*Lipsiensis*) (Anglo-Norman school, *c.* 1186)

(C.12 q.1 c.2) *sine dubio sunt coniuges:* Hoc non dicunt Clementem apposuisse, cum tamen ex uerbis Platonis hoc haberi possit, qui in re publica quam fingebat[1] uxores et liberos communes esse dixit, idest affectum dilectionis communiter exhibendum ut suis et extraneis. Non dixit uxores communes[2] quantum ad carnis usum set quantum ad dilectionem et obsequium.

    Leipzig, Univ. MS 986, fo. 155rb; Rouen MS 743, fo. 76rb.

    [1] figebant *Lp* [2] communis *Lp*

Summa De iure canonico tractaturus (Anglo-Norman school, *c.* 1186)

(D.8 pr.) *apud Platonem:* Hoc in Timeo Platonis inuenitur, ubi Plato in illa maxima ciuitate cuius rem fingebat publicam omnia dixit esse communia debent, neminem suum affectum scire,[1] omnes equaliter inuicem diligendos.

    Laon MS 371*bis*, fo. 84vb.

    [1] effectum sen[i] *Ld*

(C.12 q.1 c.2) *quidam Grecorum:* idest Plato in Thimeo. *sine dubio sunt coniuges:* Hoc non dicunt Clementem set alium apposuisse,[1] cum tamen...et obsequium.[2]

    MS Laud. fo. 131vb.

    [1] et p̄posuisse *Ld* [2] cum tamen...et obsequium *verbotenus ut in* Sum. Omnis q.i. *praeter*: haberi] fieri *Ld* qui in re publica] quia in illa re publica *Ld*

Gloss composition Ordinaturus magister (Bologna, *c.* 1180)

(D.8 pr.) printed above at n. 83. (The gloss from MS Biberach printed above at n. 32 is not part of this composition.)

(C.12 q.1 c.2) *sapientissimus:*[1] subaudi Plato. *in omnibus:*[2] idest in eo[3] uocabulo, 'omnia',[4] *sunt coniuges:*[5] intelliguntur et comprehenduntur coniuges, et est argumentum quod in uerbo generaliter prolato omnia comprehenduntur particularia, arg. di. xviiii. Si Romanorum.[6] *coniuges:*[7] (i) quantum ad affectum non ad usum. (ii) quantum ad obsequium non ad coniunctionem. (iii) A falsatoribus dictum est, uel dictum est ⟨non⟩[8] quantum ad carnis usum ut stulti putant, set quantum ad dilectionem.

> Biberach MS B 3515, fo. 16orb; Cues MS 223, fo. 122va; Leipzig, Univ. MS Haen. 18, fo. 132rb; Vatican MS Ross. 595, fo. 144ra. Cf. gl. interlin. in Paris, B.N. lat. 15398.

> [1] *Ross (al.m.)*, scil. Plato *Par, om. cett.*   [2] *Cus Ross (cf. gl. interl.* in hoc uocabulo omnia.*/(*sunt) idest continentur *Par), om. cett.*   [3] idest in m̄o *Ross*   [4] scil. praem. *Ross*   [5] sunt ho. *Cus*   [6] D.19 c.1   [7] *gl* (i) *Bib,* (ii) *Haen,* (iii) *Cus*   [8] *illegib. Cus*

Huguccio, *Summa decretorum* (Bologna, c. 1188–90)

(D.8 pr.) *inter eos:* scil. apostolos et alios tunc temporis credentes, ut xii. q.i.Dilectissimis. Scimus.[1] *nescit proprios affectus:* idest tantum...Dilectissimis.

> Admont MS 7, fo. 9vb. The second gloss is printed above, at n. 84.

> [1] C.12 q.1 cc.2, 9.

(C.12 q.1 c.2) *quidam:* scil. Plato in Timeo. *in omnibus sunt coniuges:* Coniuges debent esse communes non quo ad usum carnis set quo ad alterius officii obsequium et quo ad dilectionem etcet. *in omnibus:* idest in eo uocabulo, scil. 'omnia', *sunt coniuges:* idest intelliguntur et comprehenduntur coniuges, et est argumentum quod uerbum generale est generaliter intelligendum, ar. di. xviiii. Si Romanorum.[1]

> MS Adm. fo. 235vb.

> [1] D.19 c.1.

Alanus, *Glossa Ius naturale* (Bologna, c. 1192, second recension c. 1205)

(D.8 pr.) [*Platonem:*[1] in Thimeo.] [*proprios:* idest tanta affectione amplectitur extraneos et proprios.] *affectus:*[2] idest in qua quisque sic diligebat alienos ut proprios consanguineos.

> Paris, B.N. lat. 3909 (= Pr), fo. 1vb; lat. 15393 (= Ps), fo. 5rb; Bibl. Mazarine MS 1318, fo. 5rb; Vatican MS Ross. 595, fo. 16ra (second layer); Seo de Urgel, MS 113 (2009), folios unnumbered.—*Pr Urg:* first recension; *Ps Maz:* second rec.; *Ross:* selected glosses. Passages and glosses not found in the first recension will be printed here within brackets.

> [1] *gl. om. Ross*   [2] *gl. in Ps tantum, om. cett.*

(C.12 q.1 c.2) *Grecorum:* supra d. xxxvii. Si quid ueri. arg.[1] *in omnibus:* [arg. generaliter dictum generaliter intelligendum.] supra d. xix. Si Romanorum. arg.[2] *et coniuges:* supra di. viii. § Differt.[3] In Platone c. de feminis.[4] [set intelligas non quo ad usum set quo ad affectionem.]

> Pr fo. 35rb, Ps fo. 139rb, Maz fo. 202rb, Urg (n.n.). No glosses in Ross.

> [1] D.37 c.13.   arg.] contra *add. et del.* Urg   [2] D.19 c.1   [3] D.8 pr.   [4] *Tim.* 18C

Glossa Ecce uicit leo (French school, after 1202)

(D.8 pr.) *nescit:* idest nescire debet. ⟨uel⟩ *nescit,* tantum. Similiter[1] caritas nescit que sua sunt,[2] ⟨tan⟩tum, quia ita diligit proximum ⟨s⟩icut[3] se, et xii. q.i. Scimus.[4]

Paris, B.N. MS nouv. acq. lat. 1576, fo. 24ra; not in the St Florian MS mentioned below. Pointed brackets enclose letters hidden in the fold of the volume and hence not legible on the microfilm.

[1] Simile *Par*　　[2] *1 Cor.* 13:5　　[3] ///ĩc *Par*　　[4] C.12 q.1 c.9

(C.12 q.1 c.2) *coniuges:* quia[1] et coniuges debent esse communes, et hoc uerum est quo ad affectum[2] caritatis et servitium licitum,[3] non autem quo ad turpe aliquid committendum.

MS Par. fo. 196ra; St Florian MS XI.605, fo. 61va.

[1] *om. Fl.*　　[2] effectum *Par Fl*　　[3] licentium *Fl*

Glossa Animal est substantia (French school, *c.* 1206–10)

(C.12 q.1 c.2) *in omnibus:* idest in uniuersitate.[1] *sunt coniuges:* non quantum ad usum carnis[2] set quantum ad obsequium honestatis.

Bamberg MS Can. 42, fo. 83va; Cues MS 223 (second layer), fo. 122va; Liège, Univ. MS 127E, fo. 148rb.

[1] idest in vᶜᵒ (uocabulo?) n̄o *Bb*, idest inunitᵒ *Cus*　　[2] castitatis *Leod*

Bernardus Compostellanus, *Apparatus glossarum* (Bologna, *c.* 1202–6)

(C.12 q.1 c.2) *coniuges:* quantum ad obsequii exhibitionem, non amplexandi dilectionem. b.

Gniezno MS 28 (folio numbers illegible on film).

Laurentius, *Glossa Palatina* (Bologna, *c.* 1210–15).

(D.8 pr.) *nescit:* non ita intelligas ut nesciat filios suos et ut[1] ei liceat cum filia sua coire, set ita: idest eodem affectu suscipit extraneos quo et filios proprios.[2] xii. q.ii. Dilectissimis,[3] ff. de nundinis l.ii. in fine.[4]

Vatican MSS Pal. lat. 658, fo. 2rb; Reg. lat. 977, fo. 3ra; also MS Vat. lat. 1367 (second layer), fo. 3rb.

[1] *om. Vl*　　[2] la(urentius). *add. et reliqua om. Vl*　　[3] C.12 q.1 c.2　　[4] *Dig.* 50.11.2 (*ubi laud.* 'Plato cum institueret quemadmodum ciuitas bene habitari possit', *de negotiatoribus, Rep.* 371A, C); *allegatur etiam al. m. in Par. lat. 15393 post primam gl. Alani*

(C.12 q.1 c.2) *in omnibus:* in hoc uocabulo 'omnia'. *coniuges:* idest intelliguntur et comprehenduntur coniuges, et est argumentum quod in uerbo generaliter prolato[1] omnia comprehenduntur particularia, arg. xix. Si Romanorum.[2]

Pal. fo. 49rb, Reg. fo. 139rb (no gloss in Vl).

[1] probato *Reg*　　[2] D.19 c.1

Johannes Teutonicus, *Glossa ordinaria* (Bologna, *c.* 1217)

(D.8 pr.) *nescit:* Quisque[1] tantum diligit alium ut se. Finxit enim Plato quandam rem publicam: in qua omnia enim[2] sunt[3] communia.[4]

Bamberg MSS Can. 13, fo. 3ra; Can. 14, fo. 5va; Vatican MSS Vat. lat. 1367, fo. 3ra; Pal. lat. 624, fo. 3va; Pal. lat. 625, fo. 5vb.

Preliminary note. Even with the punctuation here proposed the Latin remains awkward with its redundant second 'enim', which the consensus of MSS does not allow to cancel. In Bartholomaeus Brixiensis's recension, the text remained at first unchanged (= *Barth. I*, e.g. Vat. lat. 1365); but in the fourteenth century, MSS will prefer 'in qua omnia sunt communia' (= *Barth. II*, e.g. Vat. lat. 1368, 1371, 1372, 1373). The printed text of this version (= *ed.*) is slightly expanded and remains constant, from the incunabula I have examined (Hain-Cop. *7882, *7912, *7913) to the official Roman text (1582) and its successors.

[1] enim *add. ed.* [2] enim *Vl Pal. 625 Barth. I et (ante* omnia) *Pal. 624:* eī *Bb. 13,* eis *(al.m.? seqr. rasura) Bb. 14,* om. *Barth. II et ed.* [3] fuerunt *Pal. 625,* essent *Bb. 14* [4] xii. q.i c.ii *add. ed.*

(C.12 q.1 c.2) *coniuges:* non quo ad usum carnis sed quo ad usum obsequii, uel quo ad dilectionem.[1] Et est argumentum quod uerbum generale generaliter intelligendum est. xix. di. Si Romanorum.[2] Jo.[3]

MSS Bamb. 13, fo. 117ra; Vat. lat. 1367, fo. 136ra; Pal. 624, fo. 148vb; Pal. 625, fo. 123va (not in Bamb. 14).

[1] xxxi. dist. Omnino (c.11) *add. ed.* [2] D.19 c.1 [3] Jo. *add. Bb Pal. 624*

Guido de Baysio, *Rosarium* (Bologna, A.D. 1300)

(D.8 pr.) *affectus:* dicit lau. sic, 'nescit' non ita intelligas...ff. de nundi. l. ii. lau.[1] Vnde dic *nescit*, idest *affectus*, idest tantum seipsum diligere, secundum hu.[2]

Vatican MS Vat. lat. 1447, fo. 8ra; ed. Lugd. 1549, fo. 9ra.

[1] *vide gl. Laurentii, supra* [2] *vide gl. Huguccionis in textu prope adn. 84 supra*

(C.12 q.1 c.2) *sapientissimus:* Plato in timeo. h.[1] *in omnibus:* materialiter tenetur, et in hoc uocabulo 'omnia' 'sunt', idest[2] intelliguntur et comprehenduntur, coniuges,[3] et facit viij. dist. § i. et c. seq.[4] [et repete et uideas quod dixi j. di. Ius autem. ij. in glos.j. res etc.][5]

MS Vat. fo. 204ra; ed. Lugd. fo. 218rb.

[1] prelato intraneo. h. *ed.*; *vide gl. Huguccionis, supra* [2] ei *ed.* [3] *vide gl. Hug.* [4] D.8 pr et c.1 [5] et repete...etc. *om. Vl; glossam laud. in ed. ad loc.* (D.1 c.7) *non inveni*

Guido Terreni, *Commentarium super decretum* (Elne [Perpignan], 1339).

(D.8 pr.) *Differt autem.* Gratianus insistit[1] circa differentiam iuris naturalis et aliorum iurium...set erant eis omnia communia. Set et a philosophis legitur traditum, inter quos Plato hoc posuit obseruandum in ciuitate bene ordinata. In hoc tamen Aristotiles Platonem reprobat ii°. pol.[2] Iure autem consuetudinis...

Vatican MS Vat. lat. 1453, fo. 5va (ex apogr. K. Pennington).

[1] incistit *Vl* [2] *Polit.* 1261b, 1262b–1264b

(C.12 q.1 c.2) *coniuges:* Hoc reprobat philosophus 2° pol. quo ad usum carnalis copule, quia ex hoc sequeretur prolis incertitudo et honor parentum tolleretur propter incertitudinem quis genuerit;[1] sequitur minor dilectio ad filios, inde oriretur odium inter ciues.[2] Nec est lex bona quod coniuges sint communes quo ad obsequium,[3] ne obsequendo committatur adulterium et obsequendo impediatur matrimonii[4] debitum reddendum.

MS Vat. fo. 100ra.

[1] genuit *Vl*   [2] cf. *Arist. Polit.* 1262a 25–33   [3] cf. *Glos. ord.*   [4] matrimonium *Vl*

APPENDIX II

The text of Pseudo-Clement, ep. 5 in Gratian (cf. at note 56 above)

Abbreviations:

Fr = Gratian, ed. Friedberg
H = Pseudo-Isidore, ed. Hinschius
Tr = Ivo, Tripartita, from Paris, B.N. MSS lat. 3858, fo. 5r/v and lat. 3858B, fo. 3v–4r
Or = Collection of MS Vat. lat. 3829 (prov. Niccolò Ormaneto)

C.12 q.1 c.2

Dilectissimis—sunt ambo (pr.–§5 at n.37 *Fr*): *H* p. 65 pr.–*ante* n.9.
Tr 1.1.23; *Or* part (i), beginning.
inscr. Item Clemens in epist. IV *Grat.* Clemens in quarta epistola (epistola iiij.) *Tr, sine inscr. Or*
rubr. Omnibus clericis communis est uita seruanda *Grat.* Communem uitam omnibus necessariam *Tr*, De bono uite communis *Or*

[Cetera que—digna sunt] (cf. n.37 0 *Fr*): *H* 65 at n.9–*ante* c.83.
Not in Friedberg's codd. ABCDF but in EGH and the editions, also in at least four MSS saec.xii/xiii I inspected. Not in *Tr* and *Or*; perhaps indication of an early revision of Gratian's text. The variant in *Fr* n.38 (sunt] uidentur EGH) is nowhere confirmed.

Quapropter—predicanda sunt (§5 concluded): *H* 65 at c.83–*ante* n.15.
Tr 1.1.24 (i); *Or* part (i) continued.
rubr. Apostolorum exempla imitanda *Tr*, cf. Obediendum esse doctrinis et exemplis apostolorum *H* c.83

Vnde consilium—adimplere satagatis (§6): *H* 66 *post* n.11–*ante* n.14.
Tr 1.1.24 (ii); *Or* part (i) concluded.

D.37 c.14

Relatum est—competenter asserere (pr.–at n.157 *Fr*): *H* 65 at n.15–66 *post* n.5
Tr 1.1.25; *Or* part (ii), with large initial.
inscr. Item Clemens *Grat.*
rubr. Ad intelligentiam sacrarum scripturarum secularium peritia est necessaria *Grat.*

Scripturas ex proprio ingenio non esse legendas *Tr*, De his qui non recte docent *Or* (*marg*)

Cum enim ex diuinis—simulata declinet (*post* n.157 *Fr*–end): *H* 66 *post* n.5–*post* n.7. Not in *Tr* and *Or*.

Summary

H 65 pr.–*post* n.14	*Grat.* 12 q.1 c.2 pr–§5	*Tr.* 1.1.23–24(i)	*Or.* (i) beg.
65 at n.15–66 *post* n.5	D.37 c.14 (i)	1.1.25	(ii)
66 *post* n.5–*post* n.7	D.37 c.14 (ii)	—	—
66 *post* n.7–*post* n.11	—	—	—
66 *post* n.11–*ante* n.14	12 q.1 c.2 §6	1.1.24 (ii)	(i) concl.
66 at n.14–end			

APPENDIX III

From the papers of the Correctores Romani (cf. at nn.59–62 above)

(i) From the book of minutes, MS Vat. lat. 4891, fo. 118r/v:

Die xvii Octob. MD.LXX. Congregatio apud Illust^mum Cardinal. Alciatum. Interfuerunt doctores R. P. Cornelius V(triusque) S(ignaturae) S^mi D.N. Refer(endarius). Doc. Thomas, Doc. Latinus, Doc. Parisetus, Doc. I. Marsa Sec(retarius). (*marg.:*) Episcopus Segninus S. D.N. Sacrista Vrbe aberat ad visitandum suum Episcopatum. Videatur an in superioribus aliquid habeat quod non sit annotatum.
(*fo. verso*)   can. ij. dilectissimis
. . . In omnibus autem sunt sine dubio et coniuges.] Desunt hec in or(iginali) et pessime sunt addita ab aliquo Nicolaita. Viderentur* quidem delenda sed propter commentarios sustinentur. notetur tamen in marg. pessime esse addita et remittatur lector ad notationem in qua rationibus impugnetur hereticorum opinio et demonstretur quam aliena sit a religione christiana et ab vnitate coniugalj. Et referatur in congregatione generali.

(*marg.*) *Videatur Ans(elmus) siue Authentica an habeat haec verba [Note that the *Correctores* in the beginning of their work used the name 'Authentica canonum' for the (lost) MS of Anselm from which the present MS Vat. lat. 4983 is copied; see *Bulletin of medieval canon law* N.S. 1 (1971), 13–14.]
(*marg. sin.*) Con(gregatio Gen(eralis). In notatione monstretur haec verba deesse in antiquis original. et sapere haeresim Nicolaitarum, de qua Epiphanius contra Epiphani [?] haereticum fo. 100.

(ii) From the draft by Michael Thomasius (Miguel Tomás Taxaquet) for the *Notationes*, MS Vat. lat. 4890, fo. 88r/v.

Causa xij q. p^a 2 c. Dilectissimis No. 1103
In uer. in omnibus autem sunt sine dubio et coniuges] uerba hec non sunt in concilijs Coloniae quatuor tomis impressis neque in duobus uetustis exemplaribus huius

epistolae, altero Vaticanae, alterò bibliothecae S^{ti} Marcj Florentiae, neque in Anselmo. quam opinionem a Platone acceptam haeretici quidam uolebant ad religionem christianam transferre, ut testatur Epiphanius haeresi 32 his uerbis: Primum quidem... perficiens. Verùm quod apud ueteres christianos haec uxorum communio vehementer damnaretur, Tertullianus in Apologetico c.39 expressè ait [et testatur his uerbis *add. marg. autogr.*] omnia indiscreta...communicauerunt.

[The quotations (here indicated by suspension points) are the same as in the printed text of the *Notationes*.]

VACARIUS AND THE CIVIL LAW

by PETER STEIN

I

IN the second half of the twelfth century English lawyers were first introduced to the Roman law of Justinian. They then received (in Heinrich Brunner's phrase) the inoculation which enabled them to withstand a full-scale Reception of Roman law in the fifteenth and sixteenth centuries. From the time of the seventeenth-century English legal humanists, it has been recognised that the agent who made the introduction was Master Vacarius. The traditional account was thus summarised by Robert Wiseman, Doctor of Civil Law, in 1657:

[The Civil Law] was brought into England by Theobald the Archbishop of Canterbury, and being publickly read in Oxford by Vacarius, it grew so general a study, and other learning was so much neglected upon it, that King Stephen incensed thereat, sent forth a peremptory command, that it should be read in England no more, that Vacarius should forbear to teach it any further, nor that it should be lawful for any to keep any books of the Roman Laws by them . . . But King Stephen's prohibition did prevaile but little; for the power of the Law, God prospering the same, waxed the more vigorous, when malice did most strive to destroy it.[1]

This account may be accepted today (apart from the specific reference to Oxford) as still true in essentials. Vacarius, however, seems to have been posthumously accident-prone in the way historians have treated him and his works.

Part of the Vacarian legend among the humanists was due to a series of uncharacteristic mistakes by the great John Selden. 'Relying on an imperfect text of the chronicle of Robert of Torigny, he identified Vacarius with Roger, abbot of Bec, whom, in turn, he confused with the jurist Roger. From these initial assumptions, Selden was led into a series of startling consequences. His first deduction was that as Roger

[1] *The Law of Laws* (London, 1657), p. 125.

119

of Bec had won fame by devoting himself (*vacare*) to law teaching, he came to be called Vacarius...'[2]

Vacarius' fame was based on his main work, the *Liber Pauperum*, and until the nineteenth century it was believed that all manuscripts of it had perished. In 1817 C. F. C. Wenck of Leipzig acquired a manuscript which he identified as of the *Liber Pauperum*, and in 1820 he published the main contents.[3] In the same year H. Dirksen[4] published some texts from another MS of the work in Königsberg, and in 1828 G. Haenel identified the *Liber Pauperum* in a MS of Worcester Cathedral.[5] About the same time two more MSS, one in Bruges, which had formerly belonged to the Abbey of Dunes, and the other in Prague, were identified and their contents discussed by Stölzel in 1867.[6] A further MS at Avranches, which had come from Mont-Saint-Michel, was identified in 1889. To us the main interest of these MSS is in the twelfth-century glosses which they contain, and the light which those glosses throw on the development of legal doctrine in the century leading up to the publication of Accursius's Great Gloss in about 1240. Nineteenth-century civil lawyers were, however, even more interested in the precise wording of the fragments from the Digest and Code which were cited by Vacarius, since they were engaged in establishing the original texts and the various changes which they had undergone.

Of all these MSS the two most important are probably the Worcester, on which De Zulueta based his edition, and that of Wenck. The latter has been thought to have perished. In 1850 F. C. von Savigny stated that it was in Dorpat (the modern Tartu in Estonia),[7] but when Stölzel inquired a few years later he was assured that it was not there and De Zulueta also made inquiries there without any result.[8] However, Savigny made a mistake in placing the MS in Dorpat. Stieber in his life of Wenck, prefaced to Wenck's *Opuscula Academica* published in 1834, says that Wenck's MSS, including that of Vacarius, were acquired by the *biblioteca Academiae Petroburgensis ante paucos annos constituta* (p. xv), that is, the University of St Petersburg, founded by Alexander I. Later, when listing the known extant MSS of the *Liber Pauperum* (all

[2] D. Ogg, *Seldeni Ad Fletam Dissertatio* (Cambridge, 1925), p. xxvii.
[3] C. F. C. Wenck, *Magister Vacarius* (Leipzig, 1820).
[4] H. Dirksen, *Civilistische Abhandlungen* (Berlin, 1820), I, 319; II, 324.
[5] F. De Zulueta, *The Liber Pauperum of Vacarius*, Selden Society XLIV (London, 1927), p. xxxv.
[6] H. A. Stölzel, 'Ueber Vacarius, insbesondre die Brügger und die Prager Handschrift desselben', *Zeitschrift für Rechtsgeschichte*, VI (1867), 234–68.
[7] F. C. von Savigny, *Geschichte des römisches Rechts im Mittelalter*, 2nd edn (Heidelberg, 1850), IV, 423.   [8] De Zulueta, *Vacarius*, p. xxv.

except that of Avranches), he mentions *Petropolitanus* (*olim Wenckii*) (p. lxv). It is today in Leningrad University Library.[9] Wenck's MS and that of Worcester are important for the richness of the glosses they contain. Each has two series, an inner gloss which was part of the original work of Vacarius, and an outer gloss containing further illustrative material and, in the case of Wenck's MS, references added by later users of the work in the twelfth century.

At the end of the nineteenth century, F. Liebermann reviewed the evidence for Vacarius' career afresh.[10] Essentially this is of three kinds: first, statements by three contemporary writers: John of Salisbury (*Policraticus*, 1159), Gervase of Canterbury (*Actus Pontificum*, about 1199) and Robert of Torigny; secondly, references in documents attesting transactions in which Vacarius took part, for example, when he acted as a witness or as judge-delegate; and thirdly, the inferences which we can draw from his own works, not only the *Liber Pauperum*, but also certain other works dealing with topics of canon law and theology. Liebermann included too much in the last category, since he attributed to Vacarius works of the Mantuan jurist Vacella, and so inferred that Vacarius had taught Lombard law as well as civil law before leaving Italy. Although Liebermann himself published a correction soon afterwards,[11] the idea that Vacarius, who was probably of a Lombard family, was an expert on Lombard law was later repeated by such authorities as P. Vinogradoff[12] and W. S. Holdsworth.[13]

There is general agreement that Vacarius was born about 1120, studied civil law at Bologna, where he attained the title of *magister*, and was brought to England by Archbishop Theobald about 1143 to help him with the legal problems arising in the administration of the province of Canterbury. In the years following his arrival he did some teaching of civil law, but in the late 1150s he transferred to the service of Roger, archbishop of York, who had previously been archdeacon of Canterbury. By this time he must have taken orders (it is unlikely that he was ordained when he arrived in England). He spent the rest

---

[9] A. Vetulani, 'Les oeuvres d'Accurse dans les Bibliothèques de Leningrad', *Atti del Convegno internazionale di Studi Accursiani*, III (Milan, 1968), 1303ff. mentions MSS, formerly belonging to Wenck, which were there in 1964. The Librarian of the MSS department of Leningrad University Library confirms that it was thought to be a *Codex Justiniani*.

[10] F. Liebermann, 'Magister Vacarius', *EHR*, XI (1896), 305, 514.

[11] F. Liebermann, *EHR*, XIII (1898), 297.

[12] P. Vinogradoff, *Roman Law in Medieval Europe* (1909), 2nd edn (Oxford, 1929), p. 63.

[13] W. S. Holdsworth, *History of English Law*, 3rd edn (London, 1923), II, 148; cf. F. Pollock and F. W. Maitland, *History of English Law*, 2nd edn (Cambridge, 1898), I, 118.

of his long life, till the end of the century, in the province of York, first as a legal practitioner and the right-hand man of Archbishop Roger and later being more concerned with his duties as a canon of Southwell and parson of Norwell.

For Liebermann it was still an open question whether Vacarius taught at Oxford or not. In 1927 De Zulueta reviewed the evidence again in the introduction to his fine edition of the *Liber Pauperum* and expressed the opinion that 'to doubt whether Vacarius ever taught at Oxford is to doubt against the evidence'.[14] Since then it has been accepted that Vacarius was the virtual founder of Oxford legal studies. However, more information has come to light about Vacarius' later career, and recently the question has been subjected to a penetrating analysis by Sir Richard Southern.[15] He sets out all the data for the life of Vacarius in detail, and they need not be repeated here. His conclusion is that Vacarius did not teach at Oxford. There is in fact only one piece of direct evidence linking Vacarius with Oxford, a statement in Gervase of Canterbury. After recounting that Archbishop Theobald brought laws and advocates into England to help him in his dispute with Henry, bishop of Winchester, King Stephen's brother, the chronicler says that among the legal experts was Vacarius, and adds 'Hic in Oxenfordia legem docuit.'[16]

There is no doubt that in the nineties of the twelfth century Vacarius' *Liber Pauperum* was the main textbook in the flourishing school of civil law which had grown up in Oxford, whose students were indeed known as *pauperistae*. Although Vacarius was still alive then, he had since at least the early 1160s been attached to the province of York as an ecclesiastical man of affairs, so that he could not have been personally associated with the Oxford school of *pauperistae* at the end of the century. On the other hand, as Southern shows, in the period before Vacarius' move to the northern province, the schools of Oxford were not developed enough to have sustained a law school. But for Gervase's remark it would be assumed that Vacarius was brought to England in the 1140s primarily to deal with the *lites* and *appellationes antea inauditae* that were then arising, that he also did some law teaching and that it

---

[14] De Zulueta, *Vacarius*, pp. xvi–xvii.

[15] R. W. Southern, 'Master Vacarius and the beginning of an English academic tradition', in *Medieval Learning and Literature: essays presented to R. W. Hunt*, ed. J. J. G. Alexander and M. T. Gibson (Oxford, 1976), pp. 257–86. I am grateful to the author for letting me see this paper before publication.

[16] *Actus Pontificum*, ed. W. Stubbs, *Historical Works of Gervase of Canterbury*, RS (1879–80), II, 384.

was at Canterbury, so that he could combine it with his advisory work. We would assume that he continued there as part of the archbishop's household until Stephen's edict against Roman law, when, as John of Salisbury, writing as a prominent member of the same household, says, 'Vacario nostro interdictum silentium'.[17] Southern argues very plausibly that the reference to Oxford in Gervase is an interpolation, and if that is so the evidence that Vacarius ever taught at Oxford is reduced to a later tradition based on the enormous popularity of his book there.

We have still to account for the fact that when a flourishing school of civil law did develop in Oxford, it was based on a book written thirty or more years before by a foreigner who never had any connection with the place. The answer must be that it was the ideal, indeed the only, book suitable for the needs of the school. It was written in England, the choice of material was dictated by the needs of English students, and it had already been used in a modest way in the teaching of civil law in England. If we seek a parallel in legal history, we will perhaps find it in the nineteenth century. In the 1820s John Austin put the science of jurisprudence on a new foundation derived from what he had learned from the German Pandectists in Bonn. With great enthusiasm he gave courses of lectures at University College, London, and published some of them. The response was so disappointing that he ceased to lecture and forgot his textbook. More than thirty years later, after the reforms of legal education in the middle of the century, there was a need for a scientific work which would provide the basis for the systematic rational treatises on law that were then demanded. Austin's full *Lectures on Jurisprudence*, published posthumously by his widow, were hailed as just what was wanted – and nowhere more than at Oxford, with which he had had no connection.

Vacarius may never have set foot in Oxford, but there is evidence that he did teach the civil law academically in England, and he managed to set a tone, which was recognised later as what was needed. It is worth attempting to characterise his attitudes more specifically.

II

Vacarius was a lawyer of the age in which he was trained at Bologna. This was the heyday of the Four Doctors, the immediate pupils of the

---

[17] *Policraticus*, VIII, 22 (808 c-d), ed. C. C. J. Webb (Oxford, 1909), II, 399.

founder of the school of glossators, Irnerius. The merit of the school of Irnerius was to have revived the study of the law of Justinian in place of the law of the *Lex Romana Visigothorum*, which had been the main source of Roman law in the early middle ages. For the glossators generally, the texts of Justinian were almost sacred; they were the authorities from which all legal decisions must proceed. Their first aim was therefore to establish reliable texts and then to catalogue and analyse their contents. Although Justinian's *Corpus Iuris* is a great treasure house of legal learning, it is appallingly badly arranged. Similar material appears in its three main parts, the Institutes, Digest and Code, but it is arranged in a different order in each, none being very coherent. Not only is it confused in arrangement, it is obscure in style, because the original material had been interpolated by Justinian's Compilers, largely for the purpose of abbreviation; it contains superfluous and out-of-date material; and it is defective, in that, despite Justinian's assurances to the contrary in an introductory constitution (*Deo Auctore* 8), it does contain antinomies and contradictions. None the less its decisions, the reasoning by which they are justified and the range of matters dealt with are unrivalled. The glossators of Bologna had a closer familiarity with its texts than any generation of lawyers have done before or since. Besides mastering the material and trying to reconcile contradictions, they delighted in controversies, preserved in the *Dissensiones Dominorum*. At the time of Vacarius, they were grouped in the orthodox school led by Bulgarus, 'the golden mouth', and the 'liberals' led by Martinus Gosia, the Gosiani. (Bulgarus and Martinus were two of the Four Doctors.)

The difference between the two schools of glossators is often portrayed as a conflict between adherence to the letter of the law, advocated by Bulgarus, and equity, espoused by the Gosians. This is misleading. Both schools were interested in just results, and both felt themselves bound by the texts of the *Corpus Juris*. The difference resolved itself into a question of interpretation of the law.[18] Bulgarus assumed that the law was equitable; he attributed to the jurist a more limited role than did Martinus. For Bulgarus, it was sufficient if the jurist found the *ratio legis*, the purpose of the rule in question, in order to interpret it correctly. For Martinus the *ratio legis* was not enough; the interpretation was still subject to control by equity. Equity was not,

---

[18] E. M. Meijers, 'Le conflit entre l'équité et loi chez les premiers glossateurs', *Tijdschrift voor Rechtsgeschedenis*, XVII (1941), 117ff. (= *Études d'histoire de droit*, IV (1966), 142ff.).

however, understood as a vague abstract idea of fairness (*equitas rudis*); it was itself to be found in the *Corpus Iuris*, but for Martinus the controlling equity for a particular rule could be found *anywhere* in the *Corpus*, even outside the *sedes materiae*:[19] it was the *equitas constituta* of Justinian's law taken as a whole.

The two schools also differed in their attitudes to other kinds of law, such as canon law and custom. The canon law was at quite a different stage of development from that of the civil law. The contents of the civil law, i.e. Justinian's corpus, were fixed and there could be no argument about their authority. That had been established six centuries before. The question was: what did they mean? The work of the civil law glossators was all interpretation of that corpus, by reference to material from within the same set of authorities. Very rarely indeed did they quote biblical texts or classical authors like Cicero; their discipline contained within itself all that was necessary for its own interpretation. Though the techniques used were those of grammar, rhetoric and logic, they were applied exclusively to what had Justinian's stamp of approval.

At the time of the Four Doctors, the canon law authorities were not fixed in this way. There were various collections, the most important being that of Ivo of Chartres at the end of the eleventh century. These consisted of statements from Scripture, decisions of councils, papal decretals, opinions of Church Fathers – a jumble of material in different forms and of differing authority. The canon lawyers were ahead of the civil lawyers in developing guides for interpretation – such as consideration of context, comparison of texts, specification of time, place and person, determination of the original cause of the statement, differentiation of general measures from particular.[20] But to a civil lawyer in the 1130s, it must have seemed less of a discipline – in the sense that Irnerius and the Four Doctors had made civil law a discipline – than a free for all.

The breakthrough in making canon law a discipline was of course the publication of Gratian's *Decretum* about 1140. We now recognise that Gratian's work marks a new epoch in the canon law, because of the scientific way in which the materials are arranged and criticised. For us the *Concordia Discordantium Canonum*, as he called it, in the first place

19 Gloss *ad* D.2.1.1., in Savigny, *Geschichte*, IV, 486, nr 24. For a general account of the glossators, F. Calasso, *Medio Evo del diritto* (Milan, 1954), pp. 521ff.; W. Ullmann, *Law and Politics in the Middle Ages* (The Sources of History, London, 1975), pp. 86ff., 96ff.
20 R. McKeon, 'Rhetoric in the Middle Ages', *Speculum*, XVII (1942), 21.

established what were the authoritative texts for his time, although unlike those of the civil law, the canon law authorities were increasing all the time with the publication of new papal decretals. Secondly, it brought out the inner coherence of these authorities and showed that what looked like blatant contradictions could be reconciled by proper interpretation. Within twenty years of publication, Gratian's work was looked on in this way, as superseding its predecessors and as having quasi-justinianian authority. But it was not hailed like that by all *when* it was published. The immediate reaction of most civil lawyers at Bologna was that Gratian was trying to do the impossible, that he was giving an air of spurious harmony to material that was intractably contradictory. They did not really recognise canon law as a rival discipline, equivalent to civil law, with its own special mysteries. For them, anyone who was properly trained in the civil law should be able to handle the soi-disant authorities of the canon law with competence and produce rational answers. It was not necessary to study the views of modern commentators like Gratian; they had little to offer. A decent civilian could produce rational answers to canon law problems on the basis of the materials collected by Ivo.

Bulgarus and his followers concentrated their attention exclusively on the civil law and tended to ignore canon law as hardly worthy of their attention. Martinus does not seem to have differed from them in his attitude to the relative scientific quality of the civil law and the canon law. But he was a realist and recognised the authority of canon law, both because of its importance in practice and because it was the *lex divina*. He was prepared to accept that in cases when Justinian's law and canon law came into conflict, the canon law, despite its unscientific character, must prevail.

Martinus' attitude is illustrated by the *Summula de computatione graduum*.[21] Civil law reckoned the degree of relationship of two people by counting the steps up to their common ancestor and down again. Canon law counted only one side to the common ancestor, so that whereas by the civil law brothers and sisters were two degrees apart and first cousins four degrees, the canon law considered them only one and two degrees apart respectively. The orthodox civil lawyers discussed the Roman texts without making any mention of the canon law.

[21] H. Kantorowicz, *Studies in the Glossators of the Roman Law* (Cambridge, 1938), pp. 91, 253; B. Paradisi, 'Diritto canonico e tendenze di scuola nei glossatori da Irnerio ad Accursio,' *Studi Medievali* (Spoleto), 3rd series, VI. 2 (1965), 47ff.

Martinus not only notes the divergence between the two systems but holds that the canon law is valid and the civil law is not. The reason is clear: 'hoc[22] videtur obviare legi divinae'.

Again with regard to agreements to submit a dispute to arbitration (*compromissum*), Roman law required for their validity stipulatory promises by each party to pay a penalty to the other if he disobeyed the arbitrator's award. Commenting on C.2.55.4, Bulgarus and his followers required the promise of a penalty. Martinus held that the agreement was binding whether or not it was accompanied by a promise of a penalty. The motive for Martinus' decision, which is reported by the canonist Hostiensis,[23] is not known but it is significant that it agrees with both the canon law and Lombard law.

Martinus' liberal approach to Justinian's texts, of which his knowledge was as wide as that of his rivals, and his attitude to other laws make him seem more progressive and modern than his rivals. In truth he was more conservative in that he represents the attitudes current before the school of Irnerius established the unconditional acceptance of Justinian's law to the exclusion of all other law and irrespective of its consequences in practice.[24]

III

At Bologna itself Bulgarus' orthodox school prevailed. It is not surprising, therefore, that Bolognese glossators, who were attracted away from the *mater legum* to other countries, were those who tended to favour Martinus' school. The most prominent of the glossators of the diaspora was Placentinus, who set up a law school on Bolognese lines at Montpellier, and was responsible for introducing the new legal learning to France. He belonged to Martinus' party and was probably more extreme than his master. Vacarius also shows distinct Gosian sympathies. Although not an uncritical adherent, for he on occasion approves Bulgarus' view, there is no doubt which side of the fence he was on and this is shown by his interest in equity, in the relation of custom to law, and in canon law.

---

[22] Either Inst. III.6.2ff. or D.38.10.1.4ff.

[23] *Lect. in Quinque libros Decretalium*, in x.1.43, de arbitris 9, per tuas, nr.11, v. indistincte; Paradisi, 'Diritto canonico', pp. 60ff. For comment on the importance of medieval arbitration, P. Stein, 'The Source of the Romano-canonical part of Regiam Maiestatem', *Scottish Historical Review*, XLVIII (1969), 107, 112.   [24] Paradisi, 'Diritto canonico', p. 54.

Vacarius' opinions on the civil law are known from the glosses to the *Liber Pauperum*, from a few glosses that have survived elsewhere and from a *Lectura*[25] on Justinian's Institutes which contains several references to Vacarius and must be notes of a course of lectures given either by Vacarius himself or by an adherent.

The *Liber Pauperum* consists of select extracts from the Digest and Code integrated by glosses. The author's first problem was to justify making what was an epitome, when the raison d'être of the glossators was the rejection of epitomes and return to the pure milk of Justinian's law in the original. He does it on economic grounds, on the need to diffuse a knowledge of the law. The implication is that Roman law was a law of reason and equity, whose principles underlay the customary law of any civilised country and therefore should be available to fill any gaps in its customary law. So it would be quite wrong to allow such knowledge to become the monopoly of the rich. There were compendia of canon law, why not also of civil law? Like all Romanists in England since then, Vacarius felt the need, which was not present in Bologna, to justify the value of Roman law. This he did by stressing its rationality and logical content – at least when arranged sensibly. The extracts were arranged in a more intelligible order than that in which they appeared in the originals. For example, Vacarius is one of the earliest glossators to comment on the *Tres Libri*, the last three books of the Code which the glossators separated from the other nine books. Extracts from the *Tres Libri* appear in the *Liber Pauperum* near extracts from the first book of the Code which deals with similar topics. Although not directed at solving specific court problems, the work was sensitive to practical needs by making the ideas of the Roman jurists and their Bolognese exponents more accessible. You could readily find a helpful lead in the *Liber Pauperum*, but you might look for ages in the Digest and Code.

Before the *Lectura* was discovered, it had seemed that Vacarius and his school had ignored Justinian's Institutes, although it was the most elementary part of the codification, the best arranged and avowedly pedagogic in aim. From the substantial correspondence of doctrine between the *Liber Pauperum* and the *Lectura* it is now clear that the Vacarian school did not ignore the Institutes, and further confirmation may be found in the twelfth-century glosses to the Institutes which

---

[25] Discovered by Dr E. Rathbone in BL Royal MS 4 B IV, fos. 203ff., and identified by De Zulueta; an edition is in preparation for the Selden Society Supplementary Series.

appear to be of English origin, published by Professor P. Legendre in 1965 from an Oxford Magdalen College MS.[26]

Vacarius gave particular attention, as his English students would expect, to the relationship of the civil law to other kinds of law. An important section of the *Liber Pauperum* (I. 8) deals with custom and its relation to the civil law.[27] The emperor is the sole legislator and the only authoritative interpreter of the law. The interpretation of the emperor can give weight to considerations of equity, whereas that of the judge is limited by the law. This is the orthodox view. But in setting it out, Vacarius adds after the interpretation of the emperor 'or custom', so equating modification of the law by custom with that by the emperor. Furthermore, says Vacarius, although the judge cannot apply equity, this refers only to the *equitas rudis* or general idea of fairness. Adopting Martinus' distinction between 'rough equity' and 'institutional equity', Vacarius holds that the judge can and should apply *equitas constituta*, or the underlying equitable principles to be derived from the law as a whole.

Custom can modify the law by interpretation; but can it actually abrogate it? The *Corpus Juris* itself did not speak with one voice on this point, D.1.3.32.1 and C.8.52(53).2 giving different views. Irnerius had compromised. Custom can abrogate the law if the custom is made with knowledge of the law, but not if it is made in ignorance of the law. Vacarius disagreed. Custom can abrogate the law because it derives from the will of the people (*consensus populi*). So long as the people are not in error as to the matter of the custom (*res*) their will is effective; whether they know of the existence of the legal rule is irrelevant. Error as to the law does not affect their will, which can be expressed tacitly. The analogy which he adduces to justify this political – or at least public law – argument is typically taken from private law. If a man sells a thing to John and then, before delivering it, resells it to Jack in ignorance of the law of sale, he cannot rescind the first sale which still binds him. The law does not draw its authority from its written form. It is the will of the people which gives it its force; so law can abrogate custom just as custom can abrogate law.

Vacarius' argument in the *Liber Pauperum* is repeated in the *Lectura* to the Institutes (*ad* 1.2.11). Significantly C.8.52.2, which is from the

[26] P. Legendre, 'Recherches sur les Commentaires Pré-Accursiens (MS, Magdalen Coll. 258)', *Tijdschrift voor Rechtsgeschiedenis*, XXXIII (1965), 353–429.

[27] De Zulueta, *Vacarius*, pp. lxxiiiff.; Meijers, 'Conflit', pp. 124ff. (= *Études*, pp. 147ff.).

title of the Code *Quae sit longa consuetudo*, is wrongly cited as from the title *De legibus et consuetudinibus*. Since it occurs in the title of the *Liber Pauperum* with the latter rubric (I. 8), the lecturer was clearly using the *Liber* rather than the *Corpus Juris*. Irnerius' opinion is given; then Vacarius is cited in opposition ('Sed hic instat Vacarius dicens...'), but as the argument proceeds against Irnerius, Vacarius becomes *nos*. So if the lecturer is not Vacarius himself, he certainly belonged to his followers.

The Vacarian line on the force of custom appears not only in the *Liber Pauperum* and the *Lectura*. It is mentioned also in a gloss in a Gonville and Caius College, Cambridge, MS of Gratian's *Decretum*.[28] The gloss quotes Vacarius' opinion that *consuetudo populi tollit legem* and denies it on the ground that *maioris auctoritatis est lex*.

This doctrine of the relation of custom and law was probably Vacarius' own. On many specific points of private law he followed Martinus' line. For example, Vacarius is the only writer to report a view of Martinus that a noxal action under the *lex Aquilia* was not 'duplex contra infitiantem'.[29] The *lex Aquilia* gave an action against one who had damaged another's property. It was for simple damages against a defendant who admitted liability (but perhaps disputed the measure of damages) and for double damages against one who denied liability. When the damage was caused by a slave, the action was brought against the slave's owner, who had the option of either surrendering the delinquent slave to the plaintiff (*noxae deditio*) or paying the damages which would have been payable if the slave had been a freeman. In this case, where the defendant was not himself the delinquent, Martinus held that the damages were not doubled even though liability was denied. There is no specific authority for this view. De Zulueta considers it an example of Martinus' *equitas rudis* or *bursalis*,[30] but in fact one could build up from other texts a respectable argument distinguishing between ordinary and noxal actions in the matter of doubling damages, and there is much to be said for it on general grounds.[31]

Although Vacarius normally followed Martinus, he was his own man and on occasion followed Bulgarus. The glossators disputed over the

---

[28] No. 676 (formerly 283), fo. 4va; C. Duggan, 'The Reception of Canon Law in England in the later twelfth century', Proceedings of Second Int. Congress of Medieval Canon Law, *Monumenta Iuris Canonici*, Ser. C.I. (1965), 371ff.

[29] *Liber Pauperum*, III, 47 (De Zulueta, *Vacarius*, pp. 100–1).   [30] De Zulueta, *Vacarius*, p. cii.

[31] B. Paradisi, *Storia del diritto italiano*, IV.1, 2nd edn. (Naples, 1967), pp. 406–7.

period of time within which a right of the Church prescribed.[32] At the beginning of his reign Justinian had conceded that actions to protect Church property should prescribe in a hundred years instead of the usual period of prescription of thirty years (C.1.2.23 and Novel 9). Later he reduced the period to forty years (Novel 111). Certain glossators, probably Martinus among them, took the view that the rules in the *Corpus Juris* were all equally valid, that temporal priority was irrelevant and that the interpretation of the divergent texts should be dictated by general equitable (and practical) considerations. They advocated the hundred-year period. Some compromised and held that the Roman church alone enjoyed centennial prescription and that others churches' actions prescribed in forty years. Bulgarus spurned contemporary considerations and argued for a forty-year period for all ecclesiastical actions, and Vacarius followed him.[33] They no doubt took the line that Justinian's later constitution had abrogated the earlier.

IV

Vacarius' concern with the civil law was primarily academic. Most of his legal career was, however, spent as a practitioner, and in practice it was canon law rather than civil law which counted. He may have learned some canon law at Bologna but it is more likely that he studied it in England. The study of canon law for Vacarius meant familiarising himself with its authorities. He did not accept that canon law involved special techniques or ideas which were different from those of the civil law. He wrote a competent tract on the canon law of marriage and the Caius MS, to which reference has been made, contains glosses on purely canon law issues attributed to him. Both the tract and the glosses suggest that his ideas were formed early in his career, whereas his theological treatises come later.

The period in which Vacarius is most likely to have studied canon law is the early 1150s, after he had been prevented from teaching civil law by Stephen's edict and before he joined the service of Archbishop Roger of York. The place may have been Northampton. This is suggested by a reference in the *Liber contra multiplices et varios errores*,[34] Vacarius' counterblast to a theological tract written by a former fellow

---

[32] Paradisi, 'Diritto canonico', pp. 27ff.   [33] *Liber Pauperum*, I, 2 (De Zulueta, *Vacarius*, p. 6).
[34] Ed. Ilarino da Milano, *L'eresia di U. Speroni nella configurazione del maestro Vacario*, Studi e Testi cxv (Vatican, 1945), p. 527 (the work is printed in full, pp. 477–583).

student of law and friend of his student days, Hugo Speroni. (Speroni came from Piacenza in Lombardy and, since Vacarius was said to be of a Lombard family, he may have been a fellow citizen.) Speroni sent his tract to Vacarius by the hand of the latter's nephew who was visiting his uncle in England in the 1170s or 1180s. Vacarius' reply likens Speroni's arguments on the nature of the Incarnation, some of which were legal in character, to those put forward by the Jews of Northampton, 'where I was staying *causa studendi*'. The meaning of the last phrase is not clear. Kuttner and Rathbone assume that he was teaching civil law;[35] Paradisi considers that he was studying theology.[36] He may have been studying canon law, possibly in combination with some teaching of civil law.

We know little of the schools of Northampton in the twelfth century, although it was the destination of at least two migrations from Oxford in the thirteenth. Mr H. G. Richardson discussed the twelfth-century evidence in 1941,[37] before Vacarius' treatise came to light, and such evidence as he cites comes from the seventies and eighties. For example, between 1176 and 1181 the king maintained in the schools of Northampton John, clerk to the queen of Spain. The purpose of such a bursary would probably have been higher studies useful in public life. Vacarius' reference to his stay at Northampton is to an earlier period of his life and, to fit what we know of the rest of his career, the most likely period would be in the late fifties.

It seems more likely that he was studying canon law than theology. As Richardson points out, Lincoln was a centre for theology in mid-twelfth-century England and, as Northampton was in the diocese of Lincoln, it is unlikely that it would have been allowed to rival the Lincoln school in theology. On the other hand, Robert de Chesney, the bishop of Lincoln from 1148 to 1166, was interested in the learned law and had a copy of the Digest specially made and glossed for his use by Gilbert Foliot.[38] He may well have encouraged legal studies at Northampton. Vacarius, it is true, wrote short tracts on theology apart from that directed against his old friend. But he never shows himself to be a theologian in the professional sense; he is rather an interested

35 S. Kuttner and E. Rathbone, 'Anglo-Norman Canonists of the twelfth century', *Traditio*, vii (1949–51), 322.   36 B. Paradisi, *Storia del diritto italiano*, iv.2 (Naples, 1964), 321.
37 H. G. Richardson, 'The schools of Northampton in the twelfth century', *EHR*, lvi (1941), 595ff.
38 *The Letters and Charters of Gilbert Foliot*, ed. A. Morey and C. N. L. Brooke (Cambridge, 1967), no. 106, p. 145 (dated 1153).

amateur who brings his considerable powers of legal argumentation to bear on the burning theological issues of the day. On the other hand, canon law was to be the main concern of his professional life. Vacarius may have been attracted to Northampton to extend such knowledge of the canon law as he might have acquired at Bologna and, at the same time, do some teaching (unofficially, if Stephen's ban still obtained) in the civil law. It is worth noting that one of the few legal glosses to mention Vacarius, outside those of the *Liber Pauperum* and the Caius MS mentioned, is a marginal addition to a collection of *quaestiones* of Bolognese origin, which was originally in the possession of St Andrew's, Northampton.[39]

Vacarius' approach to the canon law comes out clearly in his *Summa de Matrimonio*.[40] It treats the question of what constitutes a marriage as still open, which indicates that it was written before the point was settled by Pope Alexander III. To be universal, the Church law of marriage had to concentrate on some elements which could be regarded as common to marriages of peoples in all countries and at all times, such as agreement to marry, the beginning of cohabitation, and the sexual union.

Gratian's effort to obtain a consistent theory resulted in the view that the *sponsalia*, the agreement to marry hereafter, constitutes an initiate marriage, which however only becomes a consummate or perfect marriage at the moment of physical intercourse. About the same time Peter Lombard was developing the famous distinction between *sponsalia de futuro* and *sponsalia de praesenti*. If a man and woman express their agreement to be from henceforth husband and wife, these *verba de praesenti* constitute a perfect marriage. On the other hand, betrothals or expressions of intention to marry in the future are no marriage at all.

Both views had passionate adherents. About 1156, the Italian canonist Ruffinus in his *Summa* supported Gratian's view. Vacarius seems to have been familiar with both Gratian's view, and Ruffinus' defence of it, and with Peter Lombard's. But he did not think much of either. For him, the true act of marriage, the act which marks the moment when the marriage takes place, is the mutual delivery of man and woman to each other. The word is *traditio*, the civil law word for the delivery of goods following a sale or gift. There must have been

---

[39] Oxford, Oriel Coll. MS 53, fo. 355r; S. Kuttner, 'Dat Galienus opes et sanctio Justiniana', *Linguistic and Literary Studies in honor of H. A. Hatzfeld* (Washington, D.C., 1964), p. 242, n. 35.
[40] F. W. Maitland, 'Magistri Vacarii Summa de Matrimonio', *Law Quarterly Review*, XIII (1897), 133–43. (Introduction) and 270ff. (text).

some prior agreement to indicate that the man is delivering himself as a husband and the woman is delivering herself as a wife; but it is not the agreement which makes the marriage, nor is it the *carnalis copula*. The marriage is made by the *traditio*, and that, says Vacarius, is the moment when they become one flesh, not the later consummation.

Vacarius thus brings marriage into line with the conveyance of property. With the authority of the Digest behind him, he feels contempt for the bits and pieces that constitute the texts of canon law: 'ecclesiastica iura namque dissonas recipiunt sententias et varias formas, plerumque inutiles, quia non observantur'.[41] In an apparent reference to Gratian, he speaks of those who toil in vain to recall the discord of contradictions into concord. Even the Church fathers themselves are hardly treated with the respect that he gives to the Digest jurists. In a hilarious passage Vacarius pictures St Augustine coming to the nuptial bed to tell off a bridegroom who is kissing his bride to whom he is not (in the Gratian view) perfectly married (since there has not yet been *carnalis copula*). The bridegroom stands up for himself: *inciviliter loqueris Augustine*, 'you're talking nonsense; for she is my wife, having become so by *traditio*, and the first kiss is as legitimate as the last'.[42]

Vacarius' attitude to canon law remained that of a liberal civil law glossator in the Bologna of the 1140s. Canon law was the *lex divina*; and, in the day-to-day work of ecclesiastical administration, in which Vacarius was increasingly immersed throughout his career, it was also the law of the land, whereas the civil law had no such status. The dictates of canon law were binding. At the same time, viewed as a body of knowledge it did not amount to much. It was unscientific, it lacked precisely those qualities of reason and equity which, as he urged on readers of the *Liber Pauperum*, characterised the civil law. Furthermore, as Dr J. Sayers has shown,[43] in practice it was procedure that mattered rather than law. A very high proportion of cases were compromised or settled by agreement between the parties at some stage in the action. This was mainly because of the difficulties of enforcing a verdict, which had been obtained by fighting the action to the bitter end. But to get the other party to the negotiating table required a skilled use of many procedural devices, and, in developing its own procedure in the

---

[41] sec. 16; Maitland, 'Magistri Vacarii', pp. 140, 276; cf. 'ius ecclesiasticum, quod cotidie cum ipso humano genere labitur et defluit, maxime circa ea que sunt moris et consuetudinis' (*ibid.* Maitland, p. 277).

[42] sec. 21; Maitland, 'Magistri Vacarii', pp. 136, 280.

[43] J. Sayers, *Papal Judges Delegate in the Province of Canterbury 1198–1254* (Oxford, 1971).

twelfth century, canon law borrowed freely from the *Corpus Juris*. So the successful practitioner really needed a knowledge of both systems.

Thus Vacarius could genuinely respect the dictates of canon law, while feeling contempt for those who specialised in its academic study. Ignoring the superior methods of the civil law, they were choosing second-best, and he scorned them. A gloss in the Caius MS, dealing with the question whether an abbot could leave his place without episcopal permission, notes after Gratian's view: 'hanc solutionem Gratiani deridet Vacarius'.[44]

V

Not only in his canon law works, but also in his theological tracts, Vacarius applied the arguments and concepts of the civil law to alien material and derided arguments that did not fit in with his civil law notions. In the treatise *De assumpto homine*[45] he applies civil law ideas of possession to delicate problems of christology and cites contrary views with phrases like *nonne itaque ridiculum est?*[46]

The use of civil law arguments in theology was not, of course, unique to Vacarius. His contemporary, Peter of Blois, a pupil of John of Salisbury and member of the Canterbury salon, also adopted legal reasoning to elucidate theological ideas.[47] But Vacarius seems to do so with the confident superiority of the missionary who knows that his doctrine is the true one and all others are defective. For him the arguments of the civil law had a value transcending the proper matter of Justinian's corpus. They were part of the grammar of educated discourse on any learned subject. Vacarius taught that one was bound by the text of one's authorities, whether in law or in theology. But in cases of doubt one had to interpret these authorities according to *ratio*. This means both logical reasoning in general and, more specifically, the identification of the underlying purpose of the provision in question and its use as a criterion of interpreting that provision. 'In tanta itaque

---

[44] MS 676/283, fo. 142vb.

[45] N. M. Haring, 'The Tractatus de Assumpto Homine by Magister Vacarius', *Mediaeval Studies*, XXI (Toronto, 1959), 147–75.

[46] sec. 31; cf. J. de Ghellinck, 'Magister Vacarius: un juriste théologien peu aimable pour les canonistes', *Revue d'histoire ecclésiastique*, XLIV (1949), 176.

[47] *Dictionnaire de Théologie Catholique*, XII, cols. 1884ff.; Paradisi, *Storia del diritto* (see n. 36), IV.2, 19.

dubietate et contrarietate stemus simul, cerciorem vigilantem sequendo rationem'.[48]

This idea that any rational speculation could be conducted in civil law terms no doubt accounts for the great appeal of the civil law in England towards the end of the twelfth century, and the fashionable status of the *pauperistae* among the intellectual *avant-garde*. The arrogance with which they put forward their claims doubtless too explains the considerable unpopularity which they aroused among the defenders of traditional disciplines.[49]

In the sphere of law, however, Vacarius' ideas had lasting influence. His legacy was not in particular legal doctrines; rather it was the conception of the civil law as a universal jurisprudence, whose ideas underlay all systems of law. Canon law or English common law might carry more specific authority than the civil law in the decision of particular cases, but their fundamental principles and structure were to be moulded by those of the civil law. Vacarius contributed to the creation of a climate of opinion in which it was natural for canonists to call on the civil law to eke out any gaps in their own law, and Anglo-Norman canonists do seem to have made more use of the civil law than others. Similarly the Vacarian approach to law forced the common lawyers to give their customary law some structure and to organise it in a coherent way.

The main evidence for this is the work of Glanvill, written probably between 1187 and 1189,[50] the avowed purpose of which was to show that English laws, though unwritten, were just as valid, as much law, as the *lex scripta* of the civil lawyers. Glanvill's debt to contemporary legal theory, as propagated by the Vacarian school, is his dialectical method of treatment: the division of pleas into civil and criminal; of each category into King's pleas and sheriff's pleas; of royal civil pleas into those dealing with property and those dealing with possession and so on. The extent of the change brought in English legal thinking can be gauged by comparing Glanvill with the *Leis Willelme*, a work of the earlier part of the twelfth century, the only pre-Glanvillian compilation which makes any appreciable use of Roman materials.[51] The compiler of the earlier work incorporated some Roman maxims

---

[48] *Liber contra multiplices et varios errores*, ed. Ilarino da Milano, 1.3.3, p. 486. Studi e Testi, cxv (Rome, 1945), p. 486.

[49] H. Kantorowicz and B. Smalley, 'An English theologian's view of Roman Law', *Mediaeval and Renaissance Studies*, I (1943), 237ff.; E. Rathbone, 'Roman Law in the Anglo-Norman Realm', *Studia Gratiana*, xi (1967), 256.

[50] *Glanvill*, ed. G. D. G. Hall (Nelson's Medieval Texts, 1965), pp. xiff.

[51] J. Barton, 'Roman Law in England', *Ius Romanum Medii Aevi*, v. 13a (Milan, 1971), 7ff.

but he did not use the civil law in the integrative way that Glanvill did. Glanvill's success in doing what the compiler of the *Leis Willelme* failed to do is due, it is suggested, to the influence of the Vacarian school.

The conception of the function of the civil law, which Vacarius planted in English legal thought, acquired deep roots. Even in the sixteenth century, when Henry VIII abolished the teaching of canon law in the universities, it did not seem so odd that the qualification for practice in the English canon law courts should henceforth be a Doctorate of Civil Law!

WILLIAM FITZSTEPHEN AND HIS
LIFE OF ARCHBISHOP THOMAS

by MARY CHENEY

IN essays arising from his edition of the Life of St Thomas by Guernes of Pont-Sainte-Maxence, Professor Emil Walberg discussed the problem of the dating and interrelationships of the early Lives of the archbishop.[1] The present essay, which owes much to him and to the work of others,[2] attempts to evaluate in greater detail some of the evidence contained in the Life by William FitzStephen.[3] It may serve to bring into sharper focus the interest and the problems connected with this largely original Life and its author, who has been called 'the best and most satisfying' of all Thomas's biographers.[4]

Of FitzStephen, like Guernes and William of Canterbury, we know for certain only what he reveals in his work. He was a clerk, at least in sub-deacon's orders. In his preface he says that he had been in Thomas's service, accompanied him to the Council of Northampton and witnessed his death; and his statement can be accepted. His account of the council is accurate in its chronology and precise about the issues at stake; his moving account of the archbishop's last days is full of touches showing exact knowledge of Canterbury and of the men who were in one way or another involved in his death. And yet Fitz-Stephen stands apart from the rest of the biographers. The other early

---

[1] E. Walberg, *La tradition hagiographique de S. Thomas Becket* (Paris, 1929), especially pp. 74–134.

[2] Professor C. N. L. Brooke generously made available to me his then unpublished work on the manuscripts of FitzStephen's Life, for which see now C. N. L. Brooke, *Time the archsatirist* (London, 1968), and Brooke and G. Keir, *London, 800–1216* (London, 1975), pp. 88, 107–21. I have also relied heavily on the edition of Gilbert Foliot's letters prepared by Professor Brooke and Dom Adrian Morey (see n. 23). In addition I have benefited from consulting parts of Dr Anne Duggan's important thesis on the letter collections relating to the Becket dispute (see n. 29). Sir Roger Mynors and Miss Penelope Morgan gave me help in connection with Hereford Cathedral MS O IV 14, and Dr William Urry gave information confirming FitzStephen's precise knowledge of Canterbury places and Canterbury people.

[3] William FitzStephen's Life is printed, along with that of Herbert of Bosham, in M[*aterials for the history of*] T[*homas*] B[*ecket*], vol. III, ed. J. C. Robertson, RS (1877). The page references in the text of this essay refer to this edition. It is also printed in Migne, *PL*. CXC, 103–92 from the edition by J. A. Giles, in *Vita Sancti Thomae...*, I (London and Oxford, 1845), pp. 213–38.

[4] G. W. Greenaway, *The life and death of Thomas Becket* (London, 1961), p. 28.

Lives of the archbishop belong to what may loosely be called a Canterbury group, and there are many complex links between them, as Walberg showed. William FitzStephen did not belong to this group. They used the archives of the archbishop; he drew, as we shall see, on those of the bishop of London. They borrowed freely from each other's work; FitzStephen, though he probably ended his work a little later than most of them, relies almost entirely on his memory and his documents. It has been stated that Guernes met FitzStephen at Canterbury,[5] but this seems to be a slip. Guernes did indeed visit Canterbury and talk to eye-witnesses, but he does not mention William by name, or incorporate any of William's vivid anecdotes, into his own work.[6]

William names himself in his preface, calling himself the archbishop's fellow citizen, clerk, and *convictor*. At once he draws attention to the fact that he, like Thomas, was a Londoner. Justifying himself with classical precedents, he began his work with a description of the city, written in his most elaborate style and freely sprinkled with quotations from the Latin classics. He records London's ancient archbishopric, and the prophecy that it might be revived, and claims for London a share in the saint's reflected glory; such thoughts would have been anathema to the Canterbury writers. He was probably living in London, not necessarily continuously, during Thomas's exile and after his death, for he provides information about events which took place in or near the city, and which are not mentioned by other writers. He shows considerable knowledge of the doings of Gilbert Foliot, bishop of London, describes in detail events connected with his excommunication (pp. 85–92), and names the man, Robert Huscarl, appointed by Gilbert to take charge of the benefices of the archbishop's exiled clerks and relatives (p. 82). These were matters that would naturally interest a former clerk of the archbishop, now living in Gilbert's cathedral city. FitzStephen or his work may have been in London when Ralph de Diceto, dean of St Paul's, was writing his *Ymagines Historiarum*; Stubbs noted that Ralph's account of Thomas's death has 'some verbal resemblances with that of FitzStephen... but not so many as to make it probable that he used the work of that writer'.[7] Whether Ralph's

[5] R. Foreville, *L'église et la royauté en Angleterre sous Henri II Plantagenet* (Paris, 1943), p. xxxi.

[6] Walberg examined every Life for evidence of use by, or of, Guernes. He concluded that the resemblances between Guernes and FitzStephen were too slight to prove use of the one by the other.

[7] *Radulfi de Diceto Opera Historica*, ed. William Stubbs, RS (1876), II, 342, and compare pp. xli–xliii.

information was verbal or written, the connection is another link between FitzStephen and London, possibly with St Paul's cathedral. Yet another is provided by FitzStephen's account of a vision, not recorded elsewhere, seen by Master Radolphus, canon of the church of London, 'in sacra pagina doctor precipuus' (p. 143), perhaps the elusive Radulphus Theologus, who may have held the prebend of Finsbury.[8]

William does more than call himself Thomas's clerk. 'I was', he says, 'a draughtsman in his chancery...when he sat to hear lawsuits I read the letters and documents that were produced, and sometimes at his command I acted as advocate (*patronus*) in certain cases' (p. 1). He could draw up the deeds required in the archbishop's chancery, and he was more than a draughtsman. He attended legal proceedings before him, reading documents in court as Thomas, when chancellor, had done before the king, and he was sufficiently learned to act as advocate if required. FitzStephen must have been one of those whom Herbert of Bosham called 'the crowd of men whom the archbishop always had with him to deal with litigation', inferior people, he implies, who were relegated to a lower table, and whose work was practical rather than theoretical (p. 207).

FitzStephen's interest in legal matters is revealed on many occasions. Only a few illustrations can be mentioned here. He alone names the cities where Thomas studied law (p. 17). He alone records the case of the dean of Scarborough, who was tried at York in about January 1158[9] on charges of extortion and of infringing a royal *lex prohibitionis* (pp. 44–5). He alone suggests that John Marshal's claim to part of the archbishop's manor of Pagham might have succeeded under more recent legislation; John, he says, had no claim in law as the law then stood, 'quod tunc lex erat' (p. 50). Significantly, FitzStephen does not defend Thomas for his failure to appear in person when John complained to the king of defect of justice, and he uses the technical term for this non-appearance, 'quam supersisam regis dicunt' (p. 62). He alone describes Thomas's formal submission to the verdict of the king's court, 'adacta...solemni in manum ipsius missione, quasi concessionis iudicii, ut moris est ibi' (p. 53). He alone describes some of the proceedings at Northampton in terms of Roman law. On the

---

[8] John le Neve, *Fasti Ecclesiae Anglicanae 1066–1300*, I, *St Paul's London*, compiled by Diana E. Greenway (1968), p. 49.

[9] King Henry was probably at York in January 1158. The year is fixed by a reference to the death of his brother Geoffrey, which took place in July 1158.

third day, he says, Thomas was summoned *certi condictione*[10] and *actione tutele*, that is, for debt and to account for his custody of vacant bishoprics and abbeys (p. 54). He quotes Hilary, bishop of Chichester, as speaking of Thomas as 'reum repetundarum' (p. 55), and on another occasion refers to the Roman law origin of appeal procedure (p. 94). After summarising the Constitutions of Clarendon, 'those spurious statutes' which 'openly conflict with the sacred constitutions of the canons', FitzStephen makes a brief attack on the king's appeal to custom, quoting several apposite texts from Gratian and contrasting the action of the Christian king with the words of the *imperator paganus* on this subject, with a paraphrase of Code 8.52 (p. 47). He was even prepared to quote canon law against Herbert of Bosham. In the final stage of the Council of Northampton, when the archbishop went in fear for his life, Herbert recommended that he should promptly excommunicate any attacker. FitzStephen opposed this advice as contrary to the *decreta*, and inserted into the Life authorities to support his opinion (p. 58).

Interest in royal finance and administration is also occasionally revealed in FitzStephen's work. He accuses Robert Huscarl, who took charge of the benefices of the exiled clergy, of farming the benefices for low pensions and then taking payments on the side for himself, thus defrauding the royal 'fisc' (p. 28). At the dramatic conclusion of his work, he pauses before plunging into a rhetorical lament for the archbishop's death to observe that the murderers, in stealing his treasures, were robbing the king, 'to whom, if not to the church, should belong the goods of an archbishop dying intestate' (p. 144). He has something to say about the Exchequer 'where the pleas of the king's crown are heard' (p. 51), and, unlike Thomas's other biographers, he does not content himself with general statements about his power and influence as chancellor. He also gives a short account of the rights and duties of the office and discusses the use and control of the king's seal (p. 18).

This interest and this information probably came from his own experience. Several passages in the Life suggest that he was in the royal service when Thomas was chancellor. One of these is his detailed account, mentioned already, of proceedings in the king's presence at York in about January 1158. Another is the detailed account of the chancellor's embassy to France in the same year. He could record the

[10] See MTB IV, xxvii, correcting III, 53.

name of an enemy whom Thomas captured on his way home and how much he paid his knights in the border warfare between the kings of France and England (pp. 29–33). In July 1160, when the two kings met to decide between the rival popes, FitzStephen may have been present at Neufmarché in the train of Thomas the chancellor.[11] He tells a long story designed to show how 'the good chancellor' helped prelates who had incurred King Henry's anger by recognising Pope Alexander before he had given his approval, how Thomas deflected the proposed punishment in one case and in another delayed the bearers of royal writs till they could be overtaken by others with contrary orders (pp. 27–8). It was an episode calculated to appeal to administrators.

FitzStephen records that Thomas the chancellor employed fifty-two clerks on his own and the king's business. His narrative suggests that in the period *c.* January 1158 to late July 1160 he was himself one of these, an employee of the royal government in the same sort of position as Gervase of Chichester, whom the king describes in a charter as 'the chancellor's clerk and mine'.[12] Probably he only transferred definitely to the archbishop's service when Thomas resigned the office of chancellor. William was the only one of Thomas's biographers who had seen him regularly at work in his secular employment over a period of some years; his remarks on Thomas's character and actions as chancellor deserve special attention.

Unlike many others, FitzStephen stood by the archbishop to the end at Northampton. But after Thomas's flight, perhaps soon after and certainly before March 1166, he came to the king at Brill[13] and obtained his goodwill by presenting Henry with a long rhyming prayer composed specially for him (pp. 78–81). Did reconciliation with the king mean a return to royal service? That he was occasionally with the court in France is suggested by his vivid accounts, rather out of scale with the rest of the book, of episodes which took place there and are not recorded elsewhere. In May 1166 three of the archbishop's senior clerks came to the king at Angers seeking restoration of their benefices. FitzStephen can record what Henry said before Herbert of Bosham entered and remarks on the colour and style of Herbert's cloak (pp. 98–9). Similarly, long accounts are given of two occasions when

---

[11] For the date see *EHR*, LXXXIV (1969), 474–97.

[12] *Chronicles of the reigns of Stephen, Henry II and Richard I*, vol. IV, ed. Richard Howlett, RS (1889), p. 364 no. 4.

[13] King Henry was out of England from March 1166 for over four years. He was near, though apparently not recorded at, Brill several times between October 1164 and March 1166.

Roger, bishop of Worcester, brushed with the king, the first time in the later part of 1169, the second in July 1170 (pp. 86-7, 103-6). Again, he seems to have inside information; he can report advice given to the king after the bishop's departure. He was certainly in France once during this period. In his account of the Council of Northampton, he remarks that Thomas himself recalled a particular incident, at a meeting at Saint-Benoît-sur-Loire between FitzStephen, 'on his way to the Lord Pope', and the archbishop (p. 59). A likely date for this meeting would be in the summer or early autumn of 1170. Saint-Benoît lies on the route between Thomas's refuge at Sens and the region of Tours, in which peace was patched up at Fréteval on 22 July, followed by other meetings at Tours and Amboise. Possibly he was present at Fréteval and took the first steps towards returning to Thomas's service as soon as Thomas was reconciled to the king.

There is no clue in his narrative to show when he actually rejoined the archbishop. Was he the oddly described 'clerk of London origin' who went with the prior of Dover and the abbot of St Albans to carry the archbishop's complaints to the court of the Young King? This clerk delivered the sting in the tail of the mission, a short, sharp threat by Thomas that he would 'do his duty' if satisfaction was not given.[14] FitzStephen himself does not mention this detail. There can be no doubt that he witnessed the murder in the cathedral. His account is vivid and detailed, and occasionally drops into the first person. He clearly regarded himself as one of the archbishop's household, referring to his servants as 'our men' (p. 137). After Thomas's burial, he does not figure again in his story. He picked up afterwards information about happenings at court just before and after the murder; this cannot have been available to him when he was with Thomas at Canterbury. He knows which of the king's clerks wrote a particular letter (p. 114), what complaints were made against the archbishop, which noblemen spoke against him, and just how various senior royal officials were deployed at the time of his death (pp. 128-9).

FitzStephen ended his Life with Thomas's death and early miracles, rounded off with an elegant and pious conclusion and a prayer to the martyr. He assumes Thomas's sanctity, without a word of the bulls of canonisation of February 1173, but is careful to record visions in which that sanctity was promptly revealed (p. 151). Thereafter, William Fitz-Stephen, the archbishop's clerk and lawyer, disappears from sight. He

---

[14] MTB I, 114-18.

might have been expected to look for employment with another English prelate, but he has not been observed as a witness to episcopal charters.

It has been suggested that he found work of a different character. At Michaelmas 1172 a William FitzStephen accounted at the Exchequer on behalf of Ralph FitzStephen his brother, sheriff of Gloucestershire. Ralph had long been a prominent official, and in that year he took over the county,[15] possibly replacing a sheriff dismissed as a result of the Inquest of Sheriffs. William continued to account for his brother till 1176, when he himself accounts as sheriff; he remained in that office till the end of the reign. He acted as justice itinerant in 1176 and afterwards. A debt arising from his period of office was cleared in 1198;[16] another runs on till 1203, when his heirs were cleared of liability.[17] There is nothing to show that this William was a clerk, and no proof that he was not, for a clerk can have heirs, and though Albr(eda) formerly wife of William FitzStephen appears in 1198[18] (she had already appeared in the lost Pipe Roll of 1196), she appears under Yorkshire, and there is no evidence to link the ex-sheriff with her or with that county.

As long ago as 1848, Edward Foss suggested that the justice and the biographer might be one and the same man.[19] His suggestion was accepted by Robertson, who saw in FitzStephen's service to the king a reason for resentment by the archbishop's other followers and an explanation of their silence about him (p. xv). It was also accepted by Dr Greenaway,[20] but T. F. Tout had already rejected it, saying that the biographer was a chancery clerk, and was 'most unlikely to have blossomed into a sheriff'.[21] Sheriffs were indeed in this period often men of baronial families, but precisely after the Inquest of Sheriffs of 1170 a number of such men were dismissed, and replaced by household officers of the king. Elsewhere Tout himself drew attention to 'the sending to the Exchequer of the chancellor, and of clerks working under him, to discharge its secretarial duties'.[22] Because of this practice, the biographer, as clerk to Thomas the chancellor, might have had experience of the methods of the Exchequer. His appearance on the

---

[15] P[ipe] R[oll] 18 Henry II (1171–2), p. 118. The Pipe Rolls will be referred to as printed in the Publications of the Pipe Roll Society.

[16] PR 10 Richard I (1197–8), p. 178.   [17] PR 5 John (1202–3), p. 73.

[18] PR 10 Richard I (1197–8), p. 37. Compare *Early Yorkshire Charters*, ed. William Farrer, III (1916), pp. 90, 92, where a Stephen, and William his son, appear among the knights.

[19] Edward Foss, *The Judges of England* (London, 1848), I, 371–3.

[20] Greenaway, *Thomas Becket*, p. 30.

[21] T. F. Tout, *Chapters in Administrative History* (Manchester, 1937), I, 111, n. 8.

[22] *Ibid.*, I, 138.

other side of the table, presenting accounts for a sheriff, need not have been a sharp break with his past. He was no mere scribe, but a lawyer capable of acting as an advocate, and if the identification is accepted, he had a brother well placed to help him to high office. The timing of William FitzStephen's appearance as his brother's assistant may be significant, for the biographer was out of a job after the death of his employer in December 1170, and the sheriff's assistant perhaps began work at Michaelmas 1171.

A further shred of evidence may have some bearing on the matter. FitzStephen the biographer used a collection of documents relating to Archbishop Thomas, and this collection is itself copied after his Life in Bodleian Library MS Douce 287, which will be discussed later. Every document in the collection is clearly concerned with some aspect of Thomas's dispute with the king, except one. This is a text of the questions put to the jurors in the Inquest of Sheriffs,[23] which was set in motion in April 1170. Why was this one extraneous text included in a group possibly assembled as a preliminary to the writing of the Life? William FitzStephen the future sheriff was already working for his brother when the collection was made, and he might well have been interested in that Inquest. If FitzStephen the biographer was indeed the same man, this piece of the puzzle would fall into place. And yet the identification is still not positively proved. William was a very common name; two hundred Williams are said to have dined on one occasion with the Young King. And Stephen, though much less common, was not rare. A William FitzStephen was a constable of William, earl of Gloucester,[24] another is recorded in Bedfordshire,[25] and another, as we have seen, in Yorkshire. It cannot be proved that the sheriff was a clerk and clerical sheriffs were uncommon, though by no means unknown, in this period. Nor can any particular links be observed between the sheriff and the city of London; on the contrary, a connection with Devonshire is revealed from first to last by the entries in the Pipe Rolls, the first of which occurs in 1168–9.[26]

If we accept the identification, we must accept that this clerical sheriff had composed a Life of Thomas which shows knowledge of many rhetorical tricks of the writer's trade and some acquaintance with

---

[23] The text is printed from this MS and from Bodleian Library MS E Musaeo 249 (the main MS of Foliot's letters) in *The Letters and Charters of Gilbert Foliot*, ed. A. Morey and C. N. L. Brooke (Cambridge, 1967), p. 523.

[24] *Earldom of Gloucester Charters*, ed. Robert B. Patterson (Oxford, 1973), pp. 88, 116, 152, 163.

[25] PR 9 Richard I (1196–7), p. 203.   [26] PR 15 Henry II (1168–9), p. 54.

the Latin classics, as well as knowledge of canon, and at least a smattering of Roman, law. We must accept that he could hold high secular office while expressing (though not necessarily publishing) most subversive opinions about the issues disputed between the king and the archbishop. It must also be accepted that the brother of a prominent royal official stood beside Thomas at his death, exercising no authority and unpunished for his association with the king's enemy. If this spectacle is rejected as unacceptable, it must be assumed that Fitz-Stephen the biographer lived till at least October 1174, which is the latest date that can be identified in his work, and died without achieving eminence or notoriety.

Before discussing the date at which FitzStephen wrote, it is essential to take note of the surviving manuscripts of his work. A definitive study of their relationships would require full collation, which has not been attempted, and longer discussion than is possible here, but some preliminary observations can be hazarded. Setting aside composite Lives which make use of his work, there are five texts, two of which have suffered large losses. They seem to indicate the existence of an early version and various closely related revisions. The latest manuscript may present the earliest text. They are:

L BL MS Lansdowne 398, fos. 1–42v, xv century, provenance unknown. Two groups of quires are missing, with almost half the text (pp. 55–97, 129–54).

D Oxford, Bodleian Library, MS Douce 287, fos. 1–36v, late xii or early xiii century, from Lessness Abbey, Kent. One or two folios are lost at the beginning (pp. 1–5). Followed by verses on the martyrdom, John of Salisbury's Life, the *Summa cause inter regem et archiepiscopum* (MTB iv, 201–5), a collection of documents relating to the archbishop, and extracts from Henry of Huntingdon's *Historia Anglorum*.[27]

H Hereford Cathedral MS O iv 14, fos. 199r–223r, xiv century, not used by J. C. Robertson in his edition. Bound with a *Legenda Aurea* in a different hand, which was perhaps written for Thomas Cobham, bishop of Worcester, 1317–27, whose coat of arms has been identified in the decoration of fo. 1r by Miss Penelope Morgan of Hereford. The Life is followed by an account of Henry II's penance at Canterbury in 1174, a letter reporting the terms of settlement at Avranches in 1172 (MTB vii, 520), and a version of the account of Thomas from the *Legenda Aurea*. The volume was given to the cathedral library in the fifteenth century.

A London, Lambeth Palace Library, MS 138, fos. 205r–12v, early xiii century, bound with miscellaneous MSS, one of which has the *ex libris* of Lanthony Secunda, Gloucestershire. Only the first third of the Life survives (to p. 52 *approbata*).

[27] *Letters of Foliot*, pp. 14–16, and Table B, pp. xxxviii–xlviii.

J   BL MS Cotton Julius A xi, fos. 115r–52v, late xii or early xiii century, once owned by the Franciscan convent of Hereford. One folio is lost (pp. 144–6).

Let us consider these texts in a little more detail. L is a late, business-like, unrevealing text. It contains the description of London and, so far as its losses allow comparison, the passages apparently presenting eye-witness accounts of events described only by FitzStephen. It does not contain the passages demonstrably taken from other sources, which appear, as will be seen, in H, A and J.

D is an untidy little manuscript, the only one not written in a good book hand. It shows many signs of being made by a careless scribe from an untidy exemplar. One passage is meaningless (p. 28 n. 1), one on folio 5vb was cancelled at once and replaced by a different arrangement (p. 26 n. 7). On folio 21va there are three small blank spaces, as though the exemplar was illegible (compare p. 89 n. 3). One of FitzStephen's anecdotes breaks off abruptly a third of the way through; possibly the scribe failed to notice where a deletion was supposed to begin, for the whole is omitted by J (p. 104 n. 4). The scribe also failed to observe that he was intended to insert certain documents into the Life; instead he slavishly copied words such as *in hunc modum* and carried straight on, returning later to copy the documents on odd bits of parchment which were bound in with the book. Symbols showed where the documents were to go in the text; some are so obscurely placed that Canon Robertson missed one document[28] altogether (p. 92 just before n. 3). It appears in its proper place in H.

The documents were clearly not in position in D's exemplar, but there will have been some reference to them, perhaps only the incipit (p. 81). They were to be found in a collection of documents used as source material, and this collection was itself copied at the end of Douce 287. In transcribing it, D's scribe saved himself trouble by omitting the text of the documents that were to go into the Life, but he copied their protocols (as Dr Anne Duggan observed),[29] thus making it clear that this was indeed the source from which they were taken. The editors of Gilbert Foliot's letters have demonstrated that the collection derived from Gilbert's archives and that the texts in

[28] MTB vi, 560, no. 489, Archbishop Thomas to William, bishop of Norwich, *Seipsum ad penam*.

[29] A. J. Duggan, 'The manuscript transmission of the letter collections relating to the Becket dispute, and their use as contemporary sources', unpublished Ph.D. thesis, University of London, 1971, p. 204–5.

Douce 287 were copied from an existing collection, not from the originals. The last and latest items in the collection are papal letters of 27 February and 30 March 1172, concerning the restoration to office of Gilbert himself and Jocelin, bishop of Salisbury.[30] There is no copy of the bulls announcing Thomas's canonisation, though these came into Gilbert's possession in due course. Probably the collection was extracted from his archives between about April 1172 and about April 1173, by which time the bulls of canonisation must have arrived; possibly it was extracted by or for FitzStephen as a preliminary to the composition of the Life. Certainly he made extensive use of his documents for the period of the archbishop's exile. Dr Anne Duggan observes that 'in addition to the seven letters inserted into the Life, thirty further letters can be identified either from direct citation or quotation, indicating the degree to which FitzStephen relied on epistolary evidence'.[31]

D, then, is a text of the Life, accompanied by the author's collection of documents, which does not appear in any of the other manuscripts. D, like L, contained the description of London and FitzStephen's characteristic anecdotes, except for the missing part of one of them. There are, however, some differences which can best be explained as revisions made after the copying of L's ancestor (e.g. pp. 15 n. 4, 21 n. 6, 25 n. 4, 27 n. 3) and an occasional serious change, such as the addition of a phrase suggesting, against all the other evidence, that the bishops sealed the Constitutions of Clarendon (p. 48 n. 9). One paragraph breaks the flow of the narrative (p. 83) and is almost certainly an insertion, though since L is defective at this point its reading cannot be checked. The paragraph does not appear in any other text of the Life; it could have been added at the time when D was copied. This and a number of other passages, longer and more frequent at the beginning of the Life than at the end, have a fine vertical stroke through them. These strokes were not made by D's scribe, who used a broader pen, browner ink, and made his deletions horizontally. They correspond occasionally, but by no means regularly, to passages omitted in H, A and J. They were perhaps marked by someone preparing a short version or a composite Life, or even by a post-Reformation user. D presents many puzzles, but it seems certain that it was made directly from a draft after the fair copy, from which L is descended, had been made and removed. The draft may have contained revision by the author, but

---

[30] MTB VII, 506, JL 12143; MTB VII, 509, JL 11890.
[31] Duggan, 'The manuscript transmission', p. 239.

some of the differences which appear in D can hardly be due to FitzStephen or to anyone who witnessed the events of the 1160s.

H, in spite of the contrary assertion of A. T. Bannister,[32] is a version of FitzStephen's Life, but it is considerably altered. It omits the preface, the description of London, and a vision of Thomas's mother, beginning like A and J with the tell-tale words 'Igitur beatus Thomas' (p. 14 n. 3). Like them it includes a long passage from the *Summa cause* describing the Council of Westminster, though unlike them it begins at the beginning, while they omit a few lines with the date (p. 44 n. 1). Like them, it inserts three passages lifted from John of Salisbury's Life (pp. 38 n. 3, 42 n. 5, 71 n. 4). Like them it omits the whole of one of FitzStephen's anecdotes and some neighbouring material (pp. 26–33), and again like J (A is missing here) it alters and curtails the end of the Life (p. 154 n. 1). There are other resemblances; enough has been said to show that the text presented by L and D has undergone many changes in H, which are among those found in A and J. But H does not go all the way with A or with J. It includes three long passages which J omits (pp. 85–9, 98–101, 78 n. 2), and where J omits the whole of an anecdote, H makes the same irrational cut as D (p. 104 n. 4). But H can hardly be derived from D, for on folio 21ra it provides the words which fill two of the blank spaces in D, and it includes a passage omitted by D but required by the sense of the surrounding material (p. 153 n. 9). It also agrees verbally now and then with L against D (e.g. p. 18 n. 1 and n.7). He could, however, derive from D's untidy, corrected exemplar, which was clearly misleading at the point where both D and H go astray. H was written perhaps a century after A and J, but includes passages which they omit; all three must therefore derive, at various possible removes, from a common ancestor produced at latest in the early thirteenth century, when A and J were copied. It seems possible that this common ancestor was actually D's exemplar, in which passages will have been marked for deletion, but remained legible, thus allowing the maker of H (or a predecessor of H) to retain some of them. Symbols would have indicated points where insertions had to be made from the *Summa cause* and John of Salisbury's Life in the same volume, thus allowing the maker of H to copy a longer extract from the *Summa* than A and J. On the basis of this evidence, it seems permissible to speak of a first version of FitzStephen's Life represented

[32] A. T. Bannister, *Descriptive catalogue of MSS in the Hereford Cathedral Library* (Hereford, 1927), pp. 48–9.

by L and slightly modified in D, and a second version represented by H, A and J, with the reservation that H retains more of the first version than its fellows, and that no two texts are identical.

The passages inserted in the Life by H, A and J are taken from John of Salisbury's Life and the *Summa cause*. These two texts follow Fitz-Stephen's Life in Douce 287, but in this manuscript there are no indications in FitzStephen's Life to show that insertions were to be made at the appropriate points, or any indications in John of Salisbury's Life and the *Summa* to show that passages were to be extracted. This observation reinforces the conclusion already reached on textual grounds in this study and by the editors of Gilbert Foliot's letters, who suggest that Douce 287 'had a source containing the same material, which was also the foundation for the second version'. It seems certain that this lost source holds a key position in the history of FitzStephen's Life; it may well have been the author's final draft. It is not clear when or how John's Life became associated with the other material. If D's scribe was following his copy exactly, it cannot have been before the second half of 1176, for in a rubric on fo. 37rb John is described as *postea Carnotensis episcopus*. The lack of similarity, both in matter and wording, makes it almost inconceivable that FitzStephen had John's Life before him when he was writing his own first version.

The first version had been very much one man's view of Thomas Becket. It included the interesting but hagiographically irrelevant description of London, and it recorded at length events probably observed by the writer, such as the embassy to France, the Council of Northampton, and the archbishop's last days, but it passed very briefly over others. The Council of Westminster of October 1163 was not even mentioned. Two pages sufficed for the Council of Clarendon, against twenty for Northampton. Of the thirty-six pages devoted to the period of Thomas's exile, nearly half are occupied with matters perhaps observed by, or particularly interesting to, the author, including his hymn for the king, which occupies more space than the Council of Clarendon. The account of the archbishop's return and death is shot through with FitzStephen's conviction that the king and his officials never intended a genuine peace and were deeply implicated in his death.

The second version provided a shorter and more conventional picture of the martyr, with less criticism of the king and his circle. It omits passages unconnected with the archbishop's sanctity, such as the description of London, the embassy to France, the stories about Bishop Roger and the account of Foliot's excommunication, which is briefly summarised. On the other hand, it inserts the passages from John of Salisbury, which describe Thomas's pious behaviour, the jealousy of the courtiers and his sufferings, and it fills a gap by inserting the account of the Council of Westminster. Though it cuts the tale of Foliot's excommunication, it is not more friendly to him. Many of Fitz-Stephen's sharp comments remain, on his desire for the archbishopric (p. 36), his refusal to stand surety for Thomas at Northampton (p. 53), his plotting against him (p. 48), and his share, with York and Salisbury, in rousing the king's anger against him before the murder (p. 127). The king fares better; the second version cuts out the passage (already omitted by D) which all but asserts his complicity in the murder (p. 107), another with the same implications (p. 114) and another which recorded the hostility of the royal government to Thomas before his death (p. 128). It also omits a passage (p. 46 n. 4) which reflects doubly on the honour of the Foliots, naming Robert Foliot, 'postea episcopus Herefordensis', as one of those who deserted the archbishop and stating as a matter of fact that Bishop Gilbert was translated to London so that the king could use his advice against Thomas. This last cut could result from the reviser's general policy, for the passage had nothing to do with the archbishop's sanctity. But it could reveal a concern for the reputation of the Foliots. The west country provenance of two, and possibly all three, manuscripts of the second version would support, though it does not prove, a possible connection with Hereford, where Foliot influence was strong in the cathedral at least till the death of Bishop Hugh in 1234.

We have seen that FitzStephen ended his Life with the early miracles, without reference to the bulls of canonisation of February 1173. He says nothing of the settlement between King Henry and the papal legates at Avranches in May 1172, or of the king's penance at Canterbury in July 1174. But early in the Life, he mentions the purgation of prelates who had opposed the archbishop (p. 48). The purgation of Gilbert Foliot immediately preceded his restoration to office on 1 May 1172; if FitzStephen knew of this, he must surely have known of the settlement at Avranches three weeks later, and it must be supposed that he simply did not choose to carry his story on to that point. Similarly, he mentions Geoffrey Ridel and the prior of Dover, without reference to their elections to Ely and Canterbury in April and June 1173. Yet he probably knew of them, for, as we have seen, he refers to Robert Foliot, archdeacon of Oxford in Thomas's time, as 'postea episcopus Herefordensis' (p. 46). Robert was elected at the same time as Geoffrey Ridel and consecrated like him on 6 October 1174. His election was soon contested; it is most unlikely that he would have been called 'bishop' rather than 'elect' before his consecration. Could the description of Robert as bishop of Hereford have been added to FitzStephen's text? This seems unlikely, for the whole passage, in which the description is embedded, occurs only in the two manuscripts of the first version, neither of which is copied from the other. It must have been in their common source, which, as we have seen, was very probably FitzStephen's draft or one of his drafts.

This presumption is supported by one of his comments on Gilbert Foliot's doings during Thomas's exile. The bishop, he says, removed the archbishop's name from his public prayers, but reinstated him when reconciliation was expected, just as he later prayed for 'our kings' when Henry II and his son were at peace, but for 'our king' when they were quarrelling (p. 84). This passage would appear to have been written after the rebellion of the Young King in the spring of 1173, possibly even after his submission in the autumn of 1174. Walberg thought that the bishop might have acted upon rumours of the Young King's discontent, which were probably current by the end of 1172, possibly (if we trust the untrustworthy Giraldus Cambrensis) by May of that year.[33] But this seems a little strained; would the bishop have altered the form of public prayer upon a mere rumour of disaffection?

With this evidence in mind, can it be assumed that FitzStephen ended his work before the summer of 1176, because he fails to mention the translation of William, archbishop of Sens, to Rheims and the election of John of Salisbury to Chartres in July? There is nothing in the Life to suggest that any part of it was written as late as 1176, but it is clear that the argument from silence must be treated with even more than the usual caution in this case.

In his account of miracles worked by the martyr, FitzStephen refers to a great volume recording miracles worked in England and observes that no one had been found to write up those occurring abroad. The great volume corresponds, as Walberg showed, to Books I–III of the collection made by Benedict, to which a fourth book, containing miracles worked abroad, was added in or after 1179. Miracles occurring

---

[33] Walberg, *La tradition*, p. 52 n. 2.

at home and abroad are intermingled in the collection of William of Canterbury, which in its existing form cannot have been completed before *c.* 1184. Walberg suggested that a first edition was completed by the summer of 1174 at latest, and that FitzStephen, who knew only of a book of English miracles, must have written before that date.[34] But even if the hypothetical first edition existed, which is far from certain, FitzStephen would not necessarily have heard of it immediately; it cannot provide reliable evidence for exact dating.

We cannot be certain when FitzStephen began his work. But if he acquired his collection of documents with a view to writing the Life, he may have begun in the second half of 1172. The *Passio* of the martyr could have been the first section to be completed. In that section (from July 1170 onwards) there is no reference to any event after 1171, but the account of the flow of pilgrims, the stamped phials issued to them, and the great book of miracles, suggests a date not before the summer of 1172, and this was the time when it became safe and respectable openly to admire the new saint and clear that his canonisation was only a matter of time. Nothing in the text suggests that the *Passio* was intended to stand alone, but it would not be surprising if his vivid recollection of the murder prompted FitzStephen to write this vital section first. Some support is given to this hypothesis by the fact, which has often been noticed, that the part of the Life dealing with the exile is the least orderly in arrangement and the least elegantly written. Possibly it was written last and lacked the final revision intended by the author.

FitzStephen's use of documents from Gilbert Foliot's archives is a little puzzling in view of his strong criticism of the bishop. He can hardly have written at Gilbert's request, or with his patronage, but as a Londoner he must have had acquaintances among Gilbert's clerks and the cathedral clergy. Ralph de Diceto springs to mind, Ralph the historian, Ralph whose tears at Northampton FitzStephen remembered eight or ten years later, Ralph who perhaps used FitzStephen's Life, or heard from his lips his account of Thomas's death. But there may have been many others in a position to oblige the biographer by obtaining access to documents or making copies.

It does not seem likely that FitzStephen himself made the deletions and additions characteristic of the second version of his Life. He might have chosen to modify his criticism of the king, but would he have abandoned his literary masterpieces, the description of London,

---

[34] *Ibid.*, pp. 55–73.

the rhymed hymn and the accounts of episodes that he had himself observed? Would he have inserted John of Salisbury's conventional talk of foot-washing and almsgiving, and cut out his own tale of Thomas the chancellor at Neufmarché? This tale was designed to refute the charge that as chancellor Thomas had regularly ignored the needs of the clergy. Men who had lived through the bitter disputes of the 1160s would have taken the point; a reviser writing twenty, or possibly forty, years later would have cared little for such matters.

William FitzStephen's Life was not used by Elias of Evesham, the monk of Crowland, who constructed the first explicitly composite Life, the so-called Second Quadrilogus, in the last years of the twelfth century. But the revised, so-called First, Quadrilogus of 1212–13 includes a few passages from FitzStephen, one of which[35] occurs only in the first version, as Dr Anne Duggan has pointed out.[36] Extensive use of FitzStephen is made by the composite Life, apparently based on Elias's and copied in the early thirteenth century, which is preserved in MS Lyell 5 in the Bodleian Library.[37] Significantly, the compiler warns his readers that passages marked 'Willelmus secundus' come from FitzStephen; 'Willelmus' is the monk of Canterbury. The text used was of the second version, but at the end the compiler copied a long passage omitted by H, A and J (p. 26 n. 4 to p. 33 *concessum est*). Possibly he obtained a text of the first version after completing his work; possibly he used the corrected text, and, finding that he had parchment to spare, went back and copied a passage marked for deletion.

These facts suggest that FitzStephen's Life was not widely known at the end of the twelfth century. Probably there was no copy at Canterbury, the centre of the cult of St Thomas,[38] though Ralph de Diceto had perhaps used it in London. The texts of the Life itself support this supposition, revealing as they do possible dependence on a single, much corrected, copy, which became the basis of the second version. It would seem that FitzStephen was rediscovered early in the thirteenth century, with the result that we possess three texts of the Life belonging to that period and two composite Lives of approximately the same

---

[35] MTB IV, 382, n.4.

[36] Duggan, 'The manuscript transmission', p. 250.

[37] *Catalogue of Lyell MSS in the Bodleian Library, Oxford*, A. de la Mare (Oxford, 1971), pp. 5–13.

[38] The monk Gervase, writing at Canterbury in the first decade of the thirteenth century, did not use FitzStephen's Life, or include it among the authorities to which he referred his readers for further information about Archbishop Thomas. (*The Historical Works of Gervase of Canterbury*, ed. William Stubbs, RS (1879, 1880), II, 391, 396. For the date see I, xxvii–xxx.)

date in which extracts appear. A copy of the First Quadrilogus was presented to Archbishop Stephen Langton in 1220, on the occasion of the translation of St Thomas; it may have been by this means that interest was aroused in this hitherto little-known work. The second version may be a result of this new interest, which recognised the value of FitzStephen's information about the martyr, but demanded a shorter and more conventional piece of hagiography than his original Life.

THE MUNIMENTS OF
ELY CATHEDRAL PRIORY

by DOROTHY OWEN[1]

IN writing of the visitation of monastic houses Professor Cheney found that few of the records produced by their administration in the three centuries before the Dissolution had survived to the present, and he was obliged to look elsewhere for much of his material. Only when the endowments of a cathedral monastery were passed on to the dean and chapter of a Henrician foundation, and the muniments of the old monks were required as title deeds and precedents for the new canons, was it likely that any substantial part of a monastic archive would survive the Reformation. Even when such muniments escaped the attentions of the royal visitors other serious hazards threatened them during the following three centuries. Antiquaries were only too ready to buy or steal handsome charters or books; lawyers abstracted or failed to return documents entrusted to them for lawsuits; registrars and lesser officials cut charters into strips to tie up court-rolls and bound their paper books of memoranda in the membranes of medieval accounts. Besides these opportunities for loss, the national upheavals of the mid-seventeenth century left their own deep mark on all ecclesiastical records, and especially on those of the cathedral chapters, and as a result none of the former monastic cathedrals has retained anything approaching a complete medieval archive. In some cases, such as Winchester, relatively little remains, whereas in others, such as Norwich, there is a considerable quantity of material, even after the Commonwealth depredations and the collections made by Thomas Tanner from which the Bodleian Library has benefited.

A number of partial surveys of the muniments of monastic cathedrals was made for the Historical Manuscripts Commission, and Miss Midgley's Pilgrim Trust Survey of Ecclesiastical Archives also included outline reports on all of them. Full and detailed guides are, however,

---

[1] Abbreviations used here indicate Ely Diocesan Records (EDR) and Ely Chapter Records (EDC), both in University Library, Cambridge.

still not readily available. Dr Pantin, in a report on the Durham
muniments made in 1939 but never published, gave tantalising
glimpses of the riches to be found in them. This essay is an attempt,
therefore, to provide comparable information about one monastic
archive which, even though smaller and less rich than that of Durham,
is, nevertheless, very good of its kind. It traces the historical development of the Ely muniments during the later medieval period and, in
doing so, tries to indicate what the modern student may expect to
find among them. A full catalogue will appear in due course, but this
is the historical preface, without which it will not be readily compre-
hensible.

In a classic work Dr Miller has sketched the growth of the pre-
Conquest abbey of Ely.[2] He analysed the three-fold source of its
endowments: King Edgar's original grant at the re-foundation of 970;
the lands purchased for it by Bishop Aethelwold between 970 and 984;
and, finally, the many gifts made to it by representatives of all circles
of the Saxon aristocracy between 984 and 1020. With few exceptions
the evidences of these endowments no longer survive as original documents, and Dr Miller drew his conclusions from the second section of
the *Liber* or *Historia Eliensis*, the record of the abbey's re-foundation
after the Danish devastation which forms the central part of the twelfth-
century chronicle of this name.[3] Dr E. O. Blake, who edited the complete text of this chronicle in 1962, demonstrated very clearly that the
second book is drawn from a twelfth-century compilation, the *Libellus
quorundam insignium operum beati Aethelwoldi*, which survives in two
manuscript versions,[4] is in turn drawn from an Old English narrative
then surviving at Ely, and translated into Latin at Bishop Hervey's
instigation. In this latter form it was known as *Liber de terris sancti
Aethelwoldi*. This narrative, together with records of the litigation
which followed on St Aethelwold's purchases and with a few vernacular charters and wills, formed almost the whole of the abbey's muniments in the late eleventh century, when the establishment of the
bishopric of Ely and the division of the abbey's endowments to support
it was first mooted.[5] Very few of the original documents quoted or
mentioned in this second section of the *Liber* survive and none is at

[2] E. Miller, *The Abbey and Bishopric of Ely* (Cambridge, 1951).
[3] E. O. Blake, *Liber Eliensis*, Camden 3rd ser. XCII (London, 1962), p. xxxiv.
[4] BL MS Cotton Vesp. A XIX, and Trinity College Cambridge MS O 2 4.
[5] Professor D. Whitelock, in her foreword to Blake, pp. ix–x, discusses these in more detail.

Ely; of the survivors, some at least appear to be suspect.[6] There remains at Ely a grant of land at West Wratting made by King Edgar to his servant Aelfhelm in 973. The estate was later bequeathed by Aelfhelm to Ely, and Professor Whitelock has suggested that this charter, with a copy of the will, was sent to Ely while the original will remained at Westminster.[7] But the Wratting charter has no marks of Ely provenance; there is no copy of it and no reference to it in any of the medieval cartularies compiled at Ely, and it seems very probable that it reached Ely only after the confused re-sorting of cathedral muniments which followed the Restoration of 1660.[8] It is conceivable that no muniments concerning Wratting actually came to Ely and that no record would have been kept there except a memorandum in a martyrology or other choir-book: Dr Neil Ker has suggested that fragments of such an Ely book may survive in manuscripts at Cambridge and in the British Library, and, although the entries he quotes may apply equally well to Ramsey abbey, there is no doubt that the practice of enrolment in choir books continued at Ely, as it did elsewhere, as late as the fifteenth century.[9]

Although titles to estates form all the surviving or known muniments of the late-Saxon abbey, there probably were also lists of monks and of obits, lists of plate, books, relics and vestments, and administrative documents connected with the estates. The early eleventh-century *Liber Vitae* of Hyde Abbey contains a list of Ely abbots and monks which seems to have been copied from one kept at Ely.[10] Dr Ker notes the survival of a binding strip taken from a manuscript at Queens' College Cambridge, which formed part of a stock account of the abbey of the early eleventh century.[11] These apart, no other material from the pre-Conquest archives of the house has, as yet, been found.

The story is very different when we turn to the muniments accumulated by the cathedral priory after the establishment of the bishopric in 1109 and the disappearance of the abbacy. The troubled history of the early years of the bishopric and the priory, the main authorities for which are the third book of the *Liber Eliensis* and the *chronicon* preserved in a

[6] P. Sawyer, *Anglo-Saxon Charters*, Royal Historical Society Guide and Handbook (London, 1968), nos. 646, 779. Professor Sawyer is engaged on a detailed study of these charters.

[7] D. Whitelock, *Anglo-Saxon Wills* (Cambridge, 1930), pp. 133–7.

[8] D. M. Owen, 'Bringing Home the Records', *Archives*, VIII (London, 1968), 123–30.

[9] N. R. Ker, *Catalogue of Manuscripts containing Anglo-Saxon* (Oxford, 1957), pp. 35–6.

[10] BL MS Stowe 944.   [11] Ker, *Catalogue* no. 80.

fifteenth-century copy in a manuscript now in Lambeth Palace Library,[12] seems to have caused the monks to examine, arrange, copy, and even manufacture, the charters which formed the basis of their privileges. Dr Blake has demonstrated that the compiler of the third volume of the *Liber* drew much of his material from a collection of Ely privileges which has not itself survived,[13] but which is very close to Trinity College Cambridge MS O 2 41.[14] Two other versions of this collection survive, one, Cotton Tiberius A VI, apparently derived from the Trinity manuscript, the other, a fifteenth-century manuscript, Cotton Titus A I, which Dr Blake believes was copied from the *Liber* itself. These collections were plainly concerned not with the endowments of the house, apart from the question of their division with the bishopric, but with the maintenance of the priory's privileges: they consist only of royal charters to the end of Stephen's reign and of papal bulls, and they ignore all non-royal, pre-Conquest documents, if any remained at Ely, and all contemporary charters. On the other hand, it is no doubt significant that both early versions of the collection include a copy of the *Inquisicio Comitatus Cantabrigiensis*, which must itself have been regarded by the compilers as part of the evidences of the house. The arrangement of the collection of privileges seems to be entirely chronological, and nothing remains to suggest that the originals from which the first version was copied were numbered or filed in any special way. Nor do such originals as survive suggest any particular arrangement. There are no papal bulls, but a few of the other documents survive either at Ely or in the British Library, and none seems to have press-marks or endorsements earlier than the thirteenth century.[15] Critical editions of the papal bulls in the collection have been published by Holtzmann;[16] successive volumes of the *Regesta Regum Anglo-Normannorum*, and the facsimiles published by Mr Bishop and Dr Chaplais have included abstracts and texts of the royal charters to the end of Stephen's reign, and Professor Holt will deal with those of Henry II.[17]

It seems fairly certain that the monks were not at this period concerned with the arrangement and preservation of any of the muniments of their house except those which related to the maintenance of the

---

[12] Lambeth Palace Library MS 448. The *chronicon* was printed by Henry Wharton, *Anglia Sacra* (London, 1691), from this manuscript.
[13] Blake, *Liber Eliensis*, p. xxxiv.
[14] I am grateful to Dr P. Gaskell for the opportunity to examine this manuscript in detail.
[15] See appendix I below, p. 174.   [16] W. Holtzmann, *PUE*, II, 78.
[17] T. A. M. Bishop and P. Chaplais, *Facsimiles of English Royal Writs* (Oxford, 1957).

privileged status of the priory. The few endorsements of the period on surviving charters suggest that they accumulated naturally and in some disorder until the fourteenth century. By contrast, the charters of the bishopric, the originals of which have not survived, were evidently more carefully arranged. An inventory made in the mid-thirteenth century, and now preserved in manuscript Cotton Nero C III, shows that royal, papal, episcopal and private charters had been carefully numbered and arranged, probably in preparation for the survey and cartulary made in 1251 known as the Great Coucher.[18]

The surviving royal and episcopal charters of the priory from the period between 1066 and 1300 bear a letter (A for royal, B for episcopal) followed by a number. These endorsements are written in an early fourteenth-century hand which resembles that used in the greater part of the first full cartulary of the house, which was known to the Ely historian Bentham as *Liber* M, and which is now among the diocesan records.[19] *Liber* M begins as a classified cartulary, which opens with charters of kings, including the Anglo-Saxon documents, popes and bishops, arranged chronologically. The arrangement then becomes topographical, the documents being copied haphazard and without regard for chronology. They are not only title deeds but pleas, letters of institution to benefices and all sorts of administrative records which the copyist found difficult to classify. At the ends of each topographical section blank folios were left, presumably for later entries, and these have been filled, in the later fourteenth and fifteenth centuries, by miscellaneous entries quite unconnected with the rest of the section. The topographical portions of the cartulary record the priory's acquisitions during the century and a half after the accession of Henry II, and most of the documents copied relate to the estates which formed its central endowment. Only at the end (fo. 393) are there sections which late hands have labelled as the titles of special funds acquired for the precentory, refectory, hostelry, Lady altar, chamber, and almonry. The very end of the volume (fos. 597 to 623) is taken up by sections in hands of the later fourteenth century of fines and leases, extracts from rentals, plea rolls and pipe rolls, notes of arbitrations and tithe compositions and a partial table of contents.

Some, but not all, of folios 1 to 596 are numbered in arabics in the hand of the later folios and the table of contents, and there is a significant note:

---

[18] EDR G/3/27.   [19] EDR G/3/28.

Tabula super cartuarium domini prioris.

Nota quod numerus algarismi in margine cartuarii scriptus in capite inter duas columnas cuiuslibet folii ex utraque parte dictorum foliorum supra columnas servit ad istam tabulam que facta est ad cartuarium domini prioris manditorio.

Liber M, then, was the 'prior's cartulary', and a reference to it in a later cartulary of the house shows that it was still so known a century and a half after its compilation: one section there is headed:

Copie quarundam cartarum et evidenciarum cancellarie que sunt in cartuario domini prioris.[20]

It seems likely that whoever was prior when *Liber* M was compiled was responsible for it and perhaps directed it personally. If this is the case it was almost certainly the work of Prior John de Crauden (1321–41) who followed the dilapidator Fressingfield, and in whose day, which Dr Evans has called 'the flowering time of genius at Ely', the priory's finances were re-ordered and many of its finest buildings begun.[21] Since 'Lady altar' rather than 'Lady chapel' is mentioned in the text, the date of compilation must have been early in the priorate, before the start of serious work on the construction of the chapel. It probably formed part of the general 'tightening up' of administration which followed the attempts made by the chapter in 1304 and 1314 to restrict the financial powers of the prior and to require regular accounting from him.[22] Unlike larger and wealthier Benedictine houses, Ely's financial administration seems always to have been highly centralised. In the twelfth century, as Dr Miller has demonstrated, control of most of the house's income was in the hands of a single treasurer, with whom, it is clear, the prior was always able to interfere, and whom, at times, he undoubtedly dominated. Although the fourteenth-century reforms re-affirmed and even increased the principle of centralisation, they also subjected the administration to the scrutiny of auditors annually elected from among the monks.[23] Of the other obedientiaries only the sacrist had any considerable estates in his power, and a prior's cartulary represented the major part of the house's muniments.

It is conceivable that at much the same time the sacrist's muniments were also arranged and even copied. It would be surprising if Alan de Walsingham, the builder of the lantern tower, did not survey and set in

---

[20] Bodleian Library MS Ashmole 801, fo. 139.
[21] S. J. A. Evans, 'Ely Chapter Ordinances and Visitation Records', *Camden Miscellany XVII*, Camden 3rd ser. LXIV (London, 1940), p. ix.
[22] *Ibid.*, pp. 28, 30, 38. [23] *Ibid.*, pp. xii–xiii.

order everything belonging to his office during his long tenure. No trace of a sacrist's cartulary remains, and perhaps none was made, but he undoubtedly recorded copies of material affecting his office.[24] The precentor had a separate store of muniments concerning his endowment, and some of them were sent to London for a lawsuit in 1419.[25] The almoner's deeds were copied twice at short intervals, probably at the same time as *Liber* M, into cartularies, neither of them complete, which still survive. He also had a register of pittances, judging by an entry in the later cartulary ordering the enrolment of an order about a pittance: 'in martilogio capituli et in registro elemosinarii'.[26] At about the same time a fresh copy of the twelfth-century collection of liberties, with some additional material, was made and survives as one portion of Bodleian Library Laudian MS 647. It was evidently also intended to copy further sections either for the prior's cartulary or for a separate register. There is a contemporary mention of a quire *de sectis* in a fragmentary unbound gathering of miscellaneous royal charters, inquests and other memoranda relating to the Suffolk liberty, which a post-Reformation hand has called *Liber Quartus* and which evidently formed another section in the same lost work.[27]

As the fourteenth century passed the priory evidently evolved some system for the control of the muniments themselves. In 1389 some of the royal charters were temporarily entrusted to Bishop Fordham by 'Robertum de Sutton et Petrum de Norwico cancellarios capituli Eliensis',[28] and the fifteenth-century cartulary refers to a twelfth-century lease of the Suffolk liberties as being *in communi cancellario*, so that the chancery, controlled by the chancellors, was evidently the muniment room of the priory. Whether it might at other times be known as the treasury, or whether there was a separate common treasury, is not certain, although a heading *communis thesauraria* in the same cartulary, before a section of letters of fraternity and priory orders, suggests that it had a separate existence as a document store.[29]

Wherever they were kept, muniments of title continued to accumulate during the fourteenth and fifteenth centuries, and the difficulty of referring to them must have forced on the monks some improved

---

[24] He also had a customary bound in red. Lambeth MS 448, cited by D. J. Stewart, *Architectural History of Ely Cathedral* (London, 1868), p. 218.
[25] EDC 1/A/2; BL MS Cotton Vesp. A VI, fos. 90–133.
[26] BL MS Egerton 3047, fo. 119.
[27] EDC 1/A/1.
[28] BL MS Add. 9822, fo. 73.
[29] BL MS Egerton 3047, fo. 242.

method of storage. The occasion was perhaps the visitation of the house by Bishop Gray in 1466, especially if, as is likely, the bishop required the monks to produce proofs of their titles to land and churches.[30] Whatever the occasion, at some date later than 1441 when Henry VI's confirmation charter was obtained, presses or chests (*ciste*) divided into lettered pigeon-holes (*scrinie*), were installed, and the muniments, carefully endorsed with a Roman press number, and a pigeon-hole letter or number, the latter written in full, were stowed away in them. Later an individual arabic number, denoting its order within the pigeon-hole, was added to the press-mark by a different, slightly later hand.[31] Although a relatively small number of the original documents has survived, it is possible, with the help of the late cartulary, to reconstruct the scheme. The first chest contained the royal and episcopal charters, already lettered A and B and numbered. In the second were *scrinie* C to E, which contained documents for Ely itself and the neighbouring parishes in the southern half of the Isle of Ely. The third chest, in *scrinie* F to M, held the charters of estates in Cambridgeshire, Norfolk and the northern Isle, and Suffolk. The fourth chest (N to T) had the title deeds of the cellarer's and hosteller's augmentations, and of the London estates given to the priory by Bishops Hotham and Northwold. Chest five, also lettered X, held the pittancer's muniments, mortmain licences, distraints and leases, while in the sixth chest there were two boxes (*cophine*) each labelled Y and holding Ely deeds, the second of them being also labelled *communis thesauraria*. The surviving documents show that only a number of leases of the late fifteenth century, the muniments of Molycourt and Denney, which were acquired at this late period, and a variety of administrative documents classified in the nineteenth century as 'Priory and convent, numbers 101–192', were excluded from the system.[32]

To improve and simplify the means of reference, a new cartulary, arranged in the same way as the presses, was now undertaken. Since it includes the whole press-mark, including the final number, in its references for each charter, it was plainly written after the two-stage endorsements had been put on to the individual documents. This

[30] Evans, 'Ordinances', pp. ix–x, 57–64.

[31] A photograph of the surviving third chest, which was rediscovered in 1932 by Dr Evans, appears in D. M. Owen, *The Library and Muniments of Ely Cathedral*, Ely Cathedral Monographs (Ely, 1973).

[32] EDC 1/B/1, 15, 16, 17, 19, 28–9.

cartulary, which is now divided into two uneven portions, was perhaps never finished, for the larger portion, in the British Library, has a number of incomplete folios, where only press-marks and rubrics have been written.[33] The arrangement, so far as it can be determined, begins with the late royal charters not included in the prior's cartulary, a few late documents about the priory's privileges, all the episcopal charters and most of the charters in the remaining presses. The Oxford portion contains only the charters in press 4, letters N to S, and press 5, letter X, with copies at the end of additional unmarked documents. The larger section, in the British Library, has all the rest, but in some disorder after the section for press 1. It seems likely that the quires of the cartulary were not at first bound together and they may have remained loose until after the Dissolution. This would explain why the Oxford portion was separated from the rest, and why fos. 138–215, 220–36 (*cista* 3), and 244–54 (part of *cista* 4), in the Egerton manuscript, are not now bound in a logical manner. Other tidying, copying and indexing was going on at the same time as this: the first surviving priory register (now British Library Add. MS 41612) has a table of contents in the hand of the late cartulary and the second register (EDR. G/2/3) begins in the same hand.

Traces of expenditure on the making of muniments can occasionally be found in the obedientiaries' accounts, and it is clear that, wherever the documents were eventually preserved, the officer who administered the estates bore all the charges of drawing them up. There is a good example in the chamberlain's roll for 1408–9. The chamberlain, as owner of the rectory of Hauxton with Newton, had been engaged in a dispute with the vicar and parishioners of Hauxton because they had cut down the trees in the churchyard there without his licence; he had several times gone to Hauxton 'ad colloquium habendum cum vicario ibidem et parochianis'. The matter had gone to arbitration, the parishioners had given way and had submitted in a document prepared in the chamberlain's office: 'Solutum uno notario pro instrumento facto super recognicionem parochianorum ibidem de eorum maleficio 3s. 4d.'[34] The original of this document survives and a copy is entered in the cartulary.

There are various other places in which memoranda that were not directly concerned with the properties, liberties or privileges of the

---

[33] BL Egerton MS 3047 (*Liber L*) and Bodleian Library MS Ashmole 801, fos. 74–143v.
[34] EDC 5/3/27.

priory might well be recorded. As we have seen, and as was well known in other cathedrals both monastic and secular, important matters might be recorded in the *martilogium* of the church. This list of saints and benefactors for whom the monks regularly prayed was in daily use in church or chapter and must often have needed renewal. Fragments of calendars and obit rolls belonging to lists of this type remain from various periods of the priory's existence.[35] Another equally elusive, and equally important, record of the priory's life is the capitular customary where the laudable customs of the house, to which Bishop Walpole referred in his statutes of 1300, had been set down in writing.[36] An Ely customary was evidently kept among the church books for which the precentor was responsible, for in 1373 that officer paid four shillings *pro uno consuetudinario de novo ligando*. A version of the customs, in a late fifteenth-century hand, is one of the many miscellaneous tracts from Ely bound together by the first dean, Robert Steward, after the Dissolution, and now Lambeth Palace Library MS 448. The customs have been extensively quoted from this source by D. J. Stewart; it does not seem possible to determine whether this is a copy of an original record of the customs, which was presumably available in writing as early as Walpole's time, or no more than late extracts and notes.[37]

Decisions made by the chapter affecting the life of the whole community were recorded in a formal way, along with other important acts, appointments, grants of corrodies and documents passing the seal, in volumes which are generally known as registers. The earliest set of such ordinances, those of 1251–4, have only survived in a copy made much later for the bishop; it seems likely that they were never registered formally and survived only as a loose document in a file from which they were later copied for the bishop.[38] It is not clear which of the officers was responsible for the compilation of these registers, and they may well have begun, under the same impetus as the prior's cartulary, under the prior's own guidance. They fall into the class of monastic letter-books discussed by Dr Pantin who described one of them in some detail, and even if not a full record of all the priory's public transactions, they cover many aspects of its life.[39] Three of these

---

[35] Professor Wormald has published the Trinity calendar in *Benedictine Kalendars after 1100*, II, Henry Bradshaw Soc. LXXXI (London, 1946).   [36] Evans, 'Ordinances', p. 8.

[37] D. J. Stewart, *Architectural History*, pp. 217–26, 231–4.

[38] BL Add. MS 9822, fo. 57.

[39] W. A. Pantin, 'English Monastic Letter-books', *Historical Essays presented to James Tait*, ed. J. G. Edwards, V. H. Galbraith and E. F. Jacob (Manchester, 1933).

registers survive. They are the 'Leconfield' manuscript, now British Library Additional MS. 41612, a full analysis of which appeared in the Historical Manuscripts Commission's report on the Leconfield manuscripts;[40] the 'Almack' manuscript, described by Dr Pantin, which was acquired by Bishop Compton from a private owner in the late nineteenth century and is now among the diocesan records;[41] and a smaller paper quire of Prior Walsingham's time, which contains drafts or preparatory matter for the more formal register and which covers the years 1400 to 1410.[42]

The Leconfield manuscript, which was unknown to Bentham, began in the early fourteenth century as an elaborately prepared text, with red initials and rubrics, of a series of late thirteenth-century documents. It was afterwards maintained as an almost current, though spasmodically recorded, memorandum book for the years 1273 to 1366. Dr Evans has printed from it two sets of priory ordinances and it also contains (fo. 60v) an account of the sacrist's jurisdiction. The remaining entries of leases, corrodies and appointments are less unusual and very like the contents of the Almack register. This manuscript, known to Bentham as *Liber* B, covers the years 1407 to 1515; its contents have evidently been re-arranged several times so that their original order and purpose is by no means clear. Some sections were at one point intended for use as a formulary: fo. 13 is headed *C Carta Confirmatio Commissio Concessio Corrodium Certificacio*; fo. 97, *I. Indentura*; fo. 98, *P. Procuracio Presentacio*; fo. 118, *M. Manumissio*. After this point the volume begins to be a straightforward chronological register of priory leases, appointments and confirmations of episcopal leases.

It might be appropriate to mention at this point another Ely book, which Bentham knew as *Liber* A, and which is now British Library Additional MS 9822. Dr Evans printed from it three sets of episcopal injunctions for the priory and came to the conclusion that it was another priory register of a miscellaneous nature. A careful study of its contents has, however, led me to the belief that it is episcopal in origin. It eertainly contains some material relating to the priory, but the emphasis even in those sections is on the bishop's relations with the monks as visitor of the house. The major part of the entries in the volume are purely episcopal in interest. They include, for example, a copy of the

---

[40] *Historical Manuscripts Commission Report VI* (London, 1877), App. 289–300.
[41] EDR G/2/1.
[42] EDC 1/A/3. The contents are fully described in *Historical Manuscripts Commission Report XII* (London, 1899), App. IX, 394–5.

archiepiscopal award of 1401 in the bishop's dispute with the archdeacon of Ely, a number of documents about the episcopal temporalities
and copies of pleas in which the bishops, and not the priory, were
involved.

There are three other miscellaneous compilations of the fifteenth
century which are equally difficult to explain. A small paper book still
with the muniments (EDC 1/A/4) is concerned with the Suffolk
liberties and appears to relate to an expected attack on them. Two
manuscripts in the British Library, Cotton Vesp. A XIX, and Harley
329, each contain a copy of the agreement reached in 1417 between
Bishop Fordham and the prior about their respective fees in Ely, with
full lists of the tenants of each. The Cotton manuscript also includes
notes of a number of cases concerning the prior's jurisdictional liberty
in Ely, while the other is bound up with a series of notes on accounting
and conveyancing, with copies of bonds, leases and fines which seem to
have come from one of the priory's offices. Similar material, arranged
as a formulary, appears at the end of Corpus Christi College Cambridge
MS 335, and this too seems to have come from one of the administrative offices inside the priory.

All that has so far been said, with some slight exceptions, has been
concerned with the titles to ownership of priory lands, or with records
of decisions affecting the general life of the house, which were necessarily preserved for the future. The collection and expenditure of the
priory's income and the day-to-day administration of the house
generated other types of document, some of which were probably fairly
ephemeral, but which were nevertheless carefully kept and have
survived in some quantity. At times the visitor, or the monks themselves, attempted to regulate the making or keeping of these records
in the interest of better administration, and it is possible from some of
the orders, and from some of the surviving documents, to appreciate
the nature and quantity of record-making which went on in the priory.
As we have seen, the affairs of the priory were at first the responsibility
of a single treasurer who handled all the business which did not pass
through the hands of the prior or of the sacrist. These three officials
came during the thirteenth century to share their responsibilities with
an almoner, a cellarer, a chamberlain, a hosteller (or guest-master),
an infirmarer, a pittancer, a precentor and a keeper of the Lady altar.
Of these spending officers, only the sacrist and the treasurer had much

landed endowment; the rest received rents, rectorial tithes, offerings of various kinds and the profits of small farms, but for the most part relied on *la apaye*, or distribution made to them from the common fund by the treasurer.[43] There were two treasurers by 1300, and they received almost all the priory's income from manors and other landed property, which after 1261 was managed for them by two seneschals, one a monk and the other a layman. Subsequently the monk seneschal acted also as one of the two treasurers.[44]

The ordinances agreed by the prior and convent in 1304, in an attempt to restrain the priors' powers of dilapidation, repeated the bishop's earlier injunction to the monks to submit the annual accounts of all the obedientiaries to three auditors chosen from the brethren at Michaelmas. This was repeated in 1307 and 1314 and was coupled with the requirement that the prior should each year report to the monks the financial state of the whole house.[45] Here, then, is the origin of most of the account rolls we have today. They are the summary documents submitted to the Michaelmas audit, and they represent only the final stages of the accounting process in each office. The earliest reference to these rolls in post-Dissolution times is Bentham's notes made in the mid-eighteenth century;[46] since his time a number have disappeared or decayed beyond recognition, and there is no really continuous series except the sacrist's.[47] None of the surviving rolls is earlier than 1309, and it seems probable that the audit records in this form certainly date from the 1304 ordinances. Each account submitted to the audit was, of course, based on a number of subordinate accounts or vouchers which are sometimes referred to but rarely survive. One exception, which Dr Evans has published, is the hosteller's account for the purchase and amortisation of the rectory of Mepal.[48] Detailed expense accounts for building are referred to frequently: 'in diversis reparationibus ut per librum dicti computantis patet, 34s. 5d.' is a characteristic entry.[49] Rent and tithe collectors, bailiffs of individual manors and the stewards of the Suffolk jurisdictional liberty also submitted to the obedientiary detailed accounts which now survive in fragments but which were undoubtedly set aside for keeping, as were

---

[43] This is based on Evans, 'Ordinances', pp. xiii–xv.   [44] *Ibid.*, pp. 4, 24, xiii.

[45] *Ibid.*, pp. 21, 28, 30, 38. It is possible that auditors were used at Ely before this date: D. Knowles, *The Religious Orders in England*, I (Cambridge, 1948), 63.

[46] CUL. Add. MS 2957.   [47] See Appendix III.

[48] S. J. A. Evans, 'The purchase and mortification of Mepal', *EHR*, LI (1936), 113–20.

[49] Treasurer's account 1527, cited by J. Bentham, *History and Antiquities of the Conventual and Cathedral Church of Ely* (1st edn, Cambridge, 1772), fo. 79.

the court-rolls of these manors.[50] An occasional reference can be found
to the making of a rental, as in 1383, when the keeper of St Mary's
chapel paid 1s. 6d. for one such.[51]

Another duty laid on the obedientiaries at different times was the
making of annual inventories of the stock of their respective offices
to be surrendered to their successors. The 1314 ordinances ordered the
hosteller to do so, and other officers certainly did it during the next
century.[52] The chamberlain paid 1s. 1d. 'in inventario officii faciendo'
in 1343, and an inventory of the sacrist's office for the same period has
recently come to light.[53] The custom seems to have lapsed during the
next century, for in 1466 Bishop Gray enjoined the proper preparation
of inventories of all the offices 'que in archivis ecclesie fideli custodia
reponantur', at the same time as he ordered the resumption of the
keeping of clear and detailed central accounts, 'debita singula et
creditorum nomina in singulis compotis conscribantur ex quibus
verisimilis status monasterii cognosci possit'.[54]

Duties such as this were common to all obedientiaries, but some also
had certain specific obligations which produced records, some of which
have survived. The sacrist, for example, had the duty of arranging the
collection of the offerings made at the church's main shrine, that of St
Etheldreda; by the ordinances of 1314 he was required to account for
them to the auditors. Although a separate shrine-keeper appeared in
the fifteenth century, it seems likely that he was in fact responsible to
the sacrist.[55] By the same ordinances the almoner was required to keep
a note in writing of the names and dates of entry of the boys in the
almonry school, and the refectorer to submit an annual account at the
Michaelmas audit of the plate in his care.[56]

The treasurer's office, through which by far the largest portion of
the priory's revenue passed, must have required considerable numbers
of accounts, rentals and court rolls. The rush-keeper and the prior's
steward at various times accounted directly to this office; so, of course,
did the seneschals of the manors. It may well have been the treasurers,
or the prior at their instance, who in 1342 arranged to survey the priory's
manors and no doubt the detailed rental which accompanied the 1417
arbitration between the bishop and the prior was prepared in this office.[57]

---

[50] See appendix IV.   [51] EDC 5/8/8.   [52] Evans, 'Ordinances', p. 41.
[53] EDC 5/3/6/A.   [54] Evans, 'Ordinances', pp. 59–60.
[55] Ibid., p. 39.   [56] Ibid., pp. 38, 40.
[57] EDC 1/C/1, Extenta maneriorum; only the extents of the Cambridgeshire custody have survived, but fragments of others have come to light.

The responsibilities of the sacrist, defined well before the fourteenth century, were wider and more varied than those of any other obedientiary, and the records of his office must have been correspondingly more copious. They must have included inventories of plate and church furniture, though none survives; he handled all the varieties of craftsman employed about the church and supervised their stores, lists of which he must have made. In addition, since pre-Conquest times as it seems, he had claimed to exercise archidiaconal jurisdiction in parts of the Isle of Ely.[58] The sacrist's accounts of the fourteenth and fifteenth centuries regularly mention the profits of jurisdiction and probate, and it seems certain that registers of wills and of court hearings must have been made and kept.[59]

After the Dissolution the monastic muniments had a chequered history. Their safe keeping was entrusted by the Henrician statutes to the dean: 'further he is to safeguard the charters, muniments, court-rolls and writings without waste, saving their reasonable use...to ensure that a house is set aside in the church for a common treasury...the outer room is to contain the chests and pigeon-holes for the writings'.[60] The first dean of the new foundation was Robert Steward who had been the last prior and who viewed his responsibilities to the muniments somewhat liberally, especially when they were manuscript volumes rather than obvious title-deeds and court-rolls. It was Steward who abstracted as his own property and bequeathed to his heirs the Lambeth and Corpus Christi manuscripts already mentioned. The Ely muniments now in the Cottonian library, and probably the Bodleian manuscript, were evidently alienated in the sixteenth century by Steward or Andrew Perne.[61] These apart, however, there were few losses from the actual muniments before 1640.

The outbreak of the Civil War, the triumph of the Parliamentarians and the closure of the cathedral might have been disastrous for the muniments. There were two dangers: antiquarians in search of spoil would try to remove desirable specimens and would-be purchasers of cathedral estates would demand title-deeds for their purchases. The

---

58 C. E. Feltoe and E. H. Minns, *Vetus Liber Archidiaconi Eliensis* (Cambridge, 1917), p. xxii.
59 F. R. Chapman, *The Sacrist Rolls of Ely* (Cambridge, 1907, 2 vols.), II, 127, 'de jurisdictione pro testamentis probandis et correctionibus'.
60 EDC MS 1, pp. 248–9 and EDC MS 8.
61 Ker, *Catalogue of Manuscripts containing Anglo-Saxon*, no. 76, citing T. James, Ed. *Ecloga Oxonio-Cantabrigiensis* (London, 1600), p. 249.

chief antiquarian threat came from Sir Simonds D'Ewes, a well-known collector who lived close by at Long Melford. Before he died in 1650 D'Ewes had acquired a number of Ely documents, four of the best of which were copied by Sir Christopher Hatton for his *Book of Seals*. All are now in the British Library in the Harleian collection.[62]

The sale of cathedral estates was legalised by Parliament in 1649; the lands were surveyed and valued and all documents likely to be of use as titles removed to London. At first careful arrangements were made to preserve this vast collection of medieval material, but before 1660 they were in disarray and confusion, and it was several years before any official action was taken to sort and restore them. Ely did better than some other cathedrals and recovered a great deal, but stray documents were still reaching the church as late as 1678. Because the sorting was inexpert, Ely documents have been found in more recent times at Lambeth, Norwich and Worcester. There was confusion, too, between the cathedral records and those of the bishopric, and it was evidently at this point that some of the medieval priory records came into the bishop's hands.[63]

Even when the muniments were restored they remained in confusion, and in 1677 the chapter ordered a review and re-ordering of the whole. Rules were made for the proper keeping of the current records and for the preservation of non-current court-rolls and surveys.[64] This good work was continued in the next half-century by Thomas Watkins, who indexed and annotated many of the medieval records for which he was responsible as deputy-registrar of the chapter. His careful notes can be seen in many of the registers and in a collection called *Liber G*, in which he described and abstracted manorial and obedientiaries' accounts, and the *Extenta Maneriorum*, including parts of this which have since disappeared.[65] There is no sign that Watkins was interested in the medieval charters, but there were plenty of antiquarians in Cambridge who were only too interested. This was the time when Francis Blomefield and others were collecting and copying any medieval material which bore on the history of the University and of the neighbourhood. In 1766 Bentham saw and copied, 'ex autographo penes rev. et doct. Carolum Mason S.T.P.', the suspect foundation charter of 970 which was printed

[62] A. G. Watson, 'Sir Simonds D'Ewes', *Journ. of Society of Archivists*, II (London, 1960-4), 247-53, and C. E. Wright, *Fontes Harleianae* (London, 1972).

[63] D. M. Owen, 'Bringing Home the Records'.

[64] EDC 2/1/2, p. 128.

[65] Watkins's manuscript is now EDC MS. 8.

in the appendix to his *History*.[66] It seems likely that Edward the Confessor's charter, which Bentham also printed, was then in the same hands; those of Charles Mason, professor of geology and fellow of Trinity, who died in 1771. One of his Ely charters passed through the hands of Thomas Astle before reaching the British Library, where it is now Stowe charter 31.[67]

For the next half-century and more the muniments suffered no further losses, and they were little consulted until Dean Harvey Goodwin fitted up a new muniment-room in 1862.[68] The re-arrangement of the contents of this room was due to Archdeacon F. R. Chapman, who began work in 1879 and who seems to have paid the charges for what he did personally. Before he retired in 1910 Chapman had sorted, identified and arranged the obedientiary rolls, wrapping each in brown paper and numbering it. He also produced an edition of the early sacrist rolls in 1907.[69] The charters and other medieval documents were taken from their pigeon-holes, where they still remained in place, and numbered consecutively. Each was then described on a slip or wrapper and the more decayed documents were fastened on to cards, no separate list being made. A few of the manorial rolls were also wrapped and dated and the rest arranged in order in cupboards. It is clear that Chapman intended to bring out an edition of the royal charters and that his classification of these, with the episcopal documents and with the miscellanies he called 'Prior and convent', was a step to this end.[70]

After Chapman's retirement a little work was done by J. H. Crosby on the obedientiary rolls, some of which he analysed carefully.[71] After Crosby's death in 1922 no new work was done until 1930 when the Reverend S. J. A. Evans, then a minor canon, was authorised to catalogue the charters. Dr Evans began to re-arrange and re-box the charters and was able to arrange for a few repairs; the catalogue on which I am at present working necessarily follows on from his work. The rest of the story is soon told. After 1945 the medieval charters and rolls, excluding the manorial documents, were removed from the muniment-room into the cathedral library by Dr A. T. Hankey, who was then keeper of the records. From there they and the remaining contents of the muniment-

---

[66] Bentham's transcript is in CUL Add. MS 2957, 2954, p. 97. Dr A. N. L. Munby drew my attention to a sale catalogue of Mason's books, BL S-C. 500.

[67] Sawyer, *Anglo-Saxon Charters*, no. 779 where full references are given.

[68] EDC 2/1/7, p. 325 and Harvey Goodwin, *Ely Gossip* (Ely, 1892), p. 12.

[69] EDC 2/1/9, pp. 13, 274, 308.   [70] Chapman's notes are now EDC MSS 18–21.

[71] Crosby's analysis is available for use with the chapter muniments.

room were transferred in 1970, at the request of the dean and chapter, to the Cambridge University Library, where a catalogue commissioned by the Marc Fitch Fund, and repairs assisted by the Pilgrim Trust, are now in progress.[72]

The following charters, included in the text of the third book of the *Liber Eliensis*, are known to survive either in the BL or in the Ely Chapter Muniments in CUL:

6. *Carta regis Henrici quomodo abbatiam de Ely in episcopatum transmutavit.* Harl. charter 43 C 11; copy in Sir Christopher Hatton's *Book of Seals*, no. 419.

7. *Carta regis de omni libertate ecclesie.*
   Cotton charter X.8; copy in *Book of Seals*, 430.

12. *Carta regis de adquietatione custodiarum oppidi de Nordwich et de libertate onerose servitutis, qua ecclesia de Ely misere laborabat.*
   Ely charter 3.

14. *Aliud mandatum regis de Libertate v^{que} hundredorum.*
   Ely charter 4a.

15. *Carta regis de relaxatione militum qui violenter ab ecclesia de Ely requirebantur.*
   Ely charter 6.

16. *Item carta regis de condonatione pecunie que injuste exigebatur ab ecclesia.*
   Ely charter 4.

19. *Alia carta regis de relaxatione pecunie ecclesie de Chateriz quam condonavit sancte Aetheldrede in Ely.*
   Ely charter 5.

20. *Carta regis Henrici de adquietatione ville de Hadham.*
   Ely charter 2.

21. *Carta regis quod monachi et ecclesia sancte Aetheldrede in Ely de theloneo sint quieti ubique per Angliam.*
   Ely charter 5b.

26. *Carta episcopi Herevei de particulis rerum quam ad victum monachorum constituit.*
   Ely charter 51 and Harl. charter 43 H 4; copy in *Book of Seals*, no. 420.

49. *Carta regis Stephani de omni libertate ecclesie sancte Aetheldredi.*
   Ely charter 8.

54. *Carta episcopi de rebus quas monachi mutavit.*
   Harl. charter 43 H 5; copy in *Book of Seals*, 415.

[72] For the details of this, see Owen, *The Library and Muniments of Ely Cathedral.*

134. *Carta Nigelli episcopi quod monachi de Ely libere et in pace tenent ecclesias suas.*
Ely charter 55.

J. Bentham quoted in his notebooks and in his *History and Antiquities of the Conventual and Cathedral church of Ely* (1st ed., Cambridge, 1772) a number of Ely volumes belonging to the bishop to which he, or some earlier scholar, had given letters. There appears to be no evidence for the use of these letters before Bentham's time; the hand in which they are written, when the endorsement has survived, seems to be that of Thomas Watkins (registrar, 1733–75). It will be useful to set out these manuscripts here since not all were known to recent scholars by these references.

A. BL Add. MS 9822; an episcopal compilation.

B. EDR G/2/3; the 'Almack' register.

L. BL Egerton MS 3047; the larger portion of the fifteenth-century cartulary. Bentham does not mention this manuscript.

M. EDR G/3/28; the prior's cartulary.

P. EDR G/2/4; a short compilation of notes on the liberties of Ely and Bury.

R. EDR G/3/27; the Ely Coucher, a survey of the episcopal estates.

Surviving obedientiary rolls

These rolls are for the most part usable, although rather fragile. Bentham's abstracts and transcripts (CUL Add. MS 2957), and Crosby's duplicated analyses of the rolls of the chamberlain, keeper of the Lady chapel, keeper of the shrine and precentor, which are available with the muniments, are a useful guide to their contents.

Almoner 1326–1474, 14 rolls.

Cellarer 1314–1475, 39 rolls.

Chamberlain 1334–1521, 33 rolls.

Hosteller 1328–1448, 8 rolls.

Infirmarer 1451, 1 roll.

Keeper of grain 1307–1528, 55 rolls.

Keeper of rushes 1344–1433, 13 rolls.

Keeper of St Mary's chapel 1356–1492, 15 rolls.

Pittancer 1309–1512, 17 rolls.

Precentor 1329–1535, 11 rolls.

Sacrist 1292–1517, 45 rolls.

Shrine keeper 1421–95, 9 rolls.

Steward (of prior's hospice) 1360–1517, 8 rolls.

Treasurer(s) 1282–1332, 6 rolls.

Ely manorial records: EDC 7

Some medieval accounts and court-rolls, none earlier than 1300, survive for the manors named below; it is known that a number of the Cambridgeshire records were lost during the revolts of 1381. A few Ely rolls are among the records of the Court of Augmentations (PRO *Lists and Indexes*, v, vi, viii), but since the greater part of the priory endowment was transferred directly to the new cathedral chapter, these are few in number.

Isle of Ely: Leverington, Sutton, Wentworth and Witcham.

Cambridgeshire (old county): Melbourne cum Meldreth, Newton cum Hauxton, Stapleford, Stetchworth, Swaffham Prior, West Wratting.

Suffolk: Kingston, Lakenheath, Melton, Winston, the Suffolk liberty.

MONASTIC ARCHDEACONS

by JANE SAYERS

THIS paper seeks to examine the history and establishment of the four major monastic archdeaconries in England – St Albans, Glastonbury, Bury St Edmunds and Westminster – and to investigate the jurisdiction and administration of the monastic archdeacon.

I

The first stage in the establishment of an exempt area of this kind was the development of a religious cult and the land endowment of the church at the cult centre. The second stage, the confirmation (royal, papal, episcopal and popular) of the cult and of the lands, brought the precise definition of the territory and rights of the church. The four monasteries developed notably different rights at widely different times and exhibit various historical features. All had considerable pre-Conquest endowments, but the abbey of Westminster stands out from the three others as having no pre-Conquest cult, and hence no early sanctuary area where the peace of the saint operated. All the cults were associated with British or English saints, but at Westminster the post-Conquest cult of Edward the Confessor (and English kingship) followed the land endowment, which, ironically, had been made principally by the future recipient of the cult. Two of the cult centres, St Albans and Glastonbury, were probably on or near pagan religious sites, but whilst at St Albans the cult was clear-cut and the endowment followed, at Glastonbury the generally accepted venerability of the place brought gifts before a suitable cult was found, and even then, in contrast to the other three centres, there were several cults – St Patrick, St Benignus, St Bridget and St Indracht from the tenth century and the Holy Thorn and the Holy Grail from the late twelfth century – and the unsuccessful ones of Edgar and his father, Edmund, king of the West Saxons, which 'never got off the ground'. Certain distinctions can be made, too, between the development of these two early cults, of St Alban at St Albans in the first part of the fifth century and of St Patrick and others at Glastonbury in the early tenth century, and those later developed in the eleventh and twelfth centuries at Bury (St Edmund) and Westminster. At St Albans and Glastonbury the royal territorial endowment began very early and was associated, probably not totally unhistorically, with Offa (757–96) at St Albans and with Ine (680–726) at Glastonbury. Here the archidiaconal rights were later exercised over comparatively large territorial areas, whereas at Westminster and Bury, where the endowment was made between the mid-tenth and mid-eleventh century, principally by Edward the Confessor and Cnut, the area of the monastic archdeaconry was much more restricted.[1]

The confirmation and establishment of the land endowment – the acceptance of the *seigneurie* of the saint[2] – was clearly necessary before archidiaconal jurisdiction could be established. Ordinary archidiaconal jurisdiction pre-supposes a reasonably advanced diocesan system. Although the office of archdeacon was known by the ninth century, the ordinary archdeaconry, as an established institution in all dioceses, was a post-Conquest arrangement. This was probably the achievement of Lanfranc, but territorialisation did not develop generally until the mid-twelfth century.[3] There is no evidence of a monastic archdeaconry before the eleventh century.[4] The existence of the monastic archdeacon and acceptance of his (or his abbot's) position, as wielding very extensive ecclesiastical powers, was to depend on the confirmation and acceptance

[1] On the two early cults at St Albans and Glastonbury, see W. Levison, 'St Alban and St Albans', *Antiquity*, xv (1941), 337–59; C. A. Ralegh Radford in *The Quest for Arthur's Britain*, ed. G. Ashe (London, 1968), pp. 119–38; H. P. R. Finberg, 'St Patrick at Glastonbury', *West-Country Historical Studies* (Newton Abbot, 1969), pp. 70–88; and J. Armitage Robinson, 'William of Malmesbury "On the Antiquity of Glastonbury"', *Somerset Historical Essays* (London, 1921), pp. 1–25; and, for some pertinent remarks in general, Janet Nelson, 'Royal Saints and Early Medieval Kingship', *Studies in Church History*, x (1973), 39–44. On sanctuary, see J. C. Cox, *The Sanctuaries and Sanctuary Seekers of Medieval England* (London, 1911), esp. pp. 41, 86, 202–3 and 209–10; and for the land endowment of the four houses, see P. H. Sawyer, *Anglo-Saxon Charters*, Royal Historical Society Guides and Handbooks, viii (1968) (hereafter cited as *Anglo-Saxon Chs.*).

[2] See R. Génestal, 'La Patrimonialité de l'archidiaconat', *Mélanges Paul Fournier*, Bibliothèque d'histoire du droit (Paris, 1929), p. 291; J-F. Lemarignier, *Étude sur les privilèges d'exemption et de juridiction ecclésiastique des abbayes normandes*, Archives de la France Monastique, xliv (Paris, 1937), 116. Génestal showed that the monastic archdeaconries were established generally where the monks were also proprietors of the lands.

[3] F. M. Stenton, *Anglo-Saxon England* (Oxford, 1947), pp. 434 (on pre-Conquest archdeaconries) and 668; and J. Scammell, 'The rural chapter in England from the eleventh to the fourteenth century', *EHR*, lxxxvi (1971), 7, esp. n. 3, who cites all the evidence on territorialisation.

[4] U. Berlière, 'Les Archidiaconés ou exemptions privilégiées de monastères', *Revue Bénédictine*, xl (1928), 116–22.

of these privileged houses and their ecclesiastical liberties by the people of the locality, by the diocesan, by the king and by the pope. The abbot may have exercised these powers in person at first, but with the development of the corrective system, visitation, the courts and the law, he was forced to delegate. The monastic archdeacon made his appearance in the four abbeys in the years between 1071 and *c.* 1190, during the period of the territorialisation of the ordinary archdeacon in the dioceses.

Bury St Edmunds

The area of the archdeacon's jurisdiction at Bury was small but probably very ancient. It coincided with the *banleuca*,[5] which included the abbey, the churches of St James and St Mary, three hospitals and various chapels, the districts within the four crosses, Eyhtecros, Holdhawe, Weepingcross and a cross near Henhowe (or Heyecros).[6] The documentary beginnings of the monastery's supreme powers over the *banleuca* begin with Cnut's charter of 1028. The liberty of St Edmund ($8\frac{1}{2}$ hundreds), which corresponded with West Suffolk, was territorially enormous if compared with Glastonbury's liberty of the Twelve Hides (about $2\frac{1}{4}$ square miles). The essential difference was that the Bury monastic archdeacon had no jurisdiction there, but within the *banleuca* he exercised secular and ecclesiastical powers, and Bury claimed an exemption which Glastonbury never had. The very smallness of the abbey of Bury's archidiaconal jurisdiction is more closely comparable in extent with that of Westminster – over the immediate area, parts of the palace, and the parish of St Margaret – to be explained, perhaps, by their later endowment if compared with Glastonbury and St Albans.

There is no doubt that the archdeacons were monks, but from what date is not clear. At Bury the office was, at least later, associated with the extremely powerful one, within the town area, of sacrist of the abbey. In Herman (*c.* 1070), author of the *Miracles of St Edmund*, we doubtless have a monastic archdeacon and not a diocesan one.[7] The arch-

---

[5] The *leuca*, or league, equalled the Gallic mile of 1500 paces and was slightly smaller than the standard English mile. M. D. Lobel, 'The Ecclesiastical Banleuca in England', *Oxford Essays in Medieval History presented to H. E. Salter*, ed. F. M. Powicke (Oxford, 1934), pp. 122–40.

[6] See M. D. Lobel, *The Borough of Bury St Edmunds* (Oxford, 1935), p. 5, n. 8 and map of the *banleuca* at the end. The four crosses, erected by the monks, are noted in a papal bull of 1172: see W. Dugdale, *Monasticon Anglicanum*, ed. J. Caley & others (6 vols. in 8 parts, London, 1817–30), III, 99, and CUL. MS Ff 2. 29 (a fifteenth-century register of the liberties and jurisdictional rights of Bury), fo. 40.

[7] *Ungedruckte Anglo-Normannische Geschichtsquellen*, ed. F. Liebermann (Strasburg, 1879), pp. 227, 231: the text of the *Miracles* is also in *Memorials of St Edmund's Abbey*, ed. T. Arnold, 3 vols.

deaconry appears to date from 1071, when Pope Alexander II came to Bury's rescue against the machinations of Arfast, bishop of Elmham, and the outlining of Bury's exemption might well account for the appointment of a monastic archdeacon at this time or soon after. It could be that Herman is in fact the first monastic archdeacon of Bury, whose office predates any occurrence of an archdeacon within Norwich diocese, and, by some years, the division of the archdeaconry of Suffolk into two, Suffolk and Sudbury, which has been attributed to Bishop Everard of Calne (1121–45).[8]

The importance of early documentation in the struggle for exemption from the diocesan is illustrated by the abbey of Bury.[9] The establishment of the see at Norwich in 1094 or 1095 obviated another immediate attack from that quarter, and the relations between the bishops of Norwich and the abbots of Bury seem to have been quite cordial.[10] This may serve to illustrate an early acceptance of Bury's sizeable rights (though confined in terms of the archdeaconry) and its peculiarly strong position vis-à-vis the crown. For of all four abbeys, the franchise of Bury was the greatest. The abbot had the return of writs, acted as coroner, held the shire court and had civil and criminal jurisdiction over the borough and its inhabitants;[11] and it could be argued that the abbot's spiritual powers as archdeacon within the

RS xcvi (London, 1890–6), I, 26–92. Thurstan and Tolinus appear to have been sacrists under the first post-Conquest abbot, Baldwin (Dugdale, *Mon. Angl.* III, 162 no. xxxii).

8 See *Fasti Ecclesiae Anglicanae 1066–1300*, ed. D. E. Greenway, II (University of London, 1971), 61–9, esp. 61–2. The prior of Worcester exercised archidiaconal rights over the churches of the city belonging to the monks from at least 1092, according to R. R. Darlington, who treats Wulfstan's charter as 'beyond suspicion': *The Vita Wulfstani of William of Malmesbury*, Camden Soc. 3rd ser., XL (1928), p. xxxv, n. 2. At Durham, in 1093, William of St Calais committed the office of archdeacon to the prior: Simeon of Durham, *Historia Ecclesiae Dunhelmensis*, ed. T. Arnold, 2 vols. RS LXXV (London, 1882–5), I, 129.

9 *The Pinchbeck Register*, ed. Lord F. Hervey (2 vols., privately printed, 1925) I, 3–4 (JL no. 4692); also printed in Migne, *PL.* CXLVI, cols. 1363–4. It is possible that this bull is a forgery, although the general and vague terms in which it is written are quite credible, and Bury certainly was accepted as having sizeable though ill-defined liberties early on (see Lobel, 'Banleuca', p. 129). Also the facts that the pope concerned in the issue was Alexander II (and it is difficult to see why a later forger should choose him), that the see was *not* established at Bury, and that the papacy was concerning itself with legislation about episcopal sees at this time, seem to me to make it convincing. V. H. Galbraith, 'The East Anglian See and the Abbey of Bury St Edmunds', *EHR*, XL (1925), 222–8; D. Knowles, 'The Growth of Exemption', *Downside Review*, L (N.S. XXXI, 1932), 209–11; and B. Dodwell, 'The Foundation of Norwich Cathedral', *TRHS*, 5th ser., VII (1957), 1–18, do not appear to doubt the bull on historical grounds. See also *PUE*, III, no. 8, and *Pinchbeck Reg.* I, 19–20.

10 Jesus College, Cambridge, MS Q B I fo. 111v recites protests of Simon, bishop of Norwich, in 1263; of Henry, bishop of Norwich, in 1371; and of William, bishop of Norwich, in 1335 and 1344 against Bury's exempt jurisdiction, but in fact they could do little more than protest verbally.

11 H. M. Cam, *Liberties and Communities in Medieval England* (London, 1963), pp. 186–95.

borough were considerably less threatening to the diocesan than his secular powers in the $8\frac{1}{2}$ hundreds.

St Albans

Indirect evidence suggests an early origin for the archdeaconry of St Albans: otherwise it seems impossible to explain the alignment of the later archdeaconries within the see of Lincoln with the counties – Buckinghamshire, Bedfordshire, Huntingdonshire etc. – excluding Hertfordshire, the bulk of which formed the archdeaconry of St Albans, and whose remaining parishes, bordering Huntingdonshire, became absorbed in that archdeaconry after the death of Nicholas (who had borne the title of archdeacon of Cambridge, Huntingdon and Hertford) in 1110.[12]

However, the first occurrence of an archdeacon of St Albans is in 1129, at the time of the translation of St Alban by Abbot Geoffrey de Gorron (1119–46).[13] He thus precedes our first indication of the archdeaconry in the papal confirmation of 1157, where the liberty and archdeaconry of St Albans was defined as fifteen parishes: St Peter's, St Stephen's and Kingsbury in the town of St Albans, Watford, Rickmansworth, Abbots Langley, Redbourn, Codicote, St Paul's Walden, Hexton, Norton. Newnham, Barnet (all in Hertfordshire), and Winslow and Aston Abbots (both in Buckinghamshire).[14] During the thirteenth century the detached parts of the liberty and archdeaconry in Hertfordshire were absorbed into the hundred of St Albans (now called Cashio), with the exception of Caldecote adjoining Newnham. The central part of the archdeaconry consisted of an area about ten miles by ten miles in extent, roughly equivalent in size to that of Glastonbury.[15] It had, however, rather more parishes, some of

---

[12] *Fasti*, II, 50; Henry of Huntingdon, *Historia Anglorum*, ed. T. Arnold, RS LXXIV (London, 1879), 302. The Cambridgeshire archdeaconry was taken out of Lincoln with the foundation of the see of Ely in 1109.

[13] *Gesta Abbatum Monasterii Sancti Albani*, ed. H. T. Riley, 3 vols. RS XXVIII (London, 1867–9), I, 85–6.

[14] *PUE*, III no. 118; and see no. 459, Pope Celestine III's re-issue of the bull in 1193, where monks were specified for the office. At Evesham, however, it was a secular office from *c.* 1050 to the time of Thomas of Marlborough: D. Knowles, *The Monastic Order in England* (Cambridge, 1940), p. 606, n. 5.

[15] See for an outline indication *Map of Monastic Britain* South Sheet (Ordnance Survey, 1950); for more detail on the liberty and archdeaconry of St Albans, see the map in *Studies in Manorial History* by A. E. Levett, ed. H. M. Cam, M. Coate and L. S. Sutherland (Oxford, 1938), and for Glastonbury, O.S. 1-inch Map Sheet 165, on which the boundaries of the seven parishes can be clearly traced.

which were detached, unlike the sizeable Glastonbury parishes of Moorlinch and Middlezoy with their numerous chapelries.

Situated at the far end of the enormous diocese of Lincoln, St Albans was in a strong position to resist the diocesan. It was not until the 1160s that Robert de Chesney challenged the extensive rights of the abbey, but was unsuccessful in the face of powerful papal bulls obtained by St Albans between 1122 and 1157.[16] The date of the transfer of the cathedral church from Dorchester to Lincoln in 1072 must have seemed a recent event to the monks of St Albans if they looked back at their long history; and St Albans liberty, one of the most powerful eccle-siastical liberties, grew rather than shrank during the Middle Ages. St Albans came nearer the exemption of certain major European houses than any other English community, and Abbot de la Mare's book of the fourteenth century shows no signs of St Albans relaxing its hold. Indeed the apogee of its pretensions was not reached until 1487, when John de Rothbury, archdeacon of St Albans, set out to claim episcopal powers for the abbot.[17]

Glastonbury

By the opening of the twelfth century Glastonbury probably exercised some jurisdiction over the seven large parishes which lay to its west, roughly between the rivers Brue and Parrett, but it is unlikely that there was any clear-cut definition of the jurisdiction. By 1129, William of Malmesbury was claiming ancient exemption for the monastery of Glastonbury.[18] In 1144 Lucius II confirmed to Glastonbury the surrounding islands – Beckery, Godney, Marchey, Panborough, Nyland and Farningmere;[19] and the vills of Street, Moorlinch, Butleigh, Shapwick and Zoy, with their churches and chapels.[20]

---

[16] See my article 'Papal Privileges for St Albans Abbey and its Dependencies' in *The Study of Medieval Records*, ed. D. A. Bullough and R. L. Storey (Oxford, 1971), pp. 64–5; and for the ordination of 1219, CUL. MS Ee 4.20 fo. 107v.

[17] Sayers, 'Papal Privileges for St Albans', pp. 72–8, 82.

[18] Lemarignier, *Privilèges d'exemption*, p. 200. It is doubtful, however, whether Malmesbury really accepted that the church of Glastonbury had been consecrated by Christ himself, and that consequently it could not be subject to the bishop, though he does repeat the story which was obviously in circulation at the time.

[19] Panborough was part of Meare, see G. B. Grundy, *The Saxon Charters and Field Names o Somerset*, Somerset Archaeol. and Natural History Soc. (1935), pp. 113–14. All the names sug-gest Saxon colonisation. 'Ey' or 'iey' means island.

[20] *The Great Chartulary of Glastonbury*, ed. A. Watkin, 3 vols., Somerset Record Soc. LIX, LXIII–IV (1947–52), no. 175 (hereafter cited as *Glastonbury Cart.*); Secretum = Bodleian, MS Wood empt. I (hereafter cited as S.) fos. 51v–2; and Trinity College, Cambridge, MS R 5 33 fos. 89v–90 ('Pie postulatio voluntatis'). This has some relationship to the spurious charter of

Henry II's confirmation of 1154–89 added the churches of Pilton and Ditcheat.[21]

In about 1171, presumably after the death of the powerful Abbot Henry of Blois, Thomas, archdeacon of Wells, obviously fearing a rival archidiaconal jurisdiction, claimed possession of the churches. This led Abbot Robert of Glastonbury to make an agreement with the bishop that the churches of Glastonbury, Meare, Street, Moorlinch, Butleigh, Shapwick and Zoy, and three more, should form an archdeaconry to be administered by the abbot as archdeacon. In exchange for this concession, the church of South Brent was to be given to the archdeacon of Wells to form a prebend and the well-endowed church of Pilton to the bishop.[22] Such an arrangement, however, did not suit the community at Glastonbury and they appealed to Rome.

In 1189, when Henry de Soilli became abbot, he gave up the claim to archidiaconal jurisdiction over the three churches which had been added by Abbot Robert and relinquished Pilton, South Brent and Huish in return for an undisputed jurisdiction over the seven churches. The compromise was enshrined in Bishop Reginald's charter of 1191,[23] where the archdeaconry was clearly defined as consisting of the parishes of St John, Glastonbury, Meare, Street, Butleigh, Shapwick, Moorlinch and Zoy, which were to be exempt from the bishop's jurisdiction except in cases of appeal. Only the bishop could fulfil the essentially episcopal functions of institution, ordination, the dedication of churches and attending the solemn penitence of parishioners, but otherwise the monastic archdeacon of Glastonbury was to exercise full archidiaconal rights of visitation, induction and correction.[24]

The bounds of the Jurisdiction of Glastonbury, as described in 1334,[25] may have differed little from those accepted in 1191. It seems likely that

Ine, of supposedly 725 (*Anglo-Saxon Chs.* no. 250), which indicates the rights of the monks in the churches of 'Zoy', Brent, Moorlinch, Shapwick, Street, Butleigh and Pilton. It makes the extreme claim for them of excluding the bishop from any episcopal functions there. It seems likely that this charter was fabricated during the early years of the twelfth century, when what Finberg calls 'the fabulous tales of its antiquity' were circulated.

[21] *Glastonbury Cart.* no. 302.

[22] See Watkin in intro. to *Glastonbury Cart.* p. xxi; A. Morey, *Bartholomew of Exeter* (Cambridge, 1937), pp. 65–6; and *Calendar of the Manuscripts of the Dean and Chapter of Wells* I (Historical MSS Commission, 1907), p. 26.

[23] Certainly post-1189 and before 27 November 1191, the date of the election of Bishop Reginald fitz Jocelin to Canterbury. If 1191, which Watkin seems to favour (p. xxi), this would fit closely into the historical background of Glastonbury's advancement.

[24] *Glastonbury Cart.* no. 1; S. fo. 20; and Dugdale, *Mon. Angl.*, 1, 28 no. xv. Also in Adam of Domerham: Thomas Hearne, *Adami de Domerham Historia de rebus gestis Glastoniensibus*, 2 vols. (Oxford, 1727), 11, 345.   [25] S. fo. 24.

the estate boundaries were settled at the time of endowment. The bounds of Zoy are given in Ine's charter of 725[26] and of Butleigh in Egbert's charter of 801.[27] Bounds are given for estates at Pennard in 681, possibly for Shapwick in 729 and at Baltonsborough in 744.[28] The only definition after the donations were made would have been caused by assarting in the thirteenth century. It seems likely, too, that the establishment of the parochial boundaries took place at the same time as the drawing of the estate boundaries and accorded with them.

The archdeacon of Glastonbury occurs in an unusual instance in 1215, when Jocelin, bishop of Bath and Glastonbury, who was also abbot of the house, and had hence appended Glastonbury to his title, issued a statute on the sequestration of vacant churches which naturally concerned his archdeacons. Here Thomas, archdeacon of Glastonbury, undoubtedly a monk,[29] appears in conjunction with the bishop's officers, the diocesan archdeacons of Wells, Bath and Taunton, as responsible for the seven churches.[30] The final establishment of the see at Bath and Wells in 1242 and the termination of the curious arrangement whereby two of the bishops of Bath were also abbots of Glastonbury (Savaric, 1193–1205, and Jocelin, 1206–42), with their cathedral at Glastonbury, removed the anomaly of a monastic archdeacon responsible to a diocesan who was also his abbot.[31] It also initiated prolonged attacks by the bishops of Bath and Wells. In the same year Glastonbury appealed to the pope, when a case from the archdeaconry was taken before the bishop.[32] Innocent IV's confirmations of Glastonbury's rights over the archdeaconry in 1245 and 1246 followed this case, but did not stop the attack.[33] Throughout the early fourteenth century

---

[26] *Anglo-Saxon Chs.* no. 251; H. P. R. Finberg, *The Early Charters of Wessex* (Leicester Univ. Press, 1964), no. 379; and see Grundy, *Saxon Charters and Field Names of Somerset*, pp. 116–18. Finberg cites the suggestion of Mr S. C. Morland that Zoy includes Weston Zoyland and Othery: if so, it would equate with the parish of Middlezoy which included these places as chapelries. The island and manor of Zoy or Sowy contained about 1850 acres of flood-free land and three main settlements: Michael Williams, *The Draining of the Somerset Levels* (Cambridge, 1970), p. 47.   [27] *Anglo-Saxon Chs.* no. 270a; Dugdale, *Mon. Angl.*, I, 47 no. lxxxiv.

[28] *Anglo-Saxon Chs.* nos. 236 (Grundy, 75–7); 253 (Grundy, 114–16); and 1410 (Grundy, 61–4).

[29] For other Glastonbury archdeacons, all monks, see S. fo. 23v.

[30] *Councils and Synods*, ed. F. M. Powicke and C. R. Cheney, II, pt. 1 (Oxford, 1964), pp. 44–6.

[31] On Savaric Fitzgeldewin, Jocelin's predecessor, bishop of Bath and Glastonbury and also abbot of Glastonbury (1193–1205), see *The Heads of Religious Houses in England and Wales 940–1216*, ed. D. Knowles, C. N. L. Brooke and V. C. M. London (Cambridge, 1972), p. 52. Armitage Robinson in *Somerset Historical Essays*, p. 70, suggests that Jocelin abandoned the joint title of bishop of Bath and Glastonbury in 1219, but that is not the view of Knowles, etc.

[32] *Glastonbury Cart.* no. 12.

[33] *Ibid.*, nos. 9 and 180. His confirmation of the archdeaconry is also in Trinity College, Cambridge, MS R 5 33 fo. 93r-v (dat. 1245) and two pairs of it are referred to in the inventory of

repeated attempts were made by the bishops to visit. Walter de Hasel-schawe (1299–1302), previously dean of Wells, tried to visit the church of Weston Zoyland, but was prevented from entering either the church or the manse of the rectory. Bishop John de Droxenforde (1302–9) attempted to visit the church of Street, but his commissary withdrew when he was shown the privileges of Glastonbury, declaring to the assembled company, which included the abbot of Glastonbury: 'I see that you are not held to undergo our visitation, therefore I withdraw.'[34] The full-scale visitation of the seven churches, mounted by the commissaries of Bishop Ralph of Shrewsbury in 1334,[35] was the occasion of an appeal to Rome and to the Court of Arches for tuition, pending full investigation by the Holy See. Fifty years later, John, bishop of Bath and Wells, confirmed Glastonbury's jurisdiction.[36]

The extraordinary persistence of the bishops of Bath and Wells is to be explained by their proximity to the forum of confrontation, and in particular by the convent of Glastonbury's lack of exemption from episcopal control, which distinguished Glastonbury from the other three monastic archdeaconries. In the circumstances of being able to visit the monastery of Glastonbury, it was difficult for the diocesans to believe that the seven parishes were exempt from their control. There was no doubt, however, in the minds of the parishioners, some of whom recalled in 1335 having seen the charter of Bishop Reginald.[37]

Westminster

The charters used by Westminster in its establishment of an archidiaconal jurisdiction, and in its claims of liberty and exemption, were the so-called charter of St Dunstan, the bull of Clement III (1189) and the charter of Stephen Langton (1222).[38] The charter of St Dunstan supposedly defined the precinct of St Peter's, marked by crosses and

---

Glastonbury deeds in the same register (fo. 78v); and see no. 6 where Alexander IV appointed judges delegate to investigate the jurisdiction in 1261.

[34] S. fos. 24r–v, 25, and cf. *Calendar of the Register of John de Drokensford*, ed. Bishop Hobhouse, Somerset Rec. Soc. 1 (1887), 159 (fo. 140v): stitched on to the original is a torn scrap of parchment, endorsed 'Visitatio Jurisd. Glaston.', and stating that at Street church, Bruton enquired after the incumbents' exhibits, accepting that matters of conduct for the seven churches came under the archdeacon of Glastonbury (see below pp. 190–1).

[35] S. fo. 24v.   [36] Longleat Deed 10583.

[37] S. fos. 23, 25v. The jurisdiction of Glastonbury was accepted by the bishop at a visitation in 1385, see Hearne, *Domerham* 1, 273, no. xxv.

[38] See W[estminster] A[bbey] M[uniments] Bk. 1, fos. 138–9, and PRO. E 132/35 (nos. 3, 10, 15).

ditches (and hence the sanctuary area), within which priests and clerks were to be free from the payment of synodals and of Romescot. The charter is undoubtedly a forgery, as is the third charter of Edward the Confessor which mentions the immunity of the precinct and the cemetery of Westminster. Both belong to the batch of forgeries fabricated for the cause of the canonisation of Edward the Confessor in the 1140s, possibly by Osbert de Clare,[39] but there seems no reason to doubt the authenticity of the grant of Edgar which virtually outlined the archdeaconry, when he 'restored' an estate on the north side of the Thames between the Tyburn and the Fleet, to which Ethelred added a gift in 1002.[40] The canonisation of the Confessor on 7 February 1161 laid the way open for the bull of Clement III,[41] which spoke of the monastery precinct and of the church of St Margaret within the monks' cemetery, and the laymen and clerks within the same, as being free from the control of the diocesan, but the precise rights and area were not defined.

The charter of Stephen Langton of 1222 declared that the monastery of Westminster and the church of St Margaret, with its parish and all the chapels within the parish, with their tithes and appurtenances, and the clerks and laymen living within the parish should be exempt from all jurisdiction of the bishop of London. The boundaries of the parish of St Margaret were defined in 1222 as covering an area from the Tyburn to the Thames, along Watling Street (Oxford Street–High Holborn) to the hospital of St Giles, Holborn, and down to the Strand and Charing in one direction (excluding the church and cemetery of St Martin), and to the mound south west of Horseferry Road and down to the Thames in the other direction.[42]

Although an archdeacon of Westminster is not mentioned by name until 1246,[43] the office presumably existed before then, perhaps origi-

---

39 *Anglo-Saxon Chs.* no. 104. See P. Chaplais, 'The Original Charters of Herbert and Gervase Abbots of Westminster (1121–1157)', *A Medieval Miscellany for D. M. Stenton*, ed. P. M. Barnes and C. F. Slade, Pipe Roll Soc., N.S. XXXVI (1960), 89–110. It was Tait who spoke of Westminster as a 'factory of forgeries' in 'An Alleged Charter of William the Conqueror', *Essays in History presented to Reginald Lane Poole*, ed. H. W. C. Davis (Oxford, 1927), pp. 158–9, n. 2.

40 *Anglo-Saxon Chs.* nos. 670 (date much disputed but almost certainly not 951, as specifically dated, and probably after 959) and 903. See M. Gelling, 'The Boundaries of the Westminster Charters', *Transactions of the London and Middlesex Archaeol. Soc.*, N.S., XI, pt. 2 (1953), 101–4, who gives translations of the bounds and a map.

41 *PUE* I, no. 262; and see D. Knowles, 'Parochial Organization', *Downside Review*, LI (1933), 514–15.

42 WAM 12753: printed *Acta Stephani Langton*, ed. K. Major, CYS, L (1950), no. 54.

43 Matthew Paris, *Chronica Majora*, ed. H. R. Luard, 7 vols. RS LVII (London, 1872–83), IV, 589.

nating in the activities of Abbot Gervase (1138–c.1157) and the canonisation of Edward. The archdeacon exercised jurisdiction in the precincts, parish of St Margaret and parts of the palace, and was also the chief administrative officer of the sanctuary, although the sanctuary area at Westminster was not as extensive as the liberty or archdeaconry. At Bury, the *banleuca*, within which there was sanctuary,[44] was distinct from the liberty as a whole, but coincided with the archdeaconry. The sanctuary area at Westminster was about the same size, extending from King Street to Tothill Street down to Strutton Ground and Horseferry Road.[45] The sacred character of sanctuary to the medieval mind is well illustrated by the words of one of the writs of Abbot Gilbert demanding sanctuary, which states that the fugitive had sought 'the altar of St Peter and the body of King Edward'.[46]

The case of Westminster is closer to Glastonbury than to Bury and St Albans, although the house enjoyed exemption from the diocesan. This, however, was not clarified until Langton's settlement of 1222,[47] and the proximity to Westminster of the cathedral church of London meant that the bishop was never far away and had to be constantly reminded of the limitations of his power. Furthermore, the 1222 settlement had no reason to deal with the extent of the archdeacon's rights over the palace of Westminster and St Stephen's chapel which posed problems beyond that of control by the ordinary.

The rights of the palace of Westminster and St Stephen's chapel were extremely complex. The account of the serving of a citation on the countess of Warenne within the palace of Westminster, by the archdeacon of Norfolk and his official in 1420, refers to the palace as the 'most solemn' place of the kingdom, sited within the liberty of the church of Westminster. The crown defended Westminster's claims, declaring that no archbishop, bishop or other person, whosoever he might be, might exercise ordinary jurisdiction there, and the action of

---

[44] Lobel, *Borough*, p. 144. The evidence seems to suggest that it was a confirmation of an old custom, rather than an innovation, as Mrs Lobel suggests, when the burgesses sought that the borough as well as the abbey should be an asylum.

[45] N. H. MacMichael, 'Sanctuary at Westminster', *Westminster Abbey Occasional Papers*, XXVII (1971), 9–14; and see M. B. Honeybourne, 'The Sanctuary Boundaries and Environs of Westminster Abbey and the College of St Martin-le-Grand', *Journal of the British Archaeol. Assoc.*, XXXVIII, pt. 2 (1933), 316–33; I. D. Thornley, 'Sanctuary in Medieval London', *ibid.*, 293–315; and Lobel, 'Ecclesiastical Banleuca', pp. 123, 125.

[46] See J. Armitage Robinson, *Gilbert Crispin* (Cambridge, 1911), p. 37. During the course of the Peasants' Revolt of 1381, one fugitive was dragged from a pillar of St Edward's shrine, and, according to the Westminster chronicler, the failure of the revolt was due to St Edward's outrage at this insult (Thornley, 'Sanctuary', p. 299, n. 1). [47] WAM 12753.

the Norwich officials resulted in their summary committal to the Tower of London on the grounds that they must have known of the abbot of Westminster's rights.[48] The Customary of St Peter's refers to the archdeacon as being permitted to go freely to the palace and the other parts of the 'vill' of Westminster in the exercise of his duties, holding chapters and courts.[49] The rights over St Stephen's chapel within the palace were disputed intermittently until the compromise of 1394, when the abbot secured the right of inducting the dean of St Stephen's on the king's presentation, arranging certain processions and giving licence for celebrating in the oratories within the palace. Presumably his archdeacon had the usual rights over the personnel of St Stephen's chapel resident within the palace of Westminster.[50]

II

There are few surviving records of the activities of the monastic archdeacons in England. St Albans has some miscellaneous court *acta*, dating from 1425 to 1446;[51] act books and a deposition book, covering the years 1515 to 1543;[52] and testamentary material from 1415.[53] At Westminster there are some forty deeds concerning the archdeaconry, of which three are original *acta* of the archdeacon.[54] For Bury there survives the important formulary-book of William of Hoo, sacrist and monastic archdeacon from 1280 to 1294,[55] and testamentary material

[48] WAM Mun. Bk. 1, fo. 139 (PRO. E 132/35 no. 20) and WAM 5977.
[49] *Customary of the Benedictine Monasteries of St Augustine, Canterbury, and St Peter, Westminster*, ed. Sir E. M. Thompson, 2 vols., Henry Bradshaw Soc., XXIII and XXVIII (London, 1902 and 1904), II, 95; and see PRO. E 132/35, no. 19, and below p. 196.
[50] WAM Mun. Bk. 1 fos. 127, 139; and fos. 118–24 (the composition of 1394).
[51] This is contained in fos. 71 to 76b *verso* of the first surviving register of wills, Register Stoneham, in the Hertfordshire County Record Office. It occupies sixteen pages, and was obviously erroneously bound up in the middle of William of Wallingford's probate of wills, which continue in the same hand. Furthermore, the entries for Stephen London have been copied where there were blanks – on fos. 71v, last entry, 72, continuation of previous entry, and end of 76a recto. [52] Herts. County Record Office ASA 7/1, 7/2, 8/1.
[53] Archdeacon Hale gives 1408, and he had apparently seen wills dating from 1412, see W. H. Hale, *A Series of Precedents and Proceedings in Criminal Causes...from...1475 to 1640...from Act-Books of Ecclesiastical Courts in the Diocese of London* (London, 1847), p. xxxi, but they no longer exist, at least with the main deposit of records at Hertford.
[54] WAM 5981 has an impression of a fourteenth-century archdeacon's (John Borewell's) seal. E. H. Pearce, *The Monks of Westminster* (Cambridge, 1916), p. 4, n. 4, records that a die was made from Borewell's seal for ceremonial use, being handed to the archdeacon in chapter at his annual election. The office of archdeacon of Westminster continues, nominally at least.
[55] BL Harley MS 230, ed. A. Gransden, *The Letter-Book of William of Hoo Sacrist of Bury St Edmunds 1280–1294*, Suffolk Records Soc., V (1963). Jesus College, Cambridge, MS Q B 1 is a fifteenth-century Bury formulary related to this.

from 1354. For Glastonbury there is some relevant material in the *Secretum* or personal register of Abbot Walter de Monington.[56] The reason for the lack of court records of the monastic archdeacon in England is apparently their uselessness in the post-Reformation period, following the dissolution of the abbeys and their archdeaconries. This explains the better survival of St Albans records, whose archdeaconry continued within the diocese of London from 1550, whereas Westminster's archidiaconal jurisdiction vanished with the extinction of the short-lived see of Westminster in the same year.

How did the monastic archdeacon compare with the diocesan archdeacon? It seems likely that the ordinary archdeacon had assumed the two basic functions of visitation and correction and certain administrative duties by the thirteenth century, and this is probably true of the monastic archdeacon, a detailed account of whose powers and duties, as accepted in the fourteenth century, is to be found in the *Secretum*. The archdeacon visits the parishes within his jurisdiction annually and enquires about the fabric and ornaments of the churches and the condition of both clergy and laity. He proceeds *ex officio*; he also accepts instance cases. His competence is over the whole field of ecclesiastical cases: marriage, perjury, breach of faith, adultery, cases concerning testaments, laying violent hands on clerks, usury, worshipping evil spirits, witchcraft and defamation; and he may accept instance cases from parties within the jurisdiction, and from plaintiffs outside, provided that the defendant is living or staying within his jurisdiction. He imposes punishments: penances, suspension from office, interdicts and excommunication; and he absolves from the same. He celebrates monthly chapters in the archdeaconry and he examines clerks for ordination.[57]

The process of archidiaconal visitation is only obliquely referred to in the monastic archdeaconries, but it was certainly exercised. Elias le clerk of Weston Zoyland recalled Brother Edmund Barri, archdeacon of Glastonbury in the 1290s, imposing penances for *comperta* revealed at

---

[56] Bodleian, MS Wood empt. 1 (cited as S.). If this book was made for Walter de Monington then ?1341–2, and not 1340–2 as dated by Watkin (*Glastonbury Cart.* pp. x–xi). Watkin, however, believes it to be associated with John de Breynton. Can there be an identification between the *Secretum* and the register of John de Breynton which is referred to in the Feodary?

[57] S. fos. 23–23v, 25v, 26, 26v, 28. Cf. the account in 'The Friar's Tale', *The Complete Works of Geoffrey Chaucer*, ed. W. W. Skeat (Oxford, 1894), p. 359, which is remarkably similar. Geoffrey Chaucer (born *c.* 1340) began writing *The Canterbury Tales* between 1386 and 1387. On the chapter, see Scammell, 'Rural Chapter', p. 1.

his visitation.[58] Visitation was the time, too, when records were 'exhibited', the clergy producing their title deeds, letters of ordination and dispensations. According to Lyndwood, archidiaconal visitation was annual.[59] At visitations the archdeacon took procurations, which were the payments made to support the visitor in lieu of board and lodgings, or he accepted hospitality. The archdeacon also held synods to supervise the clergy and instruct them, but it was in the chapters, or private sessions of them, that correction of the clergy usually took place.[60]

At St Albans the abbot celebrated a synod of his own clerics from the fifteen churches twice a year.[61] The right to hold synods was an essential part of the archidiaconal powers and William Thorne attacked Abbot Scotland of St Augustine's Canterbury as being too complaisant in agreeing that the priests of their churches should attend the primate's synod.[62] The method of holding a synod is described for the Bury jurisdiction. The dean is ordered to cite the priests, chaplains, and others in holy orders, numbering fifteen persons from St Mary's parish, fifteen from St James's, two each from the hospital of God and of St Saviour, and three each from the hospitals of St Michael and of St Peter. All then swore oaths to be obedient to the abbot and to the sacrist. The mass of the holy spirit was celebrated, the litany sung, a sermon preached and the gospel 'I am the good shepherd' read, followed by the hymn *Veni creator spiritus*, and then the priests exhibited their letters of orders. Lastly the synodal constitutions were declared, which all had to accept.[63]

Witnesses in a case concerning the archidiaconal jurisdiction of Glastonbury which came before the Court of Arches refer specifically to the archdeacon's right to examine clerks seeking ordination. If the archdeacon approved the candidates, they were presented to the bishop. Without any further examination the bishop then conferred orders on the candidates. William Hardi of Zoy confirmed the testimony of Sir John Tys, saying that this was the procedure when his son was ordained. Nicholas Thynne of Othery, possibly a clergyman and literate, remembered being present in Bruton church in 1319 for an ordination when one of the candidates, who had not been approved by the archdeacon, was refused ordination by the bishop.[64] A further witness, Richard

---

[58] S. fo. 23v; and for Edmund Barri, see Longleat MS 10590 fo. 36.

[59] Plentiful material and exhortations in *Councils* (e.g. II, pt. I, 128) show the willingness of the archdeacons to visit. See also X. I tit.xxiii c.6 (Alexander III) and Scammell, 'Rural Chapter', p. 15.   [60] Scammell, 'Rural Chapter', pp. 14–15.   [61] *Gesta Abbatum*, I, 158.

[62] *William Thorne's Chronicle of St Augustine's Abbey Canterbury*, trans. A. H. Davis (Oxford, Basil Blackwell, 1934), pp. 54–6.   [63] BL Harley MS 645 fo. 87r–v.

[64] S. fos. 25v, 26, 26v.

Phelip of Moorlinch, recalled being present in the parish church of Zoy
at Easter 1310, when a certain Thomas de Boteleigh, clerk, presented
himself to the bishop of Bath and Wells in the chancel, duly robed for
ordination to the priesthood. But not having been approved by the
archdeacon of Glastonbury, Brother John of Worcester, he was refused
ordination until he should be presented by the archdeacon to the
bishop.[65] Institution belonged to the bishop of Bath and Wells in the
Jurisdiction of Glastonbury, but induction into corporal possession of
the living was the right of the abbot and convent of Glastonbury and
hence the monastic archdeacon.[66] Abbot de la Mare's formulary
includes an example of the abbot ordering the archdeacon of St
Albans to induct into a benefice in the exempt jurisdiction, and Archdeacon Alnwick inducted the vicar of Redbourn and the rector of
Bushey in 1430.[67] Induction was apparently the occasion when the
parson swore to inform the archdeacon of punishable (and lucrative)
misdemeanours in the parish.[68] It was also the occasion for the archdeacon to levy a fee from the inducted man.

The jurisdiction of the archdeacon over the clergy, though possibly
not older than his jurisdiction over the laity in spiritual cases, can be
traced back only very tentatively to the Northumbrian Priests' Law.[69]
But it quite clearly developed with the growth of the canon law and the
concessions of royal government (especially the Conqueror's ordinance)
from the late eleventh century onwards. Those clergy who fell short
of the requirements were the obvious prey of the archdeacons, both
ordinary and monastic, and there is nothing to distinguish between the
activities of the two here, except that parochial clergy subject to the
supervision of the monastic archdeacon were usually subject to his
house as patron. Three St Albans cases reveal the condition of the clergy.
'Ex officio' *acta* before Archdeacon Alnwick in 1434 concerned John
Mey, once chaplain of St Peter's church, St Albans, who agreed that he
was guilty of revealing the confession of Robert Hyllary, clerk of the
church, and also of public defamation; he was suspended from celebrating and later absolved.[70] A charge, doubtless brought at visitation,

---

[65] S. fo. 28.   [66] S. fo. 25.

[67] CUL MS Ee 4.20 fo. 32v; and Reg. Stoneham fo. 74, 74v; and see *PUE*, III, no. 327.

[68] Scammell, 'Rural Chapter', pp. 16–17, citing Gerald of Wales; and see Reg. Stoneham fo. 74
for the parson's oath on institution.

[69] *English Historical Documents c. 500–1042*, ed. D. Whitelock (London, 1955), no. 53, pp. 434–9.

[70] Reg. Stoneham fo. 75b *recto*. Cf. A. T. Bannister, 'Visitation Returns of the diocese of Hereford in 1397', *EHR*, XLIV (1929), 288, another case of revealing a confession. Hyllary's confession was that the woman living with him was not his wife. Parish clerks were not supposed

by certain parishioners of Chipping Barnet against their rector, John Smyth, alleged that he was lax in hearing confessions, that he did not celebrate in the parish of East Barnet and the chapel of Chipping Barnet on Sundays and feast days, and that he did not ring the bells for mass. The rector defended himself, before Abbot Wheathampstead in his greater chamber, declaring that he supplied chaplains in his stead, and he countercharged that his parishioners did not pay their tithes.[71] There is no record as to whether the rector brought an instance case against the parishioners, but the countercharge shows the way in which archidiaconal business, based on the probe of visitation, may have snowballed.[72] Charges were brought against Nicholas Grene, vicar of Abbots Langley, for not serving his cure and for non-residence. He was finally deprived.[73]

From very early times a large part of the archdeacon's work was associated with the correction of sexual offences, such as incontinency, fornication and adultery. Two confessions of incontinency, made in the presence of Thomas Pyk, archdeacon of Westminster, may have originated from visitation returns and from *publica fama*.[74] They doubtless led on to correction, which entailed a penance. The penance usually consisted of a whipping. The archdeacon did not stop, however, at enforcing beatings for sexual offences. The physical assaults on guilty parishioners would be accompanied by fines. The amounts involved have left no record and the sources are reticent about penances. Before the Conquest, secular penalties were specified for almost all ecclesiastical crimes, including sexual offences, and these were usually fines. The 'pecunial torment', to which Chaucer referred, implies payment of fines on top of a penance which would have left no record. Later sources refer clearly to fines as well as penances in *ex officio* cases.[75] A frequent form of penance in the monastic archdeaconries entailed

---

to be married, but there seems no knowledge of that in this case: see C. E. Woodruff, 'Some Early Visitation Rolls preserved at Canterbury', *Archaeologia Cantiana*, XXXII (1917), 149.

[71] Reg. Stoneham fo. 71v. The vicar of Erdesley was brought before the bishop for allowing two women to help him celebrate and ring the bells: Bannister, 'Visitation', *EHR*, XLV (1930), 447.

[72] There is an example of an instance suit between Robert Smyth, farmer of the rectory of St Stephen's, and Sir John Forthe, vicar of St Stephen's and farmer of the rectory of St Julian, in the same register (Reg. Stoneham fo. 71), heard by the archdeacon.

[73] Reg. Stoneham fo. 72v.

[74] WAM 5974–5: recorded in documentary form and sealed by the archdeacon.

[75] See A. Gransden, 'Some late thirteenth century records of an ecclesiastical court in the archdeaconry of Sudbury', *BIHR*, XXXII (1959); R. Peters, *Oculus Episcopi. Administration of the Archdeaconry of St Albans 1580–1625* (Manchester University Press, 1963), p. 62. In S. (fos. 23v, 24), for example, the witnesses refer to the imposition of penances by the Glastonbury archdeacon, but never to what they actually consisted of.

making an offering to the feretory of the shrine – usually imposed when clergy were involved. When William of Hoo imposed a penance on a rector for incontinency and for refusing purgation, thus admitting guilt, he required him to visit the shrine of St Edmund and offer one wax candle of three pounds' weight at the feretory, and to feed five poor men on the following Friday.[76] Similarly, offerings to the feretory of St Alban were ordered in early-sixteenth century cases of fornication in that archdeaconry.[77] Clearly these offences were seen as offences against the saint, who had to be recompensed and who alone could give absolution. More sinister than the payments connected with correction, but understandable and apparently common, were the payments made to the archdeacon to stay his hand.[78] The degradation of these physical punishments must have always been felt and commutation increasingly sought by those who could afford to pay.[79]

The sizeable marriage jurisdiction of the archdeacon has left little visible record. It is possible that at first the monastic archdeacon was concerned with correction and that the definite right to hear cases was not accorded to him until the twelfth century, when the law had developed considerably. In 1189 Pope Clement III licensed the abbot of Bury to hear matrimonial cases in parishes belonging to the monastery.[80] Did this mean that the abbot had at first not exercised this power, or that it had to be specified in the case of a monastic archdeaconry which had very early, and hence ill-defined, rights? In the case of an archdeaconry, like Glastonbury, which was defined later, the right was clearly there for the archdeacon to hear cases, subject to appeal to the bishop after sentence. For Glastonbury, when the bishop of Bath and Wells was attacking the jurisdiction in the fourteenth century, witnesses came forth from the parishes to tell of the cases which they remembered the archdeacon hearing between the 1290s and the 1330s. Thirteen of the seventeen cases concerned marriage and were apparently instance cases. Divorce[81] was granted on the grounds of precontract, bigamy, impotence, unlawful sexual inter-

---

[76] Jesus College MS QB I fos. 25v–26.   [77] ASA 7/1 fos. 6, 7.

[78] Scammell, 'Rural Chapter', pp. 17–18. Doubtless the bribes which the archdeacons were counselled not to accept were usually for this purpose.

[79] For commutation, see Peters, *Oculus Episcopi*, pp. 29, 76, and B. L. Woodcock, *Medieval Ecclesiastical Courts in the Diocese of Canterbury* (Oxford, 1952), p. 75.

[80] *PUE*, III, no. 416.

[81] Divorce was only absolute, 'a vinculo matrimonii', as in our sense, if it could be proved that there had never been a valid contract; otherwise, it was a separation, 'a mensa et thoro', as for adultery. The word *divorcium*, however, was used indiscriminately.

course with a relative of the other party (usually daughter) before marriage, and adultery. Four of these cases hinged on precontract.[82] The case of Joan Kympton and Nicholas Brunne, which came before the archdeacon of Westminster, was a clear case of bigamy as Joan's husband, William Twyford, was declared to be still alive and hence her liaison with Nicholas was illegal.[83] A divorce was granted to Alice Cole of Weston Zoyland on the grounds of the impotence of her husband, and to Margaret Colin and to Elena on the grounds of their husbands having had intercourse with their daughters.[84]

These were instance cases between freemen and women which were brought before the archidiaconal court. In the case of St Albans, the archdeacon of the abbey was not allowed competence to deal with the matrimonial affairs of villeins – these belonged to the cellarer.[85] Although there is no direct evidence, jurisdiction over free tenants only is likely for the other monastic archdeaconries. In the whole area of marriage jurisdiction, however, we should be wary of interpreting all cases between parties as instance jurisdiction. As has been pointed out, the distinction between office and instance cases was fine and we may well imagine that some of these cases came to light as a result of visitation. On the surface we have defended suits, but underlying this may be clerical and communal instigation. The apparitor and the clergy were known to promote cases.[86] The sentence of divorce, pronounced *ex officio* in the conventual church of St Albans in 1428, is presumably an example of clerical instigation, and, if it really was *ex officio*, illustrates that the Church could not overlook adultery even if the offended partner could.[87] Cases of correction, of adultery for example, might well lead on to divorce between the offended party and the offender. Contrariwise, an instance case for divorce on grounds of adultery or bigamy would obviously lead to correction of the offender unless he managed to flee the archdeaconry.[88]

[82] S. fos. 25, and 25v–26. [83] WAM 5989, 5990.

[84] S. fos. 23v, 25, 26. The reason for divorce is not given in the other Glastonbury cases on these folios, nor in a case before the archdeacon of St Albans: Jesus College MS QB1 fo. 124.

[85] *Studies in Manorial History by A. E. Levett*, p. 238.

[86] See Peters, *Oculus Episcopi*, p. 21; and for a clear case of initiation of proceedings by the parson, who, seeing his flock at work in the fields on a Sunday, summoned them to appear before the archdeacon's chapter: see R. Hill, 'A Berkshire Letter Book', *Berks. Archaeol. Journal*, XLI (1937), 23. For other instances of working on Sundays, which must always have roused the parson's wrath, see Gransden in *BIHR*, XXXII, and the numerous charges which occur in the records of the post-Reformation courts. [87] Reg. Stoneham fo. 73.

[88] WAM 5989, 5990. WAM 5996 shows Peter Thebaud and Joan Malwayn, described as his wife, removing themselves from the city to the archdeaconry of Westminster to avoid answer-

It seems likely that the profits from instance jurisdiction were considerably less than those from correction. Firstly the number of instance cases may well have been small.[89] Secondly, the profits probably went to the registrar and proctors and not to the owner of the jurisdiction.[90] No supporting evidence at all for the monastic archdeacons can be added to these suggestions, which have been made for the ordinary archdeacon during the later medieval period and beyond, and no accurate figures could be compiled without a run of the act books. The profits of correction of matrimonial and sexual offences are bound up with the profits of visitation. Protests were mainly against the profits from visitation and from correction, and the archdeacons were widely seen as enriching 'their own purses to the damage of poor people',[91] apparently from correction. There seems no way of estimating either, although the theory that the vigour of the archdeacons was based on their ultimate financial rewards seems outwardly acceptable.

There were also profits from the administration. The claim of the archdeacons of St Albans after 1539 to issue marriage licences, which was based on the rights of their predecessors, the monastic archdeacons,[92] was thought to be a lucrative one. By the sixteenth century, Archbishop Whitgift's table of fees for consistory courts stipulated half a mark for a licence to marry without banns, and it is possible that the fee was equally high during the medieval period.[93] No doubt, too, the certification of a marriage cost the parties something and marriages and the licences for them involved considerable profits.[94]

Controlling wills and testaments was basically an administrative function which brought profits. It is not known what probate fees were charged: probably they related to the value of the estate in

---

ing Margery Leget in a divorce case. They were, however, pursued by a letter of the commissary of the bishop of London. The definitive sentence of divorce pronounced by the archdeacon of St Albans between William Gosbyll and Elizabeth his wife in 'consistorio nostro' in 1446 on grounds of the adultery of William would have led to his correction, but there is no evidence of this because the records are so scanty (Reg. Stoneham fo. 71v).

[89] See Peters's figures for 1583 and 1588 (*Oculus Episcopi*, p. 51): 34 *ex officio*, 3 instance and 2 probate; and 17 *ex officio*, 1 instance and 1 probate.

[90] Woodcock (*Medieval Ecclesiastical Courts*, pp. 75–6) said that the archdeacon 'had no financial interest in the business of the court, apart from the fees charged for probate and small sums derived from the commutations of penance. Instance business could dwindle to zero without affecting his income'. He was, however, relieved of providing for his subordinates.

[91] Richard Burn, *Ecclesiastical Law* (4 vols., London, 1775), IV, 17 (William Lyndwood, *Provinciale* [Oxford, 1679], p. 224), citing Stratford's injunctions (Otto's injunctions printed on p. 16 of Burn imply the same). The extract continues 'it becometh not ecclesiastical persons to gape after or inrich themselves with dishonest and penal acquisitions'.

[92] Peters, *Oculus Episcopi*, pp. 11, 30–1.

[93] Burn, *Ecclesiastical Law*, II, 233.   [94] e.g. WAM 5973.

question.[95] In the thirteenth century there are a number of complaints that they were excessive.[96] The account of the goods of William Paleys, weaver of Tothill Street, Westminster, made in 1468 on an estate amounting to £6 4s 3d, shows the property going into the hands of the archdeacon of Westminster.[97] Obviously he exacted his pound of flesh, which on the basis of a tenth would have been 12s 5d. When Thomas de Bykenor, knight, died in 1416 in the palace of Westminster, the archdeacon of Westminster examined and proved the will, and, out of the goods of the deceased in the palace amounting to £20, arranged for the obsequies and funeral. Doubtless he took his cut.[98]

Hale estimated the number of wills which were proved in the archdeaconry of St Albans to have been roughly 380 between 1412 and 1439, hence about fourteen a year, and nearly 700 between 1505 and 1538, twenty-one a year.[99] The number of wills proved yearly between 1415 and 1470 averages twenty-eight a year.[100] Woodcock recorded probate fees for one year, 1505–6, for the Canterbury archdeacon. They amounted to £27 13s 4d,[101] and, although presumably in excess of those enjoyed by the archdeacon of St Albans, it may be noted that they came to nearly one-fifth of the archdeacon's total income. The proof of the will consisted of a note on the dorse and the addition of the archdeacon's seal,[102] and the registration of the will doubtless cost money.[103] At Bury there was considerable opposition to the archdeacon's control of testamentary matters. His jurisdiction was felt to be extortionate, and in 1327 the abbot was forced to promise that no fee at all should be exacted either for probate, proclamation, acquittance or administration.[104] Whether this promise was kept can only be

95 M. M. Sheehan, *The Will in Medieval England*, Pontifical Institute of Mediaeval Studies, Studies and Texts, VI (Toronto, 1963), p. 206 and n. 185, citing the provincial council of 1328, which stipulated that there was to be no fee on goods under 100s in value, and an incidence of a fee of 8d being charged in 1293 on an estate valued at 33s 8d.

96 Woodcock, *Medieval Ecclesiastical Courts*, pp. 22–3; and see below.

97 WAM 5983.   98 PRO. E 132/35 (no. 19), and WAM Mun. Bk. 1 fo. 139.

99 Hale, *Precedents*, p. xxxi. It is difficult to know what he based these figures on, particularly as the dates do not accord with the registers. Reg. Stoneham, the first surviving register, begins in 1415 (and not 1408 as Hale states) and the earliest originals in the Herts. Record Office come from 1518 (a later copy) and 1540.

100 My assessment is on Reg. Stoneham (1415–70), and on the basis of about six entries to a page (260 pp., 130 fos.).

101 Woodcock, *Medieval Ecclesiastical Courts*, p. 75.

102 Jesus College MS QB1 fo. 111.

103 S. fo. 25v – Robert Kene of 'Lym' remembered the registering of the will of Robert Drove by the archdeacon, and that the same Drove had previously been divorced from his wife.

104 Lobel, *Borough*, p. 43.

surmised: if so, the archdeacon may have managed to levy sufficient sums from other sources.

The close watch which was normally kept on the administration of wills is an indication of the profits which could accrue to the owner of the jurisdiction. In 1304 the official of the archdeacon of London wrote to the archdeacon of Westminster asking him to summon peremptorily Alice, widow and executrix of Robert, the king's tailor, who had 'fraudulently transferred' to the archdeaconry of Westminster, to render account of her administration of the will, and also to answer Elias, rector of St Mary Aldermary, the rector of St James, Garlickhithe, and Geoffrey called Belchester, chaplain, on certain matters, probably bequests.[105] The archdeacon's concern was not confined to the legatees: he had his own interests. Master John de Faringdone had something to say about the profits from intestacy in the Glastonbury jurisdiction in 1334. He recalled the case of the intestacy of Richard Sencler of But-leigh, whose goods were sequestrated by the archdeacon of Glastonbury and converted to his own uses. The official of the bishop of Bath and Wells had attempted to claim Sencler's effects in Butleigh, but relaxed his sequestration order in 1333 when he saw Glastonbury's privileges.[106] The goods of intestates were claimed in most liberties, although pro-vision was made for claimants and dependants who came forward.[107] At Westminster, with its well-developed rights of sanctuary, the abbot and convent had a confirmed right to the sequestration of goods and chattels of felons and fugitives within their liberty as well as to those of intestates.[108]

The archdeacon was only entitled to deal with the testaments and prove the wills of freemen: the testaments of villeins were the concern of the manorial courts, and, in the case of St Albans, the cellarer might prove their wills in the halimote.[109] There is every indication, however, that this was a thriving jurisdiction, bringing many testamentary cases before the archdeacon,[110] and an immense amount of administration:

[105] WAM 5969.
[106] S. fo. 28. The witness who followed, Brother Walter de Kynwardesleye, also recalled the case and confirmed that the withdrawal of the bishop's claim took place 'half a year ago' in the hostelry of Glastonbury abbey.
[107] CUL. MS Ff 2 33, fos. 149v, 159v (and see Lobel, *Borough*, p. 44, and Bodleian MS Gough Suffolk 1 fo. 72); and Jesus College MS QB1 fos. 9, 22, 26v.
[108] WAM 6219, 6234. The letter of William Montacute to Abbot Lytlington shows that the archdeacon had power to sequestrate the goods of fugitives, at least *pro tempore* (WAM 9615). The petition of Thomas Sherman for the return of his goods declares that they were seized within the sanctuary by the sacristan and by the archdeacon (WAM 6222).
[109] *Studies in Manorial History by A. E. Levett*, pp. 208–10.   [110] S. fo. 26v.

certification, relaxation on completion, the grant of letters of administration in cases of intestacy, and excommunication of those who kept
goods from executors or who did not return their records on
completion.[111]

Other cases before the archdeacon concerned perjury, breach of oath,
laying violent hands on clerks, usury, witchcraft and defamation. One
case of perjury, recalled by witnesses as coming before the archdeacon of
Glastonbury, was between Elias le clerk of Weston Zoyland, formerly
parson there, and a certain Richard de Lokyngton.[112] Two cases of
breach of oath and perjury from 1425 and 1427 came before the archdeacon of St Albans.[113] Breach of faith was often closely associated with
debt. Debt cases showed the working of the two jurisdictions, secular
and ecclesiastical. A writ was procured against a plea of debt in the Bury
sacrist's court; and the archdeacon of Westminster recorded in 1389
that Johanna Socton, the defendant in a case before his court, had
petitioned the king for a writ of prohibition on the grounds that the
suit concerned chattels and debt which were neither matrimonial nor
testamentary.[114] Laying violent hands on clergy was apparently no rare
charge. Elias le clerk again figures as the plaintiff in a case before the
archdeacon of Glastonbury, alleging that William of Zoy had violently
assaulted him.[115] Sir John Tys, staying in Glastonbury and Meare, was
brought before the archdeacon's court *ex officio* on a charge of usury,[116]
and Alice Robat of Zoy on a charge of witchcraft.[117] Usurious practices
were possibly more common in city areas; communing with spirits in
the country.[118] In 1408 the sacrist of Bury's dean heard a case of defamation in which the plaintiff alleged that Isabella, a widow, had defamed
him by saying that he had stolen certain articles from her house. His
proctor demanded Isabella's excommunication.[119] Three cases of
defamation are recorded before William Alnwick, archdeacon of St
Albans.[120] In one of them, John Palmer and his wife and John Nodde
and his wife, all of Redbourn (Herts.), were put on their best behaviour,

---

[111] See Jesus College MS QB1 fos. 9, 22, 26v; CUL MS Ff 2 33 fos. 147, 149v, 159v; and WAM
6684. [112] S. fo. 24. [113] Reg. Stoneham fo. 72, 72v.
[114] Lobel, *Borough*, p. 43 (and BL Harley MS 645 fo. 265v – breach of faith?); and WAM 5992.
[115] S. fo. 23v, and see fo. 25v. Hale, *Precedents*, cites a case of a layman breaking a priest's arm in
church (3 no. 11); and see *EHR*, XLIV (1929), 288, 449.
[116] S. fo. 24; and as a witness on fo. 25v.
[117] S. fo. 24. Eleanor, wife of Humphrey, duke of Gloucester, took sanctuary at Westminster
following a charge of treason and black magic (MacMichael, 'Sanctuary', p. 13).
[118] See e.g. Hale, *Precedents*, nos. 159, 238, 504; and *EHR*, XLIV, 287 – the chaplain of Kilpeck.
[119] Jesus College MS QB1 fo. 39r-v.
[120] Reg. Stoneham fos. 72v, 74, 75b *recto*.

after purgation, and under penalty of forty shillings, not to slander one another publicly or privately.

The archdeacon's traditional role as an excommunicator is amply illustrated. John Stowe, archdeacon of Westminster in 1388, notified William, priest of St Margaret's, within the jurisdiction, of the major excommunication of John Broke, a skinner, for the non-payment of a debt.[121] William Alnwick protected the convent of St Albans' table by ordering the vicars of the churches in the city to proclaim the excommunication of those who had killed several of their swans in 1426.[122] Monastic archdeacons, as the ordinary archdeacons, and, indeed, all ecclesiastics with jurisdictional powers, excommunicated for contumacy, the most persistent problem of the medieval court. All archdeacons called upon their fellows to publish excommunications.[123] In 1304 the archdeacon of Westminster was asked by the official of the archdeacon of London to announce an excommunication in his churches, and in 1310 the archdeacon of London's commissary asked the archdeacon of Westminster to publish the excommunication of Brother John of London, called 'le Bevere', for an offence committed within the archdeaconry of London.[124] The relaxation of sentences of excommunication entailed further administrative work.[125]

The monastic archdeacon never apparently tried to establish his own jurisdiction and separate court as did the diocesan archdeacon *vis-à-vis* the bishop.[126] This is the essential difference. The description of the archdeacon of Glastonbury as 'monk of the house and commissary of the abbot' crystallises his position as delegate of the abbot, which is found also in the other abbeys. Yet the monastic archdeacon, while functioning as the delegate of the abbot, might be extremely influential.[127] There seems little doubt that the office of archdeacon in a monastery had become a distinctly legal one by the thirteenth century. Monastic archdeacons acted as judges delegate and commissaries,[128] examining witnesses, defining boundaries and trying cases.[129] By the fourteenth century men of some scholastic quality were selected for the office,[130]

---

[121] WAM 5979. [122] Reg. Stoneham fo. 72.

[123] e.g. WAM 6684 (and Lib. Nig. Quat. fo. 124v). [124] WAM 5986, 6047.

[125] BL Harley MS 645 fo. 188; and Jesus College MS Q B 1 fos. 20v–21.

[126] Pointed out for Bury by Lobel, *Borough*, p. 42.

[127] See e.g. WAM 5965, where the archdeacon of Westminster acts as commissary of the abbot in a 1325 case about the fruits of the archdeaconry of Coventry.

[128] e.g. BL Egerton Ch. 409 and WAM 5976. [129] WAM 1262, 5982, 6113, 6684, 13530.

[130] B. Harvey, 'The Monks of Westminster and the University of Oxford', *The Reign of Richard II*, ed. F. Du Boulay and C. Barron (Athlone Press, 1971), p. 123.

and several monastic archdeacons were used as proctors before the papal curia.[131] At Westminster in 1371 the archdeacon was appointed papal conservator for Bindon by the abbot of his house, who was papal conservator for the Cistercian order in England as a whole, and, in a case some fifty years earlier, the defendant before the *auditor litterarum contradictarum* alleged that he could not litigate in England against Robert, archdeacon of Westminster, on account of his power there.[132] Robert had already claimed papal exemption from excommunication and suspension. How could a simple rector hope to fight such a man on equal terms?

By the fourteenth century the archdeacon of Glastonbury had a commissary,[133] as did the archdeacon of St Albans by the mid-fifteenth century. William Albon, commissary at St Albans in 1441, when Stephen London was archdeacon, followed him in the office in 1446.[134] The last archdeacon of St Albans (prior to the dissolution of the house in 1539), Thomas Kyngesbury, had a commissary, Christopher Leysey, whose business is indistinguishable in the Act Books from the archdeacon's.[135] Within his archdeaconry, the archdeacon was served by a dean (at Bury at least) and by apparitors.[136] In 1391 the archdeacon of Westminster appointed an apparitor: previously he had used the chaplain of St Margaret's church for citing and excommunicating within the archdeaconry.[137] There is some evidence that it was the apparitor, too, from amongst the archdeacon's henchmen, who meted out the punishments with his rod.[138]

In terms of remuneration it is difficult to compare the position of the monastic archdeacon with that of the ordinary archdeacon. A document of 1601 among the St Albans records says that the archdeacon and the register had 'in times past' several pensions of the abbot which since the dissolution are 'detained and not paid'.[139] It is not clear whether these sums were alternatives or supplements to fees, but it is quite possible that the archdeacon received certain fixed monetary payments, and that the court perquisites and fees from correction and the administra-

[131] William Amondesham, archdeacon of Westminster in 1414, proctor of the abbot of Holy Cross, Waltham (WAM 5988), and cf. William Colchester, proctor of Westminster in 1382 and possibly monastic archdeacon at the same time (WAM 18478D, and F).

[132] WAM, 5999, 6000.   [133] *Glastonbury Cart.* no. 68: by name, Walter Broun, clerk.

[134] Reg. Stoneham fos. 35–6, 36–50 and 50–60.   [135] ASA 7/1 fo. 1a *verso*.

[136] Lobel, *Borough*, p. 42; and BL Harley MS 645 fo. 266.   [137] WAM 5979, 5981, 5989.

[138] Scammell, 'Rural Chapter', p. 18, referring to Rochester diocese (the sub-apparitor) and *Registrum Hamonis Hethe*, ed. Charles Johnson, 2 vols., CYS, XLVIII–XLIX (1948), I, 441–2.

[139] *Records of the Old Archdeaconry of St Albans: A Calendar of Papers 1575 to 1637*, ed. H. R. Wilton Hall, St Albans and Hertfordshire Archit. and Archaeol. Soc. (1908), no. 156.

tion went straight into the common monastic fund. The tenacity with which the monks defended their rights as monastic archdeacons might be explained by the value of the parishes within the archdeaconries as much as by the profits of archidiaconal jurisdiction. There is evidence of the profitability of the sacrist's rights within the parishes as well as the borough at Bury, where the geographical area was small. At Westminster, where similarly the archdeaconry was small, the monastic archdeacon may have relied mainly for his profits on the sanctuary rights, although those over the palace must have been lucrative, particularly from the wills of gentry who did not quite qualify for the jurisdiction of the Prerogative Court of Canterbury.

Both Glastonbury and St Albans had a considerable number of subject parishes, Glastonbury seven and St Albans fifteen, and these merit closer investigation. The wealth of Glastonbury throughout the Middle Ages was proverbial and was equalled by no other house from the time of Domesday to the Dissolution (when its net income was £3311).[140] The estates of the Jurisdiction included particularly profitable marshland, mills and fishponds in the seven parishes, and it may be that the ecclesiastical profits compare well with the income in economic and seigneurial terms. The *Taxatio* shows the richest church, Zoy, to be worth £33 3s 8d. Moorlinch came next at £20 13s 4d, followed by St John's, Glastonbury, and Street, £16, and £16 13s 4d, and Shapwick, £15 6s 8d. The other two, Butleigh and Meare, were assessed at under £15.[141] The surveyors of 1539 recorded the payment of fifty-three shillings from the six churches (Glastonbury excluded), being the procurations and synodal payments payable 'allwayes' to the archdeacon. In pensions, Glastonbury received £7 from Moorlinch; £1 from Shapwick; £1 from Butleigh; £3 from Street; and £2 13s 4d from Middlezoy. The tithes of hay belonging to the parsonages of Shapwick and Moorlinch and of Meare were worth annually the considerable sum of £86; the tithes belonging to the parsonage of Glastonbury £72, and the tithes of corn and hay of Butleigh and Baltonsborough were leased to Elizabeth Adams for £12 and for £8 10s yearly. The total sum from the Glastonbury parsonages

---

[140] D. Knowles, *The Religious Orders in England* III (Cambridge, 1959), 473–4.

[141] On the estates of Glastonbury in the twelfth century, see M. Postan, *Essays on Medieval Agriculture and...the Medieval Economy* (Cambridge, 1973), pp. 249–77. Some of the grievances of Glastonbury against Bishop Jocelin were that he had despoiled mills and fishponds. A papal ordination stated that the fishpond of Meare was to be shared (Cambridge, Trinity College MS R 5 33 fo. 42v). *Taxatio Ecclesiastica...Nicholai IV*, ed. S. Ayscough and J. Caley (1802), p. 198.

amounted to £315 3s 4d, of which £176 10s came from archidiaconal sources; and the total sum from the spiritualities in Somerset amounted to £354 18s, of which £193 16s 4d was provided by income of various kinds from the seven churches.[142]

The net income of St Albans, according to the *Valor*, was £2102, thus putting it in fourth place. It had considerably improved its position since the Domesday survey, when its position was tenth.[143] For St Albans the *Taxatio* estimates a sum of £297 2s from the archdeaconry.[144] According to the King's Books, six of the livings were worth between £40 and £50 (between £8 and £18 at the time of the *Taxatio*) and the archdeacon was entitled to 48s from procurations and to 48s 2d from synodals.[145] As with Glastonbury, appropriation had continued relentlessly over the years: Hexton was assigned to the sacrist in 1243 and Norton to the monks' ale in 1258. The scriptor had a portion in Redbourn; the chamberlain pensions in Redbourn, Abbots Langley and Winslow; and the infirmarer in St Peter's, St Albans – possibly appropriated in 1252. This last church, with its chapels, was estimated in the *Taxatio* as worth £60, of which the vicar received £5 and the infirmarer £5 6s 8d. The next most valuable living in the thirteenth century was Winslow, worth £18, with its chapels of Horwood and Grandborough, followed by Redbourn (£17 6s 8d), Rickmansworth (£16) and Watford (£12). There were some distinct changes in value between the 1290s and the 1540s, but the position of overall wealth from these churches did not change – roughly double that accruing to Glastonbury, which, on a basis of twice the number of churches, levels out.

In conclusion, the main profits made by the monastic archdeacons probably came from the shortcomings of people, although the evidence to clinch this is simply not available. The archdeacon's operations were built upon fear and terror which the structure of society reinforced. Efficiency seems to have been the keynote of the ordinary archdeacon's activities. Indeed, the most remarkable feature of archidiaconal administration over the whole medieval period was its relentless efficiency,[146] and it is difficult to see the monastic archdeacon with his

---

[142] Dugdale, *Mon. Angl.* I, 15.

[143] Knowles, *Religious Orders*, III, 473–4.   [144] *Taxatio*, p. 37.

[145] John Ecton, *Thesaurus Rerum Ecclesiasticarum* (London, 1742), pp. 375–6. Peters (*Oculus Episcopi*, p. 10, n. 6) gives the considerably higher figure of £3 14s for procurations in the 1570s (from Act Book VII).

[146] See Scammell, 'Rural Chapter', pp. 1–21, and M. Bowker, 'Some Archdeacons' Court

smaller archdeaconry as less exacting than his diocesan counterpart. Courts in medieval England were frequented by specific social classes. When the jurisdiction of Glastonbury was attacked, the house appealed immediately to the pope. When Bishop Grosseteste commissioned his archdeacons to inquire into the morals of *all* people within his diocese, it caused loud protest from the gentry who did not accept correction from the archdeacon.[147] But the archdeacon's inquisitions into the affairs of the majority of men and women had to be tolerated. The peasants knew his court as the corrective ecclesiastical counterpart to the manorial court, and even the freemen knew little of the world of king's and bishops' courts, and of appeals to other *fora*. Instance cases brought by freemen came before the archdeacon, who also drew money from this group by providing them with essential administrative documents, for which the Church had created a need – a licence to marry, perhaps, or probate of a will. There was a fair amount of truth in the Chaucerian phrase that before the bishop caught them with his crook they were all down in the archdeacon's book.

Coupled with the profits from correction, from administration and, to a lesser extent, from instance cases, were the additional assets from the subject churches and from land-ownership in the parishes. The parishes forming the archdeaconries may not have been excessively rich, but the livings were substantial. Pensions were paid from them, the livings were gradually appropriated and the manors forming the parishes were intensively farmed. Sowy island and its surrounding moors, for example, increased dramatically in value in the mid-thirteenth century due to drainage, and so consequently did the value of its church.[148] The jurisdictional quarrels between Wells and Glastonbury were also economic disputes. The great monasteries of Glastonbury, St Albans, Bury and Westminster had been well endowed. No unworthy gifts had been bestowed on their saints. The patrimony of the saints brought money from pilgrims,[149] from the rights of jurisdiction and from the lands. They were trusts to be handed down intact. Economic advantages ensured that tradition was maintained.

Books and the Commons' Supplication against the Ordinaries of 1532' in *The Study of Medieval Records*, ed. D. A. Bullough and R. L. Storey (Oxford, 1971), esp. pp. 287–90, 311–12.

[147] Cited by Scammell, 'Rural Chapter', pp. 18–19; and cf. Peters, *Oculus Episcopi*, pp. 80–1, and Bowker, 'Some Archdeacons' Court Books', esp. pp. 308–16, who argues that it was when heresy cases became more frequent, bringing gentry before the archidiaconal courts, that protests were made.   [148] Williams, *Draining of the Somerset Levels*, pp. 47–51.

[149] Knowles, *Religious Orders*, III, 249, n.1 records the total of c. £1142 in offerings to St Thomas of Canterbury in 1220.

THE 'LEX DIVINITATIS'
IN THE BULL 'UNAM SANCTAM' OF
POPE BONIFACE VIII

by DAVID LUSCOMBE

SIR MAURICE POWICKE once argued that universities in the thirteenth century should not be studied as secluded citadels of scholastic speculation but as workshops of opinion on matters of public interest.[1] The Bull *Unam Sanctam* has long been recognised to be an example of an official statement which owes much to the attitudes of university masters.[2] It consists almost entirely of teachings about the nature of ecclesiastical society which reflect the study of authorities such as Scripture, St Bernard, Hugh of St Victor and Thomas Aquinas.[3] The chief interest of the Bull is with the theological question of the unity of the Church, and it provided a plain statement of the subordination of temporal to spiritual jurisdiction. Hunters after sources have examined it in great detail, but they have not given much consideration to the place occupied in the Bull by the pseudo-Denis the Areopagite nor has the Bull's position in the context of the earlier and later development of studies of the Dionysian corpus of writings been explained. Yet it is fully recognised that in thirteenth-century polemics the texts of the pseudo-Denis were put to kaleidoscopically varied use on questions concerning the nature of the Church, the relationship between bishops, the Mendicants and the papacy, and the location of the state of perfection within ecclesiastical hierarchy.[4]

[1] F. M. Powicke, 'The Medieval University in Church and Society', and 'Some Problems in the History of the Medieval University' in *Ways of Medieval Life and Thought. Essays and Addresses* (London, 1949).
[2] Ed. E. Friedberg, *Corpus Iuris Canonici* (Leipzig, 1879), II, 1245. Cf. F. M. Powicke, 'The Medieval University', p. 205. For a recent assessment see W. Ullmann, 'Die Bulle *Unam Sanctam*: Rückblick und Ausblick', *Römische Historische Mitteilungen*, XVI (1974), 45–77.
[3] Cf. J. Rivière, *Le Problème de l'église et de l'état au temps de Philippe le Bel: Étude de théologie positive*. Spicilegium Sacrum Lovaniense, VIII (Louvain, 1926), pp. 79–91, 394–404. Cf. p. 88: 'fidèle expression et parfois simple reproduction de la théologie commune'.
[4] Cf. the fundamental and brilliant study of Y. Congar, 'Aspects ecclésiologiques de la querelle entre mendiants et séculiers dans la seconde moitié du XIIIe siècle et le début du XIVe siècle', *Archives d'histoire doctrinale et littéraire au moyen âge*, 36ème année (1961), pp. 35–151.

In *Unam Sanctam* the pseudo-Denis is prominently cited in this context:

Nam quum dicat Apostolus: 'Non est potestas nisi a Deo; quae autem sunt, a Deo ordinata sunt', non autem ordinata essent, nisi gladius esset sub gladio, et tamquam inferior reduceretur per alium in suprema. Nam secundum B. Dionysium lex divinitatis est infima per media in suprema reduci. Non ergo secundum ordinem universi omnia aeque ac immediate, sed infima per media et inferiora per superiora ad ordinem reducuntur.

J. Rivière described this passage as a syllogism, the major premiss being provided by St Paul (*Romans*, 13:1 – all power is ordained by God), the minor by St Denis (powers are arranged in subordinate ranks), while the conclusion is expressed in the allegory of the two swords (therefore the spiritual sword must regulate the temporal).[5] Rivière also revealed the close verbal similarity between this passage (and other formulas used in *Unam Sanctam*) and its immediate source, the treatise *De ecclesiastica potestate*, I, 4, of Giles of Rome.[6] Though Rivière did not himself examine Giles's positions in relation to the writings of the pseudo-Denis, Y. Congar pointed, in a celebrated study, to the part played by Giles of Rome in the quarrels between the Mendicant friars and the Secular clergy.[7] In these debates the writings of the pseudo-Denis had encouraged many to think of the celestial hierarchy as an exemplar of the Church militant, and to criticise or to defend the hierarchical structure of the latter in the light of an interpretation of the former. How, then, was the *lex divinitatis* invoked and interpreted before, in and after the composition of *Unam Sanctam*?

Reference to the collection of Latin translations presented in Chevallier's *Dionysiaca* reveals that the citation of the pseudo-Denis in *Unam Sanctam* is not taken from the text itself.[8] The phrase *lex divinitatis est infima per media in suprema reduci* does not appear as such in the available Latin translations of chapter 5 of the *Ecclesiastical Hierarchy*[9] where Denis explains the beauty of the priestly orders and hierarchies. Phrases and terms such as *lex hierarchiae, divina lex, hierarchicus ordo, reductio, prima et media et ultima, summus et ultimus*, abound, especially in the translations made by John the Saracen and by Robert Grosseteste, but the nearest parallel is the following:[10]

---

[5] Rivière, *L'Église et l'état*, p. 396.   [6] *Ibid.* appendix II, 394–404.

[7] Congar, 'Aspects ecclésiologiques', pp. 138–42.

[8] *Dionysiaca. Recueil donnant l'ensemble des traductions latines des ouvrages attribués au Denys l'Aréopage...* (2 vols., Bruges, 1937).

[9] The reference by Congar, 'Aspects ecclésiologiques', p. 140, n. 352 to the pseudo-Denis, *Celestial Hierarchy*, c. 10 needs correction.   [10] *Dionysiaca*, p. 1330.

Lex divinitatis *in* Unam Sanctam

Lex quidem haec est Divinitatis sacratissima: per prima secunda ad divinissimam suam reducere lucem. (Eriugena)

Lex quidem ista est Thearchiae sanctissima: per prima secunda ad divinissimum sursumagi splendorem. (Saracenus)

Lex quidem ista est Thearchiae omnino sacra: per prima secunda ad divinissimum ipsius reduci splendorem. (Grosseteste)

With these may be compared further phrases in the *Celestial Hierarchy*, in which Denis demonstrates the mediating role of angels between men and God and the tripartite division of each hierarchy:

Docet autem et hoc sapienter theologia per angelos eam in nos provenire, tamquam divino legali ordine illud legaliter ponente hoc est per prima secunda in divinum reduci...ipsa lex definitur ex superessentiali omnium ordinationis principio: hoc est, per unamquamque hierarchiam primas et medias et ultimas esse et ordinationes et virtutes, et minorum esse diviniores doctores et manuductores in divinam adductionem et illuminationem et communicationem. (*Celestial Hierarchy*, c. 4, Chevallier, pp. 812–14)

Hoc enim est omnino divina taxiarchia divinitus promulgatum per prima secunda divinis participare illuminationibus. (*Celestial Hierarchy*, c. 8, Chevallier, pp. 881–2)

Lucet autem per singula secundis per prima. Et si oportet breviter dicere, primo ex occulto ad manifestum ducitur. (*Celestial Hierarchy*, c. 13, Chevallier, p. 970)

The pseudo-Denis revealed the universal character of these principles; they explain not only the arrangement of the angelic ranks but the hierarchic character of all creation:

Nonne ergo hierarchiam qui dicit, sacram quamdam universaliter declarat dispositionem. (*Celestial Hierarchy*, c. 3, Chevallier, p. 790)

...in omnibus exsistentibus per prima secundis distribuuntur quae sunt secundum dignitatem ab omnium ordinatissima et justissima providentia. (*Letter VIII to Demophilus*, Chevallier, p. 1537)

Et universitatis ordines et cumulationes in proprium optimum persalvat. (*Divine Names*, c. 8, Chevallier, p. 425)

Ipsa autem hierarchici ordinis virtus in omnibus locatur sacris universitatibus, et per omnes divinos ordines operatur propriae hierarchiae mysteria. Discrete autem huic ultra ceteros ordines in suam operationem divina lex distribuit diviniores sacrificationes. (*Ecclesiastical Hierarchy*, c. 5, Chevallier, pp. 1334–5)

The hierarchic character of creation, its tripartite divisions, are really a law of order reflecting the harmony existing within the Trinity itself and underlying the resemblances that exist between God and creation:

Ab ipsa autem iterum proportionaliter secunda, et a secunda tertia, et ex tertia secundum nos hierarchia, secundum ipsam beneornantis ordinationis legem in harmonia divina et analogia ad simul omnis boni ornatus superprincipale principium et consummationem hierarchice reducitur. (*Celestial Hierarchy*, c. 10, Chevallier, pp. 919–20)

...thearchicas leges quae et totos gubernant supercaelestium ordinum et substantiarum sanctos ornatus. (*Divine Names*, c. 1, Chevallier, p. 17)

...hierarchica lex... (*Divine Names*, c. 1, Chevallier, p. 54; *Ecclesiastical Hierarchy*, c. 1, Chevallier, p. 1103)

Pope Boniface's Bull, in reproducing the gist of the pseudo-Denis's 'law of divinity', clearly referred to a wide, cosmic view of hierarchy which had been deeply explored by many in the thirteenth century. But whereas the pseudo-Denis typically wrote of created beings which are separated from each other according to the degree to which they participate in the divine light, the Bull focusses upon the jurisdictional relationship between lay and clerical power as seen in a universal framework.

The pseudo-Denis's angelology had been given a political significance much earlier by writers such as William of Auvergne[11] and Alan of Lille.[12] The writings of Alan, in particular, had been highly influential among the early thirteenth-century masters who discussed the hierarchies of the pseudo-Denis[13] and who form an essential background to the deployment, studied by Congar, of the theme of the 'reduction', or the leading back, of creatures to the source of light during the debates between the Mendicants and the Seculars. At bottom, these quarrels were partly a dispute between supporters of centralising authority and the champions of autonomy;[14] the recourse of Boniface VIII to the pseudo-Denis's 'law of divinity' during his quarrel with King Philip the Fair may be made more explicable by examining some earlier uses of this 'law'.

Our starting point should be St Bonaventure, for not only was Bonaventure, as Congar suggested, 'peut-être l'un des plus authentiquement

---

[11] See the pioneering study of William's *De universo* by B. Vallentin, 'Der Engelstaat. Zur mittelalterlichen Anschauung vom Staate (bis auf Thomas von Aquino)', *Grundrisse und Bausteine zur Staats und zur Geschichtslehre zusammengetragen zu den Ehren Gustav Schmollers*, ed. K. Breysig, F. Wolters, B. Vallentin, F. Andreae (Berlin, 1908), pp. 41–120.

[12] See M. T. d'Alverny, *Alain de Lille. Textes inédits avec une introduction sur sa vie et ses oeuvres.* Études de philosophie médiévale LII (Paris, 1965), p. 108.

[13] Cf. H. F. Dondaine, 'Cinq citations de Jean Scot chez Simon de Tournai', *Recherches de théologie ancienne et médiévale*, XVII (1950), 303–11; M-T. d'Alverny, *Alain de Lille*, pp. 94, 98–9.

[14] Cf. M-M. Dufeil, *Guillaume de Saint-Amour et la polémique universitaire parisienne, 1250–1259* (Paris, 1972), p. 156.

dionysiens qu'on rencontre en Occident,'[15] but Franciscan spokesmen, under his leadership, were prominent in the development of ideas concerning papal primacy in the thirteenth and fourteenth centuries.[16] Bonaventure's interest in the pseudo-Denis owed much to Praepositinus of Cremona, one of the band of writers who had followed Alan of Lille in defining hierarchy as power: 'rerum sacrarum et rationabilium ordinata potestas, in subditis debitum retinens principatum'.[17] Alan and his followers used this or similar definitions, with their Pauline echo, to popularise and to transform an arsenal of concepts and terms that stemmed, not always directly, from the pseudo-Denis.[18] But among Franciscan writers prior to Bonaventure, only Alexander of Hales – 'pater et magister noster' – cited the pseudo-Denis frequently. Bonaventure and Alexander shared a remarkable passion for the works of the pseudo-Denis,[19] and the quarrel with the Seculars particularly encouraged Franciscans who knew those works to advance the thesis that at the summit of the ecclesiastical hierarchy stood the pope. Secular masters did not disagree. Indeed, though the theme of Bonaventure's *De perfectione evangelica* (written before 1256) is the 'ratio obedientiae ad unum et summum' in heaven, in ethics and in nature,[20] and though Bonaventure made a lasting contribution by describing Christ and His vicar as the 'summus hierarcha' distributing offices and dispensing charisms 'miro ordine instar civitatis supernae',[21] the same motif is equally present in the writings of William of Saint-Amour who describes the pope as 'huius Hierarchiae generalis Rector' and as 'Summus Hierarcha'.[22] But Bonaventure surpassed the Seculars in his portrayal of all the different ministries and grades to be found in the

[15] Congar, 'Aspects ecclésiologiques', p. 111.

[16] Cf. J. Ratzinger, 'Der Einfluss des Bettelordenstreites auf die Entwicklung der Lehre vom päpstlichen Universalprimat, unter besonderer Berücksichtigung des heiligen Bonaventura', *Theologie in Geschichte und Gegenwart.* Festschrift Michael Schmaus, ed. J. Auer and H.Volk (Munich, 1957), pp. 697–724, here p. 720.

[17] *Commentaria in secundum librum Sententiarum Magistri Petri Lombardi,* dist. IX. *S. Bonaventurae... Opera omnia...edita studio et cura PP. Collegii a S. Bonaventura...*II (Ad Claras Aquas, 1885); *Sermo V de sanctis angelis. Opera,* IX (1901), 622; *Apologia pauperum,* C.IX, 4. *Opera,* VIII (1898), 428.

[18] Dondaine, 'Cinq citations'; d'Alverny, *Alain de Lille,* pp. 94–9, 202–3, 225.

[19] For Bonaventure see J. G. Bougerol, 'Saint Bonaventure et le pseudo-Denys l'Aréopagite', *Actes du Colloque Saint Bonaventure, 9–12 sept. 1968.* Orsay. Études franciscaines. Supplément, pp. 33–123. A similar study with respect to Alexander of Hales might be instructive.

[20] *De perfectione evangelica,* q. IV, art, 3. *Opera,* V (1891), 189–98.

[21] *Lignum vitae, Opera,* VIII (1898), 83.

[22] *Tractatus brevis de periculis novissimorum temporum* (written 1255), partially ed. M. Bierbaum, *Bettelorden und Weltgeistlichkeit an der Universität Paris. Texte und Untersuchungen zum Literarischen Armuts – und Exemtionsstreit des 13.Jahrhunderts (1255–1272).* Franziskanische Studien, 2. Beiheft (Münster i.W., 1920), pp. 186, 187.

Church – a complex variety which had to be 'reduced' to unity as required by the 'universalis justitiae ordo'.[23] Bonaventure insisted upon the pseudo-Denis's 'law of divinity': in his Commentary on Book II of the *Sentences* (begun in 1248) and elsewhere he adapted the law and in so doing came close to the very phrase subsequently found in *Unam Sanctam*: 'lex universitatis hoc exigit, ut media reducantur per prima, et postrema per media ad suum primum principium...'[24] The high point of Bonaventure's elaborate examination of the hierarchies occurs in the *Collationes in Hexaemeron* which he delivered at Paris in 1273 at the height of the troubles with Siger.[25] In his second *Collatio* on the fourth day of creation, Bonaventure, who claims only to be summarising the *Celestial Hierarchy*,[26] describes how the Trinity (itself a hierarchy) impresses its character upon the angelic hierarchy which therefore comes to resemble God and to be assimilated to the divine Persons. The angels in turn hierarchise the Church militant and impress hierarchic features upon it. Bonaventure thinks in terms of a double movement of egression from God, a descent towards the world, and of a return or 'reduction' of all creation to God by way of assimilation to the Trinity, that is, by way of being hierarchised. In the third *Collatio* on the fourth day of creation, Bonaventure considers the Church militant, in which the orders should correspond to the celestial hierarchy which makes them visible. But there are three different ways of contemplating the ecclesiastical hierarchy. The first of these reflects the egression of the Church from God: the Church has unfolded gradually; its hierarchic character has evolved historically. In its foundation, its structure was assured by the order of Patriarchs; ultimately, it will be consummated by the members of religious orders who, being chaste, will cease to generate successors to themselves. The progression of the Church in time imitates the procession of the divine Persons which is

---

23 *De perfectione evangelica*, q. IV, art. 3. *Opera*, V (1891), 194.

24 *Comm. in secundum librum Sententiarum...dist.* XI. *Opera*, II (1885), 277. Cf. Bougerol, 'Saint Bonaventure et le pseudo-Denis', p. 70, who presents detailed references, but refers to the *Celestial Hierarchy*, c. 4 as does R. Guardini, *Systembildende Elemente in der Theologie Bonaventuras*, ed. W. Dettloff. Studia et Documenta Franciscana III (Leiden 1964), 109.

25 For studies of the *Collationes* see J. G. Bougerol, 'Saint Bonaventure et la hiérarchie dionysienne', *Archives d'histoire doctrinale et littéraire au moyen âge*, XXXVI (1969), 131–67; A. Elsässer, 'Die verschiedenen Stände in der Kirche nach der Lehre des heiligen Bonaventura', *Wissenschaft und Weisheit*, XXXI (1968), 13–29, and J. Ratzinger, *Die Geschichtstheologie des heiligen Bonaventura* (Munich–Zurich, 1959).

26 *Coll. in Hexaemeron, Visio IV, coll. II* (spoken version), ed. F. Delorme, *S. Bonaventurae Collationes in Hexaemeron et Bonaventuriana quaedam selecta*. Bibliotheca Franciscana Scholastica Medii Aevi VIII (Ad Claras Aquas, 1934); *Coll. XXI* (enlarged reported version), *Bonaventurae ...Opera omnia* (Ad Claras Aquas, 1891), V, 436.

also reflected in the angelic orders. The second way of considering the Church's hierarchy reflects the ascent of man to God: man is purified, enlightened and perfected by the ecclesiastical hierarchy which includes in its highest grade of perfectors the pope who alone has the plenitude of power and of jurisdiction over all. But the third way of considering the hierarchy of the Church consists in understanding the distinction between the active and the contemplative life. The active life is predominantly that led by the laity. Bonaventure's view of the quality of lay government in his own day was somewhat cool: whereas a man such as St Ambrose had advised an emperor, 'nunc totum est subversum' for modern princes are 'socii furum' (*Isaiah*, 1:23).[27] So, the 'reduction' of the people to God is the task of prelates, and the pseudo-Denis in his *Ecclesiastical Hierarchy* left no doubt that prelacy is the most eminent state in the active hierarchy. There is, however, another hierarchy of those most successfully perfected by the prelates. This is constructed according to the perfection of the religious state arrived at by contemplatives. Contemplatives, that is, the members of religious orders uninvolved in the prelatical or active life, stand at the apex of this hierarchy and are set above the clergy in three further grades: Cistercians and Premonstratensians, then above them Preachers and Minors, and finally on the summit perfect Contemplatives such as St Francis himself. The contemplative hierarchy may engage in the hierarchical work of purifying, enlightening and perfecting others if authorised to do so by their Ordinaries or by the Supreme Pontiff. Indeed, Bonaventure finds support in the *Ecclesiastical Hierarchy* for the papal claim to be able to override episcopal rights and the rights of the secular clergy in favour of the Mendicants, for, according to the pseudo-Denis, the hierarch has all power gathered into himself; whatever a lower grade may do, a higher can also do. Therefore, a pope may send out assistants whenever it seems expedient or whenever a deficiency in the Church requires the despatch of suitable men.[28]

Earlier writers such as William of Auvergne and Alan of Lille had distinguished and described elaborately a separate secular hierarchy corresponding to that of the Church. Bonaventure completely incorporates secular rulership into the latter which embraces both the active and contemplative forms of life. The lay order serves to procreate those

[27] *Coll. in Hexaemeron, Visio IV, Coll. III*, ed. Delorme, p. 255; *Coll. XXII, Bonaventurae...Opera omnia*, v, 440.

[8] *Expositio super regulam fratrum minorum*, c. IX, 4, *Bonaventurae...Opera omnia*, VII, 428.

dedicated to contemplation. Bonaventure's hierarchies begin their ascent with the 'ordo laicus' ('qui est producens'); they rise through the 'ordo clericalis' ('qui est productus et etiam producens') to the 'ordo monasticus' ('qui est productus tantum'); in this is achieved the ascent of men to the heavenly Jerusalem and their imitation of the heavenly hierarchy.[29]

Bonaventure's vision, which is most elaborately developed in his *Collationes*, embraces the whole universe which is fully hierarchic even in the Trinity, the planets and the individual human soul; it is supported by rich allegories, by a sweeping vision of history and by intricate analysis of the concordances between each order in every type of hierarchy. No other Franciscan master offered such a full elucidation of the Dionysian hierarchies but examples of other Franciscans who gave them a papalist interpretation can be easily multiplied. Adam Marsh, for instance, outlined the supremacy of the pope as ruler over three hierarchies, the lowest being occupied by kings, people and penitents; and he referred to St Bernard of Clairvaux on the two swords.[30] The treatise, *Manus que contra omnipotentem*, written *c.* 1259 and attributed to the Franciscan Thomas of York, also develops the conception of the supreme hierarch – the pope – by whom all power and influence is distributed in the Church.[31] In Paris, Bonaventure's successor as Minister-General in 1257, Guibert of Tournai, dedicated effusive treatises to members of royal and noble families in which he adapted the ideal of the *reductio in Deum* to the secular sphere and wrote of the king as the one who reproduces on earth the model of the Church triumphant; in the republic the king is subject to God's ministers on earth. 'Quoniam inferiora reducuntur in superiora per media, constituti sunt principes et praelati, ut per eorum ministerium reducantur in Deum angelico more subjecti.'[32]

Albert the Great and Thomas Aquinas accepted that the model of the Church triumphant was a convenient foundation of the Mendicant view

[29] On this see Congar, 'Aspects ecclésiologiques', pp. 126–7.

[30] *Letter* 246 (written in 1250), ed. J. S. Brewer, *Monumenta Franciscana*. RS (London, 1858), pp. 413ff., 436–7. Adam Marsh, of course, was a close associate of Grosseteste who, as Dr Pantin said, 'was prepared to apply a suitable dose of...the pseudo-Denis to almost any problem' ('Grosseteste's Relations with the Papacy and the Crown', *Robert Grosseteste. Scholar and Bishop*, ed. D. A. Callus (Oxford, 1955), pp. 178–215). But how much influence Grosseteste's famous applications of the writings of the pseudo-Denis had upon later Franciscan writers has still to be determined.   [31] Ed. Bierbaum, *Bettelorden und Weltgeistlichkeit*, pp. 151–5.

[32] *Eruditio regum et principum* (written in 1259), ed. A. de Poorter, *Les Philosophes Belges*, IX (Louvain, 1914), here p. 84. Cf. Congar, 'Aspects ecclésiologiques', pp. 135–6.

of the papacy as the sole presidency for all members of the ecclesiastical hierarchy, but neither indulged in a mystique of the pope as *primus* or *summus hierarcha*.[33] Albert, the thorough commentator of the pseudo-Denis, was prone to refer to the *lex divinitatis*:

Haec enim est lex divinitatis, ut per prima media, & ultima per media reducantur.
...cum lex divinitatis sit per prima media, & per media ultima reducere.
lex divinitatis est ubique per prima media & per haec ultima reducere, ut supra dictum est.[34]

Moreover, Albert applied the idea of *reductio* to the pope who gathers together the different grades in the mystical body in accordance with the 'law of divinity':

...sicut dicit beatus Dionysius: 'Lex Divinitatis est per prima media, et per media ultima reducere.' Talis autem reductio ultimorum ad media et mediorum ad prima non potest esse nisi in ordine ad unum primum. Sic igitur Divinitatis lex sicut est descensus illuminationum et charismatum ab uno, sic reductio est ad unum.[35]

However, Albert did not emulate Bonaventure in the latter's imaginatively prolific excursions to the many different hierarchic realms. He stayed, on the whole, close to the text and meaning of the pseudo-Denis. Like Grosseteste, he did not introduce topical questions into his commentaries upon the pseudo-Denis.

Aquinas did more in this matter, or at least he did so more obviously. It is now appreciated that Aquinas, the pupil of Albert, owed a considerable debt to the pseudo-Denis and other neoplatonists in elaborating a view of a universe that is united because it consists of a continuous, graded hierarchy of unequal beings, the lower levels of which participate and are included in the higher.[36] Human nature occupies the lowest

---

33 Cf. Congar, 'Aspects ecclésiologiques', pp. 132–4, and especially n. 321.

34 *Commentarii in librum B. Dionysii Areopagitae...de celesti hierarchia, Opera*, XIII, ed. P.Jammy (Lyons, 1651), 2, 52, 131. For discussion of the date of Albert's Commentaries on the pseudo-Denis (1248–52, though the Comm. on the *Cel. Hier.* may have been written before 1248) see the references collected by F. Ruello, *Les 'Noms divins' et leurs 'raisons' selon Saint Albert le Grand, commentateur du 'De divinis nominibus'*. Bibliothèque thomiste, XXXV (Paris, 1963), 12; and more recently see P. Simon, prolegomena to *Albertus Magnus. Super Dionysium de divinis nominibus. Alberti Magni Opera omnia*, XXXVII, I (Münster i.W., 1972), pp. VI–VII.

35 Cited by Congar, 'Aspects ecclésiologiques', p. 112, n. 250, from *De sacrificio Missae*, tr. III, c. 6, n. 9, ed. A. Borgnet, *Opera omnia*, XXXVIII (Paris, 1890), 103–4.

36 See most recently E-H. Wéber, *La Controverse de 1270 à l'université de Paris et son retentissement sur la pensée de S. Thomas d'Aquin*. Bibliothèque thomiste, XL (Paris, 1970), pp. 21, 90–1, 126–7, 158, 187–8, 190, 214–16, etc. Also E-H. Wéber, *Dialogue et dissensions entre Saint Bonaventure et Saint Thomas d'Aquin à Paris (1252–1273)*. Bibliothèque thomiste, XLI (Paris, 1974), p. 494. Cf. for example *Summa contra Gentiles*, lib. II, c. LXVIII: 'Hoc autem modo mirabilis rerum connexio considerari potest. Semper enim invenitur infimum supremi generis contingere supremum inferioris generis...', with reference to the pseudo-Denis, *Divine Names*, cap. VII. *S. Thomae Aquinatis Opera omnia*, XIII (Rome, 1918), 440.

level among intellectual substances and participates in intellectual being. The Dionysian schema of the emanation of all creatures from God and of their return to God through the agency of intermediate realities was adopted.[37]

Nevertheless, in accepting the pseudo-Denis's conception of universal hierarchy, Aquinas laid stress on the essential differences between men and angels. Certain essential features of angelic society were not part of the model of human society.[38] Human beings are not miniature incarnate angels, nor was man composed of an angel in respect of his soul and an animal in respect of his body.[39] The celestial hierarchy reflects differences both of nature and of grace between the orders of angels. Men, on the other hand, are equal by nature, and, although they are not all equal by grace, grace is additional to human nature and its acquisition is a hidden and an uncertain occurrence. The hierarchy among men cannot therefore be based on man's nature or divine grace.[40] Moreover, according to Aquinas, the angelic hierarchy did not constitute a *society*, for angels are servants of creatures, whereas in the Church militant men co-operate mutually for each other's advantage. The structure of the Church militant is therefore a properly social one, constituted not according to the levels of grace or of personal holiness, but according to its public powers.[41] The Church militant is visible as a sacramental and a juridical reality with a public character. Its structure rests not upon the personal or spiritual qualities of its ministers but upon the sacrament of order which confers *potestas* upon them. The power to illuminate in the Church militant (i.e. the power to excommunicate or to absolve) does not stem from the personal spiritual quality of the minister but from the authority assigned to him in the ecclesiastical hierarchy.[42] Unlike Bonaventure, Aquinas did not use the Dionysian 'law of divinity' as a pretext for discovering special resemblances to the

---

[37] Cf *Dialogue et dissensions*, pp. 412–13, 442–3; Congar, 'Aspects ecclésiologiques', p. 127 and n. 294. Cf., for example, *Summa theologiae*, IIIa, q.55, a.1: '...ut Dionysius dicit, in libro Caelest. Hier., haec est lex divinitus instituta, ut a Deo immediate superioribus revelentur, quibus mediantibus deferantur ad inferiores'; and *ibid.*, art. 2: '...Apostolus dicit, Rom. XIII, "quae a Deo sunt, ordinata sunt". Est autem hic ordo divinitus institutus, ut ea quae supra homines sunt, hominibus per angelos revelentur: ut patet per Dionysium, IV cap. *Cael. Hier.*' *S. Thomae Aquinatis Opera*, XI (Rome, 1903), pp. 515, 516.

[38] Cf. Congar, 'Aspects ecclésiologiques', p. 130 and n. 306. This line of criticism was powerfully developed by John of Paris, *De potestate regia et papali* (1302–3), ed. J. Leclercq. L'Église et l'État au Moyen Age, V (Paris, 1942), e.g. in cap. 2 (p. 179) and cap. 18 (pp. 230ff.).

[39] Cf. Dufeil, *Guillaume de Saint-Amour*, p. 160.

[40] Cf. Congar, 'Aspects ecclésiologiques', p. 131.   [41] Cf. Congar, *ibid.*

[42] Cf. Congar, *ibid.*, p. 124: 'Pour Denys, la qualité hiérarchique est une qualité d'existence... Pour Thomas, c'est une question de *potestas*...'.

angelic hierarchy in the institution of the papacy or in the Mendicant orders.

Aquinas also relaxed the Dionysian 'law' of mediation. He did not allow to angels an insuperable role as intermediaries between man and God. Divine illumination may come to each created intellect directly. The central place in the mediation of man to God is occupied by Christ. Angels, though mediators, do not occupy an ontological level which bars the complete *reditus* of man to God.[43] Moreover, angels are by nature different from each other in respect of the perfection of intelligence and will to be found in each order; men are essentially equal in respect of their spiritual potentialities. Whereas angels can only transmit light from higher to lower grades, man is not confined within such a hierarchic pattern and an inferior grade in human society may enlighten one superior to it.[44] Aquinas therefore broke with strict interpretations of the correspondences between the angelic and the ecclesiastical hierarchies, while accepting that intermediaries exist and help man to return to his beginning: '"habet" autem "hoc divinitatis ordo", sicut Dionysius dicit, "ut infima per media disponat".'[45]

Giles of Rome, of the Order of the Hermits of St Augustine, is in many respects an obscure figure.[46] In his early career he was an important Thomist and an Aristotelian whose *De regimine principum*, unlike that of Guibert of Tournai, offers nothing of interest to the student of Dionysian lines of thought. Though he was the main architect, if not actually the draftsman of *Unam Sanctam*,[47] he was also a friend, if not a tutor, of King Philip the Fair of France for whom, in fact, he wrote the *De regimine principum* between 1277 and 1279.[48] There are strong, though not conclusive, arguments in favour of attributing to Giles the authorship of the *Questio in utramque partem*, the viewpoint of which is not obviously consistent with the defence of Boniface VIII or of hierocratic principles that is furnished by his *De*

---

[43] Cf. Wéber, *La Controverse de 1270*, p. 303; Wéber, *Dialogue et dissensions*, p. 412.

[44] Cf. *Summa theologiae*, Ia, q.106, a.3, *S. Thomae Aquinatis Opera*, V (Rome, 1889), p. 485.

[45] *Summa theologiae*, IIa, IIae, q.172, a.2. *S. Thomae Aquinatis Opera*, X (Rome, 1899), p. 379, cited by Wéber, *Dialogue et dissensions*, p. 412, n. 31, who collects further references, as does Congar, 'Aspects ecclésiologiques', p. 127, n. 294.

[46] For overall surveys of Giles's life and political writings see R. Scholz, *Die Publizistik zur zeit Philipps des Schönen und Bonifaz' VIII* (Stuttgart, 1903), pp. 32–129 and U. Mariani, *Chiesa e Stato nei teologi agostiniani del secolo XIV. Uomini e dottrine* V (Rome, 1957), pp. 45–74, 113–51.

[47] Cf. Scholz, *Die Publizistik*, pp. x, 124–6; J. Rivière, *Le Problème de l'église et de l'état au temps de Philippe le Bel* (Louvain, 1926), pp. 394–404.

[48] Mariani, *Chiesa e Stato*, pp. 113–14.

ecclesiastica potestate (1300–2) and by his Commentary upon *Unam Sanctam*.[49] It is possible that Giles, archbishop of Bourges from 1295 but prior-general of the Augustinian order in 1292, veered to the cause of Boniface VIII in reaction to the strong attacks of the French Estates upon Italian occupants of benefices in France, for he went to the Roman council summoned by Boniface VIII and he remained with the pope till his death in 1303. In or after 1310, Giles defended, in his *Tractatus contra exemptos*, the rights of intermediate episcopal authority in face of the attempts of higher powers to forge immediate links with lower ones, for God himself brings man back to him by means of angels.[50]

In the *De ecclesiastica potestate*, II, 13,[51] Giles of Rome reminds one of Alan of Lille and of William of Auvergne in the detailed character of the comparisons he offers between the angelic hierarchies governing the universe and the organisation of royal government upon earth. The government of the universe and the salvation of the elect require that the orders that exist be ordained (*ordinati*) so that each presides or is presided over by another; tripartite organisation is generally character-istic of large groupings.[52]

Giles views the hierarchies of the Church militant and of heaven as *militiae* which battle in the cause of salvation.[53] These armies are arranged in ways that take into account the inequalities that exist between the capacities of individual men or angels. These arise from the differing degrees of illumination found among both angels and men.[54] The two axioms that effectively summarise Giles's general hierarchical theory are, first, that the powers that be are ordained by God (*Romans*, 13:1); and, secondly, the Dionysian law as stated in the Bull *Unam Sanctam*. The second axiom explains *how* the powers that be are ordained by God: 'lex divinitatis est infima per media in suprema reduci'.[55] Giles applies this, the law of the universe, to the theory of the

---

[49] Cf. G. Vinay, 'Egidio Romano e la cosidetta Questio in utramque partem (con testo critico)', *Bollettino dell'Istituto Storico Italiano per il medio evo e Archivio Muratoriano*, LIII (Rome, 1939), 43–136.

[50] Cap. V, 18, *Primus tomus operum D. Aegidii Romani*... (Rome, 1555), pp. 3, 14, col. 2.

[51] *Aegidius Romanus, De ecclesiastica sive summi pontificis potestate*, ed. R. Scholz (Weimar, 1929), p. 122. Cf. *Aegidii Columnae Romani Eremitarum D. Augustini...in secundum librum Sententiarum Quaestiones...industria R.P.F. Angeli Rocchensis...pars prima* (Venice, 1581), *Dist.* IX, quaest. 1, art. 2, p. 410, and *Dist.* IX, 9.II, art. 1, pp. 434–5; *Tractatus contra exemptos* in *Primus tomus operum D. Aegidii Romani*, cap. XVIII, p. 13, col. 4.

[52] *De ecclesiastica potestate*, II, 13, ed. Scholz, pp. 122, 124; *Tractatus contra exemptos*, cap. 10, p. 7, col. 2.   [53] *Tractatus contra exemptos*, cap. 19, p. 14, col. 3

[54] *In II. Sent. Quaestiones*, dist. IX, q.1, art. 2, pp. 410–12.

[55] Giles of Rome, *Commentary on Unam Sanctam*, ed. P. de Lapparent, 'L'oeuvre politique de François de Meyronnes: ses rapports avec celle de Dante', *Archives d'histoire doctrinale et littéraire*

two swords: the material sword must be linked to God not immediately but via the spiritual sword. The material sword is subject to the dominion of the spiritual sword and can only be wielded at the command and *ad nutum* of the spiritual sword.[56] Giles went far in support of papal absolutism; his assertion of papal supremacy over secular monarchs such as Philip the Fair cannot be denied on the evidence of the *De ecclesiastica potestate* or of his Commentary upon *Unam Sanctam* where he laid heavy and constant stress upon inequalities between men and upon the duty of obedience to superiors. Yet Giles, although an Augustinian hermit, was, as archbishop of Bourges, a stern defender of the rights of bishops in the matter of the exemption of religious orders from episcopal jurisdiction: exemption from intermediate jurisdiction breaches the law of hierarchy which links the lowest to the highest by means of the middle.[57] In so far as exemption removes the middle grade in the ecclesiastical hierarchy – the episcopacy – from its share in government, and in so far as exemption may result in the papacy dispensing with episcopal participation in the government of the Church, it contradicts the divine plan of universal government. Examination of Giles's use of the pseudo-Denis shows his deeply-rooted sense that lesser ranks are not superfluous, and that their functions should be defended against the pressures of greater centralisation.[58] *Unam Sanctam* does not obviously contradict this viewpoint.

The reference to the pseudo-Denis in *Unam Sanctam* is made in order to buttress the principle of a divine, hierarchic ordering of powers in the universe which entails the subordination of the temporal to the spiritual sword. Though the pseudo-Denis is quoted in a way that reflects the transformation of an original remark (as it existed in translation) into a loose *topos* that had already appeared in various verbal forms in the writings of earlier masters, especially Giles of Rome, the Bull does not, in this respect, reveal any bias towards one or other of the dominant interpretations given, for example, by Bonaventure or by the Secular masters or by Aquinas. It does not offer a statement of the position of

---

au moyen âge, xv–xvii (1940–2), App., pp. 127, 145. Cf. Giles, *De ecclesiastica potestate*, I, 4, pp. 12–13; *In Epistolam Pauli ad Romanos Commentarium*, *Lectio* xxvii. *Primus tomus operum D. Aegidii Romani*. Congar, 'Aspects ecclésiologiques', p. 140, n. 352 refers to the pseudo-Denis, *Celestial Hierarchy*, c. 10; *Ecclesiastical Hierarchy*, c. 5 suits better.

[56] *De ecclesiastica potestate*, I, 4, pp. 12–13; I, 9, p. 32.

[57] *Tractatus contra exemptos*, cap. v, 18, *Primus tomus operum D. Aegidii Romani*, pp. 3, 14, col. 2.

[58] Cf. *De ecclesiastica potestate*, ed. Scholz, pp. xiii–xiv.

bishops or of religious in the ecclesiastical hierarchy, though the Bull does conclude that obedience is owed by all to the papacy.

It is, however, a feature of later explanations of the meaning of the Bull that they return to earlier interpretations of the pseudo-Denis in order to put a construction upon the reference to the pseudo-Denis found in the Bull itself. *Unam Sanctam* was commented upon not only by Giles of Rome, but also by Cardinal John the Monk, the Dominican Guido Vernani of Rimini, Alvaro Pelayo and anonymously. John the Monk and Guido Vernani, who were both anxious to proclaim papal supremacy with as few qualifications as possible, elucidated the meaning of the Bull rather fully. The French cardinal and canonist wrote his gloss upon *Unam Sanctam* in 1302–3 and in it he played with elementary number-theory: wherever two numbers are essentially different, one contains more units than the other. As the pseudo-Denis says in *Divine Names*, c.5, essentially different things are unequal in perfection and therefore in their nearness to the unity which is God. There is a scale of perfection or of nearness to the One, and it is a scale of dignity and nobility. The pseudo-Denis showed that powers are not arranged immediately by God: earthly power is ordained by spiritual power and is led to God by spiritual power. In this way the pseudo-Denis explained the meaning of Paul's saying: 'the powers that be are ordained by God'; the Dionysian theory of mediation is a principal article of the Bull.[59] The Commentary upon *Unam Sanctam* by Guido Vernani contains almost identical passages.[60]

The anonymous Gloss upon *Unam Sanctam* raised a philosophical question concerning the meaning of the pseudo-Denis's law of mediation. The author fully accepts that temporal power is brought to God by the mediation of the spiritual power. But is temporal power subject to spiritual power in the order of causality? Is it contained within spiritual power as an effect is contained within its cause? Or is it subject to spiritual power in an order of dignity or of nobility, as it appeared to be, for example, in the Commentaries of John the Monk and Guido Vernani – and also in the Bull itself? The author is not certain that the pseudo-Denis himself described an order of causality as well as an order

59 Ed. *Corpus Iuris Canonici*, Pars III, 3 (Lyons, 1671), col. 201–12, here col. 209. See H. Finke, *Aus den Tagen Bonifaz VIII. Funde und Forschungen* (Münster i.W., 1902), pp. 160, 177–81; also Rivière, *Le Problème de l'église*, pp. 151ff.

60 Ed. M. Grabmann, *Studien über den Einfluss der aristotelischen Philosophie auf die mittelalterliche Theorien über das Verhältnis von Kirche und Staat.* Sitzungsberichte der Bayerischen Akademie der Wissenschaften. Philos.–hist. Abteilung, Jahrgang 1934. Heft 2 (Munich, 1934), pp. 144–57 here 153–4.

of dignity and nobility. Temporal power is brought to God by the mediation of spiritual power but it does not therefore follow that the holder of spiritual power also wields temporal power over lesser temporal powers.[61]

The pseudo-Denis's 'law of the divinity' found much continuing favour among supporters of papal claims in the fourteenth century. The generalised principle itself was not readily controvertible, and among those who invoked it was François de Meyronnes of the Order of St Francis. François referred in his *Quaestio de subjectione* (1320) to the rule of the pseudo-Denis ('regula b. Dyonisii') that God influences the lowest by means of the middle; divine authority is imparted to secular monarchs by means of the hierarchies.[62] François de Meyronnes distinguishes between hierarchical and political law in his *Puncti* upon the *Celestial Hierarchy* which he wrote at the request of a 'true philosopher', 'my most illustrious lord', Robert, king of Sicily and of Jerusalem.[63] Hierarchical law regulates all human actions; whereas it is possible to act outside the framework of political law without necessarily acting against it, it is not possible to act outside, or right to act against, hierarchical law. The law of hierarchy is the same for angels, saints, ecclesiastics and members of the perfect earthly polity. The perfect polity will imitate the hierarchy as far as it can. A temporal prince, such as King Robert, is worthier when he co-operates submissively with a spiritual prince than when he rules imperiously over those set beneath him.[64] A prince rules in merely temporal fashion as a Monarch if he only abides by human or political law, but he rules spiritually as a Hierarch if he adheres to divine or hierarchical law. Hierarchs in the Old Testament such as Elias, Eliseus and Samuel had authority to constitute political rulers. François de Meyronnes extols the intrinsic superiority of Robert's position as vassal of the Holy See; whenever a creature joins and participates and is assimilated into something higher than himself he is ennobled.[65]

The pseudo-Denis's 'law of divinity' also gained the attention of other champions of papal claims in the early fourteenth century.

---

[61] Ed. Finke, *Aus den Tagen Bonifaz VIII*, pp. c–cxvi; cf. pp. 181–6. For the distinction between the orders of dignity and of causality cf. Aquinas, *Summa theologiae*, IIIa, q.6, a.1, *Opera*, XI (Rome, 1903), 93.

[62] Ed. de Lapparent, 'L'oeuvre politique de François de Meyronnes', pp. 76–92, esp. 82–3.

[63] The *Puncti* are inedited; I have used a microfilm of cod. Vatican lat. 900; see here fo. 21vff. (on the *Celestial Hierarchy*, *Punctus* viff.).

[64] *Quaestio de subjectione*, I, ed. de Lapparent, 'L'oeuvre politique', pp. 82–3.

[65] *Tractatus de principatu regni Siciliae*, ed. de Lapparent, 'L'oeuvre politique', pp. 95–8.

Augustinus Triumphus of Ancona, who may be compared with Giles of Rome, as a first-class intellect in the Order of Augustinian Hermits, and as a supporter of Boniface VIII who wrote in defence of his memory in 1307–9 and marshalled all his arguments into a *Summa de potestate ecclesiastica* (1326), wrote stiffly that the meaning of the Dionysian law was that the emperor cannot legislate without the mediating influence of the papacy which stands between the empire and God.[66] On the other hand the papacy may act immediately.[67] Likewise Egidius Spiritalis of Perugia, a canonist, wrote in his *Libellus contra infideles et inobedientes et rebelles sancte Romane ecclesie ac summo pontifici* (?1338) that 'the power of the emperor is from God, but it is mediated through the church, for God acts through media. According to the blessed Denis, it is the law of divinity that the lowest are brought to the highest via the middle...it is proven that the emperor receives the power of the sword...from the pope...so too every bishop receives his power from God, but this is mediated through the church'.[68]

The theme of the overriding monarchy of Christ or His vicar ruling over the Church was also uppermost in the mind of Thomas of Ireland (before 1275 to 1329/39). He frequently repeated the phrase 'lex sacratissima divinitatis est ultima per media reducere in suprema'. Though a very minor thinker with a weakness for naive allegorisation as well as for plagiarism, Thomas nonetheless produced popular treatises that circulated widely. He extolled the Bonifatian position as it appeared to a member of the secular clergy and a Fellow of the Sorbonne who was enthusiastically fond of the pseudo-Denis, but no champion of the rights of bishops or of the religious orders.[69]

After the composition of *Unam Sanctam* and the particular conflicts which led to its drafting, the *lex divinitatis* had continued to be invoked in the light of changing problems, especially in connection with the Roman empire under Pope John XXII. The reference in the Bull to the pseudo-Denis constitutes an example of one way in which the study

---

[66] '...secundum Dionysium lex divinitatis hoc habeat ut eius influentia non transeat ad inferiora nisi per media', *Summa de potestate ecclesiastica*, Q.44, art. 1 (e.g. in the Roman edition of 1584, here p. 240).

[67] *Summa*, Q.18, a. IIII, p. 116; Q.61, a. I, pp. 321–2.

[68] *Unbekannte kirchenpolitischen Streitschriften aus der Zeit Ludwigs des Bayern (1327–1354). Analysen und Texte*, ed. R. Scholz (Rome, 1911, 1914), II, 105–29, here 115–16, 126. On Egidius, see further Scholz, *ibid.*, I, 43–9.

[69] Thomas's treatises are inedited; essential information was provided by B. Hauréau, 'Thomas d'Irlande, Théologien', *Histoire littéraire de la France*, XXX (1888), 398–404. Professor R. H. Rouse kindly allowed me to see notes he has made in preparing a book on Thomas.

of patristic texts by thirteenth-century university men bore closely upon the evolution of their attitudes to government; it serves to remind us, too, that not all these attitudes may be attributed to a simple choice between the thought of Augustine and of Aristotle. The quotation in the Bull taken from the pseudo-Denis would not have been so readily selected had not several generations of masters so intensively studied his texts and commented upon their wide significance, and had not their general viewpoints become so pervasive a part of the intellectual armoury of many of the educated clergy of the day. The law of the divinity was a general law: it bound all without exception to accept the superiority of the spirit, but it was used variously both before and after *Unam Sanctam* to support a range of varying opinions concerning the relationship of the papacy with other grades of hierarchy.

JOHN BACONTHORPE AS A CANONIST

by WALTER ULLMANN

I

THE purpose of this short contribution is to invite attention – albeit in a very sketchy outline dictated by considerations of space – to the early fourteenth-century Carmelite John Baconthorpe, a native of Norfolk, a graduate of Paris and – like the jubiland – a teacher at both Oxford and Cambridge. Baconthorpe's philosophical and theological importance has been fully appraised by modern scholarship,[1] but as far as can be ascertained with any degree of certainty his canonistic contributions have received little or inadequate attention.[2] In fact, his name does not appear in the usual handbooks and *Dictionnaires* of canon law, although his canonistic work and expertise was most certainly on a far larger scale than that of many another scholar who has been given a niche in the ordinary reference works. Leaving aside John of Athona who, incidentally, was an exact contemporary of John Baconthorpe, the fourteenth century did not produce any really memorable English canonistic scholar.[3] Although the edition of his Commentaries on the *Sentences* calls him a *canonista praecipuus* and manuscripts designate him a doctor of both laws,[4] by contemporary standards he could not have

---

[1] See B. M. Xiberta, 'De Magistro Iohanne Baconthorp' in *De scriptoribus scholasticis s. XIV ex Ordine Carmelitarum* (Louvain, 1931), pp. 167–240; supplemented by B. Smalley, 'John Baconthorpe's Postill on Matthew' in *Mediaeval and Renaissance Studies*, IV (1958), 91–145; see also P. Chrysogone, 'Maître Jean Baconthorpe: les sources, la doctrine, les disciples' in *Revue néo-scolastique de philosophie*, XXXIV (1932), 341–65; A. B. Emden, *Biographical Register of the University of Cambridge to 1500* (Cambridge, 1963) pp. 669–70. He lectured at Cambridge by 1330, became Provincial of the English Carmelites and died 1348.

[2] For some remarks cf. Xiberta, 'De Magistro', pp. 180, 182; also Smalley, 'John Baconthorpe', pp. 94, 101, 103, 120.

[3] For a succinct survey of English canonists of this period see L. E. Boyle, 'The *Summa Summarum* and some other English works of canon law' in *Proceedings of the II Internat. Congress of Medieval Canon Law*, ed. S. Kuttner and J. J. Ryan (Vatican City, 1965) at pp. 415–18.

[4] Cf. Xiberta, 'De Magistro', 175f. from Bodley MS. 82: 'Magister frater Iohannes Baconis seu Baconthorpe *doctor iuris utriusque* Parisiensis...' See also J. Bale, *Scriptorum illustrium maioris Brytanniae...catalogus* (edn Basle, 1557), I.382: '...cum summo utriusque iuris ac theologiae magistratu' (in Paris); J. Trisse, 'De magistris Parisiensibus', in B. Zimmermann, *Monumenta historica Carmelitana* (Lérins, 1907), pp. 379–80, says nothing about a degree in law: 'Sextus

been deemed a professional jurist: a Parisian Juris Utriusque Doctor is highly suspect, as there was no study of Roman law after Honorius III prohibited it at the university in 1219. But that he must have received some professional instruction in canon law is beyond question after even a perfunctory perusal of his Commentaries on the *Sentences*. His Commentaries and *Quodlibeta* show a curious lack of knowledge in matters of Roman law and civilian jurisprudence which accords well with the Paris situation.[5]

On the other hand, the relevance, accuracy and manipulation of canonistic jurisprudence and its professional accommodation into theology is sufficient justification for his being accorded a place among the canonists of the fourteenth century. He in fact serves as a particularly good example of the need of integration which a scholar of his standing quite obviously felt.[6] For since the middle of the twelfth century, that is, since juristic theology split up into its component parts[7] as a result of Gratian's *Decretum* on the one hand and Peter Lombard's *Sentences* on the other, specialisation had progressed to such a degree that there was a very real gulf separating the theologians from the jurists, and notably from the canonists, although they treated many matters common to both branches of learning. The earlier *communauté des matières*[8] of theology and jurisprudence was hardly discernible by the thirteenth century. In particular the Fourth Book of the *Sentences* contains numerous topics which were sometimes formulated completely in accord with canonistic style, but contact and mutual fructification, or what is now termed cross-fertilisation, were so rare that for all practical purposes they did not exist, despite the liberal borrowings from Gratian by Peter Lombard.

Here indeed John Baconthorpe is a most notable exception. Only a very lengthy and detailed study could throw the integration of canon law and canonistic jurisprudence in his Commentaries into sharp relief. He pays as much attention to the theologians – some of the relevant

---

(magister) fuit frater Iohannes de Bachone provinciae Angliae...fuit minimus in persona, sed maximus in sapientia et doctrina.'

[5] I have used the Cremona edn of 1618: *Quaestiones in Quatuor Libros Sententiarum et Quodlibetales.* This has been reprinted by Gregg (Farnborough, 1969). All quotations refer to this edition.

[6] Although rightly emphasising the combination of 'l'élément philosophique et l'élément théologique', P. Chrysogone, art. cit. (above n. 1), p. 341 omits in common with other writers to mention the integration of theology with canon law, which is at least as important.

[7] Cf. W. Ullmann, *The Growth of Papal Government in the Middle Ages*, 4th edn (London, 1970), pp. 359ff.

[8] The expression is J. de Ghellinck's, *Le mouvement théologique du xiie siècle*, 2nd edn (Brussels–Paris, 1948) pp. 422ff.

details are set forth with succinctness and clarity by his modern expositor[9] – as to the law and its interpreters. The hitherto unacknowledged
significance of his *Quaestiones canonicae* (i.e. his commentary on the
Fourth Book of the *Sentences*) lies precisely in the combination of
theology and canonistics.[10] This integration constituted the attempt to
restore the unity of the *theologica practica* (or *externa*) as one whole
which, as a result of specialisation, had been lost. The *Quaestiones*
demonstrate their author's singularly fertile, perceptive and wide-
ranging mind with a keen sense for synthesis.[11] With some exaggeration
one could say that the Lombard's *Sentences* emphasised the theological
aspects of the topics treated juristically by Gratian. What however was
originally a difference in emphasis, gave rise to a divisive specialisation,
with the result that by the early fourteenth century the unity of ecclesi-
ology itself was seriously threatened. Disintegration and decomposition
had begun to corrode what was once one and indivisible, what was
once one *totum*.[12]

It is against this background that John Baconthorpe must be seen. His
strongly developed aptitude for synthesis and for combinatory and con-
nective thought-processes made him realise the need of integration. The
Fourth Book dealt with the sacraments as concrete manifestations of the
ecclesiological groundwork. John's commentaries are only loosely
linked with the Lombard's subject in the *Distinctiones* and serve as mere
pièces d'occasion. Let us take a specific example. He introduces the

---

[9] See B. M. Xiberta, art. cit. (above n. 1), pp. 197–212; also pp. 218f.

[10] His *Quaestiones speculativae* (cf. IV.8.1.3, p. 361aD) have been lost: only the *Qu. canonicae* are preserved in MS as well as in the printed editions; see Xiberta, pp. 177–83. In the MS BL. Royal 9 C VII which contains the autograph emendations of the *canonicae*, 22 *Qu. speculativae* are inserted: Xiberta, 'De Magistro', p. 178. The *canonicae* were probably composed in the early 40s, possibly at Oxford.

[11] This is also pointed out – without however referring to his canonistic equipment or use of jurisprudence – in the excellent entry by A. de Saint-Paul, in *Dict. d'Hist. et de Géogr. Ecclés.*, VI (Paris, 1932), 87–9: 'il était doué d'un esprit synthètique...fecondité intellectuelle vraiment exubérante'.

[12] For the same feature in the political field cf. W. Ullmann, 'Die Bulle *Unam sanctam*: Rückblick und Ausblick' in *Röm. Hist. Mitt.*, XV (1974), 45–77. In fourteenth-century England the need of combining theology and canonistics was strongly felt. Cf. the work of William of Pagula, a parish priest writing (*c.* 1325) for the parochial clergy his *Oculus sacerdotis* which 'is a balance of law and theology', see L. E. Boyle, 'The *Oculus sacerdotis* of William of Pagula' in TRHS, 5th ser. V (1955) at 101; Boyle, *Proceedings* (above n. 3), at p. 424: this work 'is a striking, if unexpected, amalgam of theology and canon law'. See Boyle, 'The *Summa confessorum* of John of Freiburg and the popularization of moral teaching of St Thomas' in *St Thomas Aquinas: Commemoration Studies*, ed. A. A. Maurer, II (Toronto, 1974), 245ff., at 263f. A similar integration is to be found in the *Pupilla oculi* written by the Chancellor of Cambridge, John de Burgh, *c.* 1385; see Emden, *Biographical Register*, p. 107. This was frequently printed in the early 16th century. There are many other hitherto neglected tracts written in the 14th century.

question of *accidentia* relative to the Eucharist in *Dist*. xii with the very words of the Lombard, but considers that one of the *accidentia* was the juristic protection which the individual churches enjoy and which actually enables them to administer the sacraments, that is to say, ecclesiastical immunity: 'Utrum ecclesia debeat gaudere immunitate?'[13] The answer is given under three headings: the definition of immunity; the kind of immunity churches and their administrators enjoy; and the public duties, imposts, charges and the like which can and cannot be levied on the churches and their incumbents. This procedure allows him to deal theologically and juristically with topics which were commonly outside the purview of canonist[14] and theologian.[15] He did not consider that the Fourth Book covered relevant theological and canonistic topics sufficiently well: he thus hit upon the device of introducing the Fourth Book with a special Prologue consisting of 12 *Quaestiones*, of which the last three concern themselves with the foundations, scope and limitations of the papal government itself.[16] He appends a discussion on the conversion of Jews and infidels to Christianity and on the right of exercising papal jurisdiction in regard to the Holy Land. Here as elsewhere he does not intend and does not pretend to propound any new theories or interpretations, but to pursue a purely didactic purpose by attempting to weave theological and canonistic material together.

Although he could never claim to be a professional jurist, his canonistic equipment was certainly respectable. Here only a bird's eye view can be given of his authorities. Since his knowledge of Roman law and of the civilians was extremely meagre, in technical respects his juristic manipulation of problems left something to be desired. But as regards his knowledge of the canon law itself he cannot easily be faulted. He is thoroughly familiar with the whole Corpus as well as a number of individual decretals issued by Nicholas III, Boniface VIII, Clement V, John XXII and Benedict XII.[17] He has studied Gratian's *Dicta* no less

---

[13] IV.13, qu. un., p. 387bB.

[14] In her art. cit. (above n. 1) at p. 142, B. Smalley rightly noted his inclination to use canonists for exegetical purposes: 'By his use of them the fierce little man put a punch into exegesis which it had lacked.'

[15] For typical examples contrasting theological and canonistic opinions cf. IV.4.2.1, p. 335aD–E and 336aE; IV.19.1.1, p. 440aE–bA.

[16] Q. x–xii, edn cit., pp. 261rb–273rb.

[17] Some of these he quoted verbatim, e.g. John XXII's *Vas electionis* directed against Jean de Pouilly in *Extrav. comm.* v.3.2: 'quia non habent omnes constitutionem, ideo hic insero in qua sic dicitur...Datum Avinione 8 kal. Augusti, p.n.a.V' (in IV.15.3.1, pp. 415bD–416bA). He is well acquainted with the condemnation of Marsilius's tract (in *Licet iuxta doctrinam* of 23 Oct.

than the writings of a number of decretists, notably Huguccio, Laurentius, Vincentius, Guido de Baysio, all the *glossae ordinariae*, Raimond de Pennaforte's *Summa confessorum*, Goffredus de Trano's *Summa*, Innocent IV's *Apparatus*, some of the works of Bernardus Compostellanus Junior, Hostiensis' *Summa* as well as *Lectura*, the gloss by Johannes Monachus on the Sext, the commentary of the Archdeacon on the same law book, the glosses by Johannes Andreae on the Sext as well as his *Novella*, Guilielmus Durantis' *Rationale divinorum officiorum*,[18] and so on. There is no doubt that the standard work he consulted on the *Decretum* was the *Rosarium* of Guido de Baysio, to whom he refers not by his usual official designation as Archdeacon, but always as 'Guido'. Any suggestion that John referred to his teacher Guido (Terreni) who wrote an *Expositorium Decreti*, almost contemporaneously with our author's commentary (finished on 17 February 1339), must be dismissed. For Terreni's work was not primarily juristic, but a critical exposition of Gratian's sources and of the use he had made of them.[19] There is no evidence whatsoever that John even knew of his former master's work. The identity of 'Guido' is clear and unambiguous: he used the Archdeacon's work, not only on the *Decretum*, but also his commentary on the Sext (on which Terreni never commented), and the reference in both instances is 'Guido'. Whenever he cites statements of 'Guido' verbatim, they can easily be verified by using the Archdeacon as a control.[20] Considering the respective aims there were hardly any points of contact between Terreni and his pupil.[21] One of the sources frequently referred to by John – even citing the folio – is the *Registrum Romanorum Pontificum*. He obviously consulted this source whenever Gratian had incorporated a canon from one of the early

1327, see O. Raynaldus, *Ann. eccles.*, ed. A. Theiner (Bar-le-Duc, 1872) XXIV, 322–9, nos. 27ff.); or with Benedict XII's *Benedictus Deus* on the Beatific Vision of 29 Jan. 1336 (in H. Denzinger, *Enchiridion symbolorum*, 34th edn Barcelona–Freiburg, 1967) no. 530.

[18] But there is only occasionally a reference to the *Speculum Iuris*, e.g. IV.19.2.4, p. 445aD.

[19] For a magisterial discussion of Terreni see P. Fournier, 'Gui Terré' in *Hist. littéraire de la France*, XXXVI (Paris, 1927), 432ff., esp. 464ff.; B. M. Xiberta, *Guia Terrena Carmelita de Perpinya* (= Estudios Univ. Catalanis, Barcelona, 1932) II, 6off.; the object of Guido's writing was 'd'exposar more commentario el text del Decret en sos aspactes no estrictament juridica' (p. 65). The book by I. Melsen, *Guido Terreni iurista* (Rome, 1939), was not accessible to me. Cf. also R. Naz in *Dict. Droit Can.* v, 1011–12.

[20] The relevant texts tally entirely: cf., e.g. IV.13.1.1, p. 392bC with the Archdeacon's *Rosarium*, XVII.4.35 (edn Venice, 1523), fo. 236ra, no. 4; IV.18.1.3, p. 429aC with XI.3.31, fo. 184rb; IV.15.3.2, p. 417bE with XVI.1.19, fo. 215vb, no. 3. A comparison with the Archdeacon's commentary on the Sext yields the same result.

[21] Terreni was critical, if not hypercritical, of Gratian's use of sources, cf. P. Fournier (above n. 19) 466f., and when theological and canonistic opinions differed, 'taceat Huguccio, quia viri theologi omnes tenent et sequuntur Augustinum' (cit. from Fournier, p. 467).

popes. It is at once evident that this *Registrum* was nothing but Pseudo-Isidore.

About the non-juristic writers and sources very little needs to be said, because all the necessary spade work has been done.[22] What remains to be added is the frequent invocation of Pseudo-Denys whose works apparently never lost their authoritative appeal. There are also isolated instances of quotations from Cicero and Seneca.[23] His great respect for Thomas Aquinas is as significant as is his detached attitude towards Duns and his opposition, if not pathological animosity, to Peter Aureoli. John of Paris is usually viewed with a critical eye. Because hitherto unnoticed it deserves to be pointed out that he records – and apparently accepts – the non-canonical character of the Books of Maccabees: '(Aliqui) dicunt quod libri Machabaeorum non sunt de canone Bibliae, ut dicit Hieronymus in prologis super libris Salomonis'.[24] What needs stressing is the quite remarkable absence of any influence by the new kind of thought-processes as they had become rather fashionable just at the time of his writing. The naturalism, engendered by Thomism and brought into the limelight with particular incisiveness in the writings of John of Paris, Dante, or Marsilius – to mention just a few of his contemporaries – either passed him by[25] or was rejected outright, as in the case of Marsilius to whom he only refers in his citations of the decree of condemnation. There is no proof that he had really understood the implications of this work. Indeed, he may never have read it.[26]

II

The petrinological theme is the backbone in the final *Quaestiones* in the Prologue. Their central subject is the origin, function, scope and extent

22 By Xiberta, *op. cit.* (above n. 1), pp. 197ff. That he also used the *Summa confessorum* is evident, cf. Boyle, *Proceedings* (above n. 3), p. 430 (use of Pagula's *Summa Summarum*).

23 Cf., e.g., IV.20.2.1, p. 447bE.

24 IV.45.un., p. 568aB and also E. See St Jerome in his *Praefatio in Libros Solomonis*, in Migne, *PL.* XXVIII, 1243: 'Machabaeorum libros legit quidem ecclesia, sed inter canonicas scripturas non recipit, sic et haec duo volumina legat ad aedificationem plebis, non ad auctoritatem ecclesiasticorum dogmatum confirmandam.' Among the 'aliqui' may have been John of Salisbury, in his *Ep.* 143 (old numbering) in Migne, *PL.* CXCIX.126. Cf. also Peter the Venerable, *Tractatus contra Petrobrusianos haereticos*, in Migne, *PL.* CLXXXIX, 751. But, as far as I can see, the overwhelming view was that these books were canonical. The reference to St Jerome testifies to John's erudition. For an explanation of Jerome's reasons see now J. N. D. Kelly, *Jerome: his life, writings, and controversies* (London, 1975), pp. 159ff.

25 He knew, how ver, the *Politics*, cf. e.g., Prol. IV.2.1, p. 231bC–D; *Qu* 5.3, p. 245.

26 In his Postill on Matthew he seems to have adopted a similar course, and 'he shows no sign of having read it' (Smalley (above n. 1), p. 125).

of the papal government itself. His analyses follow well-trodden lines relative to the primatial function of the pope. Nevertheless, his historical perspective is noteworthy. He sees the division between East and West historically conditioned: the unity of the Church was destroyed, he declares, by the 'Greeks' who refused to acknowledge papal primacy. And the arrogation of patriarchal powers by the bishop of Constantinople formalised the schism.[27] And to him the essence of the new Marsilian doctrine was identical with the Greek standpoint: rightly therefore had his heresy, based on biblical-exegetical grounds, been condemned by the papacy.[28] He constantly refers in this context to the 'papal Register': 'Haec habes in libro qui intitulatur Registrum Romanorum Pontificum in decretis Anacleti papae.'[29] Nor is it surprising that the spurious *Epistola Clementis* makes its appearance,[30] and that he approvingly also cites Peter as *cephas* in the sense of *caput* of the apostles. Here our author falls into the same trap into which many before him had fallen, by confusing the term *kephas* with the Greek *kephale*.[3]

An ancillary problem of the papal *plenitudo potestatis* concerned the participation of the cardinals in the creation of the law.[32] 'An papa ex plenitudine potestatis possit sine fratribus suis aliqua statuere de universali statu ecclesiae?' After a lengthy discussion he concludes: 'Omnem legem tam universalem quam particularem licitam, quam cum cardinalibus potest condere, potest per se.'[33] In this function he sees a 'commissario plena potestas generaliter concessa'[34] since the pope has in any case all the laws in his breast.[35] Because for our author

---

[27] Temporarily healed by II Lyon: '…quadraginta tres errores…in concilio Lugdunensi, quos habui de libraria ecclesiae Roffensis…' (Prol., 10.1, p. 262aA–D). In IV.48.12, p. 575bC this becomes 'Libraria de Roccaforte' and in IV.50.1.1, p. 578bA this is: 'Libraria de Rocha forte'.

[28] Prol. 10.1, p. 262aC.

[29] See P. Hinschius, *Decretales Pseudo-Isidorianae* (repr. Aalen, 1963), p. 79: *Ep*. 2, c.24; *Ep*. 3, c.30, p. 83 = Gratian, *Dist*. XXI. 2, to which he refers.

[30] Cf. Ps. Anacletus, *Ep*. 3, c. 29, and Prol. 10.1, p. 262bC–D.

[31] Even Innocent III had made the same mistake: *Sermo* II in Migne, *PL*. CCXVII 658A; *Sermo* XVIII (*ibid*. 517B), but cf. *Sermo* XXI (*ibid*. 552C), where he began to have doubts about this meaning. In his decree of condemnation of Marsilius John XXII had the same view: Raynaldus, ed. cit. (n. 17 above), p. 324. It all originated with Ps. Anacletus, *Ep*. 3, c. 33, ed. cit., p. 83: 'Cephas, id est caput.' This is not noted by H. Fuhrmann, *Einfluss und Verbreitung der ps. isidorischen Fälschungen* (Stuttgart, 1972–4).

[32] See p. 263aC. On the problem of the divine or human origin of the cardinalate, cf. W. Ullmann, 'Eugenius IV, Cardinal Kemp and Archbishop Chichele' in *Essays in Medieval History presented to Aubrey Gwynn* (Dublin, 1958), pp. 359–86.

[33] He quotes the Archdeacon's *Rosarium*, XXV.1.6. (edn Venice, 1523, fo. 274, no. 1) who in his turn quoted Laurentius Hispanus: 'Dicit lau. quod generalem legem universali statui ecclesiae condere non potest papa sine cardinalibus, sed particularem.' John evidently went much further.   [34] See p. 263bB.

[35] The reference is to the enactment in the Sext by Boniface VIII which made the Roman law passage of C.VI.23.19 the official papal standpoint: VI: I.2.1.

the pope was the pivot of the whole ecclesiologically conceived society, 'in omni casu potest per se in quo potest cum cardinalibus'. The sole barrier to papal legislative power he finds in the Old and New Testaments, and in this view he moves along accepted doctrine.

Another contingent question of the papal plenitude of power referred to the pope's right to designate his successor, a topic rarely discussed by the canonists: positive canon law was perfectly plain on the issue[36] which for him was no compelling reason for not examining the problem at length.[37] What exercised his mind was the example of Peter who had appointed his successor in the person of Clement I. Hence could not every pope as successor of St Peter do the same? For Peter 'ordinavit Clementem successorem in auribus totius ecclesiae'. To soothe his conscience John saw this as a genuine election which 'vocatur inspiratio spiritus sancti, quae est canonica'. Once more there was consultation of the book 'qui vocatur registrum Romanorum Pontificum', where in the first chapter he found the 'actual' letter which Clement himself had written to St James in Jerusalem.[38] According to John, Linus and Anacletus were Peter's assistants,[39] whereas Clement was consecrated bishop and after Peter's death became his successor. Indeed, he is quite right in saying that the 'Register of the Pontiffs' (Pseudo-Isidore) had no entry relating to Linus and Cletus (though he might have known that Cletus and Anacletus were identical) from which he concluded that they were no popes.[40] But the problem still remained, despite the *Epistola Clementis*, for if Clement was the

[36] Cf. Alexander III in III Lat., c. 1 (partly in x: 1.6.6) and Gregory X in II Lyon, c. 2 (partly in VI: 1.6.4).

[37] From the late 4th cent. the appointment of the Roman archdeacon amounted to his designation as the future pope, as, for instance, evidenced by the decree no. 5 of the Roman synod of 1 March 499: *MGH. Auctores antiquissimi*, XII.399ff. at 404. The only certain designation of a successor was by Boniface II in 531, see *Lib. Pontificalis*, ed. L. Duchesne (repr. 1955) I, 281, who appointed the unfortunate Vigilius, but had to retract on protest. The case re-echoed throughout the medieval period, cf. e.g. Peter Damian, *Lib. gratissimus*, c. 16, *MGH. Libelli de Lite*, 1.38, lines 30–5; Deusdedit, *Libellus contra invasores et symoniacos*, c. 13, *ibid.* II, 312, lines 4–6; Gerhoch of Reichersberg, *Opusc. de edificio Dei*, c. 155, *ibid.* III, 190f. From one of these sources or their derivatives John learned of the problem. This incident is also the occasion on which the principle that *prima sedes a nemine iudicatur* was applied, see *Lib. Pont., loc. cit.*

[38] *Epistola Clementis*, ed. Hinschius, *Decretales Pseudo-Isidorianae*, pp. 30ff. About details cf. W. Ullmann, 'The significance of the Epistola Clementis' in *Journ. of Theological Studies*, n.s. XI (1960), 295ff. A check proves that John's quotations are perfectly correct.

[39] The *gl. ord.* on VIII.1.1 saw the problem differently and adopted a different solution: '…videns autem Clemens quod hoc esset perniciosum exemplum quod aliquis sibi eligerit successorem, renuntiavit papatui et tunc electus est Linus, eo mortuo electus est Cletus, quo mortuo denuo fuit Clemens electus, et sic Clemens secundum unam computationem fuit secundus, et secundum aliam fuit quartus. Disputat hic mundus, quartus fueritve secundus?'

[40] For the various kinds of computation cf. art. cit. (above n. 38), pp. 302ff.

first successor of St Peter, who elected him after Peter's death? 'Per quos fiebat electio Clementis?' His answer is:

Pro illo tempore haec fuit bona electio, nam cum assensu cleri et populi consuevit antiquitus episcopi fieri electio.[41]

In subsequent ages

semper electio pertinuit ad clerum, sed fidelis populi consensus adhibendus erat, quia docendus est populus, non sequendus.[42]

John goes very far in the application of the electoral principle which he bases on Pseudo-Anacletus:[43] the election of a pope was specifically ordained by Christ:

Fuit ex ordinatione Christi, nam Petrus a Christo et per electionem apostolorum fuit institutus in forma electionis in futurum.[44]

In the last resort this unusual view could only be derived from the preamble of the *Epistola Clementis*.[45] According to John the electoral principle was even applied to Christ as can be concluded from Is. 42. 1. He does not, and in all likelihood cannot, adduce any authority for this remarkable thesis.

In the end he shelters behind the example of Moses who was bidden by God not to elect, that is, appoint his own successor, from which he deduces that 'nec summus pontifex debet eligere successorem' partly in order to avoid simony, partly to exclude subterfuges and similar reprehensible devices.[46] Nor could the appointment of Clement by Peter provide a precedent because this was, our author avows, 'praedifinitum per spiritum sanctum', and what is thus arranged is outside the ordinary laws. He is bound to concede that the papal plenitude of power suffered 'exceptionem in hoc casu'. Indubitably Peter had been

---

[41] Referring to *Dist.* LXIII.20 and 11, and *Dist.* XXIII.1.

[42] He may have had in mind the decree of 769 (*MGH. Concilia*, II, 86, no. 14) embodied in *Dist.* LXXIX.4. The memorable expression *Populus docendus, sed non sequendus* originates with Celestine I, *Ep.* 5, in Migne, *PL.* L, 437, cf. W. Ullmann, *Principles of Government and Politics in the Middle Ages*, 3rd edn (London, 1974) p. 134, though *docendus* was sometimes changed into *ducendus*, e.g., by Alcuin, *Ep.* 132, c. 9 in *MGH. Epp.* IV, 199 (addressed to Charles); here also the rejection of the adage: *Vox populi, vox Dei*, 'cum tumultuositas vulgi semper insaniae proxima sit.' For the Roman synod in 898 under John IX it was also self-evident that 'populum non sequendum esse, sed docendum', see J. D. Mansi, *Conciliorum Collectio* (Venice, 1773) XVIII, 223E.

[43] *Dist.* XXII. 2 = Ps. Anacletus, *Ep.* 3, c. 32, ed. Hinschius, *Decretales*, p. 83.

[44] Prol. X.3, p. 264bD: 'Ipsi (apostoli) inter se idipsum voluerunt, ut reliquis omnibus praeesset apostolis et caput...'

[45] See *Epistola Clementis*: 'vocatus et electus,' ed. Hinschius, *Decretales*, p. 30.

[46] Invoking Gratian, VIII.1.6.

chosen by the apostles as their head, and it was they who had bequeathed this arrangement to posterity as an immutable law:

Dices igitur canones apostolorum, qui reperiuntur in registro Romanorum pontificum, sunt immutabiles.

Pseudo-Isidore had not yet spent his force in the fourteenth century. There were very few canonists, or for that matter theologians, who had taken the trouble to consult the 'original source'. From the canonistic standpoint it is the consultation of the source rather than the substance of the novel argumentation which is significant, especially when one considers how stereotyped, if not monotonous, fourteenth-century canonistic literature had become. The novelty of approach (as well as of interpretation) is all the more refreshing as it was advanced by a scholar whose mind was not, by training, cast into the somewhat rigid mould of the jurist who was hypnotised by the *lex lata*.[47]

The electoral principle entails consideration of the cardinalate. Not apparently much exercised by the contemporary discussions concerning the divine or human origin of the cardinalate as an institution, his *point d'appui* is once again the *Epistola Clementis* – 'ut in registro Romanorum pontificum, cap. I'. According to John's interpretation, the cardinals had existed before Nicaea because, like patriarchs and archbishops, they had been appointed by the apostles.[48] Peter himself had assistants: what is therefore of particular importance in this context is that the cardinals had an intimate connection with the Roman Church which (Ps.) Anacletus (*Dist.* xxii.2) called 'cardo (et caput) omnium ecclesiarum'. From here it was only a short step to the explanation of the cardinals as *cardines* which indeed was the common standpoint.[49] Of the Innocentian view concerning the Levitic origin of the cardinals there is no allusion anywhere.[50] Instead at great length and with exact folio reference he quotes from the 'papal register' that the earliest popes had considered the prelates appointed by the apostles as *collaterales assistentes* or counsellors.[51]

The relationship between the cardinals and other ecclesiastical

---

[47] About the different approaches of theologians, philosophers and jurists to the idea of justice and law, cf. Ullmann, *Principles* (above n. 42), pp. 290ff.

[48] 'Ante illud concilium sub Sylvestro (!) celebratum instituti fuerunt...'

[49] This view of *cardo-cardinalis* has a long history and was also quoted in the Leo–Humbert letter to Kerullarios (cited in *Growth*, above n. 7), p. 321. For the early historical (as distinct from 'doctrinal') development see S. Kuttner, 'Cardinalis' in *Traditio*, III (1945), 129ff. which is basic.

[50] For details cf. W. Ullmann, art. cit. (above n. 32), esp. pp. 369ff.

[51] 'Haec in Registro Romanorum Pontificum, fo. 5 et fo. 19...'

dignitaries constituted one of the most hotly debated questions in medieval juristic scholarship.[52] In a concise and succinct manner John makes the very distinction that was to become the official standpoint exactly a hundred years later. He maintained that basically the *ratio ordinis episcopalis* and the *ratio iurisdictionis papalis* determine the relationship between cardinals and other prelates. The distinction between what is technically called the *potestas ordinis* and the *potestas iurisdictionis* supplies a firm juristic basis for establishing the right order. A century later Eugenius IV was to make exactly the same distinction in unravelling the cluster of problems surrounding the archbishop's relations to a cardinal. Let our author speak himself:

> Licet archiepiscopi et patriarchae sunt maiores ratione ordinis episcopalis, tamen cardinales sunt maiores ratione iurisdictionis papalis.[53]

It is evident that he considered the cardinalate an ecclesiastical office that could be attached to any rank: hence the cardinal-deacon was hierarchically superior to an archbishop. For him the cardinals are judicial assistants of the pope, again the view authoritatively expressed later by Eugenius IV. According to John they assist the pope in trials concerning bishops, archbishops, patriarchs, in controversial matters relative to faith and morals, and evidently in the formulation and enactment of legislative measures.[54] Furthermore, by reason of their intimate judicial link with the pope they are called *legati a latere*, because they form part of the pope's body, an adaptation of the respective Roman law statement that the senators formed part of the emperor's body.[55] This topic leads our author to discuss the legatine system and the prerogatives which the cardinals enjoy in the exercise of their functions as *legati a latere*. He presents a neat and competent summary of the respective enactments[56] and devotes considerable space to the powerful protection of the cardinals, notably in respect of offences committed against them. These offences are to be treated as high treason, because the eventual target of the crime was the papal majesty itself. Hence punishment was

---

[52] For this cf. W. Ullmann, 'The legality of the papal electoral pacts' in *Ephemerides Iuris Canonici*, XII (1956), 312ff.

[53] Art. 4, p. 265bE–266aA.

[54] The wording of Eugenius IV's decree *Non mediocri dolore* (details in art. cit., above n. 32), should be compared with that of our author.

[55] See C. IX.8.5, incorporated in Gratian, VI.1.22. He also adduces the *gl. ord.* on X: 1.30.9 which concedes that this judicial function also applies to the *capellani papae* when acting as papal legates.

[56] Cf. X: 1.30.8, 9, 10; he also refers to X: V.33.23 (= IV Lat. c. 5) and VI: 1.15.1.

extended beyond the actual wrong-doer to his descendants in direct line
as well as to collateral relatives.[57] The crime entailed the social, economic
and moral ruin of the defendant, his family and relations, as they were
deprived of the right to acquire property or to dispose of it by testamentary means. Hardly any other crime incurred such stringent
penalties as the crime of *lèse majesté*, in itself a first-rate pointer to the
underlying governmental ideology.

The substance and meaning of the papal vicariate of Christ presup-
posed clarification of Christ's own powers: here he follows Thomas
Aquinas' *Summa theologiae* (III.59) closely and contributes little in
substance. Since in common with Thomas he considers that Christ had
judicial powers (*iudiciaria potestas*) in regard to all human things
(*quantum ad omnes res humanas*), John can readily employ the teleological
argument:

Res humanae ordinantur, *ut* per earum usum debitum assequetur homo vitam
aeternam, et vitae aeternae iudex est Christus.[58]

This is the message of the wholeness point of view: the totality of the
life of a Christian *qua* Christian matters. No conceptual distinction can
be drawn between religious, moral, political and other norms. This
indivisibility was a basic Christian presupposition and furnishes an easy
explanation for the view expressed by an exact contemporary of
Baconthorpe that life was merely a *vita transitoria* in which the worldly
things are no more than 'organa et instrumenta ad finem ultimum ordinata'.[59] Indeed, it was the standpoint that had been argued in countless
tracts from the fourth to the fourteenth centuries. Further, according to
John, Christ had 'potestatem dispositivam, distributivam et trans-
lativam quantum ad omnes res huius mundi'.[60] Consequently, Christ
was 'rex regum super omnes reges terrae'. In this very same context
John viewed property as an effluence of grace, a claim unbeknown to
him already made by Gregory VII,[61] and by Innocent IV and Hostiensis
(whom he invokes).[62] Therefore, 'potest dominium dare aliis et con-

---

[57] See VI: v.9.5. On this cluster of problems cf. W. Ullmann, 'The significance of Innocent
III's decretal "Vergentis"' in *Études...dédiées à Gabriel Le Bras* (Paris, 1965), 729ff.

[58] At p. 267aA.

[59] Hermannus de Schilditz, *Contra haereticos*, ed. R. Scholz, *Unbekannte kirchenpolitische Streitschriften des 14. Jahrhunderts*, II (Rome, 1914), 135, cf. also 142. This totality standpoint was
expressed lucidly by another contemporary of John, Conrad of Megenberg, *De Translatione
Romani imperii*, c. 12, ed. *ibid.* II, 292: 'Liquidum est religionem christianam quodam *totum*
esse.' [60] At p. 267aB, referring to Ps. 23:1.

[61] *Reg.* VII.14a, ed. E. Caspar, *MGH, Epistolae Selectae*, t. II (repr. Berlin, 1955), 487: the two
apostles can 'omnium hominum possessiones pro meritis tollere unicuique et concedere'.

[62] Innocent IV in his *Apparatus* (edn Frankfurt, 1535), ad X:III.34.8, fo. 430vb, no. 10; Hostiensis,
Lectura in Decretales (edn Paris, 1512), *ibid.*, fo. 124va.

cedere sicut placet'.[63] Property was not based on any natural law or natural rights, but was a favour, a grace, a *beneficium* conceded.[64]

To these views John adjoins his very detailed analyses concerning the substance and ramifications of papal power. In a different context he had stated that the pope's function was principally juristic: 'Papa est arca iuris, cuius est omnes libertates ecclesiasticas statuere.'[65] Although he did not operate with the concept of the pope as *indignus haeres b. Petri*, he nevertheless assumed the juristic transfer of powers to have taken place topographically: 'Locus autem quem elegit Dominus est sedes Petri et apostolica.'[66] And this transfer concerned the same rights he had attributed to Christ – the *ius dispositivum, distributivum* and *translativum*, a categorisation and a thesis all his own: I have not found it before, nor does he himself cite an authority. For the function of the pope as universal monarch he invokes partly the law and partly doctrine.[67] Innocent III's thesis that 'Romanus pontifex non tantum puri hominis, sed veri Dei vicem gerit in terra et divina auctoritate fulcitur'[68] is correctly seen by John as the expression of papal *maioritas*, that is, legal and judicial sovereignty concerning all Christians 'totius orbis indistincte'.[69] His exegesis presents the traditional unipolarity point of view. What is here remarkable is the absence of any reference to *Unam sanctam* or the numerous other unambiguous and relevant papal statements nor is there any recourse to a two-sword theory or the juristic implications of the Donation of Constantine. Evidently, papal sovereignty includes the non-justiciability of the pope: the papal tribunal was the final court of appeal 'in omni causa tam civili quam ecclesiastica'.[70] This unappealable jurisdiction extends also to the deposition of kings – the relevant passage is a literal copy of the Archdeacon's[71] – as well as of emperors.[72]

Let us now briefly survey the last *Quaestio* in the Prologue in which

---

[63] At p. 267aC.

[64] About this concession principle, cf. *Principles* (above n. 42) pp. 54f., 76f.

[65] IV.3.2.2, p. 318bD, referring to *Dist.* XXI.1 and 2.   [66] Art. 4, p. 269aA.

[67] Such as X:1.7.3; IV.17.13, and the relevant glosses and commentaries, as well as to *Dist.* XXII.1, which is attributed to Nicholas I, but is Peter Damian's. For the genesis and later development, cf. *Growth*, (above n. 7), p. 437 n.4, to which should be added another statement of Damian's in his letter to Hildebrand: *Opusc.* 5, in Migne, *PL.* CXLV, 91.

[68] X:1.7.30; cited at p. 268bB.

[69] Referring to the *Lectura* of Hostiensis, ad X:IV.17.13 (edn Paris, 1512), fo. 38va.

[70] Art. 4, p. 269aA. For some observations on this topic cf. W. Ullmann, 'The medieval papal court as an international tribunal' in *Virginia Journal of International Law* (= Essays in honour of H. C. Dillard), XI (1971), 356ff.

[71] *Rosarium* ad XV.6.3 (edn Venice, 1523), fo. 213rb.

[72] Relying on X:1.6.34 and the *gl. ord. ibid.*

he deals with two seemingly unrelated problems, the conversion of
Jews and infidels, and the papal rights in regard to the Holy Land. This
at first sight unusual grouping can be explained by a common denomi-
nator: the treatment and position of non-Christians by Christians. Law
and doctrine had never left any doubt about the essential element of
consent in baptism.[73] Yet, he holds, papal legislation shows that there
were ways and means by which indirect and gentle pressure could be
exercised to make the Jews convert:[74] the Church 'indirecte quodam
modo eos cogit'.[75] Moreover, as Huguccio had already pointed out,
Jews could be subjected to higher public payments, 'ut sic facilius
trahantur ad fidem'.[76] The pope may prohibit usury among Jews
because 'hoc est contra utrumque testamentum'.[77] Christians have an
undoubted right to send missions to infidel countries: if they object,
secular princes may be called upon to assist missionary efforts: 'potest
ergo papa cogere infideles ad fidem coactione (saltem indirecta)'. In
regard to the Holy Land John considers that numerous statements in
both the Old and the New Testaments amply justify papal intervention
which is also warranted by history, he declares: the conquest of the
Persians by the Emperor Heraklios in 628–9 who rescued Palestine from
the infidels[78] – a most unusual argument which no other author had
adduced – and the eventual reconquest by Godfrey of Bouillon through
which a *ius conquisitionis* accrued to the papacy. And since the pope
qua pope succeeds Christ – 'quia Romanus pontifex succedit Christo'
(a debatable formulation) – he was juristically the *haeres terrae promissionis*. However, all this was by then a purely academic discussion.

Additional canonistic points came also to be treated in John's
Quodlibeta.[79] One of these concerned the petrinological thesis in regard
to the revocation of a previous papal decree or statement. The *Quodlibet*

[73] Prol., *Qu.* x, p. 270aE.
[74] x:v.6.4, 15; also 8, 10, 13; Gratian, xxviii.1.13.   [75] At p. 271aB.
[76] In the *Rosarium* ad xxiii.6.4 there is no mentioning of Huguccio which proves that John had
consulted him directly (and most Huguccio MSS are of fourteenth-century provenance).
The Archdeacon said this: 'Nota argumentum pro consuetudine hispaniae ubi exiguntur
tributa a sarracenis et iudaeis, etsi terras non habebant secundum la.' Apart from Laurentius
no other canonist (or civilian) is quoted.
[77] Innocent IV in his *Apparatus* ad x:iii.34.8, fo. 430v. Hostiensis in his *Lectura, ibid.* (edn Paris,
1512) fo. 124va, is of the same opinion, though he does not mention Innocent: 'Oves autem
non sunt solum fideles, set etiam infideles per creationem, licet non sint de ovili, unde sequitur
quod papa super omnes habet potestatem et iurisdictionem de iure, licet non de facto.'
[78] For this see G. Ostrogorsky, *Geschichte des byzantinischen Staates*, 3rd edn (Munich, 1963),
86f. Heraklios returned the Cross to Jerusalem in 630.
[79] Appended to the Cremona edn of 1618. Their exact chronological relationship to the Commentaries needs to be established. There may be several recensions.

in question[80] was a sequel to the Marsilian attack on the petrinological theme and to some pronouncements by John XXII: had the pope by virtue of his primatial position the right to revoke a decision of his precedessor? Indeed, this problem was later to assume major dimensions in the shape of papal infallibility. He had already touched on the power of the keys in the appropriate places of the *Sentences*.[81] The *Quodlibet* is headed by the carefully worded question:

Utrum illud quod est ordinatum per *clavem scientiae* in fide et in moribus semel per Romanum pontificem ita perseveret immobile, quod successori revocare in dubium vel contrarium asserere non licuit, sed de his, quae per *clavem potestatis* ordinaverit, secus sit.

Restrictions of space do not allow a detailed examination of this problem here, but so much may be said with confidence that John made a distinct contribution to this important issue, because he viewed it from both the theological and canonistic angles. Indeed, by a very dexterous handling of the law, including decrees which were of no universal interest, such as Clement V's *Meruit*, he trod a path which is far from being appreciated by modern scholarship. Not the least significant feature (which appears to have gone unnoticed) of this *Quodlibet* is that in it he touches on, and examines, the meaning of such technical matters as the clause employed in papal documents (the Privilegia): 'salva auctoritate Romanae ecclesiae'.[82] That he did concede to the pope revocatory powers, has recently been pointed out.[83] But his argumentation demands that degree of close attention and respect which it has not yet received. As soon as the problem was aired, he realised its explosive potentiality. To him the problem of revocability or infallibility had nothing to do with sovereignty: this was an exclu-

---

[80] *Quodlib.* III.17, pp. 774–9.

[81] IV.17. His Postill on Matthew is an appendix to his IV.19 about which see Smalley, art. cit. (above n. 1), especially p. 103.

[82] See p. 778aE and 779aA. For this clause cf. F. Thaner, 'Entstehung und Bedeutung der Formel Salva...' in *Sitz. Ber. Vienna, phil. hist. Kl.*, LXXI (1872), 807–51; J. B. Sägmüller, *Zur Geschichte der Entwicklung des päpstlichen Gesetzgebungsrechts* (Rottenburg, 1937). The formula is Ps. Isidorian: Ps. Stephen, *Ep.* 2, c. 9, ed. Hinschius, p. 185; Ps. Julius, c. 12, *ibid.* p. 469. It appeared in Gratian, *Dist.* LXXX.1; III.6.12 and 9.7, also in the famous D.p.c.15, XXV.16. In view of W. Holtzmann's thesis in *Studia Gratiana*, I (1953), 325–49 that Gratian had no influence on the papal chancery before Clement III and the consistent use of this formula from the 40s onwards, the problem is in need of examination. The significance of this diplomatic matter has not fully been realised by H. Fuhrmann, *Einfluss und Verbreitung*, p. 352, n. 291; cf. also W. Ullmann in *Zeitschrift der Savigny-Stiftung, Kan. Abt.*, XLVI (1960) at 432.

[83] B. Tierney, *Origins of Papal Infallibility* (Leiden, 1972), p. 188, who is perhaps a shade too brief in the citation of passages (e.g. of that on p. 779a–b). Cf. also IV.17 and 15.11, pp. 515–518bC.

sively legal concept which could not be accommodated within the terms of the *magisterium*. Sovereignty was the effluence of the exercise of the *clavis potestatis* and concerned government: it is a meaningless concept within the precincts of the *magisterium* or teaching where the *clavis scientiae* operates. He used perfectly understandable terminology. Hence whether a statement or decree was revocable depended on whether it was issued by a pope in his capacity as a *gubernator* or in that as a *magister*. In the former capacity he acted as a sovereign monarch whose rulings could be modified or revoked by a (sovereign) successor, in the latter capacity he acted as a teacher, and the idea of sovereignty simply did not enter here.

Although it might at first sight seem strange, John also treats the Immaculate Conception within the petrinological framework. This instance testifies once more to his principal aim to achieve an integration of theological and liturgical matters which had elements in common with canon law. As his contribution has only been cursorily touched on by modern scholarship, a few remarks seem apposite. In a number of places[84] he attempted to prove the thesis that Mary was free from original sin and was conceived immaculately.[85] He draws his arguments partly from Augustine's *De natura et gratia*,[86] *De Genesi ad litteram*[87] and other exegetical works and some New Testament passages, here and there supported by snippets from Aristotle, by Anselm's *Cur Deus homo*[88] and Pseudo-Anselm's *De conceptu virginali* – the author of this *De conceptione B.V.M.* was Eadmer[89] – a tract, he says, that is to be seen in many places:[90]

Inveni istum librum in domo Fratrum Minorum Cantabrigiensium et postea inveni Parisiis eundem tractatum in manu unius communis stationarii.[91]

---

[84] III.3.2.4–5, pp. 34ff.; IV.2.3.3–5, pp. 307ff.; IV.3.1.2–3, pp. 314ff.; *Quodlib.* III.13–14, pp. 763ff.

[85] In II.2.30.2–3, pp. 642b–645b, he had propounded a different view which is singled out by I. Brady, 'The development of the doctrine of the Immaculate Conception in the 14th cent. after Aureoli' in *Franciscan Studies*, XV (1955), 175ff., at 195. John's contemporary, Hermann de Schilditz, wrote the first tract in Germany on the topic, *c.* 1350: *Tractatus de conceptione gloriosae virginis Mariae*, ed. A. Zumkeller (Würzburg, 1970), pp. 109ff. For the three MSS of this tract cf. editorial comment, pp. XIVff.

[86] Ed. in *Corpus scriptorum ecclesiasticorum latinorum* (Vienna), XL, 233–99.

[87] Ed. *ibid.* XXVIII, 1–435.   [88] Esp. cc. 16, 18, see p. 309bD.

[89] Ed. in Migne, *PL*, CLIX, 301–18 and by H. Thurston and Th. Slater, *Tractatus de conceptione s. Mariae* (Freiburg, 1904). Details in R. W. Southern, *St. Anselm and his Biographer* (Cambridge, repr. 1966), pp. 290ff. Apparently M. Manitius, *Geschichte der lateinischen Literatur im Mittelalter*, III (Munich, 1931), 92 still considered this a genuine Anselmian product.

[90] 'Hunc librum vidi in multis locis…incipit autem liber Anselmi de conceptione sic: Principium…' (p. 309bE).

[91] *Quodlib.* III.13, p. 763bB, also quoted by Xiberta, 'De Magistro Iohanne', p. 207 and Southern *St. Anselm*, p. 295 from Brady, 'Immaculate Conception', p. 196, n. 77.

But in order to strengthen his case, a juristic buttressing appeared to him advisable, hence his invocation of a number of canon law passages.[92] The institution of a formal feast day celebrating the Immaculate Conception was to his mind long overdue. To this end he makes a passionate plea to the papacy that by virtue of its primatial function it should decree the establishment of this feast. In support of this plea he refers to the many relevant discussions among theologians in Paris, Oxford and Cambridge who were all of one mind:

Nam a multis annis disputatum est inter theologos in universitatibus Parisiensi, Oxoniensi ac Cantabrigiensi, et ubique determinatur, quod sanctum est conceptionem b. Mariae celebrare, habito respectu ad eius sanctificationem, et in dictis universitatibus celebratur per statutum.[93]

Only the papacy could put its seal on this custom, for its magisterial primacy extends also to liturgical matters. Both Innocent III[94] and Gregory X had shown the proper dimensions of this function,[95] and so did contemporary popes, such as John XXII and Benedict XII.[96] But there was even more justification for the papacy to act in the matter of the Immaculate Conception, because the Roman Church itself celebrated this feast;[97] and, since the true religion was preserved in the apostolic see,[98] it was only right and proper for the 'vicarius Dei in terris' to confirm this custom. Papal silence would inflict damage on religion.[99] John quotes lavishly from Pseudo-Anselm (i.e. Eadmer) and goes into the details of the miracle that was revealed to the abbot of Ramsey, Elsinus, apparently the first to have introduced this feast, at least in his abbey.[100] The *Quodlibeta* also refer to the opponents of the feast: there was the *glossa ordinaria* on the *Decretum* which poured ice-

---

[92] On the nature of Privilegia (which John invokes) see Innocent III in x:v.40.5, refined and elaborated by Innocent IV (vi:v.7.1) and commented on by himself in his *Apparatus* ad x:v.33 in fine (edn Frankfurt, 1535, fo. 538rb).

[93] iv.3.1.3, p. 316bB; *Quodlib.* iii.14, p. 767bB. See also iv.2.4.2, p. 316aC concerning the sermon preached by Alexander Neckam at Oxford. Duns and his teacher William of Ware were also advocates of the feast, cf. K. Binder, 'Heinrich von Gent über die Empfängnis der Gottesmutter' in *Festschrift für Franz Loidl* (Vienna, 1970) pp. 13–29, at 23f. Henry was an opponent.

[94] See x:i.1.2.   [95] vi:i.1.c.un. = II Lyon c.2.

[96] On the Beatific Vision. The date (29 Jan. 1336) gives some clue to the time of his writing. The same problem also forms the topic of iv.50.1 and 2, pp. 579ff.

[97] See iv.2.4.2, p. 316bE.

[98] He refers to Gratian, xxiv.i.11.   [99] Referring to xxiv.i.13.

[100] *Quodlib.* iii.14, p. 765bE: '…ibi recitat (scil. Anselmus) quomodo istud festum fuit miraculis revelatum abbati Helsmo Ramensi in Anglia…' See also *ibid.*, p. 767aE. This is from the *Miraculum s. Mariae*, in Migne, *PL.* clix, 323–6. For details and background see R. W. Southern, 'The English origins of the "Miracles of the Virgin"' in *Mediaeval and Renaissance Studies*, iv (1958), 176ff., at 195–8.

cold water on this concept.[101] The professional canonists moved in good company, as he tells us, since no lesser man than Bernard of Clairvaux had strongly opposed the formal celebration of the Immaculate Conception.[102] It is understandable that John was gratified by the recent statute issued by the provincial council of Canterbury in January 1328 which decreed the observation of this feast.[103]

III

Space can here be found for only a few remarks on the numerous other topics treated by this much-neglected juristic theologian. A selection is not easy because his commentary on Book IV ranges over a very wide field of canonistic jurisprudence. His exposition is only loosely linked with the topic set by the Master of the *Sentences*. As a characteristic instance of John's method may be taken his commentary on *Dist*.vii. Its subject, the sacrament of confirmation, was dealt with by the Lombard in two short Articles, one on its essence, the other on its relation to baptism. Now John briskly deals with the theological side of confirmation,[104] only to hasten to the juristic question concerning the legitimate administration of the sacrament. Apart from Thomas Aquinas, Richard Middleton, and others, his main authorities are the relevant chapters in Gratian's *De consecratione*. John appends a number of associated problems, such as consecration of chrism, the power of the local bishop to delegate confirmation to priests in his diocese, and so on. But all this is merely an introduction to the quite unexpected question of the exact relationship between confirmation and election. Clearly, of this the Lombard had said nothing, but John joins the two topics and devotes three lengthy *Quaestiones* (fourteen columns) to them. Here he

---

[101] See *gl. ord. (De cons.* III.1; I used the edn Antwerp 1537): 'De facto conceptionis nihil dicitur, quia celebrandum non est sicut in multis regionibus fit, maxime in Anglia, et haec est ratio, quia in peccato concepta fuit.' To judge by the siglum, this was Huguccio's view. In his *Rosarium (ibid.,* IV.3, edn Venice, 1523, fo. 338vb) the Archdeacon treats this in connection with 'the two births' (of St John 3:3–5): '...unde conceptio b. Mariae non debet celebrari, sed nativitas ex utero bene celebretur et s. Johannis, quia fuerunt in utero sanctificati et eis fuit dimissum originale peccatum, secundum hu'. For Henry of Ghent, see above n. 93.

[102] See p. 764bC and p. 768aD. Bernard's letter to the canons of Lyon in Migne, *PL.* CLXXXII, 332–6.

[103] See p. 765aA: '...concilium provinciale Cantuariense noviter anno Domini MCCCXXVIII, mense Januario declarat...'. See D. Wilkins, *Concilia* (edn London, 1737), II, 552. W. Lyndwood, *Provinciale* (edn Oxford, 1679) comments on this decree under the title 'De Feriis' (p. 101a–b), where in addition to many canonists he also quotes Bernard's letter. With the exception of the last word ('libenter') the quotation is faultless.

[104] IV.7.1–3, p. 348b–349b.

poses virtually all important matters relative to election: the qualification of electors, of the elected, personal and impersonal conditions of valid elections, impediments to ratification, the principles of quantitative and qualitative majority, the various forms of election procedures, the rôle of scrutineers, voting by proxy, factors nullifying an election, such as participation of excommunicated persons or of suspended officers, and so on. Based on a thorough knowledge of canonistic literature, this is a very respectable canonistic *opusculum* on elections, the importance of which is only heightened by the appended question on the effects of customary law and usages on elections.[105] It is in this partly theoretical, partly practical context that he treats of the concept of customary law, its juristic ingredients, its derogatory power, the relative importance customary law may display in the elections of various officers, such as in abbatial or episcopal elections, and similar questions. No doubt this was an ingenious way of introducing his audience or his readers to a jurisprudential topic of considerable magnitude. Dexterity of manipulating complex matter can certainly not be denied to our author – witness his handling of customary law in relation to (what he himself calls) *ius positivum*,[106] or his anatomy of the Roman-law-based view that *pontifex omnia iura suo pectore habet*.[107]

Another subject only remotely linked with the *Sentences* is that of excommunication, its validity and effects.[108] Since excommunication was a juristic act and therefore the effluence of jurisdictional power, he reverts to the exercise of the *potestas clavium* to throw light on it from yet another angle. Of the theologians – and he ranks himself among them: 'cum igitur nos theologi concedimus...'[109] – he singles out Thomas, Duns, the *Scoti*, Peter Aureoli, not without crossing swords with him once again, while within the field of canon law he invokes the whole galaxy of eminent canonistic names as well as the enactments from Gratian down to the Clementines. This is a veritable tract on excommunication.[110] Among the topics examined are the constitutional and ecclesiastical qualifications of the officiating organs; the rôle of the unjust and unlawful sentence, including the famous statement by Gregory I ('Utrum iuste vel iniuste obliget, pastoris tamen sententia gregi timenda est');[111] *error iuris* and *error facti* as well as *ignorantia iuris* in relation to the validity of the sentence; the distinction between ex-

---

[105] *Qu.* 4, p. 355aC.   [106] *Ibid.* p. 355bA.   [107] *Ibid.* p. 356aA (VI:1.2.1).
[108] *Sentences*, IV.17–19.   [109] Art. 3, p. 425aC.   [110] See pp 426aE–439bD.
[111] On this and its transmission cf. *Principles* (above n. 42), p. 107, to which should be added: Anselm's *Collectio canonum*, ed. F. Thaner (repr. 1965), VI.139, p. 334.

communications which are null and void *ab initio* and those which are unjust; the grounds of appeal; the social consequences of excommunication; and so on. A highly significant feature of this 'tract' is the attention it gives to the excommunication of juristic persons, one of the really thorny problems after Innocent IV. Considering that he was a theologian, John shows himself extraordinarily well-informed on this topic. To him the *universitas* as a juristic person was a *persona imaginaria et non vera*: it possesses no *animam rationalem veram*,[112] and therefore, notwithstanding contrary opinions, excommunication can be decreed only against *universos animatos*, but not against the *universitas* itself.[113]

The obligatory character of commitments solemnly undertaken in an oath was frequently discussed since the problem first emerged during the Investiture Conflict:[114] John clearly saw the necessity of dealing with this question. The baptismal vow serves him as a springboard for an analysis of other vows (simple and solemn) and of oaths.[115] The canonistically important conclusion relates to papal dispensatory powers from vows and oaths.

Licet de plenitudine potestatis dispensare possit (scil. pontifex Romanus) super omne ius ecclesiae, ubi tamen erraret contra voluntatem Dei, non posset valere, quia ubi errat commissarius ab intentione committentis, nihil valet.[116]

Another practical problem he discusses was the modification of the promises contained in a vow or oath by extension or restriction, and the possible need of dispensation,[117] necessitated by changing circumstances or by misunderstanding or error.

In an ecclesiological context the descending theme of government and law assumed its concrete shape in the hierarchical ordering of society, hence the prominence of ecclesiastical ranks, their gradation and validity, notably of orders conferred by heretics. The divergence between theologians and canonists on this latter problem was an additional incentive for our author to find a synthesis, precisely because the topic embodied all the classical features of the *communauté des matières*.[118] Even the briefest of outlines of all the problems covered in

---

[112] Art. 3, p. 437aC–E.
[113] See VI:V.11.5. On the subject of excommunication of juristic persons see P. Michaud-Quantin, *Universitas* (Paris, 1970) pp. 327ff.
[114] Cf., e.g., Bernard of Constance, *Liber canonum*, in MGH., *Libelli de Lite*, I.507, c. 37.
[115] IV.3.3.2, p. 321ff.
[116] Art. 3, p. 328bE, referring to X:III.8.4 and 5.38, which is really ingenious. For the *commissarius* cf. above at n. 34.
[117] *Ibid.* Art. 4, p. 330a–b, and Art. 5, pp. 330–332bE.   [118] IV.25, pp. 495ff.

over sixty columns would assume monographic dimensions. Evidently, the 'hardy annuals' receive their due attention, such as the constituents of the sacramentality of orders;[119] whether the episcopal rank was an order or merely a higher grade of the priesthood; ordination impediments; dispensation from irregularities; and so on. In parenthesis it should be observed that this discussion too has a strong practical tinge, notably in regard to servitude and villeinage, property, manual labour and *mendicitas*.[120] Nor does he omit to deal with the nuns.[121] There is an inner coherence in this quite remarkable 'tract' on the orders, within which obedience and its consequences occupy an important place.[122]

Compensation for wrongs inflicted and restitutions of illegitimately acquired rights are characteristic of all legal systems. The medieval canon law, too, dealt with these subjects.[123] Despite the technicalities involved, John does not shirk this issue which was quite obviously of practical concern. Here again the *Sentences* provided only the most tenuous link with the topic of legal restitution. Under this heading[124] John treats of the need of turning a moral obligation into law and of the responsibility of the church (as distinct from its incumbent) for restitution. How far have the judicial personnel and the officers employed in and by the courts a duty of restitution and compensation?[125] Are arbitrators, auditors, executors, assessors, judges delegate, notaries, bedells, messengers and similar officers included in this personnel? In this lengthy examination of another sixty columns he also deals with such subjects as the withholding of just wages, excess of fair profit, compensation for damage caused by simony or usury,[126] indemnification for breach of contractual obligation, compensation for crimes committed in the prosecution of war, such as personal injuries, outrage against the person (rape),[127] restitution for shipwreck suffered, and so on. The mass of material here digested and dexterously manipulated is indeed most impressive.[128]

---

[119] *Ibid.* pp. 512–513bA. This topic prompted even the Archdeacon to consult Thomas Aquinas: *Rosarium*, xxv.1.6, no. 5, (edn Venice, 1523) fo. 275ra: 'Dicit Thomas in summa sua, quod...'.

[120] *Ibid.* pp. 500–501b; 520bE–523aD.   [121] iv.25.6, p. 512.

[122] *Qu.* 14, pp. 523ff.   [123] X:ii.13; vi:ii.5; *Clem.* 1.39; Gratian ii.2; iii.1.

[124] iv.21–22, pp. 452ff.   [125] Art. 4, referring to vi:ii.14.1.

[126] *Ibid.* pp. 466bA–475bB; *Qu.* 5–6, pp. 475ff.   [127] *Ibid.* pp. 459ff.

[128] Mention should at least be made of other practical canonical problems, such as the reasons and effects of the interdict and the qualification of those who can pronounce and dispense from it; clerical immunity (iv.11.4, pp. 384ff.); the right of asylum, its *raison d'être* and foundation in ecclesiastical doctrine (iv.13.1, pp. 392ff.); matrimony (iv.26ff., pp. 533ff.); consecration, desecration and reconsecration of churches and cemeteries, the appropriateness of the locality for divine services, etc. This exposition is a full-length commentary on X:iii.40.10; vi:iii.21.

Lest it be thought that John was only interested in substantive law, two topics in procedural law should at least receive a passing remark. The multitude of civil litigations and criminal trials prompted the introduction of simplified proceedings known as 'de plano et sine strepitu ac figura iudicii'.[129] John stipulates a number of safeguards so that the cause of justice does not suffer, although the procedure is 'contra ius commune'.[130] The other procedural point concerns the probative value of evidence. He treats this as an issue of the difference between the private and public knowledge of the judge.[131] It was an old problem and had excited many jurists: should the judge adjudicate or sentence on the basis of the evidence given in court, or can he also use his own privately acquired knowledge?[132] Here he adopts an independent attitude and rejects the canonists' general opinion that the judge should reach his verdict 'secundum allegata et probata'.[133] This rejection betrays his theological outlook and lack of practical experience in the administration of the law: his reasoning commands respect, nevertheless. Suppose, he says, that the defendant John is charged with committing theft in London on 10 December, and on the evidence before the judge the charge is proved, yet the judge knows perfectly well that John was in Rome on that day. If he now sentences John, he acts against his better knowledge and therefore sins; if he acquits him, he acts 'contra iustitiam publicam'. In disagreeing with the *communis opinio* he applies the descending theme of government and law in a rather unusual way. To him the *iudiciaria potestas* has to decide a case finally and, within an ecclesiological society, this power was first given to St Peter and thence to his successors who hand it on to lower placed officials. The pope (or, for that matter, a lower judge) cannot himself decide against the truth. This analysis is, perhaps, one of the best instances of our author's utter integrity. What makes this section still more significant is the light it sheds on the concept of law when seen in the pure and unadulterated air of theological premisses.[134] This topic,

c.un. and 23.2. He examines such questions as nose bleeding of the celebrating priest at mass (because blood is being shed); someone entering the church having been wounded outside in an affray; death occurring as a result of violence inside or outside the church; 'coitus maritalis sive extramaritalis' inside the church, all with further distinctions and subdivisions: IV.10.1–2, pp. 376ff.

[129] X:II.19.11 and *Clem.*: V.11.2 and II.1.2. [130] IV.25.16, pp. 531–3.

[131] IV.1.3, pp. 282ff.; also II.40, pp. 688ff.

[132] Cf. W. Ullmann, *The Medieval Idea of Law* (London, repr. 1968), p. 129 and the civilian passages cited there. [133] IV.1.3, p. 283bD–E.

[134] See Art. 3, p. 284aE: Judicial decisions should conform to truth. 'Ergo ius humanum desinit esse eius ligans aut solvens apud eum, qui certus est de veritate contraria.'

as so much else in John Baconthorpe's work, would repay thorough study by medievalists whose concern is historical jurisprudence.

In studying John Baconthorpe, the reader is confronted by a man of exceptional erudition. He is conversant with a far greater number of academic disciplines than most of his contemporary academics. His *Quaestiones canonicae* are primarily didactic and may well be classed the forerunner of the comprehensive academic handbook which synthesised theology and canonistics and aspired at an integrated practical theology. This integration was to overcome the fragmentation that threatened the traditional unity of outlook. What others of such divergent persuasion as Dante, Engelbert of Admont, Alvarus Pelagius and Augustinus Triumphus tried to do in the field of government and society – that is, to restore the latter's unity by the universality of the monarch's rule, in order to neutralise the new disintegrating forces – the Carmelite attempted to do by returning to the one and indivisible juristic theology. His *Quaestiones* are simultaneously more and less than the conventional canonistic works. They are more, because they attempt to bridge the yawning gap between theology and jurisprudence; they are not tied to specific juristic categories; they are not intended as professional expositions of canonistic jurisprudence, but are conceived on a comprehensive scale. But against these indubitable merits must be set some demerits: there is hardly any Roman law or the viewpoint of a civilian taken into account. And were not many of the problems common to both canonist and civilian? Did not the very first titles of the first Book of the Codex deal with precisely the topics which formed a large part of our Carmelite's commentaries? Is not in fact canonical jurisprudence built on the firm foundations of Roman jurisprudence? Then as now, nobody could profitably pursue any canonistic topic unless he had at least an elementary grounding in Roman law. This grounding he lacked, as a perusal of his commentaries soon reveals. And within canonistic jurisprudence there are some notable lacunae, such as the lack of consultation of the numerous *ordines iudiciarii*. The topics are unevenly and selectively treated.

Yet whatever shortcomings there are, they are heavily outweighed by the positive achievements of the work. Our knowledge of the intellectual landscape of the fourteenth century would be materially enriched, if this undeservedly neglected canonistic theologian were to find a sympathetic interpreter and expositor who can be assured of a rich harvest. The achievements of lesser men have had a greater share of attention than this man's efforts, aiming as he did at a practical integration of several disciplines. Here indeed lies a vast and fallow field of research.

WALTER REYNOLDS AND
ECCLESIASTICAL POLITICS 1313–1316:
A POSTSCRIPT TO 'COUNCILS
& SYNODS, II'[1]

by JEFFREY DENTON

THE inadequacies of Tout's treatment of the political position of the clergy in his distinguished assessment of Edward II's reign are yet to be remedied,[2] despite the pioneering work of Maude Clarke and Kathleen Edwards.[3] And *Councils & Synods II* ends, aptly enough, in the sixth year of the reign, at the death of Archbishop Winchelsey in May 1313. Winchelsey's death marks the beginning of a crisis for the English clergy. The years 1313 to 1316 were a period of emergency comparable to the years 1294 to 1297. Some notable issues concerned the clergy in both periods: how far and in what circumstances they could be taxed on their spiritualities directly by the king; whether their representative assemblies should take place in parliament or in purely ecclesiastical councils; how they could maintain their special position in law, their 'liberties', in the face of the encroachment of the king's government and of the king's ministers. The problems were interlinked.

The new archbishop, Walter Reynolds, has often been maligned by historians: 'a mere creature of court favour'; 'unworthy and incompetent'; 'intellectually and morally Reynolds was, of all the medieval archbishops of Canterbury, least deserving of respect'; perhaps he was 'wholly unfitted for the office'.[4] These comments reflect the views of some contemporary chroniclers, notably the outspoken author of the

---

[1] I have benefited greatly from the criticisms and advice of Dr J. R. Maddicott and Professor J. S. Roskell.
[2] T. F. Tout, *The Place of the Reign of Edward II in English History*, 2nd edn (Manchester, 1936), pp. 205–11.
[3] M. V. Clarke, *Medieval Representation and Consent* (London, 1936) and K. Edwards, esp. 'The political importance of the English bishops during the reign of Edward II', *EHR*, LIX (1944), 311–47 (and see now G. A. Usher, 'The career of a political bishop: Adam de Orleton', *TRHS*, 5th ser. XXII (1972), 34–47). J. R. Wright's thesis ('The relations between the Crown and the English Church during the pontificates of Clement V and John XXII', Oxford D.Phil., 1966) is a detailed survey of many of the problems of the relations between clergy and crown, but it is not primarily concerned with the political and constitutional role of the clergy.
[4] W. Stubbs, *Constitutional History*, II (4th edn Oxford, 1906), 351, Tout, *Ed. II*, p. 71, Tout in *DNB*, XLVIII, 80 and M. McKisack, *The Fourteenth Century* (Oxford, 1959), p. 296.

Vita Edwardi Secundi and Robert of Reading.[5] But criticism of Reynolds must be viewed in a political context. As a royal clerk he represented the secularist as opposed to the sacerdotalist opinion of the position of the clergy.[6] Winchelsey's policies, on the other hand, had been directed against the clerks in royal service. The division within the clerical ranks can be viewed, from different angles, in the often contrasting policies of Clement V and Boniface VIII and in the often contrasting attitudes of such theorists as John of Paris and Giles of Rome; in England the division was easily measurable in terms of the difference between Reynolds and the scholar-archbishops who had preceded him, Kilwardby, Pecham and Winchelsey. Under their guidance a self-protective policy prevailed in the English Church. Theirs was unmistakably a Church-centred world; and Pecham and Winchelsey especially had been unwavering in the concentration of their interests upon the distinctive position of the clergy. They were separatists. Walter Reynolds was only the second archbishop since the Conquest, following Hubert Walter, to hold his office along with, if only for a short time, the chancellorship of the realm; it must have seemed like posthumous success for Edward I's attempts to secure Canterbury for Burnell.

Reynolds was not, of course, a layman: he was described by Robert of Reading as *laicus*[7] to emphasise his involvement in secular government. He cannot conceivably have been illiterate (if this is how we translate *illiteratus*),[8] but he was unlettered by comparison with his predecessors or many of his contemporaries.[9] In some chronicles the attack upon him is represented by the statement that very large sums were paid to the pope for his appointment.[10] There is little point in discussing how far the chroniclers were accurate in these matters: they indulged in hyperbole. They were presenting a point of view. To his opponents Reynolds

---

[5] *Vita Edwardi Secundi*, ed. N. Denholm-Young (London, 1957), pp. 45–6, and *Flores Historiarum*, ed. H. R. Luard, RS (1890), III, 154–6.

[6] For the 'secularist' view see John of Paris, *On Royal and Papal Power*, ed. J. A. Watt (Toronto, 1971), p. 14, and for the large number of bishops who were civil servants in the early 14th century see W. A. Pantin, *The English Church in the Fourteenth Century* (Cambridge, 1955), pp. 11–18.

[7] *Flores Historiarum*, III, 155.

[8] See K. B. McFarlane, *The Nobility of Later Medieval England* (Oxford, 1973), pp. 235, 238.

[9] See J. R. Wright, 'The supposed illiteracy of Archbishop Walter Reynolds' in *Studies in Church History*, v, ed. C. J. Cuming (Leiden, 1969), pp. 58–68.

[10] W. E. L. Smith, *Episcopal Appointments & Patronage in the Reign of Edward II* (Chicago, 1938), p. 19; H. G. Richardson, 'Clement V and the see of Canterbury', EHR, LVI (1941), 99; and W. E. Lunt, *Financial Relations of the Papacy with England to 1327* (Cambridge, Mass., 1939), p. 480, n. 5.

was *pseudo-archiepiscopus*.[11] Likewise, latter-day chroniclers are more likely to regard Reynolds as unworthy if they take the side of the separatists. We must work towards an appreciation of the policies which Reynolds attempted to follow. One chronicler believed that he was a wise choice as archbishop because he was held in the highest regard by the king, behaved circumspectly in his dealings with everyone and tempered the prevalent bitterness between the king and his magnates.[12] As we shall see from the early years of his archiepiscopate, much of the evidence for his political standpoint is indirect and biased, for what we hear most clearly is the voice of the clergy's opposition to him. We cannot, of course, doubt at the outset that in the continuing crisis about supreme jurisdiction, brought to a head by Boniface VIII, Reynolds was on the side of co-operation with royal government.

In the tense political situation in England in 1313 the appointment of a new archbishop, after the death of Winchelsey on 11 May 1313, was of the greatest importance to the king. By secret collaboration with the pope, Edward made his own nomination and overrode the election by the monks of Canterbury of Thomas Cobham, who would, with little question, have followed the policies of Winchelsey.[13] Reynolds's appointment by Clement V must be seen in the context of the negotiations in the summer of 1313 between the pope and the kings of both France and England: both kings took the cross and were granted large papal loans, in the case of Edward II in exchange for the mortgaging to Clement V of the revenues of Gascony. There was rejoicing to mark the outcome of the conciliatory policies, with a succession of banquets in Paris and processions in the streets during the first week of June. But could conciliatory policies be made to work in the English Church?

On 1 October 1313 the bulls translating Reynolds from Worcester to Canterbury were issued,[14] and the new appointment aptly coincided with a settlement between the king and the magnates.[15] Reynolds was

[11] *Flores Historiarum*, III, 156.

[12] *Johannis de Trokelowe et Henrici de Blaneforde...Chronica et Annales*, ed. H. T. Riley, RS (1866), p. 82.

[13] See Smith, *Episcopal Appointments*, pp. 17–19; E. H. Pearce, *Thomas Cobham* (London, 1923), pp. 22–8; Richardson, *EHR*, LVI (1941), 97–103; and J. H. Denton, 'Canterbury archiepiscopal appointments: the case of Walter Reynolds', *J. Med. Hist.*, I (1975), 317–27.

[14] *Reg. S. de Gandavo*, ed. C. T. Flower and M. C. B. Dawes, CYS (1934), I, 477–8; *Worcester Registrum Sede Vacante 1301–1435*, ed. J. W. Willis Bund, Worcestershire Hist. Soc. (1897), p. 144; *Foedera*, II, i, 288 (PRO SC7 (Papal Bulls) 44/11); *Regestum Clementis V* (Rome, 1885–92), no. 9713 (*CPL*, II, 115); and Wilkins, II, 430–1 (Canterbury, Dean and Chapter Muniments (hereafter Cant. D. & C.), Reg. Q, fos. 89v–90v). [15] Below p. 257, n. 51.

granted the temporalities of the see on 3 January 1314, received his
pallium on 13 February and was enthroned at Canterbury on 17
February.[16] The political and constitutional implications of his appointment cannot fail to have been recognised as far-reaching. Perhaps the
most pressing problem facing the clergy (especially during the vacancy
in the papal see between the spring of 1314 and the autumn of 1316)
was taxation. It was the most important single issue affecting their
intention to determine policy for themselves in ecclesiastical assemblies
outside parliament; and the king's right or otherwise to tax the spiritual
income of the clergy was linked directly to the clergy's ability to bargain
for the redress of grievances. Clement V had stated his belief that the
archbishop nominated by the king should be amenable in the matter of
granting aids.[17] But the English clergy's attitude to taxation had been
sharpened by Boniface VIII's bull *Clericis laicos*.[18] While Benedict XI
had decreed in 1304[19] that the penalties in *Clericis laicos* should apply
only to those laymen exacting money, and those aiding and abetting
the exaction, and not to those freely giving and receiving, yet he had
adhered to the spirit of the bull by stressing that the earlier decrees
should be observed whereby consent to taxes should only be given after
due deliberation and in cases of necessity, and that even in such cases
the pope must be consulted. But in 1306 Clement V had completely
revoked *Clericis laicos* and the bulls which followed from it.[20] Clement's
repeal must at least have prevented those who had acted contrary to the
bull from incurring sentences of excommunication.[21] And the inclusion
of the revocation in the register of Bishop Swinfield of Hereford shows
that it was known about in England. Nonetheless, the practical consequences of Clement's annulment appear to have been small and it
perhaps received little publicity. In May 1311 the clergy of the northern
province meeting in council were clearly unaffected by it, for they used

[16] *CPR 1313-17*, p. 77 (and see 87-8); Lambeth Palace Library, Reg. Reynolds (hereafter Lambeth, Reg. Reyn.), fo. 4r; Cant. D. & C., Reg. Q, fo. 91r; and J. R. S. Phillips, *Aymer de
Valence, Earl of Pembroke 1307-24* (Oxford, 1972), p. 72.
[17] Richardson, *EHR*, LVI (1941), 102.
[18] See *Councils II*, 1149.
[19] 12 May, 'Quod olim': *Le Registre de Benoit XI*, ed. Ch. Grandjean (École française de Rome,
1905), no. 1269; *Corpus Iuris Canonici*, ed. E. Friedberg, II (Leipzig, 1881), 1287-8 (Extr.
Joan. XXII, iv, 13); and Oxford Bodleian, Fairfax 9 (Warter Chartulary), fo. 4r.
[20] 1 Feb., 'Pastoralis cura': *Reg. Clement V*, no. 906; *Corp. Iur. Can.*, II, 1178 (Clem., iii, 17);
and *Reg. R. de Swinfield*, ed. W. W. Capes, CYS (1909), pp. 426-7. Cf. J. H. Denton, 'Pope
Clement V's early career as a royal clerk', *EHR*, LXXXIII (1968), 313; and *Les Registres de Boniface
VIII*, ed. G. Digard et al. (École française de Rome, 1907-39), I, 941 n. 1.
[21] For examples of absolution from excommunication see *Councils II*, 1182, n. 3 and many cases
in LRO Reg. III (Dalderby), e.g. fos. 33r, 34v, 93r-94v, 103r.

Clericis laicos as one explanation of their inability to make a grant to the king.[22] Clement's bull was essentially a political gesture. He safeguarded the decrees previous to *Clericis laicos* concerning taxation, decrees upon which Boniface's own policy had been based, but declared that *Clericis laicos* itself had caused, and would continue to cause unless annulled, dangerous disruption and bitterness: 'nonnulla scandala, magna pericula et incommoda gravia sunt secuta et ampliora sequi nisi celeri remedio succurratur'.

Yet *Clericis laicos* had assisted the clergy in England under the guidance of Winchelsey to clarify their rights and to establish firm principles governing the taxation of spiritualities. It may be true that many clergy hated, almost as much as did the king, the insistence on a papal licence for all payments, and it seems that they only exploited the need for papal consent when they wished to oppose payment;[23] but because of *Clericis laicos* grants of direct subsidies by the English clergy had been made more firmly dependent than ever before on proper clerical decisions. In one of the Christ Church Canterbury registers there was transcribed, between documents of 1320 and 1321, a statement purporting to be Boniface VIII's reply to the consultation of the English prelates concerning *Clericis laicos*.[24]

There is a marked absence of official correspondence between Boniface and England concerning the interpretation of *Clericis laicos*. This *responsum* was possibly communicated to the English prelates following a request to the pope for advice either during the January council of 1297 or shortly after it.[25] But more likely it was not a reply to the English clergy at all and was taken, word for word, from *Coram illo fatemur* (28 February 1297) addressed to the French prelates.[26] It contrasts with the pope's later concession to Philip of France,

---

[22] *Councils II*, 1340–1; and see below, p. 268.

[23] See Lunt, *Financial Relations to 1327*, p. 407, n. 4.

[24] Cant. D. & C., Reg. I, fos. 368v–369r: 'Responsum domini Bonifacii pape viii ad consultationem prelatorum Anglie super constitutione nova de emunitate ecclesiarum que sic incipit "Clericis". Licet enim constitutionem illam ediderimus pro ecclesiastica libertate non tamen fuit nostre mentis intentio regi vestro aliisve principibus secularibus in tam arte necessitatis articulo, ubi ab extrinsecis iniusta timetur invasio et ab intrinsecis eiusdem regni subversio formidatur ac etiam prelatorum ecclesiarum personarum ecclesiasticarum eiusdem periculum iminet, viam subventionis excludi, quominus ipsi prelati ecclesie ecclesiasticeque persone libero arbitrio ac sponte de nostra licentia pro communi defensionis auxilio in quo proprium cuiuslibet interesse conspicitur principibus ac sibi ipsis provideant iuxta suarum modulum facultatum.'

[25] See the Dunstable annalist and the reference to the chronicle of Walter of Guisborough in *Councils II*, 1166 & n. 2.

[26] See *Reg. R. Winchelsey*, ed. R. Graham, CYS (1952, 1956), I, 178 and *Annales Monastici*, ed. H. R. Luard, RS (1864–9), IV (Worcester Annals), 531.

as embodied in *Etsi de statu*,[27] for the pope granted that the king of France could tax the clergy in an emergency without consulting the pope, and the decision as to what constituted an emergency was left to the conscience of the king. The supposed *responsum* to the English prelates was also about the granting of money in an emergency: it states that the pope had not intended to prevent the clergy, acting with papal permission, from contributing to national defence at a time of crisis, provided that they did so freely and spontaneously. Thus the need for the consent of the clergy themselves had been firmly stated. And the right to consent necessarily gave the clergy the right independently to determine what constituted an emergency situation.

This is how *Clericis laicos* had been interpreted in England. And in these respects the bull had given emphasis to the decrees of the Lateran Councils of 1179 and 1215.[28] Whether or not we accept the *responsum* as in fact addressed to the English clergy, it is significant that it appears *c.* 1320 as a statement, presumably of continuing relevance, upon *Clericis laicos*. For the English clergy the bull had highlighted their rights and privileges in their relations with the laity. It had put them in a stronger position, despite the king's coercive powers, to refuse requests for direct taxation of their income. And the bull was in harmony with the general thinking of many churchmen. In a letter probably belonging to 1313 we find Simon of Ghent, bishop of Salisbury, taking action following damage done by parishioners to trees in a cemetery and beginning his letter with these words: 'Experimenta temporum manifeste declarant clericis laicos infestos existere.'[29] This simply abbreviates Boniface's declaration: 'Clericis laicos infestos oppido tradit antiquitas quod et presentium experimenta temporum manifeste declarant.'[30]

The corollary of the acceptance by the clergy of papal protection against the incursions upon their spiritual income by 'inimical laymen' was their acceptance of the pope's especial right to tax their income virtually at will. It has long been clear from the work of Lunt that the problem of taxing the clergy was largely solved by Edward I, and also by Edward II, through the pope's willingness to give a very large share of the proceeds of papal taxes of the English Church to the king. This

[27] *Reg. Boniface VIII*, no. 2354. See H. Rothwell, 'The confirmation of the charters, 1297', *EHR*, LX (1945), 18–21.

[28] T. S. R. Boase, *Boniface VIII* (London, 1933), p. 132.

[29] *Reg. Gandavo*, CYS, I, 472.

[30] For the canonical tradition of *laici infesti clericis* see *Councils II*, 399 and n. 1, and for the text of *Clericis laicos* see L. Santifaller, 'Zur Original-Überlieferung der Bulle... "Clericis Laicos"', *Studia Gratiana*, XI (1967) (Collectanea Stephan Kuttner, I), 84–6.

procedure of raising money for the king's needs was used unashamedly by Clement V and the clergy were powerless to resist. An analysis of the situation concerning taxation in the period 1313 to 1316 must begin with the papal tenths. Ever since the crisis of 1297 it was primarily through these papal tenths that the king taxed the clergy; in this sphere of taxation he avoided the need for the clergy's own consent and also reduced the possibility of recalcitrance and complaint.

In 1313 and 1314 there were two overlapping papal tenths. The first of these was the last of a series of tenths referred to collectively as a sexennial tenth. The papal portion of this sexennial tenth was only an eighth of the whole; and the papal collectors, the bishops of Lincoln and London, exercised their office as *de facto* servants of the crown. Money was paid directly to the Exchequer, or to the Wardrobe, or to royal officials and royal creditors. In all but name these were royal subsidies. 'After the final audit of the account of the collectors with the Exchequer the deputies became responsible to the Exchequer for the arrears. The king ruled with regard to the liability of some members of the clergy for the tenth, granted exemptions and pardoned favored payers their debts.'[31] The king's government had greater control over the collection of these papal taxes than was possible with subsidies granted directly by the English clergy. This sexennial tenth was comprised as follows: a biennial tenth had been collected in 1306 and 1307, a triennial tenth between 1309 and 1312, and the terms for the payment of the final tenth, granted wholly to the king, were 24 June and 25 December 1313.[32] At Winchelsey's death the clergy were thus already committed to the payment within 1313 of a tenth of their income entirely to the king.

The collection of further papal tenths, another projected sexennial tenth, was decreed by Clement V at the Council of Vienne in 1311.[33] Because of Clement's death in April 1314, only the first year of this tenth was in fact collected. The terms for its collection were 1 October 1313 and 1 April 1314, and the bulls ordering collection arrived in England in June 1313.[34] This tenth therefore overlapped with the previous tenth, so that within a period of less than ten months the

[31] Lunt, *Financial Relations to 1327*, pp. 393–4.

[32] W. E. Lunt, 'Clerical tenths levied in England by papal authority during the reign of Edward II' in *C. H. Haskins Anniversary Essays* (Boston and New York, 1929), pp. 157–65; and Lunt, *Financial Relations to 1327*, pp. 382–95.

[33] For what follows see Lunt, *Financial Relations to 1327*, pp. 395–404.

[34] They were made known to the suffragan bishops by the prior of Canterbury in the July parliament: Cant. D. & C., Reg. Q, fo. 101r, and see 103v.

clergy were being required to make their payments for *two* papal tenths. On any showing the demand of a fifth of their income within a year was a heavy drain on the clergy, the heaviest in fact since the crushingly burdensome demands of 1294, 1295 and 1297. This is one reason, no doubt, why the conciliar tenth was difficult to collect. But this tenth was, of course, intended for the pope and intended for a crusade. The money was collected by the bishops of each diocese and deposited in safe places awaiting further papal instructions. Predictably, on 28 April, only eight days after Clement's death, the king ordered the retention of all the money collected and asked for statements of the sums held by each bishop.[35] As in 1294 and in 1303, a papal vacancy led to the seizure of papal taxes. The prelates were required, during the summer and autumn of 1314, to loan all the money to the king.[36] The repayment of the loans was repeatedly delayed. The new pope, John XXII, excused the king from repayment for five years, and, in fact, the money was never recovered. Thus, the conciliar tenth too passed into the royal coffers.

The fact that clerical income was being heavily taxed in 1313 did not deter the king from attempting to get money from the English Church in a different way. He had failed to obtain the grant of a shilling in the mark from the clergy in 1311.[37] In the important May council of 1312 the clergy had consented instead to a subsidy of a fortieth (4*d.* in the mark) for the archbishop of Canterbury's needs as metropolitan and for the needs of the churches of the province.[38] Edward had tried to enlist the support of the royal monasteries in opposition to this subsidy, claiming that a tax without his consent on the income of monasteries established by the alms of his predecessors was a tax prejudicial to the crown. The pressure from the king prevented payment in some quarters,[39] but the subsidy was certainly granted and the terms for collection had been 20 July and 21 September 1312. The money was ordered to be stored in safe places by each diocesan until further orders. Winchelsey drew from the proceeds in order to pay the procurations of the papal nuncio, the cardinal priest of St Prisca.[40] But within a few

[35] *CCR 1313–18*, 99.

[36] Memoranda (dated 14 July) of recognisances for loans from each diocese are entered in the king's memoranda roll: PRO E159/87 m. 72. See *Parl. Writs*, II, ii, app. 78–83.

[37] *Councils II*, 1305–6, and Lunt in C. H. *Haskins Essays*, p. 179, n. 169.

[38] *Councils II*, 1356, 1367–8, 1372–3; and F. R. H. Du Boulay, 'Charitable subsidies granted to the archbishop of Canterbury, 1300–1489', *BIHR*, XXIII (1950), 152–4.

[39] *Reg. H. Woodlock*, ed. A. W. Goodman, CYS (1940–1), I, 614.

[40] *Ibid.*, and *Reg. Gandavo*, CYS, pp. 438–9.

weeks of the archbishop's death the king was attempting to lay his hands on all that remained of the money.[41] In a royal writ of 16 June (dated at London; the king was in fact at Pontoise),[42] Edward outlined his dire needs in relation to the Scottish war, stressing that the money was required for the salvation of both the kingdom and the Church, and ordered that all the money be sent without delay, and not later than the second week in July, to the bishop of London and the prior of the Hospital of St John of Jerusalem. The king implied that the tax had been granted at his request and claimed that its purpose was the business of the kingdom, even the defence of the kingdom against enemies. He stated that all this had been told to him both by the earl of Gloucester and Hereford, who was present when the request for the subsidy was made, and by the bishops of Norwich and Bath and Wells. The two bishops had, indeed, been commissioned to inform the king of the clerical subsidy, but the bishop of Norwich was quick to deny the king's version of what he had been told.[43] Whoever was the author or initiator of the royal writ, he completely misrepresented the original reasons for the clerical subsidy.

This royal writ of 16 June 1313, attempting to take from the bishops money designed and collected for exclusively clerical purposes, was addressed to each of the bishops and to the prior of Christ Church Canterbury as keeper of the spiritualities of Canterbury. On 23 June the prior ordered the dean of the province, the bishop of London, to deal with it since it was a matter touching the whole province.[44] But the prior clearly did not himself intend to submit to the royal policy, for in a letter of 29 June he wrote again to the bishop of London, and now to the prior of the Hospital of St John of Jerusalem as well, pleading that he knew nothing at all about the collection of the tax in the diocese of Canterbury.[45] There also survive immediate and separate replies to the writ from the bishops of Winchester, Salisbury, Rochester, Norwich and London, denying that the king had any proper right to the money: what had been collected by the order of an ecclesiastical council could only be diverted to other uses by the order of another council.[46] The bishop of London sent his reply to the king's chancellor, Walter

[41] *Councils II*, 1378.
[42] Wilkins, II, 426 (Cant. D. & C., Reg. Q, fos. 97v–98r), and *Parl. Writs*, II, ii, app. 63 (*CCR 1307–13*, 537–8).
[43] PRO SCI (Anc. Corresp.) 20/107.
[44] Wilkins, II, 427 (Cant. D. & C., Reg. Q, fo. 98r).
[45] Reg. Q, fo. 98v.
[46] *Reg. Woodlock*, CYS, I, 614; and PRO SCI 20/107, 34/51 and /199, 35/84.

Reynolds. It is hard, at the very least, to believe that Reynolds had been ignorant of the royal order. The king, it appears, asked for the money again when the prelates and clerical proctors met at the July parliament, and consequently the clergy of the northern province were summoned to a council to meet in September to discuss whether they too should grant the king a similar tax.[47] The outcome in the northern province is not known, but certainly the clergy of the southern province had successfully opposed the attempted royal seizure.[48] The money remained a reserve fund for each of the bishops.[49] Had it been a papal tax the story would have been different.

After April 1314, following the death of Clement V and the consequent termination of the collection of the conciliar tenth, it became a matter of urgency for the king to be able to tax the clergy's income directly.[50] At the same time there was renewed uncertainty about the constitutional relationship between the crown and English ecclesiastical councils. Under Winchelsey's guidance it was in their own councils that the clergy had determined for themselves what their policy should be regarding royal taxation of their income. Edward I's attempts in

[47] See *Reg. W. Greenfield*, ed. A. Hamilton Thompson, Surtees Soc. (1931, 1934, 1936, 1938, 1940), V. 126–7 (Wilkins, II, 436, printed his own abbreviation of this summons); and *Reg. Palatinum Dunelmense*, ed. T. D. Hardy, RS (1873–8), I, 415–6, and 430–1 (proxy).

[48] Cf. Lunt in *C. H. Haskins Essays*, p. 181. Some of the prelates at the July parliament did, however, begin the process of making loans to the king to be offset in payments from the papal tenths or in payments for military service: Lunt, *Financial Relations to 1327*, p. 392; and see Wilkins, II, 429.

[49] See *Reg. Gandavo*, CYS, pp. 522–3. Reynolds as archbishop obtained as loans £84 of the proceeds from the bishop of Coventry and Lichfield and £500 from the bishop of Lincoln: Lambeth, Reg. Reyn., fos. 122r, 286r (cited in Du Boulay, *BIHR*, XXIII (1950), 154 and I. J. Churchill, *Canterbury Administration* (London, 1933), I, 545). And see *Calendar of the Reg. of J. de Drokensford*, ed. E. Hobhouse, Somerset Rec. Soc. (1887), p. 84; and *The Registers of J. de Sandale & R. de Asserio*, ed. F. J. Baigent, Hampshire Rec. Soc. (1897), p. 88.

[50] The importance for the king of the taxation of the clergy can be shown by a comparison of the amounts involved during this period in the taxes of clerical income (both papal tenths and direct taxes) and the taxes on lay movables granted in parliament. The lay taxes were the main source of extraordinary income for the king. It is not possible to discover from either the subsidy rolls (PRO E179) or the receipt rolls (E404) the total amounts collected from the clerical taxes. But they can be estimated with some confidence from the valuation of 1291 upon which they were based: a total valuation of £170,000 for the Canterbury province and £40,000 for the York province (Stubbs, *Const. Hist.*, II, 580). The continued collection of arrears of earlier taxes no doubt helps to balance out deficiencies of collection. Thus, the sums were approx. £21,000 for each of the papal tenths of 1313–14, £3,000 from the York province in 1314 (12d. in the mark), £17,000 from the Canterbury province in 1315 (tenth), and £21,000 granted from both provinces in 1316 (tenths): a total of £83,000. The taxes on lay movables of 1313, 1315 and 1316 amounted respectively to approx. £40,000, £37,000 and £39,000 (J. F. Willard, 'The taxes on lay movables in the reign of Edward II', *EHR*, XXIX (1914), 317–21): a total of £116,000. And included in the assessments for the lay taxes was the personal property of the clergy on their temporalities not annexed to spiritualities.

1294 and 1295 to bring meetings of the clergy under the control of the king had been shortlived. But Edward II now revived the policy of his father.

A parliament, with full representation of prelates and clergy, had met in the autumn of 1313 at Westminster. The earl of Lancaster and his followers had been pardoned, and a grant of a fifteenth and a twentieth of lay movables had been made.[51] Another parliament, again to include the prelates and clergy, was summoned to meet on 21 April 1314.[52] On 24 March Edward, because of the attacks of Robert Bruce, decided to be at Newcastle-on-Tyne on 27 April and therefore cancelled the parliament. But he urgently needed money from the clergy and thus, using the same mode of summons as for a parliament, he ordered the prelates and clergy of the southern province to be at Westminster on 17 May and the prelates and clergy of the northern province to be at York on 3 June, to treat with royal ministers about granting a direct subsidy.[53] In addition to a personal summons to each bishop, the king summoned the two archbishops to attend using the peremptory *venire faciatis* clause, as a result of which both archbishops themselves also summoned the bishops and clergy of their provinces.[54] The most recent clerical assembly summoned directly by the king was in 1294, but this assembly of 1314 bears an even closer resemblance to the council of January 1283 to which the clergy had been summoned by the *venire faciatis* writ to appear before the king or his deputies.[55]

There must have been opposition in the northern province to the form of the summons, for it was followed by a second summons from the archbishop of York of a regular kind for his clergy to meet on 26 June 1314. On this date, two days after the battle of Bannockburn, the northern council granted 12*d.* in the mark to the king.[56] But in the

---

[51] *Parl. Writs*, II, ii, 100–19; *CPR 1313–17*, 21–6, 43–6, 49–51; J. R. Maddicott, *Thomas of Lancaster 1307–22* (Oxford, 1970), pp. 150–1; Phillips, *Pembroke*, p. 67; *Vita Ed. II*, ed. Denholm-Young, p. 43; and *Trokelowe*, ed. Riley, RS, p. 80.

[52] *Parl. Writs*, II, ii, 119–21.   [53] *Ibid.*, 122–3.

[54] W. Wake, *The State of the Church and Clergy of England...* (1703), app. 36–7 (hereafter Wake, *Clergy*); Wilkins, II, 442; *Parl. Writs*, II, ii, 122–3; *CCR 1313–18*, 96; *The Liber Albus of the Priory of Worcester*, ed. J. M. Wilson, Worcestershire Hist. Soc. (1919), no. 631; *Reg. Gandavo*, CYS, pp. 482–5 (with proxy); Lambeth, Reg. Reyn., fo. 35v; CUL MS Ee 5 31, fo. 145; Cant. D. & C., Reg. I, fo. 328, and LRO Reg. III (Dalderby), fo. 297v (proxy, describing the meeting as a 'tractatus').

[55] *Councils II*, 939–44, 1125–34.

[56] See *Reg. Greenfield*, ed. Hamilton Thompson, II, 190–1, v, 137–9, 140–1; *Reg. J. de Halton*, ed. W. N. Thompson, CYS (1913), II, 97–8 (proxy); and *Reg. Dunelmense*, RS, I, 574–8, 636–7, 641–2. The 12*d.* in the mark applied in the York diocese but was not a standard rate for the whole province.

southern province a crisis had arisen. The council of the southern clergy at Westminster was unable to proceed because of the objections of the clerical representatives. The abbots, priors of cathedral churches, deans, archdeacons, and proctors of chapters and of diocesan clergy, apparently met as a group in isolation from the archbishop and suffragan bishops. On 20 May they presented eight major objections, the *Rationes Cleri*, to the way in which they had been summoned and followed this on 22 May with a *Petitio* to the effect that the council should be abandoned.[57] Whatever the attitude of individual bishops the voice of the rest of the clergy was clear. They were standing by the principles of ecclesiastical immunity fought for by Winchelsey, and they referred directly to the example which he had set. It was stated in the royal mandate for the council that an aid was due from the clergy; they insisted that they were bound by their own laws in making aids. The clergy had been summoned to meet before laymen; but they pointed out that laymen were in no position of authority in ecclesiastical matters over the clergy. They flatly denied that they could be summoned by the authority of the king to meet in an ecclesiastical council. If they accepted that summons, the king could order them to meet as often as he wished, and he could punish them for refusing to meet, as he already punished those who disobeyed *venire faciatis* writs. Reynolds was unable to prevent the clergy from abandoning the assembly. Threats of coercion were made against the clergy by certain laymen at this abortive council; but the whole question of making a grant was postponed, and on 24 May Reynolds summoned another council to meet at St Paul's on 8 July.[58]

The new archiepiscopal summons comprised necessary adjustments in view of the clergy's opposition. But Reynolds was patently unrepentant. While he did not now cite the king's writ verbatim, he repeated most of it and even elaborated upon it. In relation to taxation he avoided the royal *debetis* but insisted on the need for a clerical subsidy and accepted the king's statement that assistance from the clergy, as from the whole realm, had been agreed upon in the parliament of

---

[57] The *Rationes Cleri* and the *Petitio* are printed from Cant. D. & C., Reg. I, fos. 328v–329v in Wake, *Clergy*, app. 37–9, Wilkins, II, 442–4 and *Parl. Writs*, II, ii, 123–4. For other MS copies see Lambeth Palace Lib., MS 1213 (Reg. of St Aug.'s Cant.), pp. 36–8 and BL Add. MS 41612 (Ely Chapter Reg.), fos. 53v–54v. For comment see Clarke, *Representation*, p. 133 and E. W. Kemp, *Counsel and Consent* (London, 1961), pp. 92–3.

[58] Wake, *Clergy*, app. 39–41; Wilkins, II, 444–5 (Lambeth, Reg. Reyn., fos. 105v–106r); Cant. D. & C., Reg. I, fos. 330r–331r; LRO Reg. III (Dalderby), fo. 301r (proxy) and see 300r; and CUL MS Ee 5 31, fo. 147r (proxy).

September 1313. This was a *de facto* summons of the clergy by the king. The reason which Reynolds gave for the need for a new summons was simply that the first citation had not reached some deans, abbots, priors, archdeacons and clergy in some parts of the province. This must have been seen at the very least as reluctance on the part of the archbishop to admit the validity of the clergy's strong opposition. The July council certainly seems to have met;[59] but no grant was forthcoming from the clergy, perhaps because the king's retreat from Scotland, following his defeat at Bannockburn, temporarily reduced the strength of the claim of *urgens necessitas*, and the king was in any case in the process of acquiring from the clergy the proceeds of the first year of the conciliar tenth following the pope's death. Bannockburn also put the opposition to Edward in a much stronger political position.

The York parliament in September 1314, at which the clergy from both provinces assembled, brought concessions to the Ordainers, including the appointment of a new royal chancellor, John de Sandale, to take the place of Reynolds, who nevertheless remained an especially active member of the king's council.[60] The matter of a clerical subsidy had still not been settled. The September parliament was followed by a parliament at Westminster which continued through the early months of 1315. For the summons of the clergy to the parliaments of September 1314 and January 1315 the king used the normal direct summons to each bishop, with the *premunientes* clause. But he also once again issued in both cases a provincial summons to the archbishop of Canterbury with the offending *venire faciatis* clause. On both these occasions the bishops of the southern province were not in fact themselves summoned by the use of the *venire faciatis* writ; but, without question for the January parliament, the clergy of the southern dioceses *were* summoned by that writ and the consequent archiepiscopal summons, as though to an ecclesiastical council but in fact to a parliament and by the authority of the king.[61] A confusion between parliaments and councils was being deliberately fostered. Once again there were to be protests about the

---

[59] Wilkins, II, 447–8.
[60] Tout, *Ed. II*, pp. 90–2; Maddicott, *Lancaster*, pp. 164–6; Phillips, *Pembroke*, p. 76; and below, pp. 271–2.
[61] *Parl. Writs*, II, ii, 126–8, 136–9 ; *Reg. Gandavo*, CYS, pp. 544–6; *The Reg. of W. de Stapeldon*, ed. F. C. Hingeston-Randolph, (London–Exeter, 1892), pp. 121–2; Cant. D. & C., Reg. I, fo. 333v; LRO Reg. III (Dalderby), fos. 302v, 309r, 310v, 311v–312r (executions of writs and proxies), and CUL MS Ee 5 31, fos. 155v, 159 (executions and proxies). I have found no evidence that in the case of the Sept. parliament the archbishop responded to the *venire faciatis* writ. See Clarke, *Representation*, pp. 134–5 and Kemp, *Counsel and Consent*, p. 94.

archbishop's summons, but all the bishops were said to have executed it, with the exception of the bishop of Exeter. The bishop of Salisbury pointed out that most legal experts feared that the mandate was pre-judicial to the clergy; but he rated highly the need to follow the law-abiding course of obeying the summons and did not wish to be blamed for the danger that was likely to ensue if the clergy failed to grant an aid for the defence of the realm.[62]

The clergy of the southern province had thus been drawn early in 1315 into a meeting of parliament in which they were required to agree a direct subsidy to the king. They probably met as a separate assembly to discuss the matter of taxation, as they had done in the Bury parliament of 1296.[63] But on that previous occasion no grant had been made and an ecclesiastical council had been summoned. Certainly, in 1315, it was in a separate clerical assembly on 3 March in the house of the Carmelite Friars, next to the New Temple, that the clergy of the Canterbury province presented a strongly-worded *Protestatio* about the mode of summons.[64] They insisted that they would not in future be able to obey such a summons. Their objection was two-fold. Because of the separate citations, of the prelates by direct royal writ and of the diocesan clergy by an additional archiepiscopal summons, there were many abbots and priors who had been altogether excluded. The unity of the clergy was thereby threatened. On a more fundamental issue the clergy objected that they had been cited to a secular court which had begun its proceedings in the king's own Chamber, 'tam ratione fori quam etiam loci contra canonicas et patrum sanctorum instituta'. The summons having been denounced for the future, the clergy conceded that they were prepared to do what they could, within the laws of the Church, to assist the kingdom in its great need.

However much they protested, the fact remains that the clergy had assembled in response to what they regarded as an irregular summons; and, more important still, they conceded a direct tax of a tenth of their spiritual income in this parliament, the first direct and purely royal tax of the southern province since the grant of a fifteenth in 1307.[65] The laity conceded another subsidy of a twentieth and a fifteenth and were granted in return assurances concerning a new perambulation of the

---

[62] *Reg. Stapeldon*, ed. Hingeston-Randolph, p. 122; and *Reg. Gandavo*, CYS, pp. 550-1 (and see *Reg. of R. Martival*, ed. K. Edwards *et al.*, CYS (1959-75), II, 347).

[63] *Councils II*, 1150.

[64] *Reg. Stapeldon*, p. 122; and *Parl. Writs*, II, ii, 139 (Cant. D. & C., Reg. I, fo. 334r).

[65] Lunt in *C. H. Haskins Essays*, p. 181; and *Reg. Dunelmense*, RS, II, 960-3, 969-71, 975-8.

forests and concerning the observance of the Ordinances of 1311, Magna Carta and the Charter of the Forest.[66] The clergy likewise attached conditions to their grant of the tenth.[67] They were in a strong bargaining position, and in their *Conditiones* required that peace be made between the king and the magnates, that there should be a firm commitment to the observance of the Ordinances, that all concessions made against the terms of the Ordinances should be revoked,[68] that their tenth must be used only to meet the pressing needs of the kingdom, and that it must be collected by churchmen and not by laymen. In addition, the clergy sought in separate articles ('ut petitur in articulis') a redress of grievances ('reformatio') concerning ecclesiastical liberties, and restraints upon the king's ministers who violated ecclesiastical rights and property. They required that concessions to the clergy concerning their liberties should be ensured by the issuing of a royal *constitutio*, with penalties for non-observance including the promulgation of sentences of excommunication. It was probably to these articles that the king referred, using the term *requisitiones*, in a letter to all the bishops dated 15 March 1315.[69] The urgency of other business and the departure of the earls and magnates for Easter had prevented him from making replies to these articles concerning the state of the clergy and of the English Church. He promised to reply in the new session of parliament on 13 April; but it appears that he was unable to do so. Nevertheless, the collection of the tenth proceeded.[70]

At a time when the king was having to make concessions, the clergy had fully accepted its traditional role of alliance with the magnates in opposition to the crown. But a tax had been granted in parliament, and this could certainly be viewed as a major achievement for Reynolds, whose close personal contact with Edward is illustrated by his presence

[66] *Parl. Writs*, II, ii, app. 89–90. See J. Conway Davies, *Baronial Opposition to Edward II* (Cambridge, 1918), p. 400.

[67] *Parl. Writs*, II, ii, app. 92 (Cant. D. & C., Reg. I, fo. 334) and *Reg. Swinfield*, CYS, pp. 497–8 (from new foliation 189r).

[68] See *Foedera*, II, i, 265 (*CCR 1313–18*, 167); and *Calendar of Chancery Warrants 1244–1326* (HMSO, 1927), p. 407.

[69] *Parl. Writs*, II, ii, app. 88–9; *Foedera*, II, i, 264 (*CCR 1313–18*, 163); and *Reg. Drokensford*, ed. Hobhouse, p. 87.

[70] Wilkins, II, 451 (Lambeth, Reg. Reyn., fo. 61r), 454 (*Reg. Woodlock*, CYS, pp. 972–3, and see 628, 974–84, 987–9); *Reg. Martival*, CYS, II, 27–30, 52–61, 73, 76, 149–52; *Reg. Stapeldon*, ed. Hingeston-Randolph, pp. 122–3; *Reg. Gandavo*, CYS, pp. 519–21; *Reg. Drokensford*, pp. 83–4, 87–8, 96–8; LRO Reg. III (Dalderby), fos. 316v, 318v, 326v, 335r; Worcester Record Office, Reg. Maidstone, fos. 26v–27r, 28, 35r; Cant. D. & C., Reg. I, fos. 345v–346r; *Foedera*, II, i, 263–4; *CPR 1313–17*, 271; *Cal. Chanc. Warrants 1244–1326*, p. 419; and PRO E159/88 m. 217, and /89 esp. mm. 166r–169r.

at the burial of Gaveston at Langley on 2 January and by his dining with the king on 3 February and 20 April 1315.[71] The tax aroused the bitterest of invective in the chronicler Robert of Reading: he claimed that the pseudo-archbishop, an intolerable impostor, was putting all his energies into overturning ecclesiastical liberties; that he had used deceit to persuade the clergy to meet and urged them to pay a tax by false preaching; and that the clergy were deluded by his seductive and deceptive promises, for having conceded that the tax should only be used for an expedition against the Scots, he then acted as the worst plunderer of all by using the king's ministers to extort the money from the bishops, an adulterous act of rapine against the Church, the bride of Christ.[72]

The conflict came to a head in 1316, one of the most critical years for the crown since 1297.[73] The burdens of defence in Wales and of plans for a renewal of war in Scotland led to heavy prises and continuing demands for loans of money; and the Great Famine was at its worst.[74] The two terms for the clerical tenth of 1315 had been 3 May and 14 September: more money was now required. The royal writs summoning the clergy to the Lincoln parliament of 27 January 1316 were the same as in 1314 and 1315. The prelates, episcopal and monastic, were summoned by direct writs, with the *premunientes* clause included in the bishops' writs, and the clergy of the southern province were summoned in addition by a *venire faciatis* writ to the archbishop.[75] In the consequent archbishop's citation the bishops themselves, as well as the diocesan clergy, were summoned as they had been in the spring of 1314. The royal policy, supported if not directed by Reynolds, of bringing the meetings of representative ecclesiastical councils into parliament had not weakened.

But, in view of the clergy's opposition at the previous parliament, Reynolds once again made adjustments in his provincial writ.[76] He

---

[71] BL MS Cotton Cleo. D iii, fo. 56v (Chronicle of Hailes Abbey); PRO E101/375/17 (Daily Household Account 1 Dec. 1314–7 July 1315); and see Davies, *Baronial Opposition*, app. no. 46.

[72] *Flores Historiarum*, RS, III, 170.

[73] See Maddicott, *Lancaster*, pp. 183–6.

[74] See I. Kershaw, 'The Great Famine and agrarian crisis in England 1315–22', *Past & Present*, LIX (1973), 3–50.

[75] *Parl. Writs*, II, ii, 152–4; *Reg. Martival*, CYS, III, no. 19; *Reg. Greenfield*, ed. Hamilton Thompson, I, 161, V, 279–80; and *Reg. Dunelmense*, RS, II, 1099.

[76] Wake, *Clergy*, app. 41–2 (as *Reg. Woodlock*, CYS, 652–5, and see 658, and CUL MS Ee 5 31, fos. 161v–162r); *Reg. Martival*, CYS, II, 49–50, 61–2; LRO Reg. III (Dalderby), fo. 334r, and *Parl. Writs*, II, ii, 155 (from Cant. D. & C., Reg. I, fo. 343v and for the certificate and proxy see CUL, MS. Ee. v. 31, fo. 162r). And see *Reg. Swinfield*, CYS, p. 506 and below, n. 78.

summoned the clergy to meet separately in the cathedral church of Lincoln and on 24 January, before the opening of parliament. This appears to have been a deliberate attempt to circumvent the clergy's previous complaint that they had been summoned to a secular court which had begun its proceedings in the king's Chamber. And, to meet the second complaint of March 1315, Reynolds extended his provincial writ so as to summon all abbots and priors to appear in person and all religious houses to be represented by proxy. It is difficult to see in what ways this noteworthy parliament of Lincoln[77] was not also combined with an ecclesiastical council of the southern province. At any rate it was clear that the southern clergy had been summoned to a separate assembly before the meeting of parliament, an assembly to be held as though at the doors of parliament ('quasi in ianuis').[78] The archbishop's summons embodies a striking *non sequitur*: it says that since the king has requested him to convoke the provincial clergy to be at Lincoln on 27 January the archbishop orders the clergy to appear before himself on 24 January. Despite this staggered start to the proceedings a uniting of the secular and ecclesiastical institutions was without doubt intended. Of all the archbishop's citations this was the most remarkable.

Reynolds claimed that illness prevented his attendance at Lincoln, and he commissioned the bishops of Norwich, Exeter and Salisbury to preside for him in the congregation of the clergy.[79] The new bishop of Salisbury, Roger Martival, came to Lincoln with a strong feeling of resentment against the royal policy, which was endorsed by Reynolds and by other bishops, of postponing once again the repayment of the loans made from the papal crusading tenth of 1313–14; but, predictably, further delay in the repayment of the loans had to be conceded.[80] According to the consequent royal writs, this concession was made in parliament. According to the bishop of Salisbury it was made in the congregation of prelates and clergy of the Canterbury province held at Lincoln by the authority of the archbishop: this was presumably the council which had been summoned for 24 January. It is true that the clergy met separately at least once after the opening of parliament. But this separate assembly was of the clergy of both provinces, a meeting

---

[77] Davies, *Baronial Opposition*, pp. 408–24.

[78] *Reg. Martival*, CYS, II, 59–60; and separate proxies for parliament and clerical assembly in LRO Reg. III (Dalderby), fos. 337v, 338v and BL Add. MS 41612, fos. 28r–29r.

[79] *Reg. Drokensford*, ed. Hobhouse, p. 104.

[80] *Reg. Martival*, CYS, II, 58–61, 80–1, 92–3; *Reg. Woodlock*, CYS, pp. 975–80, 987–9; *Parl. Writs*, II, ii, app. 99–100 (*CPR 1313–17*, 440–1, 455), and Lunt, *Financial Relations to 1327*, pp. 401–2.

facilitated no doubt by the absence of Reynolds and the vacancy at York, and it took place in the cathedral church of Lincoln on 6 February. It was to this assembly that a denial by the bishop of Exeter of the right of the archbishop of Canterbury's official to promulgate sentences of interdict, suspension or excommunication against suffragan bishops was presented.[81]

On the question of the grievances concerning ecclesiastical liberties a petition of the archbishop, bishops, prelates and clergy of the southern province was put forward at the Lincoln parliament. It requested that they should have a favourable reply to those *gravamina* which had not yet received a satisfactory answer and to some new *gravamina* not previously presented, and in addition they asked that regarding the few *gravamina* to which satisfactory replies had been made, these should be observed inviolably henceforth by being embodied in a statute ('per statutum super illis edendum'), for they claimed that replies simply given by the king's council were of little or no effect.[82] On 7 February the earl of Hereford on the king's behalf announced in the parliament that answers should be given to the outstanding petitions of the prelates concerning the state of the Church, and that such answers as were advisable for the welfare of the king, kingdom and Church should be determined by consultation between the prelates, magnates and king's council.[83] What then happened in the parliament is shown in part by the *Articuli Cleri* issued as letters patent later in the year.[84] The preamble reveals that at the Lincoln parliament some earlier *gravamina* were recited, together with replies to them now accepted or amended, and replies were made to new *gravamina*. It appears that the *Articuli Cleri* of 24 November were drawn up at the Lincoln parliament between 7 and 20 February. But, whether or not the preamble to the *Articuli Cleri* gives the right impression of what happened at Lincoln, it is certain that the clergy were far from satisfied with the proceedings

---

[81] *Reg. Stapeldon*, ed. Hingeston-Randolph, p. 96.

[82] PRO SC8 (Anc. Petitions) 1985, printed in H. G. Richardson and G. O. Sayles, 'The clergy in the Easter parliament, 1285', *EHR*, LII (1937), 230, n. 1.

[83] *Parl. Writs*, II, i, 169, II, ii, 156; and *Rotuli Parliamentorum*, Record Commission (1783), I, 350.

[84] Below, pp. 269–70. PRO C 49 (Parl. & Council Proceedings, Chancery) 4/17 may have been drawn up at the Lincoln parliament: it is an exact list under the heading 'Gravamina cleri Anglie quibus sufficienter est responsum' of all the grievances and replies embodied in *Articuli Cleri*. Another undated list under the same heading (C49/43/13) has only one grievance and reply found in *Art. Cleri* (c. 2; and see 1280 grievances c. 5: *Councils II*, 877); another from 1300–1 grievances c. 19 (*Councils II*, 1213) is similar to *Art. Cleri* c. 3 from 1280 c. 8 (*Councils II*, 878–9); the remaining four (1280 c. 6, 1300–1 cc. 12, 24, 28: *Councils II*, 877–8, 1212, 1215–16) found no place in *Art. Cleri*.

at the parliament. For one thing, their important request that favourable replies should be embodied in a 'statute', which had been a condition of the grant of a tenth in 1315, had not yet been met.

There was 'stone-walling' from the clergy at Lincoln on the matter of taxation. While the laity were to concede a further tax on their movables,[85] it is clear that by 16 February the clergy had pleaded for further consultations outside parliament. The king on that date wrote to the archbishop of Canterbury and the dean and chapter of York asking for convocations of the two provinces to be summoned, in the Canterbury province on 28 April and in the York province on 9 May. The king reported that the clergy had consented so far as they were able to a subsidy, but that the absence of many clergy, including the archbishop himself, prevented full consent.[86] The royal writs thus fixed the dates of new ecclesiastical councils; and the king openly proposed to send members of his own council to receive the replies of the clergy and to report back to him.

Reynolds's citation for the new council of the southern province to meet at St Paul's on 28 April[87] was in the first place an attack upon the bishop of London for failing, as dean of the province, to certify execution of the mandate for the council of Lincoln. He should presumably have certified execution of the summons to those commissioned by the archbishop to act for him at Lincoln; his failure to do so had nullified the summons. Reynolds was, it seems, blaming the bishop of London, whom he apparently disliked,[88] for the failure of the clergy to make a grant at Lincoln; but perhaps the bishop had been confused, understandably, as to whether the mandate which he had executed was for the clergy to meet in an ecclesiastical council or in a parliament. In any case, there were several reasons for the clergy's unwillingness to concede another tax.

However much the prelates may have implied at Lincoln that they were willing to make a grant to the king, the clergy at St Paul's in April adamantly opposed it, as we see from their petitions, which have sur-

---

85 A sixteenth and fifteenth: see *Parl. Writs*, ii, ii, 163–5, and J. F. Willard, *Parliamentary Taxes on Personal Property* (Cambridge, Mass., 1934), pp. 10–11.
86 Wake, *Clergy*, app. 42; Wilkins, ii, 456 (Lambeth, Reg. Reyn., fo. 73); *Foedera*, ii, i, 285–6; *Parl. Writs*, ii, ii, 158; *CCR 1313–18*, 325; *Reg. Halton*, CYS, ii, 118; and *Reg. Dunelmense*, RS, ii, 785–6.
87 Wake, *Clergy*, app. 42–3; Wilkins, ii, 456–7 (from CUL MS Ee 5 31, fos. 166v–167r, with proxy); *Reg. Martival*, CYS, ii, 80, 97–8; *Reg. Woodlock*, CYS, pp. 665, 671; and LRO Reg. iii (Dalderby), fo. 344v (proxy).
88 *Flores Historiarum*, RS, iii, 156.

vived in a miscellaneous register of the priory of Southwark.[89] Once again, the regular and secular clergy of the province formed a class apart from the bishops and presented fierce opposition to the policies of their archbishop, and not simply because of the current national hardships of famine and disease.[90] Their *Petitiones* represent at least two stages in the discussions at the provincial council. They begin with two statements from the regular and the secular clergy separately. The *religiosi*, after stressing the hardship that they were suffering, pointed out that the conditions which had been placed upon the grant of a tenth in the previous year had not yet been met by the king. They can only have been referring to the insistence that there should be a redress of grievances and that the king's favourable replies to grievances should be embodied in a *penalis constitutio*.[91] Likewise, the secular clergy emphasised that there had been no remedies for their grievances and they petitioned that the archbishop should urge upon the king the drawing up of remedies in a penal statute issued in full parliament. We learn from the third petition that all the clergy were then asked to reconsider the position under three headings: how to proceed concerning the grievances; whether they could not agree to a subsidy; and what advice to give the king concerning the protection of ecclesiastical freedom and the defence of the kingdom. Reynolds clearly hoped to persuade them to be more conciliatory and to reach a compromise.

But the clergy were adamant. On the first matter, they suggested, quite unrealistically, that the king should arrange for wise churchmen who knew the law of God to act for him on the question of their grievances and to determine replies in accordance with the dictates of canon law. With regard to the subsidy, they added to their previous statement that they were especially unable to assist the king since the subsidy seemed to be required of them as though by custom. On the question of giving advice, they stated their belief that God would be disposed not to favour anyone who was contemptuous of Mother Church. The fourth section of the petitions reaffirms some of the earlier claims, but it is also an assertion of the good faith of the clergy regarding the archbishop's summons and their willingness to treat and advise on matters concerning the king and the kingdom, provided that the archbishop did not attempt to pass beyond the limits of their powers as

---

[89] BL MS Cotton Faustina A. VIII, fos. 175v–176r: see J. H. Denton, 'The *communitas cleri* in the early fourteenth century', *BIHR* (forthcoming).
[90] Their statements can be compared with Kershaw, *Past and Present*, LIX (1973), 30, and see *Trokelowe*, RS, pp. 92–6.   [91] Above, p. 261.

proctors and as long as there was no change in the form of the summons as used for this council. Finally, in the fifth petition, the clergy, both regular and secular, pleaded that Reynolds should obtain from the king an excusal from appearing before him in the way in which they were being ordered and summoned, for, by reason of the archbishop's summons, they could appear only before the archbishop and in the place cited. To act otherwise, they claimed, would bring to the church unprecedented servitude and to the archbishop everlasting shame. Thus, the clergy linked their refusal to grant a tax with the demand for a statute to remedy their grievances and with the insistence that they were not prepared to be ordered to appear before the king in parliament just as if they were being summoned before the archbishop in an ecclesiastical council. Silence suggests that Reynolds had to accept the opposition of the clergy; certainly, no grant was made.

In the northern province absenteeism at the council of 9 May[92] caused the re-convening of the clergy for 7 June.[93] At this council a small tax of 4*d*. in the pound was agreed upon for defence against the Scots, perhaps as a *depositum* for the use of the clergy of the province in case of need.[94] The northern clergy, like the southern, were reluctant, it seems, to make a grant to the king; but nothing is known of their discussions. The king's need and the danger from the Scots increased during the summer, and Reynolds's summons for another provincial council in the south to meet on 11 October at St Paul's, the third southern council of the year, contained a vigorous plea that the clergy should give assistance to the king.[95] The archbishop made it abundantly clear that he regarded the situation as one of *urgens necessitas*. And in two letters, of 1 October and 4 October, the king himself urged his great need of a subsidy upon the southern prelates.[96]

The account in the *Vita*[97] of the October council is strongly biased towards the opinion of the *communitas cleri*. Reynolds, the chronicle reports, asked for a half or a third of clerical income and gained the support even of those few bishops who had been elected by the Church rather than appointed at the instance of the crown. The rest of the

[92] Summons: *Reg. Greenfield*, ed. Hamilton Thompson, v, 290–2; and *Reg. Halton*, CYS, II, 118–9.
[93] *Reg. Greenfield*, v, 293–4; *Reg. Dunelmense*, RS, II, 802–5; and *Reg. Halton*, II, 120–2.
[94] *Reg. Greenfield*, v, 248–50.
[95] Wilkins, II, 458 (Norwich, Dean & Chapter Muniments, Reg. IX (Prior Langley), fo. 10v); *Reg. Martival*, CYS, II, 146; LRO Reg. III (Dalderby), fo. 354r (proxy), and CUL MS Ee 5 31, fo. 170v (proxy).
[96] *Parl. Writs*, II, ii, app. 107–8; *Foedera*, II, i, 297–8 (*CCR 1313–18*, 433, 436); and Lambeth, Reg. Reyn., fo. 74v.   [97] *Vita Ed. II*, ed. Denholm-Young, pp. 76–8.

clergy, however, continued to oppose the grant of any tax arguing that special papal authority was required. In other words they argued against the plea of *urgens necessitas*. The author of the *Vita* expounds the sacerdotalist viewpoint: the clergy must intercede by prayer; the king must wage war from the royal treasury not from the Church's treasury which belongs to the poor; the priesthood must be exempt from secular burdens. 'Would that the lord king remembered that he has received the power of the sword from the Church not for its oppression but to protect it.'

The proctors of the clergy came under strong pressure to accept the case of necessity and had to give way. But the tenth to which they agreed was to be paid at two terms separated by a year (2 February 1317 and 1318);[98] and, once again, conditions were attached to the grant.[99] In the first place, the clergy required in these *Conditiones* that ecclesiastical goods should be protected from the depredations of sheriffs, their ministers, or others, and that writs to that end should be granted to the clergy without payment. Secondly, full royal backing should be given to the king's acceptable replies to some of the clergy's grievances ('responsiones...fiant perpetue et reales ac pene adjeccione vallate'); fitting replies to the other grievances should be drawn up by the king's deputies and deputies of the clergy, and these too should be embodied in a document issued with royal authority. On this crucial matter of the clerical grievances the clergy clearly regarded the royal deputies as representing both the king and the magnates. The clergy suggested that their nuncios should have direct access to the king, so that if his deputies were unable to reply on their own the king himself could agree, with the consent of the magnates, to the clergy's reasonable petitions. The last clauses of the clerical statement of conditions included an ineffectual requirement that the money loaned from the papal tenth should be off-set from the first term's payment. And the clergy stated their intention that the new tenth would cease in the event of any future papal tax upon the clergy. Just as they suspected, the new pope, John XXII, crowned on 5 September 1316, was soon to make new grants of taxation to the king.[100]

---

[98] For the collection of the tax see *Parl. Writs*, II, ii, app. 108–9 (*CCR 1313–18*, 380); Lambeth, Reg. Reyn., fo. 75r; LRO Reg. III (Dalderby), fo. 360; *Reg. Drokensford*, ed. Hobhouse, pp. 4, 6, 120; *Reg. J. de Sandale*, ed. Baigent, pp. 20–1; *Reg. A. de Orleton*, ed. A. T. Bannister, CYS (1908), p. 46; *Reg. Woodlock*, CYS, pp. 983–4; and *The Reg. of T. de Cobham*, ed. E. H. Pearce. Worcestershire Hist. Soc. (1930), pp. 3, 6.

[99] *Reg. Martival*, CYS, II, 173–5.

[100] Lunt, *Financial Relations to 1327*, pp. 404–7.

The king appears to have assumed that a grant would be forthcoming from the southern clergy, for on 11 October, the same day as the council met, he wrote to the dean and chapter of York stating that he had been promised an aid from the prelates and clergy of the province of Canterbury, and he asked that another northern council should meet at York on 26 October in order to do likewise. A council was summoned for that date,[101] but it appears to have been postponed, for it was at a council in York on 23 November that a subsidy of a tenth was conceded by the northern clergy too.[102]

With tenths granted in both provinces the king issued as letters patent, dated 24 November at York, the famous *Articuli Cleri.* As letters patent of the same date, and also entered on the Great Roll of the Statutes, the king re-issued and re-affirmed part of the first clause of Edward I's Statute of Westminster I (1275), prohibiting the purveyance of ecclesiastical goods.[103] This re-issue contained an admission that unlawful prises had taken place and reinforced the king's orders to his sheriffs in June 1315 and April 1316 for the observance of the Statute of Westminster.[104] The importance of *Articuli Cleri* lies in the order for implementation of some royal replies to clerical grievances. Thirteen replies to clerical complaints were given statutory authority. This was in response to the clamouring of the clergy since the plea for a *constitutio* was first made early in 1315.[105]

The grievances and replies in *Articuli Cleri* raise problems which reach far beyond the confines of this essay. But we may wonder at the outset whether it gave greater freedom to the exercise of ecclesiastical law in England. To many of the clergy it can have brought only cold comfort. A few of their complaints were recognised as legitimate. But more than half the grievances and royal responses had been drawn up as long ago as 1280.[106] And these long-standing royal replies now issued as letters patent had certainly not all been regarded as satisfactory by the

---

[101] Wake, *Clergy*, app. 43–4; Wilkins, II, 462; *Reg. Halton*, CYS, II, 129–31; and *Reg. Greenfield*, ed. Hamilton Thompson, v, 295.

[102] *Reg. Greenfield*, v, 253–4 and see 280–1, and *Reg. Halton*, II, 132–4.

[103] Both letters appear in many MS copies including the patent rolls (*CPR 1313–17*, 607–8), and PRO C74/1 (Great Roll of the Statutes), mm. 33v, 34v, whence *The Statutes of the Realm*, Record Commission (1810–28), I, 171–6. For printed editions of *Art. Cleri* see also H. Spelman, *Concilia, Decreta, Leges, Constitutiones...* II (London, 1664), 483–6; W. Lyndwood, *Provinciale* (Oxford, 1679), pt iii, 37–9; Wilkins, II, 460–2, and *Historical Papers and Letters from the Northern Registers*, ed. J. Raine, RS (1873), pp. 253–60.

[104] *Annales Londonienses*, pp. 234–6 (*Chronicles of Ed. I & Ed. II*, RS (1882–3), ed. W. Stubbs, I); *Calendar of Letter Books of the City of London, E*, ed. R. R. Sharpe, (London, 1903), p. 63; and *CCR 1313–18*, 235, 334.　　　[105] Above, p. 261.

[106] See the 1280 *gravamina*, cc. 2, 5, 8, 9, 10, 13, 18 (*Councils II*, 874–85).

clergy. The long reply, items 1 to 4 in the printed editions, to the first grievance of *Articuli Cleri*, concerning writs of prohibition, had not found approval when most of it had been re-stated in 1300–1.[107] And the renewed emphasis now given, specifically by the king's council ('Hic additur sic de novo per consilium domini regis...'), to the right of clerks in royal service to be absent from their benefices would without question have been strongly opposed by Winchelsey.[108] The new replies to four of the thirteen complaints of 1309,[109] and, lastly, the replies to two new complaints concerning benefit of clergy were, it is true, couched in terms of concessions to the clerical point of view; but they are conceding, for the most part in general terms, only what was in any case considered established custom, as in the statement of the freedom of ecclesiastical elections and the acceptance of the sole right of ecclesiastical judges to determine the suitability of a presentee to a benefice. *Articuli Cleri* gave clarification on some points relating to the clergy's liberties,[110] but, like the writ *Circumspecte Agatis* of 1286,[111] it was not a statute in the sense that it changed the law. Perhaps it represents some attempt by the king's council to find areas of agreement between the prelates, if not the clergy at large, and the crown, though naturally as a royal document it cannot conceal its concern for the protection of royal jurisdiction. To argue that it brought to a close the long period, beginning with Grosseteste, of clerical petitions for redress of grievances is to exaggerate its importance.[112]

Articuli Cleri signifies the end of this particular crisis for the clergy. The issues which had concerned the *communitas cleri* between 1313 and 1316 continued to be debated,[113] culminating in the crisis involving Archbishop Stratford and the crown in 1340–1. But no direct clerical tax was granted to Edward II by the clergy of the southern province after 1316,[114] and developments after that year were largely determined by the stand which the clergy had already taken.

[107] *Councils II*, 1209.
[108] See *Reg. R. Winchelsey*, ed. R. Graham, CYS (1952–6), p. 1017 and *Councils II*, 880 n. a.
[109] Cc. 1, 5, 8, 9 (*Councils II*, 1271–3).
[110] Lyndwood included three of the royal replies under the title 'De immunitate ecclesie' in his *Provinciale*: see C. R. Cheney, 'William Lyndwood's *Provinciale*' in *Medieval Texts and Studies* (Oxford, 1973), p. 163.
[111] See H. G. Richardson and G. O. Sayles, 'The early Statutes', *Law Quarterly Review*, L (1934), 565.
[112] Cf. F. M. Powicke, *The Thirteenth Century*, 2nd edn (Oxford, 1962), p. 484.
[113] Clarke, *Representation*, pp. 137–53, and Kemp, *Counsel & Consent*, pp. 95–106.
[114] The requested subsidy of 1322 (Lunt in *C. H. Haskins Essays*, pp. 177, 181) was not in fact conceded by the southern clergy (Kemp, *Counsel & Consent*, pp. 96–7).

Reynolds's archiepiscopate probably brought few innovations in respect of the routine of Canterbury administration. There is every indication that he defended the rights of the see. Yet, on a political plane, especially in terms of relations with the king, he was attempting to bring about fundamental changes. The crisis of his early years as archbishop was exacerbated by the papal vacancy of over two years and the consequent pressure upon the clergy to grant direct aids, by the king's financial needs, caused especially by the Scottish war and by the extremely severe effects of famine. But the crisis was largely Reynolds's own making. He appears to have aimed at securing the full co-operation of the English Church with the royal government in which he had been closely involved from the beginning of the reign. In pursuing his aims, aims so different from Winchelsey's, he was proving as obstinate as the latter had been. His allegiance to the crown was at the heart of his moderating attitude towards clerical taxation and had driven him to attempt to change the very nature of clerical assemblies by bringing them into parliament, the clergy to be represented there possibly in the way to be described, as part of a programme of reform, in the *Modus Tenendi Parliamentum*.[115] Reynolds's methods may seem devious, as in the changing form of his citations to councils, for he was challenging the clergy's established claim to control its own spiritual wealth and to determine policy for itself in its own peculiar and exclusive assemblies. In these respects he was opposing entrenched views of clerical privilege. He was intent upon undermining the belief that the laity, least of all the king, were inimical to the clergy.

There can be no doubt that Reynolds was in a very strong political position throughout these early years as archbishop. He had become chancellor in July 1310. After April 1312 he was more usually styled keeper of the great seal, the title of chancellor probably being avoided because he had not been accepted as chancellor in parliament in accordance with the Ordinances of 1311.[116] After he ceased to be official keeper of the great seal in April 1314,[117] he none the less remained the leader of the king's council.[118] When Edward was in Scotland in 1314 Reynolds was referred to as the king's lieutenant in England,[119]

---

[115] See esp. J. S. Roskell, 'A consideration of certain aspects and problems of the English *Modus Tenendi Parliamentum*', *Bulletin of the John Rylands Library*, L (1968), 411–42.

[116] Tout, *Ed. II*, pp. 285–8.

[117] His chancellorship ended on 16 April according to a note in a register of Southwark (BL MS Cotton Faustina A VIII, fo. 175r); but see Tout, *Ed. II*, p. 287.

[118] Davies, *Baronial Opposition*, pp. 331–6.

[119] PRO E159/87 m. 100r.

and, in a letter attempting to gain remission for Reynolds of the large payment which the pope sought for his translation to Canterbury, the king included among the archbishop's heavy expenses those which he was incurring 'in negotiis nostris et regni nostri...in parliamentis nostris et aliis congregationibus'.[120] J. Conway Davies has brought together the evidence which illustrates the very important unofficial position which the archbishop held at the heart of royal administration, as 'working head of the council', between 1314 and 1316. 'His influence seems to have been concentrated upon the administration of the council. Here he displaced the chancellor and was able to maintain his position even against Lancaster after the latter had been appointed chief counsellor.' With the archbishop so involved in royal government it is no surprise to find clerks referred to by Reynolds as clerks both of the king and of himself.[121] His responsible position had secured for him, in addition to the many concessions made by Clement V,[122] grants of financial importance from the king.[123] And some archiepiscopal duties had to give way to royal duties, for he visited in person neither his own diocese nor the dioceses of Rochester (in 1314) and Ely (in 1315), a papal grant permitting him to visit by deputy.[124] When he excused himself from visiting Ely he sent not only a copy of the papal bull but also a royal 'excusatory' writ.[125]

It needs no stressing that Reynolds's activities in the king's council affected the clergy directly. Their plea for redress of grievances had naturally gone to the king's council, which certainly had been largely responsible for drawing up the *Articuli Cleri*, notably the statement that royal clerks must not be required to reside in their benefices. A Chancery warrant of 4 December 1316 provides a striking example of the archbishop's influential position.[126] The king had received a roll containing some requests from the prelates and clergy of the southern province, possibly the eleven conditions which they had attached to

---

[120] *Foedera*, II, i, 257.
[121] *The Liber Epistolaris of Ric. de Bury*, ed. N. Denholm-Young, Roxburghe Club, (1950), nos. 255, 459.
[122] See Smith, *Episcopal Appointments*, p. 18, and Churchill, *Canterbury Administration*, I, 507; and for the bulls see Wilkins, II, 433–6, 438, 440–2 and *Reg. Clement V*, nos. 10062–5, 10147, 10151–5, 10157–9 (*CPL*, II, 119–21).
[123] Davies, *Baronial Opposition*, p. 332.
[124] Churchill, *Cant. Admin.*, I, 307–11. In his own diocese he did begin the visitation proceedings in person, at Christ Church Canterbury on 27 Feb. and 4 Mar. and at the abbey of Faversham on 5 Mar. 1314: Cant. D. & C., Reg. Q, fo. 91 and Eastry Correspondence, I, no. 59.
[125] BL Add. MS 41612, fo. 33v.
[126] *Calendar of Chanc. Warr. 1244–1326* (HMSO), p. 451.

their grant of a tenth in their council of 11 October.[127] The king sent these requests to Reynolds and the chancellor, treasurer and other members of the king's council in London, with a mandate to take action upon them. So, the archbishop was in a position to determine the outcome of his own provincial clergy's petitions to the king. By contrast, the lower clergy must have been well aware of the weakness of *their* position. Despite a few indications of disaffection with the policies of Reynolds on the part of Stapledon, bishop of Exeter, Ghent, bishop of Salisbury, and Segrave, bishop of London, the clergy who were voicing their opposition in clerical assemblies gained remarkably little support from the bishops. Admittedly, the episcopate was far from united, but its political tendency in these years was to co-operate with the crown.[128] When Greenfield, archbishop of York, organised a pseudo-parliament at Doncaster in May 1315, he was concerned with the defence of the north rather than with the defence of clerical privileges.[129] At times of emergency, especially when papal taxes had dried up, the clergy could not in the end resist the granting of royal aids. And the conditions which they attached to their grants were, of course, requests rather than provisos. Many such conditions could be met, like the insistence upon the clerical control of the collection of taxes; some achieved at best further definition of the clergy's rights, as in *Articuli Cleri*; while others expressed a desire and a hope, like the request that the money be spent only on the kingdom's proper needs. The crisis had culminated in a year of frequent ecclesiastical councils, as in 1297, but there were no concessions comparable with *Confirmatio Cartarum*.

Yet, the outstanding feature of these years was the persistence of the clergy in urging their point of view. No leader emerged among the *communitas cleri*, but in a series of statements the secular and regular clergy revealed a consistent programme of separatism. The *Rationes Cleri* and *Petitio* of May 1314, the *Protestatio* and *Conditiones* of early 1315, the *Petitiones* of April 1316 and the *Conditiones* of October 1316[130] all go to demonstrate the strength of feeling and determination among the clergy, who have taken up the issues for which Winchelsey had

[127] Above, p. 268.

[128] Edwards, *EHR*, LIX (1944), 326–31, 346–7; and for the activities in 1316 of Martival, bishop of Salisbury, as a king's councillor see now *Reg. Martival*, CYS, II, 112–13.

[129] Clarke, *Representation*, pp. 161–2, and Maddicott, *Lancaster*, pp. 168–9.

[130] Wake, *Clergy*, app. 37–9; Wilkins, II, 442–4; and *Parl. Writs*, II, ii, 123–4; *Reg. Stapeldon*, ed. Hingeston-Randolph, p. 122; *Parl. Writs*, II, ii, 139 and app. 92; and *Reg. Swinfield*, CYS, pp. 497–8; BL MS Cotton Faustina A VIII, fos. 175v–176r; and *Reg. Martival*, CYS, II, 173–5.

fought. Reynolds has driven the clergy, apart from the episcopate and ecclesiastics who were royal clerks, into hard opposition. Whatever the compromises in practice, for example the tax granted in the parliament of 1315, the clergy's attitude to taxation and to the status of their assemblies was unequivocal and reflected an entrenched belief in the overriding value and importance of clerical privilege. Whether or not its policies were of long-term advantage, the lower clergy had achieved a high degree of political effectiveness in relation to the defence of clerical privilege. While the road of separatism in fact led away from wider political involvement, it is none the less true that the community of the clergy had united in political action, using powers based upon the long-established right of consent to royal taxation of their spiritualities.[131] And it is largely because of the forceful strength of clerical opinion that we can respect the emphatic statements of Richardson and Sayles that 'the coalescence of parliament and convocation was fundamentally impracticable' and that there was 'an essential incompatibility of the ecclesiastical organisation with the secular'.[132]

[131] See W. E. Lunt, 'The consent of the English lower clergy to taxation during the reign of Henry III' in *Persecution and Liberty: Essays in Honor of G. L. Burr* (New York, 1931), pp. 117–69 and H. S. Deighton, 'Clerical taxation by consent, 1279–1301', *EHR*, LXVIII (1953), 161–92.
[132] *EHR*, LII (1937), 230–1.

BIBLIOGRAPHY OF THE WRITINGS OF
C. R. CHENEY

compiled by GEOFFREY MARTIN

1931   *Episcopal visitations of monasteries in the thirteenth century.* Publications of the University of Manchester, Historical Series, LVIII (Manchester, 1931), viii+190 pp.
'The papal legate and the English monasteries in 1206', *EHR*, XLVI (1931), 443–52.

1932   'A visitation of St. Peter's priory, Ipswich', *EHR*, XLVII (1932), 268–72.
Review of G. W. Greenaway, *Arnold of Brescia* (Cambridge, 1931), *BIHR*, X (1932–3), 32.
'The authorship of the De expugnatione Lyxbonensi', *Speculum*, VII (1932), 395–7.
Review of J. W. Thompson, *The Middle Ages, 300–1500* (New York, 1931), *History*, XVII (1932–3), 162–4.
'Letters of William Wickwane, chancellor of York, 1266–8', *EHR*, XLVII (1932), 626–42.

1933   *Review* of E. M. Thompson, *The Carthusian order in England*, (London, 1930), *History*, XVII (1932–3), 359–60.
Reviews of J. Evans, *Monastic life at Cluny, 910–1157* (London, 1931) and L. M. Smith, *Cluny in the eleventh and twelfth centuries* (London, 1930), *History*, XVIII (1933–4), 41–3.
Review of E. Faral, ed., *Poème sur Louis le Pieux et épîtres au roi Pépin par Ermold le Noir* (Paris, 1932), *History*, XVIII (1933–4), 82.

1934   *Review* of A. H. Thompson, ed., *The register of William Greenfield, lord archbishop of York, 1306–15* (London, 1931), *EHR*, XLIX (1934), 158–9.
Review of N. Denholm-Young, ed., *The cartulary of the medieval archives of Christ Church* (Oxford, 1931), *History*, XIX (1934–5), 177–8.
Reviews of E. H. Pearce, *Hartlebury Castle* (London, 1926); M. A. Babington, *Canterbury Cathedral*, (London, 1934); R. J. Fletcher, *History of Bristol Cathedral* (London, 1932); H. F. S. Stokes, *Glastonbury Abbey before the Conquest* (Glastonbury, 1932); F. B. R. Troup, *The consecration of the Norman minster at Exeter* (Yeovil, 1932), *History*, XIX (1934–5), 178.

1935   *Review* of J. G. Edwards, V. H. Galbraith and E. F. Jacob, eds, *Historical essays in honour of James Tait* (Manchester, 1933), *EHR*, L (1935), 128–31.
Review of W. A. Philips, ed., *History of the Church of Ireland, II: The movement towards Rome, the medieval Church, and the Reformation* (London, 1934), *History*, XIX (1934–5), 334–5.

Review of K. L. Wood-Legh, *Studies in church life in England under Edward III* (Cambridge, 1934), *EHR*, L (1935), 327–9.

'Legislation of the medieval English Church', *EHR*, L (1935), 193–224, 385–417.

'The Diocese of Grenoble in the fourteenth century', *Speculum*, X (1935), 162–77.

'Norwich Cathedral priory in the fourteenth century', *Bulletin of the John Rylands Library*, XX (1936), 93–120.

1936 'The punishment of felonous clerks', *EHR*, LI (1936), 215–36.

Review of W. J. S. Simpson, *Religious thought in France in the nineteenth century* (London, 1935), *History*, XXI (1936–7), 95.

'Early Banbury chap-books and broadsides', *The Library*, XVII (1936–7), 98–108.

'A monastic letter of fraternity to Eleanor of Aquitaine', *EHR*, LI (1936), 262–4.

Review of G. G. Coulton, *Five centuries of religion, III, Getting and spending* (Cambridge, 1936), *History*, XXI (1936–7), 262–4.

(with J. Cheney and W. G. Cheney), *John Cheney and his descendants, printers in Banbury since 1767* (Banbury, 1936), 81 pp.

1937 Review of E. H. Carter, *Studies in Norwich cathedral history* (Norwich, 1935), *EHR*, LII (1937), 154–5.

Reviews of (Anon.), *La Trappe in England* (London, 1937); and C. S. Phillips, *The Church in France, 1848–1907*(London, 1936), *History*, XXII(1937–8), 188–9.

Review of J. C. Russell, *Dictionary of writers of thirteenth-century England* (London, 1936), *EHR*, LII (1937), 692–6.

'La date de composition du *Liber poenitentialis* attribué à Pierre de Poitiers', *Recherches de Théologie Ancienne et Médiévale*, IX (1937), 401–4.

1938 Review of G. Baskerville, *English monks and the suppression of the monasteries* (London, 1937), *EHR*, LIII (1938), 131–4.

Review of R. F. Bennett, *The early Dominicans* (Cambridge, 1937), *History*, XXII (1937–8), 379.

Review of C. H. Jenkinson, *A manual of archive administration*, 2nd edn (London, 1937), *History*, XXIII (1938–9), 84.

'A propos des registres de marguilliers', *Revue d'Histoire Ecclésiastique*, XXXIV (1938), 801–3.

Review of M. Hüffer, *Die Reformen in der Abtei Rijnsburg im XV. Jahrhundert* (Münster, 1937), *Journal of Theological Studies*, XXXIX (1938), 430–31.

1939 Review of M. V. Clarke, *Fourteenth-century studies* (Oxford, 1937), *Medium Aevum*, VIII (1939), 83–4.

1940 Review of E. F. Jacob, ed., *The register of Henry Chichele, archbishop of Canterbury, 1414–43*, II (London, 1938), *Medium Aevum*, IX (1940), 49–53.

1941 *English synodalia of the thirteenth century* (London, 1941), x + 164 pp.

Review of A. H. Thompson, ed., *Visitations in the diocese of Lincoln, 1517–31*, I (Lincoln, 1940), *Economic History Review*, XI (1941), 109–10.

1942   *Reviews* of C. Mellows and W. T. Mellows, *The Peterborough chronicle of Hugh Candidus* (Peterborough, 1941), and W. T. Mellows, *The foundation of Peterborough Cathedral* (Kettering, 1941), *Journal of British Archaeological Association*, 3rd series, VII (1942), 71–2.

1944   *Review* of A. H. Thompson, ed. *Visitations in the diocese of Lincoln, 1517–31*, II (Lincoln, 1944), *Economic History Review*, XIV (1944), 203–4.

      Review of R. A. L. Smith, *Canterbury Cathedral priory* (Cambridge, 1943), *Oxford Magazine*, LXII (1943–4), 290.

      Reviews of E. F. Jacob, *Essays in the Conciliar epoch* (London, 1944), and A. G. Little, *Franciscan Papers, Lists and Documents* (Manchester, 1943), *Oxford Magazine*, LXII (1943–4), 218–19.

1945   *Handbook of dates for students of English history*. Royal Historical Society Guides and Handbooks, IV (London, 1945), xviii + 164 pp.

1946   *Review* of J. R. H. Moorman, *Church Life in England in the thirteenth century* (Cambridge, 1945), *Journal of Theological Studies*, XLVII (1946), 99–104.

      'Some papal privileges for Gilbertine houses', *BIHR*, XXI (1946–8), 39–58 [republished in a revised form in *Medieval Texts and Studies* (1973), 39–65].

      Review of British Records Association, *Notes for the guidance of editors of record publications* (London, 1946), *BIHR*, XXI (1946–8), 78–9.

1947   'The medieval statutes of the diocese of Carlisle', *EHR*, LXII (1947), 52–7.

      Review of J. W. Adamson, *The illiterate Anglo-Saxon, and other essays on education, medieval and modern* (Cambridge, 1946), *Humanitas*, I, no. 3 (Feb. 1947), 36–9.

      Review of C. Wittmar, *Inventaire des sceaux des archives de la ville de Strasbourg de 1050 à 1300* (Strasbourg, 1946), *EHR*, LXII (1947), 265–6.

      Review of *Revue du Moyen Age Latin: études, textes, chronique, bibliographie* (Lyons, 1945), *Medium Aevum*, XV (1946), 64–6.

1948   *Review* of F. M. Powicke, *King Henry III and the Lord Edward* (Oxford, 1947), *EHR*, LXIII (1948), 110–14.

      'The alleged deposition of King John', *Studies in Medieval History presented to F. M. Powicke*, ed. R. W. Hunt, W. A. Pantin, and R. W. Southern (Oxford, 1948), 100–16.

      'A neglected record of the Canterbury election of 1205–6', *BIHR*, XXI (1946–8), 233–8.

      'Master Philip the Notary and the fortieth of 1199', *EHR*, LXIII (1948), 342–50.

      Obituary of Albert Frederick Pollard, 1869–1948, *Manchester Guardian*, 5 August 1948.

      Introduction to *Shoemaker's window: recollections of a Midland town before the railway age*, by George Herbert, ed. C. S. Cheney (Oxford, 1948), pp. 1–4.

      'King John and the papal interdict', *Bulletin of the John Rylands Library*, XXXI (1948), 295–317.

1949   *Review* of J. C. Davies, ed., *Episcopal acts relating to Welsh dioceses, 1066–1272* I (Cardiff, 1946), *EHR*, LXIV (1949), 100–103.

      'King John's reaction to the interdict on England', *TRHS*, 4th series, XXX (1949), 129–50.

Review of A. H. Thompson, *The English clergy and their organization in the Later Middle Ages* (Oxford, 1947), *History*, XXXIV (1949), 126–7.

Review of A. H. Thompson, ed., *Visitations in the diocese of Lincoln, 1517-31*, III (Lincoln, 1947), *History*, XXXIV (1949), 171.

Review of F. Kempf, *Die Register Innocenz III: eine paläographisch-diplomatische Untersuchung* (Rome, 1945), *EHR*, LXIV (1949), 365–8.

Review of A. Watkin, ed., *The great chartulary of Glastonbury*, I (Taunton, 1947), *History*, XXXIV (1949), 284.

1950　*English bishops' chanceries, 1100-1250* (Manchester, 1950), xii + 176 pp.

Review of N. S. Kroon, *Det Svenska Prästmotet unden Medeltiden* (Stockholm, 1948), *Journal of Ecclesiastical History*, I (1950), 120–1.

'The "paper constitution" preserved by Matthew Paris', *EHR*, LXV (1950), 213–21 [reprinted in *Medieval Texts and Studies* (1973), 231–41].

'Gervase, abbot of Prémontré: a medieval letter-writer', *Bulletin of the John Rylands Library*, XXXIII (1950–1), 25–56 [reprinted in *Medieval Texts and Studies*, 1973, 242–76].

'Innocent III', *Chambers Encyclopaedia*, (Revised edn), VII (London, 1960).

1951　Review of S. Painter, *The reign of King John* (London, 1950), *EHR*, LXVI (1951).

'Quum and quoniam', *BIIIR*, XXIV (1951), 44–5.

'Church building in the Middle Ages', *Bulletin of the John Rylands Library*, XXXIV (1951–2), 20–36 [reprinted in *Medieval Texts and Studies* (1973), pp. 346–63].

Review of R. M. T. Hill, ed., *The rolls and register of bishop Oliver Sutton, 1280-99*, I–II (Lincoln, 1948–50), *Journal of Ecclesiastical History*, II, (1951) 237–9.

1952　Review of T. D. Tremlett and H. N. Blakiston, eds, *Stogursey charters* (Taunton, 1949), *History*, XXXVII (1952), 69–70.

Review of W. O. Hassall, ed., *The cartulary of St. Mary Clerkenwell* (London, 1949), *History*, XXXVII (1952), 70.

'Harrold Priory: a twelfth-century dispute', *Publications of the Bedfordshire Historical Record Society*, XXXII (1952), 1–26 [reprinted in *Medieval Texts and Studies* (1973), 285–313].

'The letters of Pope Innocent III', *Bulletin of the John Rylands Library*, XXXV (1952–3), 23–43 [reprinted in *Medieval Texts and Studies* (1973), 16–38].

1953　'Les bibliothèques cisterciennes en Angleterre au XIIe siècle', *Mélanges S. Bernard* (Dijon, 1953–4), 375–82. [Republished in a revised form in *Medieval Texts and Studies* (1973), 328–45.]

Review of B. L. Woodcock, *Medieval ecclesiastical courts in the diocese of Canterbury* (London, 1952), *EHR*, LXVIII (1953), 306–7.

(with W. H. Semple) *Selected Letters of Pope Innocent III concerning England, 1198-1216* (London, 1953), xliv + [i] + 227 (x 2) + [21] pp.

1954　Review of L. Santifaller, *Beiträge zur Geschichte der Beschreibestoffe im Mittelalter, mit besonderer Berücksichtigung der päpstlichen Kanzlei*, I (Graz-Cologne, 1953), *EHR*, LXIX (1954), 173.

Review of K. Major, ed., *The Registrum Antiquissimum of the cathedral church of Lincoln*, VII (Lincoln, 1953), *EHR*, LXIX (1954), 651–2.

Review of C. H. Jenkinson, *A guide to seals in the Public Record Office* (London, 1954), *EHR*, LXIX (1954), 652.

Review of B. Dodwell, ed., *Feet of fines for the county of Norfolk, 1198–1202* (London, 1952), *History*, XXXIX (1954), 138.

1955   Review of W. Holtzmann and E. W. Kemp, eds, *Papal decretals relating to the diocese of Lincoln in the twelfth century* (Lincoln, 1954), *EHR*, LXX (1955), 314–15.

Review of A. Watkin, ed., *The great chartulary of Glastonbury*, II (Taunton, 1952), *History*, XL (1955–6), 357–8.

Review of H. E. Salter and M. D. Lobel, eds, *The Victoria History of the County of Oxford, III: The university of Oxford* (London, 1954), *Journal of Ecclesiastical History*, VI (1955), 243–5.

'Decretals of Innocent III in Paris, B.N. MS Lat. 3922A', *Traditio* XI (1955), 149–62.

1956   'The records of medieval England: an inaugural lecture delivered in the University of Cambridge, 25 November 1955' (Cambridge, 1956), 21 pp. [reprinted in *Medieval Texts and Studies* (1973), 1–15].

'The eve of Magna Carta', *Bulletin of the John Rylands Library*, XXXVIII (1955–6), 311–41.

Review of A. Gwynn, ed., *The writings of Bishop Patrick* (Dublin, 1955), *Journal of Ecclesiastical History*, VII (1956), 120–1.

From Becket to Langton: English church government, 1170–1213 (Manchester, 1956), x+212 pp.

'Introduction: The Dugdale Tercentenary' in *English historical scholarship in the sixteenth and seventeenth centuries*, ed. L. Fox (London, 1956), pp. 1–9.

Review of G. V. Scammell, *Hugh du Puiset, bishop of Durham* (Cambridge, 1956), *Cambridge Review*, LXXVIII (1956–7), 517.

1957   'Close Roll fragments of 16 and 17 John (1215, 1216)', *The Memoranda Roll for the tenth year of the reign of King John*, Pipe Roll Society, LXIX (n.s., XXXI), (London, 1957), 127–44.

1958   Review of A. Watkin, ed., *The great chartulary of Glastonbury*, III (Taunton, 1956), *History*, XLIII (1958), 49–50.

Review of M. Pacaut, *Alexandre III: Étude sur la conception du pouvoir pontifical dans sa pensée et dans son oeuvre* (Paris, 1956), *EHR*, LXXIII (1958), 286–8.

Review of A. B. Emden, ed., *A biographical register of the University of Oxford to A.D. 1500, I: A to E* (Oxford, 1957), *Journal of Ecclesiastical History*, IX (1958), 249–51.

Review of M. Pacaut, *Louis VII et les élections épiscopales dans le royaume de France* (Paris, 1957), *EHR*, LXXIII (1958), 705–6.

Review of H. Bresslau, *Handbuch der Urkundenlehre*, I (3rd edn) and II (2nd edn) (Berlin, 1958), *EHR*, LXXIII (1958), 751.

1959   Review of N. F. Cantor, *Church, Kingship, and lay investiture in England, 1089–1135* (Princeton, N.J., 1958), *Speculum*, XXXIV (1959), 653–6.

Review of A. B. Emden, *A biographical register of the University of Oxford to A.D. 1500, II: F to O* (Oxford, 1958), *Journal of Ecclesiastical History*, x (1959), p. 127.

Review of J. P. C. Roach, ed., *A history of the County of Cambridge and the Isle of Ely, III: the City and University of Cambridge*, Victoria History of the Counties of England (London, 1959), *Journal of Ecclesiastical History*, x, (1959), 254–5.

'Three decretal collections before Compilatio IV: Pragensis, Palatina I, and Abrincensis II', *Traditio*, xv (1959), 464–83.

1960 'The earliest English diocesan statutes', *EHR*, LXXV (1960), 1–29.

Obituary of Sidney Painter, *The Times*, 18 February 1960.

Review of F. K. Ginzel, *Handbuch der mathematischen- und technischen-Chronologie* (Leipzig, 1906–14; unaltered reprint, 1958), *EHR*, LXXV (1960), 381–2.

Review of A. B. Emden, *A biographical register of the University of Oxford to A.D 1500, III: P to Z* (Oxford, 1959), *Journal of Ecclesiastical History*, XI (1960), 119–20.

Review of C. M. Fraser, *A history of Antony Bek, bishop of Durham, 1283–1311* (Oxford, 1957), *Cambridge Review*, LXXII (1960–1), 20.

1961 'The so-called statutes of John Pecham and Robert Winchelsey for the province of Canterbury', *Journal of Ecclesiastical History*, XII (1961), 14–34.

'Cardinal John of Ferentino, papal legate in England in 1206', *EHR*, LXXVI, (1961), 654–60.

Review of H. Bresslau, *Handbuch der Urkundenlehre: Register zur zweiten und dritten Auflage*, ed. H. Schulze (Berlin, 1960), *EHR*, LXXVI (1961), 698–9.

Review of F. J. Tschan, ed., *History of the archbishops of Bremen by Adam of Bremen* (London, 1959), *Journal of Ecclesiastical History*, XII (1961), 262–3.

Review of W. L. Warren, *King John* (London, 1961), *History*, XLVI (1961), 238–40.

'Rules for the observance of feast days in medieval England', *BIHR*, XXXIV (1961), 117–47.

'William Lyndwood's Provinciale', *The Jurist*, XXI (1961), 405–34 [reprinted in *Medieval Texts and Studies* (1973), 158–84].

'A group of related synodal statutes of the thirteenth century', *Medieval Studies presented to Aubrey Gwynn, S.J.*, ed. J. A. Watt, J. B. Morrall and F. X. Martin (Dublin, 1961), 114–32.

'Provincial and national councils of the Church in England, 602 x 603 – 1536', *Handbook of British Chronology*, ed. F. M. Powicke and E. B. Fryde, Royal Historical Society Guides and Handbooks, II, 2nd edn (London, 1961), 545–65.

(with M. G. Cheney) 'A draft decretal of Pope Innocent III on a case of identity', *Quellen und Forschungen aus italienischen Archiven und Biblioteken*, XLI (1961), 29–47.

1962 'A letter of Pope Innocent III and the Lateran decree on Cistercian tithe-paying', *Cîteaux: Commentarii Cistercienses*, Fasc. II (1962), 146–51 [reprinted in *Medieval Texts and Studies* (1973), 277–84].

Bibliography

Review of F. M. Powicke and E. B. Fryde, *Handbook of British Chronology* (London, 1961), *EHR*, LXXVII (1962), 713–14.

Review of M. Howell, *Regalian right in medieval England* (London, 1962), *Journal of Ecclesiastical History*, XIII (1962), 230–1.

1963 'Magna carta Beati Thome: another Canterbury forgery', *BIHR*, XXXVI (1963), 1–26. [reprinted in *Medieval Texts and Studies* (1973), 78–110].

1964 Review of W. Janssen, *Die päpstlichen Legaten in Frankreich von Schisma Anaklets II bis zum Tode Coelestins III, 1130–98* (Cologne-Graz, 1961), *EHR*, LXXIX (1964), 153–4.

Review of P. Herde, *Beiträge zur päpstliche Kanzlei- und Urkundwesen in XIII Jahrhundert* (Kallmunz-Opf, 1961), *EHR*, LXXIX (1964), 364–7.

Review of H. G. Richardson and G. O. Sayles, *The governance of medieval England from the Conquest to Magna Carta* (Edinburgh, 1963), *History*, XLIX (1964), 207–10.

(with F. M. Powicke) *Councils and synods, with other documents relating to the English Church, II: A.D. 1205–1313* (Oxford, 1964), liv + xiv + 1450 pp.

Review of J. T. Appleby, *The chronicle of Richard of Devizes of the time of King Richard I* (Edinburgh, 1963), *Journal of Ecclesiastical History*, XV (1964), 250–1.

Review of J. Sawicki, *Concilia Poloniae: Études critiques et sources, X: les synodes du diocèse de Wroclaw et leurs statuts* (Warsaw, 1963), *Journal of Ecclesiastical History*, XV (1964), 255.

Review of P-R. Gaussin, *L'abbaye de la Chaise-Dieu (1043–1518)* (Paris, 1962), *EHR*, LXXIX (1964), 784–6.

1965 Review of C. Duggan, *Twelfth-century decretal collections and their importance in English history* (London, 1963), *EHR*, LXXX (1965), 142–3.

'Aspects de la législation diocésaine en Angleterre au XIIIe siècle', *Études d'Histoire du Droit Canonique dédiées à Gabriel le Bras* (Paris, 1965), I, 41–54 [reprinted in English in *Medieval Texts and Studies* (1973), 185–202].

'The Church and Magna Carta', *Theology*, LVIII (1965), 266–72.

'The downfall of the Templars and a Letter in their defence', *Medieval Miscellany presented to Eugène Vinaver*, ed. F. Whitehead, A. H. Diverres and F. E. Sutcliffe (Manchester, 1965), 65–79 [reprinted in *Medieval Texts and Studies* (1973), 314–27].

Review of C. D. Ross, ed., *The cartulary of Cirencester Abbey, Gloucestershire* (London, 1964), *Journal of Ecclesiastical History*, XVI (1965), 235–6.

'A papal privilege for Tonbridge priory', *BIHR*, XXXVIII (1965), 192–200. [reprinted in *Medieval Texts and Studies* (1973), 66–77].

Review of S. M. Brown and J. F. O'Sullivan, *The register of Eudes of Rouen* (New York, 1964), *Medium Aevum*, XXXIV (1965), 142–3.

'Statute-making in the English Church in the thirteenth century', *Proceedings of the Second International Congress of Medieval Canon Law, Boston College, 12–16 August 1963*, ed. S. Kuttner and J. J. Ryan, *Monumenta Juris Canonici, Series C. Subsidia*, I (Vatican City, 1965), pp. 399–414 [reprinted in *Medieval Texts and Studies* (1973), 138–57].

1966   *The study of the medieval papal chancery* (Glasgow, 1966), 38 pp.

Review of P. Herde, ed., *Marinus von Eboli Super revocatoriis und De confirmationibus* (Tübingen, 1964), *EHR*, LXXXI (1966), 372–3.

Review of C. H. Lawrence, ed., *The English Church and the Papacy in the Middle Ages* (London, 1965), *EHR*, LXXXI (1966), 818.

Review of F. R. H. du Boulay, *The lordship of Canterbury* (London, 1966), *Theology*, LXX (1967), 36–8.

'A recent view of the General Interdict on England', *Studies in Church History*, III, ed. G. J. Cuming (London, 1966), 159–68.

1967   Review of O. Hageneder and A. Haidacher, eds, *Die Register Innocenz III*, I Bd: *I Pontifikatsjahr: Texte*, (Cologne, 1965), *EHR*, LXXXII (1967), 109–11.

Review of C. H. S. Fifoot, ed., *The Letters of Frederic William Maitland* (Cambridge, 1965), *EHR*, LXXXII (1967), 359–61.

Review of C. E. Wright and R. C. Wright, eds, *The diary of Humfrey Wanley, 1715–1726* (London, 1966), *Archives*, VIII (1967–8), 44–5.

Review of G. le Bras, C. Lefebvre and J. Rambaud, eds, *Histoire du droit et des institutions de l'Église en Occident, VII: L'âge classique, 1140–1378* (Paris, 1965), *EIIR*, LXXXII (1967), 564–7.

'Cheney and Sons: two centuries of printing in Banbury', *Cake and Cockhorse*, III (1965–8), 167–75.

Hubert Walter (London, 1967), x+198 pp.

'An annotator of Durham Cathedral MS C.III.3', *Studia Gratiana*, XI (1967), 37–68.

'England and the Roman Curia under Innocent III', *Journal of Ecclesiastical History*, XVIII (1967), 173–86.

'Appendix III: The Calendar', *The Oxford Companion to English Literature*, ed. P. Harvey, 4th edn (London, 1967), 932–61.

Review of S. Grayzel, *The Church and the Jews in the thirteenth century: a study of their relations during the years 1198–1254* (New York, 1966), *Journal of Ecclesiastical History*, XVIII (1967), 250–1.

Review of J. Taylor, *The Universal Chronicle of Ranulf Higden* (Oxford, 1966), *Journal of Ecclesiastical History*, XVIII (1967), 251–2.

'On the Cheltenham (Phillipps) Manuscripts and Some Others Described in *Papsturkunden in England* 3.73–87', *Traditio*, XXIII (1967), 512–16.

(with M. G. Cheney), *The letters of Pope Innocent III, 1198–1216, concerning England and Wales: a calendar with an appendix of texts* (Oxford, 1967), xxxiv+ [ii]+308 pp.

1968   Reviews of A. Morey and C. N. L. Brooke, *Gilbert Foliot and his letters* (Cambridge, 1965) and Z. N. Brooke, A. Morey and C. N. L. Brooke, eds, *The letters and charters of Gilbert Foliot, abbot of Gloucester, 1139–48*...(Cambridge, 1967), *History*, LIII (1968), 75–6.

'The twenty-five barons of Magna Carta', *Bulletin of the John Rylands Library*, L (1967–8), 280–307.

Bibliography

'Itinerary', 'Index', 'Errata', *The Register of John Pecham, Archbishop of Canterbury, 1279–1292*, ed. F. N. Davis and others, D. Douie. Canterbury and York Society, LXIV, LXV (Torquay, 1968, 1969), vol. I, ix–xvi; vol. II, 255–315, 316–24.

Review of W. Urry, *Canterbury under the Angevin kings* (London, 1967), *Medium Aevum* (1968), 229–31.

1969 'Notes on the making of the Dunstable annals, A.D. 33–1242', *Essays in Medieval History presented to Bertie Wilkinson*, ed. T. A. Sandquist and M. R. Powicke (Toronto, 1969), 79–98 [reprinted in *Medieval Texts and Studies* (1973), 209–30].

Review of A. Terroine and L. Fossier, *Chartes et documents de l'abbaye de St. Magloire, II, 1280–1330* (Paris, 1966), *EHR*, LXXXIV (1969), 152–3.

Review of J. Th. Sawicki, *Bibliographia synodorum particularium* (Vatican City, 1967), *Revue d'Histoire du Droit*, XXXVII (1969), 124–5.

1970 *Review* of G. Constable, ed., *The Letters of Peter the Venerable* (London, 1969), *EHR*, LXXXV (1970), 118–21.

1971 'Helen Maud Cam, 1885–1968', *Proceedings of the British Academy for 1969*, LV (1971), 293–309.

(with M. G. Cheney), 'Letters of Innocent III: Additions and Corrections', *BIHR*, XLIV (1971), 98–115.

Review of R. M. T. Hill, ed., *The rolls and register of bishop Oliver Sutton, III–IV* (Lincoln, 1954–69), *Journal of Ecclesiastical History*, XXII (1971), 261–3.

'Textual problems of the English provincial canons', *Atti del Secondo Congresso Internazionale della Società Italiana di Storia del Diritto, I: La critica del testo* (Florence, 1971), 165–88 [reprinted in *Medieval Texts and Studies* (1973), 111–37].

1972 *Notaries public in England in the thirteenth and fourteenth centuries* (Oxford, 1972), xii + 205 pp.

Review of J. F. Benton, *Self and society in medieval France: the memoirs of Guibert of Nogent* (New York, 1970), *EHR*, LXXXVII (1972), 162.

Review of G. J. Cuming and D. Baker, eds, *Studies in Church History, VIII: Councils and Assemblies* (Cambridge, 1971), *Journal of Ecclesiastical History*, XXIII (1972), 267–8.

'Hubert Walter and Bologna', *Bulletin of Medieval Canon Law*, n.s. II (1972), 81–4.

'Law and letters in fourteenth-century Durham: a study of C.C.C.C. MS 450', *Bulletin of the John Rylands Library*, LV (1972–3), 60–85.

Review of C. E. Wright, *Fontes Harleiani* (London, 1972), *Archives*, X, (1971–2), 174–5.

1973 'Richard de Bury, Borrower of Books', *Speculum*, XLVIII (1973), 325–8.

Review of R. Marsina, ed., *Codex diplomaticus et epistolaris Slovaciae, I: 805–1235* (Bratislaw, 1971), *EHR*, LXXXVIII (1973), 582–4.

Review of L. E. Boyle, *A Survey of the Vatican Archives and of its Medieval Holdings* (Toronto, 1972), *Archives*, XI, (1973–4), 97–8.

Medieval texts and studies (Oxford, 1973), viii + [ii] + 371 pp.

Review of H. E. J. Cowdrey, ed. and trans., *The Epistolae Vagantes of Pope Gregory VII* (Oxford, 1972), *Medium Aevum*, XLII (1973), 261–2.

Review of G. Constable and B. Smith, eds. and trans., *Libellus de diversis ordinibus et professionibus qui sunt in aecclesia* (Oxford, 1972), *American Historical Review*, LXVIII (1973), 1031–2.

Review of W. G. H. Quigley and E. F. D. Roberts, eds, *Registrum Johannis Mey, Archbishop of Armagh 1443–56* (Belfast, 1972), *Journal of Ecclesiastical History*, XXIV (1973), 417–18.

1974 *Review* of H. Diener, *Die grossen Registerserien im Vatikanische Archiv, 1378–1523* (Tübingen, 1972), *EHR*, LXXXIX (1974), 163.

'Some features of surviving original papal letters in England', *Annali della Scuola Speciale per Archivisti e Bibliotecari dell'Università di Roma, Anno XII, 1972* (1973), 1–25.

Review of S. Kuttner, ed., *Proceedings of the Third International Congress of Medieval Canon Law, Strasbourg, 3–6 September 1965* (Vatican City, 1971), *EHR*, LXXXIX (1974), 652–3.

1975 *Review* of Henri Bresc, ed., *La correspondance de Pierre Ameilh, 1363–9, archevêque de Naples, puis de Embrun* (Paris, 1972), *EHR*, XC (1975), 175.

GENERAL INDEX

The following abbreviations are used: abb. = abbey; abp = archbishop; archd. = archdeacon; bp = bishop; card. = cardinal; pr. = priory.

General Index

General Index

Falaise, Edict of, 69, 72
false moneyers, 57 and n.
false testimony, 30
Famine, the Great, 262, 266, 271
Faral, E., 77n., 89n., 90n.
Farningmere (Somerset), 182
Farrer, W., 145n.
Fathers, Church, 107, 125, 134
Fauroux, Marie, 3–13nn. *passim*, 23n.
Faustinus, 105 and n.
Faversham, abb., 272n.
Fawtier, R., 36n., 62n.
feast, patronal, 25
feast day, 239 and n., 240
Fécamp, abb., 5, 7n., 67n.; abbot of, 32, 59
    and n.
Félibien, Dom, 4n.
Feltoe, C. E., 171n.
feodary, 189n.
feretory, of a shrine, 193
Finberg, H. P. R., 178n., 183n., 184n.
Finke, H., 218n., 219n.
Finsbury, 141
Flanders, count of, *see* Charles the Good,
    William Clito
    county of, 53n., 75n.
    towns of, 55n.
Fleet, 186
Fletcher, R. H., 85n.
Fliche, A., 21nn., 36 and n.
Florence of Worcester, 55n., 64n., 66n.
Flower, C. T., 249n.
Fontenelle, *see* Saint-Wandrille
Fordham, John, bp of Ely, 163, 168
Fordwich, 60n., 71n.
forest laws, 26; *and see* Charter of the Forest
Foreville, R., 5nn., 8n., 16n., 19–39; 140n.
forgeries, 3, 8, 10, 11, 12, 54n., 105, 180n.,
    186 and n.
forgers, 38, 102, 107
formulary-books, 188 and n., 191
fornication, 192, 193
Foss, Edward, 145n.
Foster, C. W., 34n.
Fournier, P., 102nn., 109n., 227nn.
France, 3, 20, 34, 35, 36, 38, 39, 75n., 127, 142,
    143, 144, 151, 152, 216, 251; king of, 249,
    252
Francis, St, 211
Franciscan friars, 209, 211, 212 and n., 219;
    and see Mendicant friars
    order, Minister-General of, 212
François de Meyronnes, 219
Frankish Church, 62
Frankish *inquisitio*, 49n.
Frankish origin, 73

frankpledge, 48, 60
freemen, 197, 203
Fressingfield, prior of Ely, 162
Fréteval, 144
friborh, 48
Friedberg, E., 67n., 102n., 103n., 104n., 116,
    205n., 250n.
Fuhrmann, H., 102nn., 104n., 105n., 229n.,
    237n.
Funk, F. X., 65n.

Gagnér, S., 94n.
Galbert of Bruges, 49n.
Galbraith, V. H., 11 and n., 12n., 166n., 180n.
Gascony, 21, 249
Gaskell, P., 160n.
Gasquet, Cardinal, xi
Gaudemet, J., 36n., 62n., 63n., 93n.
Gaul, 37
Gaveston, Piers, 262
Gelasius I, Pope, 32
Gelling, M., 186n.
Génestal, R., 178n.
gentry, 201, 203 and n.
Geoffrey (Brito), abp, of Rouen, 22, 23n., 24,
    31, 32
Geoffrey, brother of King Henry II, 141n.
Geoffrey, called Belchester, 197
Geoffrey de Clinton, 46n., 50n.
Geoffrey de Gorron, abbot of St Albans, 181
Geoffrey de Mandeville, 74
Geoffrey of Lèves, bp of Chartres, 35
Geoffrey of Monmouth, 77–91
Geoffrey of Mowbray, bp of Coutances, 23n.
Geoffrey Ridel, 152, 153
Gerard de Camville, 50n.
Gerard of Angoulême, legate, 36
Gerhoch of Reichersberg, 230n.
Germany, 238n.
Gerona, council of, 36
Gerould, G. H., 85n.
Gervase, abbot of Westminster, 187
Gervase, serjeant, 56
Gervase of Canterbury, 121, 122, 123, 155n.
Gervase of Chichester, 143
Gesta abbatum Fontanellensium, 2, 3, 8
Ghellinck, J. de, 135n., 224n.
Ghent, 2, 55n.; *and see* Simon
Gibbs, M., 34n.
Gibbs, V., 87n.
Gibson, M. T., 122n.
Gilbert, bp of Évreux, 31
Gilbert, son of Richer of Laigle, 14
Gilbert Crispin, abbot of Westminster, 16, 187
Gilbert Foliot, bp of Hereford and London,
    68, 81, 82, 132, 139n., 140, 148–54 *passim*

General Index

General Index

Protestants, 106n.
province, 19–39 *passim*, 250, 255–72 *passim*; *and see* Canterbury, Rouen, councils
Psalms, 85
psalter, 10
Pseudo-Anacletus, 105n., 229–32
Pseudo-Anselm, 238, 239
Pseudo-Clement, and *Epistola Clementis*, 93n., 101–6, 108, 109, 112, 116–7, 229, 230, 231 and n., 232
Pseudo-Denis the Areopagite, 205–21, 228
Pseudo-Isidore, 101, 102 and n., 104, 105 and n., 106n., 116, 228, 229, 230, 232, 237n.; *and see Registrum Romanorum Pontificum*
Pseudo-Julius, 237n.
Pseudo-Stephen, 237n.
publica fama, 50n., 64n., 65, 68n., 192
parochianorum, 49n., 64n.
punishment, 127, 143, 189, 193, 199, 200, 233, 250; *and see* mutilation
capital, 60nn.
purgation, 152, 193, 199
Pyk, Thomas, archd. of Westminster, 192

Queste del Saint Graal, 79n.

Radolphus, Master (?Radulphus Theologus), 141
Raimond de Pennaforte, 227
Raine, J., 269n.
Ralegh Radford, C. A., 178n.
Ralph, bp of Shrewsbury, 185
Ralph, count of Bayeux, 26
Ralph Basset, 58
Ralph de Diceto, 140, 154, 155
Ralph d'Escures, abp of Canterbury, 32
Ralph FitzStephen, 145
Ralph of Ivry, Count, 4
Ralph Passelewe, 55 and n.
Ramsey, abb., 55, 56, 159, 239
Ranulf II, earl of Chester, 71n.
Ranulf Flambard, 55 and n.
rape, 26, 243
Rathbone, E., 95n., 128n., 132 and n., 136n.
ratio, 135–6
Rationes Cleri, 258 and n., 273
Ratzinger, J., 209n., 210n.
Ravenna, statute of, 55n.
Raynaldus, O., 227n., 229n.
recreantisa, 60n.
Redbourn (Herts.), 181, 191, 198, 202
reditus (of man to God), 215
reductio (reduction), 208, 210, 211, 212, 213
Reedy, W. T., 51n., 52n., 75nn.
Rees, U., 12n.
reeves, 45, 47, 48n., 56, 58; royal, 44

Reformation, 157
Reginald fitz Jocelin, bishop of Bath, abp of Canterbury, 59n., 183 and n., 185
Regino of Prüm, 61, 63
registrar, 195
Registrum Romanorum Pontificum, 227, 228
regnum and *sacerdotium*, x
Rehm, B., 105n.
relics, of saints, 2, 3n., 7, 44, 159
Restoration (1660), 159
Reynolds, S., 51n., 55n.
Reynolds, Walter, abp of Canterbury, 247–74
Rheims, 153
council of (1119), 15, 23nn., 31, 32n., 36; (1148), 2n.
rhetoric, 1, 4, 125
Richard, bp of Bayeux, 32
Richard I, duke of Normandy, 2, 3, 4, 5 and n., 14
Richard II, duke of Normandy, 3, 4, 6, 7, 8
Richard I, king of England, 33, 145nn., 146n.
Richard Bucuinte, 59n.
Richard de Belmeis I, bp of London, 81
Richard de Lokyngton, 198
Richard de Lucy, 59n., 69, 74
Richard fitz Troite, 50n.
Richard of Dover, abp of Canterbury, 64n.
Richardson, H. G., 44n., 46nn., 51n., 58nn., 73n., 132 and n., 248n., 249n., 250n., 264n., 270n., 274
Richer of Laigle, 14
Richter, Ae. L., 103n., 105nn.
Richter, M., 81n.
Rickmansworth, 181, 202
Riley, H. T., 181n., 249n., 257n.
Rivière, J., 205n., 206 and nn., 215n., 218n.
Robat, Alice, 198
Robert, abbot of Glastonbury, 183
Robert, abp of Rouen (d. 1037), 29
Robert, archd. of Lincoln, 67n.
Robert, archd. of Westminster, 200
Robert, bp of Coutances, 23n., 27
Robert, brother of St William, 59n.
Robert, earl of Gloucester, 82 and n., 87 and nn.
Robert, king of Sicily and of Jerusalem, 219
Robert, the king's tailor, 197
Robert Courson, legate, 22, 38
Robert Curthose, duke of Normandy, 21, 27, 30, 31, 34, 49n.
Robert de Chesney, bp of Lincoln, 132, 182
Robert de Montfort, 50n.
Robert Foliot, archd. of Oxford, bp Hereford, 152, 153
Robert Huscarl, 140, 142
Robert 'Malarteis', 57–8

General Index

INDEX OF MANUSCRIPTS CITED

Index of Manuscripts Cited